THE STORY OF WOODROW WILSON

TWENTY-EIGHTH PRESIDENT OF
THE UNITED STATES, PIONEER
OF WORLD DEMOCRACY

BY RUTH CRANSTON

SIMON AND SCHUSTER, NEW YORK

MANUFACTURED IN THE UNITED STATES OF AMERICA
BY THE HADDON CRAFTSMEN, INC., SCRANTON, PA.

FOR THE MEN AND WOMEN
WHO WILL BUILD THE NEW WORLD
THIS STORY OF
A GREAT PIONEER
WHO LAID THE FOUNDATION

PUBLISHER'S NOTE: To conserve paper we have divided *The Story of Woodrow Wilson* into only six chapters and a short introductory section. In the body of the text the numerous subsections that might have been separate chapters are headed by Roman numerals only. For the convenience of the reader we have also prepared a detailed Table of Contents in which each of these subsections has a descriptive title.

CONTENTS

Contents

Contents

Contents

Chapter VI. Legacy: His League That "Failed"

ILLUSTRATIONS

FOREWORD

THE *purpose of this book is to present within a single volume the life and achievements of Woodrow Wilson, with emphasis upon that part of his life which has particular significance now: Wilson's fight for peace, and his pioneer work for world security and world organization.*

The author's temerity in adding to the already large number of Wilson biographies may reasonably be challenged. "Why another book about Wilson? Hasn't Ray Stannard Baker said it all?"

Mr. Baker's eight volumes—the authorized Life *and* Letters of Woodrow Wilson—*carry the story only to the 1918 Armistice; they do not include the Peace Conference, the Senate fight, or an account of Mr. Wilson's final years. Mr. Baker covers the Peace Conference in a separate three-volume series,* Woodrow Wilson and World Settlement; *and Dr. Denna F. Fleming has written a splendid history of the Senate fight in* The United States and the League of Nations. *We have also volumes of lively personal reminiscence by various friends and relatives, and a number of recent books which deal effectively with some special phase or portion of Wilson's career.*

But there exists no one-volume story of Wilson covering the entire sixty-eight years of his life in detail, plus a somewhat detailed account of the Peace Conference, the Senate fight, and, finally, a record of the institution for which he literally gave his life: the League of Nations.

These considerations influenced the writer to undertake the present volume. Old friendships, family ties, strong personal admiration also played their part, and perhaps most of all, the writer's sense of individual indebtedness and gratitude to the League of Nations and the men who administered it, the work she has seen it accomplishing for mankind in many countries.

No one-volume book can include everything, or even all of the important things. I have therefore tried, after briefly picturing

Foreword

the formative influences of Wilson's early life and his accomplishments as educator and Governor, to present the outstanding achievements of his two terms in the Presidency; his efforts, first as mediator in the early part of the World War I, then as war leader and as peace-maker; I have dwelt on the aspects of the Peace Conference which hold the greatest interest for Americans —his work on the League Covenant, his fight at Paris for the American amendments to the Covenant, and his opposition to further amendments and reservations in the Senate struggle; later, the great fight he put up on his ill-fated Western tour, when he so nearly won the battle for the League and the Treaty which he finally lost through the crushing illness that struck him down.

I have given the major events of the bitter battle waged by the small group of "irreconcilable" Senators determined to crush the League and every Wilsonian policy; their success through the mechanism of our system of committee government, in spite of the general will of the people and a substantial majority of pro-League Senators; finally a brief sketch of Mr. Wilson's last years and a quick, though I trust not superficial, survey of the League which he brought into existence.

Thanks to Mrs. Wilson's kindness, I had as background for this writing the vast collection of Mr. Wilson's private papers and documents, his personal and official correspondence, the Peace Conference documents—including letters and memoranda from people all over the world; his pre-Presidential letters and papers and those covering the period from his retirement in 1921 until his death. I have spent two and a half years at this work. They went like a flash of light.

My personal recollections of Woodrow Wilson begin with a June day many years ago when he addressed my graduating class at our Goucher College commencement. My father sat next to him on the platform; Dr. Wilson's daughter Jessie—my classmate for four years—sat near me. Wilson was President of Princeton then—a tall, energetic man in the prime of his life and power, scholarly yet dynamic. We were all proud of "Jessie's father."

Foreword

A few years after that I stood in his office at the White House to receive from him my special permission to cross the ocean to work in a French canteen. America had not yet entered the war. My father was anxious about my going. The President had given me a personal letter for my protection. "Don't you worry," he said, laying his hand on my father's shoulder; "don't you worry —she's going to be all right!"

Forty-eight hours later Germany declared unrestricted submarine warfare. I was in the Capitol and heard Mr. Wilson deliver his historic address breaking off relations with Germany. I was in France when he came to the Peace Conference. I heard many of the speeches quoted in this volume—Mr. Wilson's speeches and the speeches in the Senate fight. My family lived in Washington for twelve years. My father knew many of the Senators, and I frequently saw them. Later, I worked for the better part of ten years in Geneva on various international committees, side by side with the men in the League and the International Labor Office—some of them Mr. Wilson's own colleagues. I attended many League Assemblies and Council meetings: the meetings on Manchuria, Ethiopia, the Disarmament Conference, and numerous others. I saw the League at the height of its power and in the tragic days of its disintegration. Some of my closest friends fought with all their might against appeasement— whether of Japan or Germany—and for strict adherence to the Covenant. So I have watched this story being written at both ends of the line.

In later years I came upon Margaret Wilson again in New York, and we saw each other frequently before she went away to India. She talked to me long and intimately about her father— the incidents of his early life as well as his fight for the League and the events of his later years. A number of the allusions and anecdotes in this book are the result of those conversations, though at the time we had no idea that I was to do a biography of Woodrow Wilson. That proposal came six years later. When it came I was reluctant rather than eager to accept.

I had been repeatedly warned—especially by old Princeton residents—that the revelations I would come upon would destroy

Foreword

"the Wilson legend of greatness" and shatter my own private "Wilson dream." During the weeks before I began my work I received testimony from many people as to all the varying shades of Mr. Wilson's wickedness. I can confess now that I went to my task with some apprehension. After two years of minute study of Mr. Wilson's life through his intimate papers and revealing personal notes, my admiration has increased a thousandfold.

I have been particularly impressed in this work with the wide gaps between the current statements about Wilson and the facts of his life as shown in the daily record. During the past year or two "Wilson's failure" has become a national theme song, chanted every hour of the day and through every medium—newspaper column, radio, pulpit, play, lecture platform: "Wilson's obstinacy," "Wilson's pigheadedness," his "determination not to consult the Senate" (he consulted it thirty-three times in a single year!), "Wilson's refusal to compromise"—without which, we are told, the League would have succeeded, the United States would have joined, and we should have had an efficient world organization long ago.

Most of these statements started with his political enemies during his lifetime and were handed down and repeated again and again until a whole nation believed them.

Happily, the theme now is changing. As we come to know more about international organization and the things Wilson worked for, we gain a greater appreciation of our twenty-eighth President. In another fifty years he too will have his marble memorials and national highways; people will forget that they once criticized and scoffed at him; it will be the fashion to cheer and hurrah over Wilson as over Lincoln and Washington.

Meanwhile there is only one plea his adherents need make: Look at the record. Study Wilson's concrete acts and accomplishments—then, if you will, talk about Wilson's failures. Study the factual record of the accomplishments of his League of Nations and the men who ran it. Then, if you still feel like it, talk about the failure of Wilson's League.

To present this record as completely and accurately as possible is the object of the present volume.   R. C.

MAN OF DESTINY

ARIS, on a sunny winter morning of December 14, 1918—Paris
a-thrill and a-quiver. Today the President of the United
States was coming, the President of the New World!

Flags were flying, bands playing, people hurrying through the
city with happy, excited feet. "All Paris" and as much of France
as could get there packed the streets and crowded the rooftops.
Day of days and victory of victories for Paris!

1870 was a date to laugh at this morning; Germany a word to
toss off with a contemptuous *"Bah—les Boches!"* Captured German cannon filled the Place de la Concorde. The statue of
Alsace-Lorraine, freed from her long mourning, shone with flags
and flowers and glittering wreaths. Triumphant French soldiers
lined the stately avenues and massed their banners at the bridges.
Huge placards on public buildings bore their salutation of welcome: *"Vive Wilson! Vive le Grand Président! Vive Wilson le
Juste!"*

Church bells ringing, students singing, the crowds surging up
the Champs Elysées toward the Arch and round the station
where he would come in. Ambassadors leaned from balconies;
shopgirls were squashed in doorways and long windows, cafés
packed with eager customers standing on chairs, tables, counters
—anything. Men and boys perched precariously on telegraph
poles and chestnut trees, policemen trying unsuccessfully to be
severe.

"Vive Wilson! Vive les Etats-Unis!" Only a few minutes now—
he was coming!

French mothers waved little American flags in crepe-banded
fingers; French *mutilés* waved their crutches and shouted with
the rest; trembling hands lifted black veils to gaze for a moment
—faces that had almost forgotten how to smile, smiled once
more. Faces too disfigured ever to smile again managed a twisted
gleam of hope. Blind men clinging to their brothers and sisters

xiii

Man of Destiny

shivered and cried: "Isn't it wonderful? *Feel* how glorious it is!"

The helmets of the Garde Républicaine glittered in the sunlight. Now the Generals—the American General Pershing, Marshal Haig, the Maréchale of France—officers of other nations, Poles, Greeks, Belgians, Australians. Then side by side the French and the Americans—two nations friends since Lafayette led his men against the Hessians.

Hark—the American national anthem. He was coming. "Look, Justine—watch for him, Pierre. You'll never forget this day, my boy. He'll pass right by here—any minute now!"

Yes, he was coming. He who used to stride up and down the Princeton woods in his student days and declaim to the trees the great words he was one day to utter before parliaments and statesmen; he who fed upon the ringing phrases of Burke and Pitt, John Bright and Gladstone, was here today to utter his own historic terms. He whose major passion for thirty years had been the study of government and the grand spiritual truths of his Scottish ancestors, today held the highest governmental position and the moral leadership of the entire world. Woodrow Wilson held the people of the world in his two hands that morning—to sway, to mold, to guide and direct as he pleased.

"I got up at four o'clock to be here to greet him," said a gnarled old peasant in a blue blouse. "I came all the way from Rouen," said another. "I'm a blacksmith from the Vosges," a third big fellow confessed sheepishly.

Blacksmiths, farmers, bankers, businessmen—up the avenue they swept in a vast welcoming wave, rendering, in the words of every person who witnessed it, the highest tribute ever paid to a living man.

To Wilson it was a moment of supreme dedication, service, responsibility: his own responsibility and that of his nation. Because she was the greatest, hers was the greatest duty. This was always his central theme. Because she possessed the most, she owed the most. Because she had suffered least, she must be prepared to give more now than all the others—who had suffered everything. Great privileges impose great obligations. This was

Man of Destiny

the dominant theme of every gathering at which Wilson presided—not "America first" but "Humanity first," with America and every nation pouring out its best for all mankind.

Thus he came to his own great moment. The carriage that bore him through the city beside the President of France swung through the square with its hundred thousand joyous people and turned into the avenue. The bells rang out, the cannon boomed, a great shout went up. For the first time in half a century the chains were drawn back, the Arch of Triumph was thrown open —his carriage swept through.

Wilson had taken Paris. Wilson had captured the imagination of the world.

THE STORY

OF

WOODROW WILSON

CHAPTER I

THE

MAKING OF

THE MAN

I

Fifty-three years before that December morning in Paris, a little boy in Augusta, Georgia, said to his father, the Reverend Joseph Wilson: "Do you know, Father, I believe the very best profession is to be President of the United States."

"Do you really think so, now?" asked his father teasingly. "And are you intending to have a try for it?"

"Well," said Tommy Wilson reddening, "maybe I might be a *Senator*."

They were gazing into the flashing saws of one of Augusta's big cotton mills. The Reverend Joseph Wilson was a man of great gifts and considerable originality, which he exhibited in the education of his son. He was a master of precise and beautiful English, and on Sunday afternoons after his church duties he would sit down with the boy and pour into his wondering ears the great classics of verse and prose that gave Woodrow Wilson the respect for words and their magnificent use that stayed with him all his life.

On Mondays Dr. Wilson usually took the afternoon off and set forth with his son on some excursion in the city or country. The two would visit the factories and machine shops of Augusta; Tom was initiated into the mysteries of furnaces, boilers, engine rooms, shown the history of a bit of steel or a bale of cotton from the crude to the finished product. He always remembered the impression made upon him then of "gigantic engines, the roar of furnaces, or the darting up of sheets of flame, the great forges presided over by imps with sooty faces."

He did not learn his alphabet or go to school until he was nine years old. But these frequent tours of investigation into living things and visible processes, with a running commentary by his father on the laws of nature and of human society as they went along, taught the boy much that he could never have got from books. They also laid the foundation of that democratic respect for all types of men and their work that later made him such a great humanitarian.

Wilson's people on both sides were Scotch-Irish—a race of sturdy fighters; stouthearted men, who knew what they believed and were not slow to express themselves. He used to tell his students jokingly that "no one who amounts to anything is without some Scotch-Irish blood." Grandfather Wilson was a printer, known for his positive opinions and his courage in stating them. His papers—in Pittsburgh and Steubenville, Pennsylvania, where the family lived—discussed the questions of the day with bluntness and conviction. Grandfather Woodrow, born in Paisley, educated in Glasgow, and afterwards minister in the North of England, came to America in 1843 with his family, to preach the gospel. They settled at Chillicothe, Ohio. But Jessie Woodrow, one of the daughters, attended the Young Ladies' Female

The Making of the Man

Seminary of Steubenville; and one day, looking over a garden wall, she saw and liked young Joseph Wilson.

Well she might, for this Joseph was a remarkable fellow: tall, handsome, with a great shock of black hair and piercing brown eyes. "My incomparable father," Woodrow Wilson used to call him. "If I had my father's face and figure I could say anything!"

Like all *his* father's sons, Joseph of course learned printing. His brothers went into business, but Joseph was the scholar of the family. He made a brilliant college record, at the institution now known as Washington and Jefferson. Later he decided to study for the Presbyterian ministry, and he was graduated from Princeton Theological Seminary in 1846 with the degree of Bachelor of Divinity. Instead of entering at once upon a pastorate, he taught for a time at the Steubenville Male Academy. While there he met Jessie Woodrow. The two were married on June 7, 1849.

Woodrow Wilson's parents were both, as one might expect, unusual people. Dr. Joseph Wilson was a fine preacher as well as a scholar and a wit. He preached in Beecher's pulpit and Talmadge's and remained an outstanding figure in the Presbyterian Church over a period of forty years. Brilliant in conversation, full of life and gaiety, he was a companion whom his son adored, not only in childhood but to the end of his days.

"I have never seen filial affection equal to that of Woodrow Wilson for his father," wrote one of his Princeton friends, Professor Winthrop Daniels. Old friends wherever the Wilsons lived said the same. Even after he was a man of forty the son planned his vacations so that he could see as much as possible of his father; he consulted him before reaching any important decision, went to him for criticism on all his speeches and writings, and awaited his verdict with far more anxiety than he showed towards Congressmen and crowned heads. He considered his father the finest speaker he had ever heard, and the greatest man in the universe.

His mother was just as remarkable in her way—a woman of unusual spirit, with lively gray eyes and a wide, intelligent brow;

The Story of Woodrow Wilson

firm, and of great strength of character. She had sailed across the ocean with her father when she was only seven years old, on the long, fearsome voyage to America. A storm had come up, and little Jessie, on deck, was clutching a rope when a big wave hit the ship, buried the bow in the water, and swung the little girl far out over the sea. However, she held on fast and swung back again; and became the mother of the courageous, hard-holding twenty-eighth President of the United States.

She was more sedate than his father—a typical gentlewoman, said the neighbors, quiet and dignified in her manner. Scotch to the marrow she was, deep in her affections, independent in her convictions, capable of strong loyalty and of strong indignation when aroused. (As, for example, when certain gentlemen of the Church had the effrontery to take her scientist brother James to task for his outspoken belief in the new doctrine of evolution!)

"Everyone who knew her," wrote her son, "felt the charm of her unusual grace . . . the clear perceiving mind. . . ." How much he thought of her, how deeply and constantly she was in his heart was shown when he was at the height of his power and in the midst of the most exacting work of his life. Just before the opening of the Peace Conference he took one of his precious three days in Britain to visit her home. He was staying at Buckingham Palace at the time, on a visit of state. Early on a Sunday morning, December 27, 1918, the royal train of the King of England drew into a little station near the Scotch border. It was Carlisle, the town where she was born and where she and his grandfather lived until they went to America. The whole population turned out to greet her famous son and escort him to the church where Grandfather Woodrow had preached and where little Jessie Woodrow had sat in the pew looking up at him. There they sang a hymn and said a prayer. And there, with an emotion he found it difficult to conceal, "the most renowned man in the world" paid a tribute to his mother that no one who heard it ever forgot.

From her he inherited his shyness, his intense reserve and retiring disposition (there was nothing retiring about his father), his love of simplicity and dislike of ostentation; and, perhaps, his instinctive affinity for English institutions.

His mother and father had been married seven years when he was born. They already had two daughters, Anne and Marion. Another son, Joseph Jr., arrived in 1866. The family had lived in a number of places during those early years while Dr. Wilson began building the reputation as a preacher and teacher which brought him increasing distinction. After filling various charges he was called to the First Presbyterian Church of Staunton, a fine old town in a beautiful valley of Virginia. Here he and Mrs. Wilson moved with their daughters in 1855, and here, on December 28, 1856, their son Thomas Woodrow Wilson was born.

II

H E WAS a fine, healthy child—"just as good as he can be," wrote his mother; "plump, and remarkably quiet," said an aunt. "That baby," observed his Grandfather Woodrow, "is dignified enough to be Moderator of the General Assembly."

When Tommy was one year old his father accepted a call to Augusta, Georgia, where the family lived for thirteen years. Thus, although Wilson was born in the State called "the Mother of Presidents," his actual residence in Virginia was brief.

Augusta, where he spent the important formative years of his childhood, was an attractive city of the old South, with many fine homes and plantations. The life of its fifteen thousand people revolved about its rolling mills, railroad shops, and cotton and spinning mills. The Wilsons lived in a comfortable red brick parsonage across the street from the Presbyterian Church. The church, a substantial building with a tower and a white spire, was set in a dignified square in the center of town, and was the focus of the religious life of the community, its members outnumbering the aristocratic Episcopalians. To be minister of such a church in those days was to rank with the foremost leaders of the time. To be a Presbyterian was to be predestined to leadership.

The Story of Woodrow Wilson

The little boy grew up in an atmosphere of pleasant superiority and a home of more than average comfort for a minister's son. In addition to the Doctor's salary from teaching and preaching, there was a small legacy from Mrs. Wilson's brother and the family never knew the pinch of poverty or various restrictions which many ministers' families have to suffer. This had an important bearing on Thomas Woodrow's education, which he was able to continue through three universities, until nearly his thirtieth year.

When Tommy finally did go to school he attended Professor Derry's Academy, and Professor Derry used to boast that he was the only man who ever had licked Woodrow Wilson. This usually happened after the circus came to town, for Thomas Woodrow, like most of the other boys, played hooky. They would stop at the cotton mill on their way home and lay in some cotton pads to mitigate their inevitable punishment—applying these, as Wilson recounted later, "in the places where they would do the most good."

Among his companions at the time was Pleasant Stovall, whom he later appointed Minister to Switzerland, and Joseph Lamar, later Associate Justice of the Supreme Court. Tommy played baseball and Indians with his friends, learned to ride exceptionally well—a straight little figure atop his father's big black horse —read prodigiously, and was fascinated by ships. His greatest game was playing Admiral in the American Navy. Professor Derry records him a "very indifferent student"—not because he wasn't bright, but principally it seemed "because he just wasn't interested."

Apparently the chief interest of his early youth was a club which he organized himself and which was called the Lightfoots. The club had various secret and mysterious purposes. Its insignia was a lurid red devil taken from an advertising poster for deviled ham. Its members played baseball, challenging other teams of the neighborhood. Tommy Wilson was not one of the best players, but he was president of the club just the same. Meetings took place in the loft of Dr. Wilson's barn, and Tommy was in his element presiding. He made a constitution for the club—before

8

The Making of the Man

he was ten years old—and all debates were conducted according to rules of strictly parliamentary procedure.

The boys were thrilled by the appearance of the first trolley cars, clanging perilously down the street, and loved to manufacture "scissors" out of crossed pins laid on the track. Tommy had friends and cousins who lived at the Sand Hills and in the big corn and cotton plantations round about Augusta, and he frequently rode out to spend the day and have a good game with them.

His father was a great playfellow for a growing boy. Ministerial dignity would be cast aside, and the two would go into a wild game of tag around the garden, while the rest of the family looked on, from the window, laughing. "I've got him, the young rascal—I've got him!" the Doctor would call excitedly, grabbing the flying Thomas triumphantly by the trouser leg.

The father was a cruel tease and a master of witty repartee—some of it barbed. The boy had to take his share of the verbal drubbing. He grew up hearing his adored father's swift and telling digs at people and questions, and the admiring laughter these sallies provoked. Later he developed a similar gift of his own—perhaps by way of unconscious imitation. His overswift and sometimes cruel tongue stood in his way in public life.

But the teasings were just occasional fireworks on the father's part. Life at home was close, devoted, congenial. The family loved to sing together of an evening. Tommy developed a fine tenor and all his life enjoyed singing, especially the old songs and hymns. They also loved books and reading aloud: Scott, Dickens, and books of travel and poetry. Many an evening they spent like this, the mother knitting beneath the lamp, the two sisters side by side on the sofa, the little boy Tommy perched near by while his father read from *David Copperfield* or *Pickwick Papers*.

Dr. Wilson had a fine, deep voice which he used to perfection, playing upon it to convey every shade of meaning and emotion. Woodrow Wilson never forgot his father's voice or how his father's great laugh would ring out when he came to some passage that especially pleased him. That voice sank into the

9

consciousness of the listening child. Throughout his life Wilson loved the roll of grand and beautiful words, and himself became one of the greatest modern masters of English, with a voice that thrilled and fascinated his hearers.

His father believed that there could be no clear thought unless it could be put quickly and definitely into words. "Tommy, what do you mean by that?" he would demand sternly, when his son brought him an article or a speech to criticize in later years. Tommy would explain what he meant, usually in much simpler terms. "Then why don't you say so?" asked the older Wilson indignantly. A splendid discipline for a future statesman and maker of covenants and constitutions.

He was still very young when he came upon a word he never had heard before but which was to play an immense part in his own destiny.

"Abe Lincoln's been elected—now there'll be war! Abe Lincoln's been elected, yes *sir!* Now there sure *will* be war!"

A little boy swinging on his father's gate—two men going by, talking in excited tones, repeating that word over and over: this, he said afterward, was his very earliest recollection.

War. That word he never had been taught. He ran into the house to ask his father what it meant. And his father drew him onto his knee and explained "war" to the boy who was later to become a war President.

It was daily and dramatically explained to him in the years that followed: when troops marched through the quiet streets of Augusta; when his father's church became a hospital full of groaning wounded, and the churchyard a prison camp with blue-uniformed soldiers under guard; when great battles were being fought and the people prayed all night after rolling cartridges all day; when Sherman's army was actually "marching through Georgia" and might descend on the town of Augusta at any moment. Finally Tommy stood with the rest of his family and watched the President of the Confederacy, Jefferson Davis, led away defeated between Federal soldiers. Later still, on a sad but peaceful day when it was all over, he gazed up into the "noble"

The Making of the Man

face of General Robert E. Lee, who remained always one of his favorite heroes.

Then came the Reconstruction chaos, when freedom-drunk Negroes and carpetbag adventurers who cared neither for law nor for the people lorded it over the land, crushing great families and devastating their homes. In such scenes the boy passed his impressionable early years.

The Wilsons were not Southern-born, but they were strong Southern sympathizers. Dr. Wilson, with his independent Scotch spirit, believed in the right of secession. When the break came in the Presbyterian Church he sided with the South, and the first Southern assembly was held in his church. But neither he nor his son was an extremist, and they never spoke with hate or bitterness. Woodrow Wilson referred to the war as "a dark chapter of history." He knew what his relatives and friends in the South had gone through. He was "neither justifying nor condemning but only comprehending," he said in an article on Reconstruction, years later.

When his son was fourteen Dr. Wilson was called to a professorship at the Theological Seminary at Columbia, South Carolina—a city terribly devastated by the war, just beginning to raise its head again. Columbia Seminary was bitterly poor in material things, but it had a great tradition for learning and leadership. Here the growing lad was surrounded by an extraordinary group of scholars and thinkers who exercised a profound influence on his life.

In Columbia Tommy attended Mr. Barnwell's school. Mr. Barnwell himself did most of the teaching, having sometimes fifty boys whom he taught at the rate of seven or eight dollars a month. Tommy Wilson was well liked by his teacher and the other pupils, but here again he was not very good at his studies. Indeed, his father and his Uncle James were seriously concerned over the boy's progress. They both had been honor men, at the top of their classes. They held family conferences with the old Scotch grandfather to decide what to do with a boy who could not do better than Tommy was doing in his school.

But Tommy's real education came from knowledge gained

The Story of Woodrow Wilson

outside the formal scholastic routine: from his father's lectures at the Seminary, where he slipped in and listened from the back row, hidden from the older students; from the books he read in the library, to which he was given a special key; above all, from the stirring conversation of those splendid scholars and colleagues of his father—great philosophers and preachers, doctors, scientists, pioneers from far-off China and Africa in the mission field, all of them *leaders*, men of vision, of sacrifice, of devoted service to their fellow-creatures. Day after day at the Seminary and in his own home the boy would listen to these men discussing the problems of that tumultuous postwar period: States' rights and Federal government; the race problem, problems of returning soldiers, problems of education and rehabilitation.

What a preparation for the man who forty-five years later faced reconstruction problems beside which those of the Civil War faded to insignificance. At the time they seemed colossal, and the men around Tommy Wilson—baffled by the confusion and suffering—turned for reassurance to the "eternal verities," the dauntless life of the spirit.

The life of the Wilson family naturally centered on religion. From his earliest childhood the Church remained the pivot of the boy's existence. He attended services, joined in the hymns and responses, listened with awe and exaltation to the great voice of his father proclaiming the message of the Psalms or the Gospels. His father's sermons sometimes went over the heads of the simple people of his congregation, but they ably fulfilled what was perhaps their real mission—to prepare and fortify a coming world leader with faith and strength to meet whatever might happen.

In the dark days of the Civil War and the darker days of the Reconstruction the thoughts of the men and women around Tommy Wilson turned more than ever to religious consolation. What if mountainous troubles and sorrows did encompass people here? There, in those eternal principles, lay an everlasting surety and hope. This was one of the very earliest elements instilled into the boy: belief in principle, reliance on principle, readiness,

The Making of the Man

to sacrifice anything, go through anything, even to die for principle if necessary. For principle is truth, and endureth forever.

Every member of his family, all the great men around him were as sure of it as of their own names. Woodrow Wilson grew up believing in this truth as he believed in his own father. When all men forsook you and your cause seemed utterly lost, you could still remain calm knowing that principle is never beaten but that in the end it must triumph "as surely as God reigns." He was to live to test his conviction to the uttermost.

At home, throughout his youth, there were family prayers each day, the reading of the Bible, the sharing of personal religious experience on the part of his parents and sisters. In Sunday school he learned the shorter catechism. "What is the chief end of man?" his old Scotch grandfather would ask sternly. It was a hard struggle, for he found it difficult to commit things to memory. He shivered at the thought of what the longer catechism might be. But he came to know and love the Bible, which remained his daily guide and inspiration throughout his life. Sooner or later a boy brought up in such an atmosphere had to come to his own religious experience and his own view as to the chief end of man.

When Tommy was sixteen he became greatly attracted to a young man named Brooke who was studying for the ministry at Columbia. This young man possessed a deeply spiritual nature and the gift of inspiring others. He held meetings in his room which Tommy and some of the seminary students attended. Soon the attendance grew so large that the meetings had to be moved to the seminary chapel—a small brick stable with a few pictures on the walls, a simple rostrum, and some plain wooden benches. In this humble stable Woodrow Wilson's personal experience of the Christian life was born.

On July 5, 1873, the official record of the First Presbyterian Church of Columbia states that Thomas W. Wilson with two other young men of the Sunday school applied for membership in the First Presbyterian Church. "After a free confession in which they severally exhibited evidences of a work of grace in

The Story of Woodrow Wilson

their hearts, they were unanimously admitted to membership in this church."

Wilson counted this religious awakening as one of the major turning points of his life. From that time on, as he told a friend, "argument was adjourned" for him so far as religion was concerned. He accepted without question—though no doubt with his own personal interpretation—the doctrines of his father's church. (One daughter remembers a twinkle in his eye when the Church in later years reversed some of its tenets on infant damnation.) The important things for him were the great basic principles, direct spiritual experience, the Bible, and his daily prayers. These he continued in his own home after he had one, and until the very day of his death.

"I do not see," he said, "how anyone can sustain himself in any enterprise in life without prayer. It is the only spring at which he can renew his spirit and purify his motive." He himself, said one of his friends, "prayed like a man who knew God not only as a fact in history but as an experience in his own soul." His writings and addresses are richly interwoven with references to the things of the spirit and to his religious convictions. His career can be understood only in the light of these and against the background of the doctrines and attitudes inculcated in his early years. Some of these doctrines had implications clearly evident in the later philosophy and fixed ideas of the man. Predestination, for example: a man who is predestined and a foreordained agent of God has nothing to fear—from governments or rulers, would-be assassins or anybody. Several members of Wilson's family tell how he would reassure them at times when they worried about his physical safety: "Don't you know," he would say, smiling, "that I am immortal till my work is done?"

Another firm belief of the Presbyterian is that the Presbyterians are unquestionably right, on matters of principle. He and his friends are right; and he expects his friends to think as he does—naturally, or they would not be his friends. This bred-in-the-bone doctrine caused Woodrow Wilson some of his most acute suffering when his friends disagreed with him, as in the case of Professor Hibben at Princeton, and others. It also caused

14

his scathing indictment of those who acted from principles foreign to his own, and alienated from him certain men to whom he gave a sound tongue-thrashing. He was sometimes harsh in his judgments, tenacious in his hatreds as in his loves. In short, he had the weaknesses of his strengths, the defects of his virtues. Yet without his tenacity and conviction we should never have had a League of Nations.

Religious faith; his mother and father and their stalwart Scotspeople; the Civil War; the scholars and pioneers of the Reconstruction era—these were some of the primary influences that went into the making and molding of Woodrow Wilson. There was also his passionate interest in strong men who led and governed. "Who is that?" asked his young cousin, looking up at a portrait that hung over his desk while the youthful Wilson sat practicing his shorthand.

"That is Gladstone, the greatest statesman in the world! Wait —I'll read you about him!" the boy replied eagerly.

Meanwhile it was time he was getting on with his education. Mr. Barnwell's School at Columbia was no longer considered suitable for the fast-developing youth. In the autumn of 1873 he was sent along with young Brooke to Davidson College at Mecklenburg, North Carolina, his family fondly hoping that from there he would go on to study for the ministry.

III

T. W. WILSON's report card for the term ending December 22, 1873, shows the following record:

Logic and Rhetoric	95	Composition and English	96
Greek	87	Declamation	92
Latin	90	Deportment	100
Mathematics	74		

As usual, he had made only an average record—lowest in Mathematics and, after Deportment, highest in Composition and English. His mathematics was generally, as he said, "terrible."

The Story of Woodrow Wilson

The truth was, he had been very badly prepared and entered Davidson with several conditions, being obliged to make up a heavy amount of back work.

Davidson was a Presbyterian school with Scotch traditions. It boasted one huge pillared building, where most of its activities took place. Life was primitive at this Southern college of the late nineteenth century: the boys had to cut their own wood and fetch their own water from the pump outside; many of them earned their own way. But some great men came out of Davidson. One of them was Robert Glenn, afterwards Governor of North Carolina.

Glenn remarked irritably to another member of the baseball team, of which he was captain, that "Tommy Wilson would be a good ballplayer if he weren't so damned lazy." Tommy played center field and was an average batter. He was not lazy, but his main interest lay in his debating society. There were two debating societies at Davidson as at every Southern college of the time. T. Wilson had become a member of the "Eumenean."

The object of the society was "the acquirement of literary knowledge, the promotion of virtue, and the cultivation of social harmony and friendship." The discipline was severe. T. Wilson is listed as having been fined ten cents for "sitting on the rostrum" (fine marked "Pd"). Subjects for debate were relevant to the time: "Was the Death of Lincoln Beneficial to the South?" "Was John Wilkes Booth a Patriot?" "Was the Introduction of Slavery into the United States Beneficial to the Human Race?"

T. Wilson at once began looking into the constitution of the society. He obtained a new record book and himself copied out the entire constitution. The record does not show whether he recommended any changes, but almost certainly he did.

His first public appearance is set down as December 1, 1873, when he debated in the negative the question: "Resolved, that Republicanism is a better form of government than a limited monarchy." He delivered an "original oration" on January 17 and debated the question of compulsory education—in the affirmative—on February 20. In May he was marked "excused"

The Making of the Man

from several meetings because of illness. Never very strong, he was finding the effort to make up his work too much for him.

In June he went home, not in good enough health or sufficiently well prepared to enter a university that autumn. He remained at home for the following fifteen months, studying and reading, leading a rather solitary existence.

In the fall of 1874 his family moved to Wilmington, North Carolina. Tommy did not care much for Wilmington, but it had one great attraction—the docks. His early passion for the sea revived, and he spent much of his time poking around the vessels. He wanted to run away to sea but was persuaded by his mother to give it up. Pirates—treasure—enchanted islands—far places—"I lived a dream life when I was a lad," he said; "the world seemed a place of heroic adventure."

One boy whom he met at Wilmington—five years younger than he but a member of his father's church—was Edwin Alderman, afterwards President of the University of Virginia, and an honored friend of Wilson's later years. In 1924, after Mr. Wilson's death, Dr. Alderman delivered his great Memorial Address before the two houses of Congress; an address remarkable for its beauty, feeling, and penetrating analysis of the man whom he first knew back in the Wilmington days when young Wilson would appear at home from college—"a tall slender youth of curious homeliness, detachment, and distinction."

At that particular time Wilson had few friends of his own age. He had grown very fast and was awkward and shy "but very dignified and courteous," one friend remembers. "You should have seen him escorting his mother down the street or handing her into her pew on Sunday morning." He read a great deal in his father's magazines—especially the *Edinburgh Review* and the New York *Nation*. His interest in famous personages also continued. One young man whom Wilson saw a good deal of at this time, John Bellamy, remembered how he liked to sit and talk for hours about great public men—Cromwell, Lincoln, Stonewall Jackson, General Lee—to analyze their characters and

17

question what it was that made them great.

In the autumn of 1875, when he was nearly nineteen, he seemed sufficiently well prepared to enter Princeton, his father's alma mater and another stronghold of Presbyterianism firmly approved by the Wilson clan. Dr. McCosh, the President, had been down on a visit to Dr. Wilson and looked the lad over approvingly. "A fine boy—he'll be comin' to Princeton, no doubt."

So on the eleventh of September, 1875, a tall young man from North Carolina, wearing a round hat and carrying a "ministerial-looking black bag," walked into the village of Princeton. Nobody noticed him much, except for a few friendly upperclassmen. The quiet town, long accustomed to its yearly influx of Freshmen, did not perceive that a future President of the University, and one who was to be the center of a bitter, dramatic struggle, had arrived.

IV

NOTHING startling occurred during young Wilson's Freshman year. He did not set the world on fire. He had some hard tussles with his Greek and Latin. He was not among the twenty-one Freshman "Honor Men" listed in June. The main things he did, aside from his studies, were to make some good friends in an eating club known as the Alligators and to join a debating society—the Whigs.

But in the beginning of his Sophomore year something happened that changed the course of Woodrow Wilson's life—and the lives of millions of other people. As we have seen, he had a strong interest in statesmen and politics, particularly English politics, and had read everything he could find about them. When he reached Princeton he spent long hours in the library, looking into the speeches of Burke and John Bright and the essays of Bagehot, though Gladstone remained his chief hero.

One day he ran across some copies of the British *Gentleman's*

The Making of the Man

Magazine. His eye fell on an article describing "Men and Manner in Parliament." It was brilliantly though anonymously written, by a man in intimate daily familiarity with the parliamentary scene ("The Member from Chiltern Hundreds"), and it stirred young Wilson deeply, waking in him an intense desire to be part of that scene. He found another article by the same writer, called "The Orator," which so fired his imagination that he remembered always the particular corner of the library—near the south stairs—where he read it. The article spoke of the supreme qualities of oratory, "earnestness and conviction," and asserted that of the 653 members of the House of Commons, only three could be properly classed as orators: Mr. Bright, Mr. Gladstone, and possibly Mr. Fawcett. It called Mr. Bright "the orator par excellence of the House because of his great sincerity and honest conviction—a mighty power."

These and other articles, especially one on "The Democratic Party in the United States," made a profound impression on young Wilson. They made the world of great men and great affairs in which he always had been romantically interested suddenly almost unbearably real. More than that, they wakened him with a rush to the consciousness of his own powers. The things he had been reading about—he could do these things himself. *He* could stir men and women with the magic of eloquence, he could debate, he could govern, he could lead the people with great principles and fiery words. He now saw clearly and consciously as he always had known subconsciously and instinctively what he was here to do: the meaning of his own life, his task upon this earth, and his high calling. Statesmanship —for him, Thomas Woodrow Wilson: to be a consecrated, devoted public leader of the first rank.

Jubilantly he wrote his family about his great discovery, confident that they would rejoice with him. But the family seemed disappointed—especially his father, who had hoped that the boy would add to the long family record and bring his brilliant gifts to the service of the Presbyterian Church. "Oh, my boy, how I wish you had entered the ministry!" his father would cry out, even to the end of his days.

The Story of Woodrow Wilson

But nothing could budge Wilson, once he really had made up his mind. From this moment he took his education into his own hands. Henceforth he had a clear and single purpose: to prepare himself for public life. He therefore began to devote his every energy to becoming an authority on government and to developing the qualities required for leadership.

He had an instinctive feeling for what he needed. His most intimate classmate, Robert Bridges, says of him that his college career was remarkable for "the confident selection of his work" and his "easy indifference" to all subjects not directly in line with his purpose. "Wilson's business in college," says another, "was to train his mind to do what he wanted it to do, and what he wanted he knew." His stenography became a great help to him in making digests of what he read—and he read constantly, always noting what he wanted to remember. To his reading he added strenuous practice in writing and extemporaneous speaking, striving for ease and exactness in expression, nimbleness in debate. He followed this course from the moment of his great decision and kept it up to the day he was graduated. The debating clubs of the college helped him.

The student body at Princeton was divided into two debating "Halls"—the American Whig Society and the Cliosophic Society. Wilson belonged to Whig Hall, an organization founded by James Madison. Here the young man was in his glory. He became one of the leading spirits of his Hall and began in good earnest the practice of elocution. It was a frequent sight to see him in the Princeton woods declaiming from a volume of Burke. During his vacations at home he would go into his father's empty church and practice speaking from the pulpit.

Later on he himself organized another debating society called the Liberal Debating Club, fashioned after the British Parliament. One group of members represented the Government and had to maintain the confidence of the chamber or "go out of power." He was more and more convinced of the superiority of the British form of democracy, and political events in this country tended to strengthen his conviction.

In 1876, while Wilson was in college, came the Hayes-Tilden

The Making of the Man

election contest, when an Electoral Commission had to decide a political scandal involving double returns from four States. The Commission finally gave the election to the Republican candidate, Mr. Hayes, though Mr. Tilden needed only one more electoral vote to win, and everybody knew that actually the three Southern States in dispute were overwhelmingly Democratic and for Mr. Tilden. But our electoral mechanism permitted the "carpetbag" Republican government in control in the South during those Reconstruction days to turn in a report of "fraud" in various precincts and thus dominate the situation. Many public-spirited people took the view of young Wilson that our governmental machinery needed to be thoroughly re-examined, and possibly drastically changed. The students in many colleges discussed the issue hotly.

At that very same period a young Texan whom Wilson did not meet until forty years later—a boy by the name of Edward House, also much stirred up about the Hayes-Tilden controversy —was disposing of his college studies at Cornell as imperiously as Wilson disposed of his at Princeton. Young House kept running down to Washington with his friend Oliver Morton, hanging about Senator Morton's parlor, drinking in all the backstage gossip and personalities, and beginning already his eager search for "some really great American leader for the future."

Little men were in the saddle in those days. What had become of the great Americans of former times? Why were there no more Patrick Henrys, Daniel Websters, Clays, and Calhouns? England and the countries of Europe had their great orators. What had happened in America?

"Have you ever thought," Wilson asked one of his classmates, "what is the reason for the decline of American oratory?" He believed it was due to our "deadly" system of committee government. In England great orators and leaders continued to exist because all questions were debated in open forum in the House of Commons; governments kept or lost their power because of the personal force of the leaders, and because the country really supported or opposed them. But in America, land of the free, a hierarchy of powerful committees settled everything in ad-

21

The Story of Woodrow Wilson

vance: Congress was invited to confirm, not to challenge or debate, their decisions.

This idea churned within him during the next two years; he kept thinking and making notes about it. Later it became one of the chief themes of his political writing and speaking. In his Senior year he wrote a powerful article entitled "Cabinet Government in the United States." It was published in the *International Review*, a leading American journal of the time.

One of the younger editors of the periodical that accepted his article, with its passionate plea against government by committee, was Henry Cabot Lodge, who years later used one of those very committees to wreck Woodrow Wilson's greatest political project.

Life was not all work for this serious-minded young man. He played baseball and headed the Athletic Association, though he was never an outstanding athlete. He serenaded young ladies and took part in various undergraduate pranks. He was a normal college boy, interested in everything that was going on, mingling with everybody, liked by all. In '77 he went on the board of the *Princetonian*, the college weekly, and later became its manager.

Wilson was always popular with his classmates. With all his dignity, he had a great deal of charm. He talked brilliantly, he could sing a song, dance a cakewalk, tell a good story; he helped the younger students and devoted himself to the interests of the college. "There was not a touch of the pedant or the dig about him," said one of his college friends. "He was as keen on the life of the college as any of us—cheered as wildly at the games, stood up for the rights of the undergraduate body as firmly as anybody."

The legend of his being "cold" and "hard to get along with" seems odd, considering his obvious genius for attracting friends. He made friendships at Princeton which endured to the end of his life, especially with Robert Bridges, Hiram Woods, and Charlie Talcott. With Talcott he entered into "a solemn covenant" which exercised a powerful influence on the lives of both young men: "a covenant that we would school all our powers and passions for the work of establishing the principles we held in

The Making of the Man

common; that we would acquire knowledge and drill ourselves in all the arts of persuasion so that we might persuade others and lead them to our ways of thinking."

Early in his course Wilson went to live in Witherspoon Hall and soon became the central figure in the crowd known as the "Witherspoon Gang." They got together in the early evening and discussed everything under the sun. Through all the years Wilson cherished those ties; he sent messages to their reunions when he was President and referred with affection to "the boys at Witherspoon."

"Give my love to the gang . . . how I wish I could have got over for reunion. . . . Hope you found the boys well and in good spirits. . . . I believe I love the fellows of that crowd and value the genuine friendships existing among us more now than I ever did before. . . . I feel an occasional heartsickness because of the dispersion of the old crowd and the necessity which keeps us apart."

He grew steadily—in his writing, his debate, his character, and in the estimation of his fellow-students. On them he made a strong impression of *power*.

"There was," writes his friend Bridges, "a certain integrity in his ideal from boy to man that gave his friends a peculiar confidence in his ultimate destiny as a leader of men. He used to say jokingly, 'When I meet you in the Senate I'll argue that out with you!' But the boys did not take it as a joke altogether— nor did he. He had all along that instinct of unusual capacities —of a future for which he was consciously preparing, almost indeed consecrating himself."

"When I meet you in the Senate . . ." He even wrote out a number of cards in a youthful, flowing hand:

THOMAS WOODROW WILSON
Senator from Virginia

The Governorship also occurred to him, or perhaps the Secretaryship of the Navy; but the Senate remained his preferred goal.

Meanwhile he read omnivorously in his special subjects, acquainting himself not only with American and English politics but studying French and German and other European political systems. He read the history of many European nations and sought to understand the background of their governments and institutions. All his reading was done thoughtfully, thoroughly. Wilson never skimmed through anything. He had the genius' incurable passion for taking pains.

Thus he reached the important milestone of his Senior year. He now had become star debater of the Whig Society, and everybody expected him to represent his Hall in the big college contest for the Lynde Debate Prize and to win it. The debate was one of the big events of Commencement, and the prize one of the highly coveted honors of the Senior class. The subject was "Free Trade vs. Tariff for Protection," which Wilson knew thoroughly. He was, of course, a free-trader, a disciple of his hero Cobden. The more he studied the subject the stronger his views became.

But when the time came for the preliminary debate in Whig Hall, he drew the protective-tariff side. Wilson tore up the slip and refused to debate. "No—never! First, last, and forever I'm a free-trader. Nothing under heaven will make me argue for a principle I do not believe!" Another young man became Whig Hall's representative in the debate—and lost.

Wilson has been frequently criticized for this episode, for "having lost a prize which he could easily have won," not only for himself but for his Hall. He has been accused of pigheadedness and exaggerated scruples. But sincerity and conviction were the basic principles of his whole life, as they were of John Bright's. Whatever the cost, he would not betray them. Meantime, graduation approached, and that ominous question mark: The Future. Political leadership of course—but how to achieve it?

One is tempted to speculate as to what might have been the outcome of Woodrow Wilson's career if at this time there had existed in America something like the British system of private secretaryships in official life. If on leaving college he could have

The Making of the Man

attached himself to some great man, learned from him and from the daily routine of affairs the give-and-take of human association, he might have obtained a knowledge of men which would have proved an invaluable supplement to his theoretical study.

But alas, there is no such excellent training in America. He had to make shift with what he could. In America the law provides the favorite stepping-stone to politics. The law as a profession did not appeal to Wilson—but how else could he carry out his purpose and become a statesman and a leader? This was a hard problem for a Southerner and a Democrat, barely fifteen years after the Civil War.

He thought it out with characteristic definiteness: "The profession I chose was politics. The profession I entered was the law. I entered the one because I thought it would lead to the other. . . . Congress is . . . full of lawyers!"

Therefore on his graduation from Princeton in 1879 young Wilson applied for admission to the Law School of the University of Virginia, at Charlottesville. The "Senator from Virginia" was on his way!

V

AT CHARLOTTESVILLE the future President lived two miles from Monticello, the former home of Thomas Jefferson, and every day he passed the house where President Monroe once lived. The University was just recovering from the disasters of the war. The student body numbered only 328, the law students 79, the year that Wilson entered. Food was poor, conditions primitive, the rooms sparsely furnished and cold. You had to want an education in those days and to work for it in more senses than one. No wonder the luxury of college clubs in later days revolted him. The expenses of a student at Princeton in Wilson's student days came to $306 a year; at the University of Virginia, $312.

He was warmly welcomed as a Southerner of an honored family who already had made a name for himself. His article on

The Story of Woodrow Wilson

cabinet government had preceded him and lay on the University library table when he arrived. He was greeted with enthusiasm and drawn at once into various college activities: the Glee Club, the Athletic Society, the Phi Kappa Psi fraternity, and, of course, a debating society. Wilson joined the "Jefferson," which, with its rival the "Washington," occupied the center of the intellectual life of the University. T. W. Wilson swiftly became "Jeff's" outstanding speaker. His "Washington" rival was William Cabell Bruce, later United States Senator from Maryland. The two debated many questions, remaining on terms of "severe politeness" outside.

Other men of unusual gifts at the Law School at that time included Richard Byrd of Virginia, father of the present Admiral Richard Byrd; Leroy Perkins, afterwards Senator from Mississippi; and John Bassett Moore, whom Wilson was one day to appoint Counsellor of the State Department and who later became a celebrated international lawyer and a judge on the World Court at The Hague.

Wilson became president of the Jeff Society and of course soon gave notice "that he would at some future time introduce a resolution to appoint a committee for revising our Constitution"! For many weeks the members discussed the principle of the society in relation to the new Constitution. They also debated the two subjects in which their president was most interested: the tariff, and the feasibility of adapting the British scheme of ministerial responsibility to the United States. The Constitution was finally adopted, and the university magazine remarked that "it reflects great credit in every respect on its framers, Messrs T. W. Wilson, Andrews, and LeFevre."

Wilson admired his teachers—especially Dr. John Minor, head of the law department—as intensely as he was bored by the law. "I am struggling hopefully through its intricacies," he wrote Charlie Talcott at the end of 1879. He had to go through his courses in order to become a lawyer and enter politics, but he never pretended to enjoy them. Nevertheless he was chosen judge of the moot court in his second year—an honor coveted beyond any other, in all schools of law.

The Making of the Man

His passion for his own studies continued unabated. Here no labor was too great, no discipline too strenuous. The college library record shows the stiff list of books that T. W. Wilson drew out. He concentrated on history and orations and used to tramp off in the woods to a quiet spot where he could declaim the Attic orators.

Something from within drove him on. The sense of preparation for anticipated greatness? He wrote, at twenty-three, to his friend Charlie Talcott, with whom he had made the "solemn covenant": "Those indistinct plans of which we used to talk grow on me daily, until a sort of calm confidence of great things to be accomplished has come over me which I am puzzled to analyze. . . . I can't tell whether it is a mere figment of my own inordinate vanity or a deep-rooted determination which it will be within my power to act up to."

His fellow-students reflected this impression of greatness. Here, as at Princeton, he was an unchallenged leader, not only because they admired his brilliant intellect but because they genuinely liked him. Here too his fellow-students speak of his charm, his "fine courtesy," his "distinction of manner," his "affability with everyone." Here again, though nothing of an athlete, he was chosen as an outstanding leader to present the medals at the close of the university field day. The magazine reports that he made "a perfect little medal-delivery speech."

"The fellows of his fraternity," writes a friend, "greatly wanted to give a banquet—a dollar dinner—where Wilson would be the principal speaker, but the time never arrived when every man had the dollar, so they never had the dinner."

The crowning event of his life at Charlottesville was his oration on John Bright. By this time he had such a reputation that the entire college turned out to hear him—including the ladies of Charlottesville, who requested that a special exception be made for them. Other friends came from towns near by.

The oration did not confine itself to distant England and John Bright. It struck home on a dangerous topic: the Civil War and the attitude of the South toward it. Referring to John Bright's opposition to the Confederacy, Wilson faced the issue squarely, taking an attitude which he maintained throughout his life and which he later developed into a striking and valuable book: *Division and Reunion.*

"I yield to no one precedence in love for the South," he said. "But *because* I love the South, I rejoice in the failure of the Confederacy. Suppose that secession had been accomplished? Conceive of this Union as divided into two separate and independent sovereignties! To the seaports of her Northern neighbor the Southern Confederacy could have offered no equals; with her industries she could have maintained no rivalry; to her resources she could have supplied no parallel. . . . We cannot conceal from ourselves the fact that slavery was enervating to our Southern society and exhausting to our Southern energies. . . . The Northern Union would have continued stronger than we, and always ready to use her strength to compass our destruction.

"With this double uncertainty, then, of *weakness* and *danger*, our future would have been more than dark—it would have been inevitably and overwhelmingly disastrous. Even the damnable cruelty and folly of reconstruction was to be preferred to helpless independence. All this I see at the same time that I recognize and pay loving tribute to the virtues of the leaders of secession, to the purity of their purposes, to the righteousness of the cause which they thought they were promoting—and to the immortal courage of the soldiers of the Confederacy."

In the South such an address naturally made a tremendous stir. Newspapers throughout the State commented on it. The following month Wilson did another brilliant study—this time on Gladstone—which appeared in the April number of the university magazine. Ex-Governor Hubbard publicly paid him handsome compliments and declared, "that young man will be an honor to his State."

But all these varied activities—his studies, his reading, his writing and debating, his constant practice of elocution and public speaking—proved too much for a never overstrong body. In the early winter of 1880 he had a physical breakdown and to everybody's regret had to leave the University and go home. His doctor found his digestive apparatus seriously out of gear. He was told that if he did not take great care of his health he might become a confirmed dyspeptic.

It was a hard blow, having to retire from the scene of his triumphs just at the height of his success. "How can a man with a weak body ever get anywhere?" he asked disgustedly. But, like another famous Democratic leader, he set himself to conquer his infirmity. He decided both to restore his health and to finish his law work, and he therefore continued reading law by himself. Resolutely he settled down to a year and a half of solitary hard study.

"I am again steadily at work on the law," he wrote his friend Heath Dabney at the University, "and making very satisfactory progress with it. . . . Having gone so far under competent guidance, I now know the landmarks of the subject . . . enough to enable me to explore it with safety and advantage, and I am naturally very much encouraged to find that I can travel so well alone."

He missed his friends greatly, as his letters show. He was not happy in Wilmington; his health still troubled him, and the future appeared most uncertain. But he stuck to it. He continued his reading and worked at his oratory—"I practice elocution hard and systematically every day," he wrote one of his cousins. . . . "I intend to spare no trouble in gaining complete command of my voice in reading and speaking. . . ."

By the spring of 1882 he felt himself sufficiently prepared and in good enough health to take his examinations and face the great adventure of entering into active law practice. The question was, *where?* He talked it over with his family and finally decided on Atlanta. It was the only Southern city that had recovered from the exhaustion of the war and seemed destined to become a big business center. It therefore appeared most promising to an ambitious young lawyer with hopes of a public career. So, with high courage, backed by the confidence of a devoted family, he set out to try his fortune.

VI

WILSON arrived in Atlanta June 1, 1882, took his examinations, and was admitted to the bar in October, with license to practice in Georgia at once, and in the Federal Court the following March. The first thing he did on reaching Atlanta was to hunt up a friend from the University of Virginia—Edward Renick, also poor, also the son of a minister, also highly gifted and just beginning the practice of law. The two decided to form a partnership. They took an office in the center of town and hung out their shingle:

RENICK AND WILSON
ATTORNEYS AT LAW

They boarded at the same house—Mrs. Boylston's, on Peachtree Street—and became devoted friends. Renick's charming manner appealed to the shy, reserved Wilson. Wilson's power and gifts of leadership won Renick's ardent admiration.

The two were of one mind on many things: how to rehabilitate the South; how to create a responsible Federal government; how to circumvent the Northern business interests that seemed determined to prevent the South from having anything. They talked for hours every night—two passionate postwar planners.

But no clients came. In 1883 Atlanta had 143 lawyers: apparently sufficient for its 37,000 inhabitants, without Messrs. Renick and Wilson. The two were stout-hearted, but the future looked grim. Months went by, and "that boy down at Atlanta still isn't earning a penny!" said Wilson's father. He kept up his reading in history and politics, practiced his oratory and elocution, paid instructive if discouraging visits to the local legislature; but he made no headway at all in his chosen profession.

Nevertheless, two important things happened to Wilson while he lived in Atlanta. He addressed a Congressional Commission, and he met the woman he was to marry. The Congressional Commission came first. It was the Tariff Commission of Congress, at that time going about the country taking evidence.

The Making of the Man

Wilson and Renick hotly disapproved of its activities, which they saw as simply further efforts on the part of Northern business interests to assure their special privileges. The witnesses were almost invariably men with some small manufacturing business, each of whom naturally wanted a tariff to protect his interest. Nobody spoke in the interest of the general public or put the larger issues involved.

Wilson's friends urged him to appear before the Commission and speak. An obscure young lawyer with no practice, undistinguished, unheard of, he hesitated. Yet actually no man in the South knew more about the tariff problem. He had studied exhaustively the precepts of Cobden, Bright, and other authorities; he had followed closely the debates in the House of Representatives. He knew what he believed and could say what he believed in words that carried conviction. Because of his burning belief, he consented.

The young man who had forgone a prize and $125 rather than argue for a protective tariff now argued eloquently against it before a commission of national authorities. The meeting took place in the breakfast room of the Kimball House: the six Commissioners gathered round the table, tilted back in their chairs and puffing at their cigars, with a sardonic tug at their side-whiskers; the "audience" consisted of the mayor, the local Congressman, four or five young men whom Wilson knew, and a few reporters; and the awkward young lawyer, flustered, shy, but with a certain austere dignity.

Wilson had agreed to talk, he wrote his friend Dabney, "influenced by the consideration that my speech would appear in their printed report rather than by any hope of affecting their conclusions." Embarrassed by "the frequent and ill-natured interruptions" of the Commissioners, he yet spoke well enough to receive some thoroughly approving remarks from the Congressman when he had finished, attesting that he showed in his speech that he knew what to say and how to say it. "A man in dead earnest . . . extremely well equipped with the facts," said another listener.

He represented the general public and the Southern and

Western agricultural interests as opposed to the industrial Eastern interests which sought what he claimed was "government bounty."

"I maintain that manufacturers are made better manufacturers," he said, "whenever they are thrown back upon their own resources and left to the natural competition of trade rather than when they are told, 'you shall be held in the lap of the government, and you need not stand upon your own feet.' . . ."

"Are you advocating the repeal of all tariff laws?" one of the Commissioners asked him.

"Of all protective tariff laws; of establishing a tariff for revenue merely," said the young advocate firmly.

That very night, while interest in the tariff was still warm, he gathered a group of young men around him and organized a branch of the Free Trade Club of New York. This persisted as a debating club for years.

With the Commission came a young reporter on the staff of the New York *World* with whom Wilson was greatly taken. This young man was also a Southerner, a friend of Renick's, and a keen student of political questions. He had been traveling about with the Commission, upsetting its dignity and poking fun at its pompous conclusions. Indeed, he was principally responsible for having persuaded Wilson to make his address. He and Renick and Wilson had some long talks, warming the unused chairs of the R. and W. law office. Thirty years later Renick's unsuccessful partner appointed him Ambassador to the Court of St. James. His name was Walter Hines Page.

VII

WILSON's mother led him to his wife. The understanding woman whose deep, proud nature made her long to help her proud son was his one and only client. She turned over to him the management of her own small property, which until that time had been under the care of his Uncle James Bones. The transfer and business arrangements necessitated a visit to

Ellen Axson and Woodrow Wilson at the time of their marriage. *Courtesy Mrs. Eleanor Wilson McAdoo*

"The Alligators," Wilson's eating club at Princeton.

Wilson is the one holding his hat. *Courtesy Ray Stannard Baker*

With Taft on the White House portico just before leaving for Wilson's First Inaugural. *Photo: Harris & Ewing*

The Making of the Man

his uncle's home at Rome, Georgia. It turned out to be the most important visit of Wilson's life.

He had quite a collection of cousins, aunts, and other relatives at Rome, and—since business at Atlanta was hardly pressing—very contentedly spent some days there. While in Rome, naturally, he went to church. Ellen Axson, daughter and granddaughter of a Presbyterian minister, also went to church. She sat in the corner of her pew, "a girl with a flowerlike face, bronze-gold hair, eyes of deep brown, and features alight with the wonderful color she never lost." Young Wilson looked—and looked again. He made inquiries, found out who she was. Next day, showing some of the strategic power for which he was later to become famous, he called upon her father, the Reverend Mr. Axson.

"He received me with unsuspecting cordiality . . . under the impression that I had come to see only him," Wilson wrote later. "I asked rather pointedly after his daughter's health, and he in some apparent surprise summoned her to the parlor." The three then proceeded to an animated discussion, introduced by the father, as to "why night congregations have grown so small"!

That evening Woodrow Wilson took Ellen home from a family gathering at his cousin's and, as he returned to his uncle's house later, stood on the bridge in the quiet of the night and swore to himself that he would marry her. Young, unknown, without a penny to his name, far from the greatness he dreamed of—yet "by the eternal he would be great, and he would marry Ellen Axson and no other!"

It was a whirlwind courtship. He stayed on in Rome. They saw each other every day; there were walks, rides, picnics. He wrote to her; she wrote him brief little notes in return. He hung about her house, confessing he could not keep away. He was irresistibly drawn, like a magnetic needle to its lodestar.

For Ellen was more than beautiful. She was wise, she was steady, she was good. Ardently alive, interested in a wide variety of things and people, she opened up to the young student of politics and history other phases of life with which it was time he became acquainted: the poetry of the Brownings, the philosophy of Kant and Hegel, a wider view of the literature of the period, and the world of art. Here she was thoroughly at home, having a gift for painting.

But most of all she opened to him her own rich and lovely personality. By that mysterious communication which one human being makes to another, there was conveyed to Woodrow Wilson, past all the conventional stiltedness, formality, and sentimentality of the time, the fact that here was a spirit, brave, true, intelligent, qualified by every attribute to stand beside his spirit through the years and to be to him what he longed to be to her: a true life companion. For she had in the depths of her quiet self the qualities of mind and heart which beautifully balanced the intensities and extremes of his.

Something of all this young Wilson at least partially perceived that night when he stood on the bridge at Rome and swore by all the gods that it should be "Ellen Axson and no other!" It took him a longer time to convince Ellen. Not because she did not feel some of the same presentiment and attraction—she did, definitely, from the first; but because of the very loyalty and fidelity, the strong sense of duty and self-giving which made her the great wife she afterward became.

Her mother had recently died. Her father was seriously, even tragically, ill. She was head of the Manse and guardian of the three younger children who seemed to have first and inescapable claim upon her. Shortly before she met "Mr. Woodrow," as she demurely called him, she had taken—as young ladies quite frequently did in those days—a vow never to marry.

But events aided Wilson. After a considerable and not very productive correspondence following the Rome visit, fate threw him a favor. On his way to Baltimore in September he stopped off for a little while at Asheville, North Carolina. Going along the main street of the town, as he looked up he saw a girl sitting on the veranda of the hotel—in a hat that with a cry of joy he recognized.

"Ellen!" He flew up the steps to meet her. She had been called home from a visit north by the continued illness of her father. She too was waiting between trains in Asheville. They walked up and down the veranda together, talking earnestly. This time Wilson would not take no for an answer. He was determined, and he carried her with him. When they said good-by, they were engaged.

VIII

IN THE spring of 1883 Wilson decided to give up the law and to earn his living by becoming a professor. He saw now how hard, if not impossible, it was for a man without an independent fortune to weather the initial years of building up a law practice. The year at Atlanta had been one of disillusion but also of clarification and awakening. His glimpses of the Georgia State legislature—the ignorance, greed, and narrowness of the men he daily beheld on the floor there—showed him the contrast between the crude realities of political life and his dazzling dreams. They also brought him to a new and clearer knowledge of himself.

The bar was not the place for him. Neither was the political organization. Whatever influence he might be able to exert would have to make itself felt through other agencies. Walter Page had talked enthusiastically of the new group of scholars at Johns Hopkins University, in Baltimore. Wilson decided that he would go to Johns Hopkins for some postgraduate courses and fit himself for a professorship. He never for a moment gave up his ultimate goal of "profound and public-spirited statesmanship." But if he could not reach that goal through the law and the political organization, he resolved to do it by means of education and writing. His application for admission to Johns Hopkins shows his completely clear intention:

My purpose in coming to the University is to qualify myself for teaching the studies I wish to pursue, namely, history and political science, as well as to fit myself for those special studies of constitutional history on which I have already bestowed some attention. I am prepared to be examined upon the constitutional machinery of the English Government . . . upon the general course of Colonial history . . . upon the phases of the free-trade controversy, and upon the general topics of political economy which I have studied in Professor Fawcett's writings and in the lectures of the late Professor Atwater of Princeton.

He arrived in Baltimore on September 18, 1883, two days after he had become engaged to Ellen Axson. He had made these decisions before his engagement, but there is no doubt that his love for Ellen and his desire to marry were powerful factors in his plans. He took her fully into his confidence, telling her of his inmost aspirations as well as his recognition of practical necessities. She approved his decision, urged him to go ahead without hesitation on his chosen course. From the very first moment she held him to his main purpose and his own best interests, even if it meant postponing their marriage.

Thus he settled into the life of a postgraduate student in a delightful Southern city, with some old friends—such as Hiram Woods of the Princeton days—to carry him off for an occasional good dinner and evening of talk. He also met some stimulating new companions at the University and wrote daily letters to Ellen, now at art school in New York.

Johns Hopkins, he declared joyfully, was just then "the best place in America to study." Organized only a few years before and launched on a great campaign for high scholarship, it had attracted a remarkable group of leaders. Dr. Herbert Adams was his professor in International Law; Dr. Richard Ely in Advanced Political Economy; Dr. Jamieson in English Constitutional History. Wilson lived in a furnished room near some congenial university men and spent long hours at the celebrated Bluntschli Library. He reveled in the brilliant lecturers who came occasionally from abroad—especially James Bryce and Edmund Gosse.

But the center of interest was Dr. Adams's "Historical Seminary" on Friday evenings. Famous men gathered about the long red seminary table on those nights—and some who were to become famous: Albert Shaw, afterwards editor of the *Review of*

The Making of the Man

Reviews; Edward Bemis and Davis R. Dewey, distinguisher economists; E. R. L. Gould, at one time Chamberlain of New York
City; Arthur Yager, whom Wilson was to appoint Governor of
Puerto Rico; the fast-developing Wilson himself, and a number
of others. It was the sort of group and the sort of instruction
Wilson liked best, the sort reflected in his own plans at Princeton later: informal methods, "instructors and lecturers like older
brothers to us [as one of the group, Dr. Shaw, wrote]. . . . Instructors and students participating on an equal basis."

Wilson made his characteristic and brilliant contribution to
the discussions. Of course in time he also organized a Hopkins
House of Commons, putting the members through the usual
strenuous debates and reforms that he set in motion everywhere
he went. Adams and Ely encouraged him in his constitutional
studies. He was asked to speak before the Seminary on Adam
Smith and started in at once to read Smith's entire works. Ely,
eager for the spreading of economic knowledge, proposed to Wilson and Davis R. Dewey that they collaborate on a history of
American economic thought. Although this book was never published, the research which he did in preparing his part of the
manuscript gave Wilson an economic knowledge rare among
public men—a magnificent background for his economic reforms
as President.

Absorbed in all this arduous work, he permitted himself few
social distractions—the glee club, an occasional ball game, the
theater on one or two great occasions. He saw Henry Irving and
Ellen Terry in *Hamlet*, he attended a few evening parties. A
lifelong friend, Mrs. Reid of Baltimore, with whom Wilson corresponded for many years, gives an interesting vignette of his
appearance one night at a reception—the young genius who had
caused somewhat of a flurry, and (already) curiosity and criticism
in Baltimore's scholastic circles.

"I was talking with a group of immaculately dressed youths
when I noticed," says Mrs. Reid, "a tall young man, with a
formal oversensitive manner. 'Look at Woodrow Wilson,' said
one of the group about me. 'Now how does he manage that

bedside manner and make his dress clothes look like a preacher's? He's terribly clever, but he's provincial.' "

Edith Reid took a long look at him. "If he's provincial," she said, "he's making the provinces look bigger than the city. He has personality; he is distinctly the personage in this room. . . . It was a remarkable face," she continues, ". . . strong and heavily marked, naïvely young but full of power." Later in the evening she had a conversation with young Mr. Wilson. "There was a diffident graciousness in his manner and in the quality of his voice that marked him as coming from the South; but the moment the talk touched on the problems of the country all diffidence and youth were lost, and he led the conversation with vivid brilliancy."

They talked chiefly "of his work and ambitions, of the Government of the United States, and of his satisfaction over the inauguration of Grover Cleveland. . . . He made a swift-running appraisement of our Presidents from Washington on to Cleveland." She was struck by his eagerness for a political career and says, "It seemed to me then as it seems to me now that he was made for an English statesman and not for an American politician." But he took very little time off for parties or social relaxation. He was working unceasingly, those two years at Hopkins. Between Adam Smith and his economic manuscript, his research in constitutional history and his own articles and writing, he overtaxed himself to such an extent that in January (after reading steadily through the whole of the Christmas holidays) he had to go home and be nursed. He admitted to Ellen that he *had* "overdone it a bit" just then.

But thoroughness takes time, and Wilson was inexorably thorough. Whether it was a letter to a friend or a lecture or an essay, everything he did had to be done as perfectly as he could do it. His power in the speeches of his Presidential years was not accidental or the mere inspiration of the moment. It came from years upon years of conscientious preparation and self-discipline. He gave his best in every line he wrote or spoke, trying constantly to improve his powers of expression, practicing his elocu-

The Making of the Man

tion faithfully day by day, knowing that letting it go for even a single day makes a difference.

He worked particularly hard because he was going to be a teacher, and considered the art of oratory vitally important to that profession. "Oratory," he said, "is not . . . swelling tones and an excited delivery, but the art of persuasion, the art of putting things so as to appeal irresistibly to an audience. And how can a teacher stimulate young men to study, how can he fill them with great ideas and worthy purposes, how can he draw them out of themselves and make them become forces in the world without oratory? Perfunctory lecturing is of no service in the world. It's a nuisance."

He was indignant at the weak and unconvincing exposition of some of his own professors in their college lectures. He prepared even informal speeches to his seminary friends with the same meticulous care he would have used in constructing a speech for Congress. The finished product was evidently satisfactory: his speaking was warmly applauded.

"I enjoy it," he wrote to Ellen after one triumphal evening, ". . . it sets my mind—all my faculties—aglow. . . . There is," he adds, "absolute joy in facing and conquering a hostile audience . . . or thawing out a cold one." He complains that "exact knowledge overcrowds everything else in a university, and the art of persuasion is neglected on principle."

But the outstanding experience of those years at Hopkins was the writing and publication of his first book. He was continually absorbed in his studies of American government—the living tissue of government, not the dead machine. During these years of his early manhood statesmanship in our country was at its lowest level, just as by maddening contrast Great Britain with her Bright and Gladstone and other brilliant leaders was at her highest. Once we had had our own great leaders and debaters—Webster, Calhoun, Lincoln, Douglas. Once our institutions had performed the functions for which they were created. Now they were twisted into tools of corruption by small and selfish men. Under committee rule there was no responsible leadership. Congress could not, like the British Parliament, be instantly called to account or turned out for its blunders. We had become the victims of our own system of checks and balances.

All these matters concerned Wilson deeply. He had begun to set forth his views in the article published while he was at Princeton. Then he carried his ideas a step further and outlined the actual changes required to transform the American Constitution into an implement of responsible government. He published this study in an article, "Committee or Cabinet Government," which appeared in the *Overland Monthly* for January, 1884. It was a remarkable piece of work and attracted much attention, especially among his teachers and comrades at Johns Hopkins. He was encouraged to develop his study further and then began to work out material for a book.

"I've been writing today," he tells his fiancée, "an historical sketch of the modifications which have resulted in making Congress the omnipotent power in the Government . . . this is to serve as an introduction to essays on Congress itself. . . . I wish to examine at length the relations of Congress to the Executive and that legislative machinery which contains all the springs of Federal action." He was "on fire to do a great and useful work, a work that would reform the institutions of the nation."

He toiled away at his task, reading some of his chapters aloud to his fellow-students, begging for their criticism. All summer, while at home on vacation in Wilmington, he worked at it. Soon after his return to Johns Hopkins in October the precious manuscript was completed. He wrapped it up in fear and trembling and sent it to Houghton Mifflin in Boston: *Congressional Government—A Study in American Politics—*by Woodrow Wilson."

Five weeks went by. "No—not a word from H. M. and Co.," he wrote Ellen. Then, on November 28th he writes that he has "some exceptionally good news." *His book was accepted!*

"They have actually offered me as good terms as if I were already a well-known writer. The success . . . takes my breath away—it has distanced my biggest hopes."

Then comes the exciting moment when he holds the bound

The Making of the Man

copies of his first book in his hand. He "took time only to write her name upon the fly-leaf" and sent the first copy on to Ellen. The second went to his father, "the patient guide of his youth, the gracious companion of his manhood, his best instructor and most lenient critic," to whom the book was dedicated and who wept with love and pride when he received it.

And then the reviews, some filling him with exultation, some with fury; the praise from old friends—Renick, Bridges, Page—who wrote him a fine review in his paper of the time, the *North Carolina Chronicle*; the congratulations and enthusiasm of his university friends: all the thrills and mixed emotions and excitements that come to a young author, especially an author with Wilson's intense and hypersensitive nature.

The book had an immediate and triumphant success. The first edition sold out within a few weeks. The reviews were on the whole remarkable, especially Gamaliel Bradford's in the *Nation*, which began: "We have no hesitation in saying that this is one of the most important books dealing with political subjects which have ever issued from the American press. We have often been asked by students of politics and by foreign visitors for some book which would explain the real working of our Government and have been obliged to confess that there was none in existence. . . . This want Mr. Wilson has come forward to supply."

The book was translated into a number of foreign languages. Critics on both sides of the Atlantic gave it warm praise. James Bryce admired it unstintedly and quoted from it in his *American Commonwealth*. Rear-Admiral Chadwick thought so highly of it that he had a copy placed in every ship of the Navy. Altogether an extraordinary achievement for a university student of twenty-eight—in addition to all the work of his regular courses. It launched Wilson as a political scientist of the first order.

He had worried about finding a college place after leaving Hopkins. But now he was in demand. He received invitations from the Universities of Michigan and Arkansas, from Tulane, and also from a new college for women, Bryn Mawr, just being

The Story of Woodrow Wilson

organized near Philadelphia under the auspices of some members of the Society of Friends. Its brilliant young Dean, Miss M. Carey Thomas, was the daughter of one of the Johns Hopkins Trustees, and the Hopkins professors were taking a special interest in it. Dr. Rhoads, a fine old Quaker, was President; but the real leader was the Dean.

The founders were eager to secure outstanding young men to organize its various departments. For the department of history and political economy they were agreed that Wilson would be ideal. One day before class he was haled into Dr. Adams's office to meet the Dean and Dr. Rhoads, and very shortly afterward the invitation was extended.

Wilson took some time about his decision. He did not fancy being under Miss Thomas. He would have preferred to teach in a men's college. But he was in love, he was poor, he wanted desperately to get married. The would-be statesman stood considering a position to teach history in an embryo women's college just in the throes of being born. Hardly a brilliant beginning! However, the college was in the East, convenient to political and intellectual centers, and within easy reach of his publishers and magazine editors.

"At Bryn Mawr," he wrote Ellen, "I should receive a comfortable salary, should have more leisure for private study, should have leisure to learn *how* to teach before seeking a more conspicuous place . . . and should have plenty of congenial work.

"It is not my purpose . . . to spend my life in teaching," he assured her. "It is my purpose to get a start in the literary work which cannot at first bring one in a living. I should of course *prefer* to teach young men, but . . . I could do my duty . . . without fretting, provided my ultimate object is not interfered with or postponed meanwhile." Pretty sound reasoning for an impractical idealist. Wilson possessed, even this early and straight through life, an extraordinary combination of lofty idealism and canny Scotch common sense.

In the end he told Ellen she must be the one to decide. If she thinks "that the position is one she would be sorry to have

42

me accept, I will at once withdraw. . . . I will not take, contrary to her choice and judgment, this first step we shall take together." Ellen voted in the affirmative. The die was cast, and an acceptance went to Philadelphia. Dr. Rhoads wrote young Mr. Wilson approvingly: "Thine of the 24th with its enclosure is at hand, and I am truly glad thou hast decided to come to Bryn Mawr. I trust it will prove no less advantageous to thyself than to us."

On June 24, 1885, Woodrow Wilson and Ellen Axson were married and in the autumn went to their new home to begin life together.

IX

THE wedding took place in Savannah, in Ellen Axson's grandfather's house. Her grandfather and Wilson's father performed the ceremony in the presence of a delighted gathering of Wilsons, Hoyts, and Axsons. The bride was radiant in her traditional tulle and orange blossoms; the young groom tall and distinguished-looking. We are told that "a handsomer couple was never seen in Savannah."

They honeymooned in a cottage in North Carolina appropriately named "Arden." They walked in the woods, read Browning, discussed their lives and the life of the race (like millions of young couples before and after them), and Ellen reiterated what she had already told her brother: "He is the greatest man in the world, and the best."

So began one of the world's great romantic attachments, curiously little stressed in the general appraisal of Wilson's character and destiny. "Man's love is of his life a thing apart" could never be said of Woodrow Wilson. It was the core and mainspring of his existence. "There never lived a man to whom love was a more critical matter than it is to me," he wrote Ellen in the early days of their courtship.

His intense, pent-up nature, given over for so long to dry political studies, turned to the sun and light of her love with desperate eagerness. When at one time, during her father's illness, she considered breaking off the engagement, he was in the lowest abyss. Thus, after two long years of waiting when they were finally united, his joy was ecstatic.

From the instant he saw her, he loved her. From the moment they were married she was literally and in everything the center of his life. He consulted her on every move, showed her every line he ever wrote, brought her all his problems and perplexities, discussed his political views with her—"You will grow weary of a man who will be insisting on your hearing his views of the world many times every day"—and leaned on her for guidance, help, and inspiration in a fashion curious for so masterful and sometimes domineering a person.

But he was never domineering with Ellen. The letters he wrote her over a period of thirty years show a tenderness, devotion, adoration even, that persisted through all the trials and tests they met together, that rose triumphant over poverty and hardship, calumny and attack, tragedy and disaster—until her last illness, when he hovered wretchedly about her room at the White House, unable to sleep or eat, part of his living self being torn away.

It began in the honeymoon cottage at Arden, but swiftly moved into the realistic scenes of the life of a young professor in a college just struggling to be born. It is hard to think of Bryn Mawr College as we know it now, with its beautiful buildings, fine laboratories, perfect equipment, and splendid grounds, as an embryo institution. During the academic year of 1943-44 six hundred and forty students enrolled at Bryn Mawr. The year that Wilson went there—the first year of its existence—the college had forty-two students and two buildings, plus three small cottages for housing the faculty. Professor Wilson and his young wife lived upstairs in one of them.

Conditions were uncomfortably primitive: kerosene lamps, not much heat in the houses, country roads ankle-deep in mud. The buildings were almost bare of books and apparatus. The great asset was the group of brilliant young professors, men and women, whom the Trustees and the extraordinary young Dean

The Making of the Man

had gathered together. Wilson plunged into his work with the same intensity and thoroughness he had shown at Johns Hopkins. His lectures, beautifully prepared, made a powerful impression on his students. "The most interesting and inspiring college lecturer I ever heard," one of them said. His life with Ellen was completely happy.

Yet he was restless, dissatisfied. Profoundly intellectual, intensely masculine, he found it irksome to be under a woman and to teach women. The Dean—a Doctor of Zurich, if you please, and five days younger than Wilson—was by no means easy to get on with. Wilson wanted to be out in the thick of things; he was restless for the great world, restless for the fight— "hungry to teach a class of men," as he wrote to Robert Bridges.

Instead, this soaring spirit made for the debating floor and the rostrum was confined within cramped quarters (even though the bride was "the sweetest thing in the world"), with soon the added responsibility of two babies arriving in swift succession; chafing under many restrictions, seemingly every day farther away from the work he loved, the career he longed for. He worried about his own intellectual quality. "Undergraduate instruction . . . compels you to live in the commonplaces—the A.B.C. of every subject," he wrote one friend. "You get weary of the plodding, and yet you get habituated to it, and find all excursions aside difficult—more and more so!"

"What *is* a fellow to do? How is he to earn bread and at the same time find leisure for the thoughts detached from the earning of bread?" How many ardent, aspiring young souls have asked the same question!

He longed to travel, to study in one of the great universities abroad where some of his friends were now working, "to know the world" (which he never did, except to a very limited degree, by travel). But the "comfortable salary" had turned out disappointingly meager—a bare fifteen hundred dollars. He began desperately to look about for a way to make a living for his growing family and at the same time pursue the studies he loved so passionately.

He wrote several magazine articles which added to his prestige, if not greatly to his income. He spoke at one or two places. On the urging of his friend Bridges, he went to New York and made an address to the Princeton alumni—his first public talk—eagerly hoping that it might lead to something, perhaps even an invitation to a professorship at Princeton. Some well-known and influential men were to be at the alumni gathering. "The College and the Government" was his topic, and he prepared for it long and carefully. He spent hours rehearsing every line. As a result he was *too* well prepared: he took his theme and his audience too seriously.

The address was a thorough failure. "Awfully solemn, nearly an hour long. Wilson was so terribly in earnest," writes one of the alumni. To his shame and fury many of the men went out before the end. Chauncey Depew, who was present, guyed him good-naturedly about it afterwards. It took Wilson years to get over that meeting. Oratory, to which he had given so much time!

1888 was a terrible year. His mother died, and the loss over-whelmed him. His wife was ill, expecting another child. His family was increasing, and he saw no prospect of earning any more for them to live on. He was overburdened with work; the assistant promised him when he went to Bryn Mawr was apparently not forthcoming. "Thirty-one years old, and nothing done!" he exclaimed bitterly on his birthday.

Most young men would think that to have published an outstanding book recognized all over America and Europe, to be in demand by magazine editors, to be holding a college professorship at thirty-one, was something. But not Wilson. His ambition was immense, his self-disgust stupendous.

His friend Renick, now working in the Treasury Department at Washington, had suggested that he apply for an Assistant Secretaryship of State. "Seems to think I have a good chance of success, as the office is not much in demand by politicians." Wilson responded with pathetic eagerness. There's nothing he would love so much as "an inside seat in some department of the Federal Government." "Don't you pity me, with all my old political longings set throbbing again?" he wrote his friend Bridges.

The Making of the Man

Here at last might be an opening to the life he had always craved. A day or two later he departed with high hopes for Washington. Renick met him. The two friends conspired together, in joyful reunion, and set forth to conquer official Washington as once they had tried to storm Atlanta. They made the rounds of the offices, interviewed various department heads, found several who were interested in *Congressional Government*—but no opening for a poor young professor entirely without political influence or important friends in the Administration.

At the end of the second day Wilson put his arm affectionately about his friend's shoulder. "It's no go, old fellow—let's give it up. Thanks just the same—thanks enormously."

Stung with defeat, discouraged, heartsick, he decided he would at least do one thing on his Washington trip that he had never done before—pay a visit to Congress. He left his friend and walked down Pennsylvania Avenue and up Capitol Hill, alone. The Senate was in executive session, but he could watch the House of Representatives until traintime.

Mounting those suave green slopes to the front of the Capitol, where on March 4th the inaugural rostrum stood, hesitating a moment before that white-domed magnificence, he looked back down the avenue to the tall shaft of the Washington Monument. Then entering the imposing Capitol itself, walking slowly through those colonnaded halls he had hoped to tread as "the Senator from Virginia!" he gazed into the marble faces of his heroes on their stately pedestals: Webster, Washington, Lincoln, Calhoun—lingering with a kind of envious sadness, savoring all the nostalgic legends and memories. Finally upstairs and through the swinging green doors into the visitors' gallery of the House of Representatives.

There he sat, looking down on them—an anonymous visitor in the public gallery, a tired, slightly shabby young man with a thin, eager face—overwhelmed with his own problems yet even then coolly critical, detached, acutely intent on the body of men to whom he had given so much thought, about whom he had written with an insight and penetration far beyond his thirty

47

The Story of Woodrow Wilson

years. There he sat, watching them, leaning a little forward, his hat clasped between his long, sensitive hands.

The next time that august body saw Woodrow Wilson was on the day when he addressed it, together with the Senate, in his first message as President of the United States.

CHAPTER II

EDUCATOR

AND

GOVERNOR

I

PERHAPS one reason why in later years Wilson could make himself understood by the common man was that he himself went through so many of the common man's experiences: racking his brains how to get a better position, tramping along country roads trying to think out ways to earn more money to take care of his wife and babies; chafing at being dependent on his father, longing for more education, not knowing how to get it; turned down at jobs he wanted desperately. He had experienced just what thousands of other young men have gone through, had dreamed great dreams, hoped high hopes, cherished tremendous aspirations on a purse as slim as a shoestring. Eager to serve,

The Story of Woodrow Wilson

longing to remake the world—as what generous, brilliant youth does not?—and all the while proud, high-spirited, knowing he had power, feeling instinctively the sense of authority and leadership, the ability to provide for twenty families—if only he could find his right place and begin!

The long, uphill struggle broke at last. In 1888 Wilson received an invitation to teach history and political economy at Wesleyan University, in Middletown, Connecticut and immediately accepted. Here he got a much better salary. Here he taught men. Here—as usual—he established a Wesleyan "House of Commons" which flourished mightily and added to his prestige with the student body. Here his happy home life continued: a third daughter was born to the Wilsons at Middletown. Here he wrote, completing his vast book on *The State* which he had been toiling at for three years, and immediately beginning another: *Division and Reunion.*

Here again he formed strong and lasting friendships—with the Hazens, the Westcotts, the Winthrop Danielses, the Freemans. He made occasional sorties to other colleges and institutions. His speeches and lectures attracted increasing attention. He spurred the football team to unaccustomed triumphs, coaching it with his fighting spirit rather than his technical skill, so that the little college of Wesleyan won over Amherst, Pennsylvania, Williams, Rutgers, and Trinity. He also gave a brilliant series of lectures as visiting professor at Johns Hopkins. And here at Wesleyan in 1890 he received the longed-for call to Princeton, to fill the chair of jurisprudence and political science made vacant by the death of Professor Alexander Johnston. Wesleyan wanted to keep him and offered to create a chair for him if he would stay. But the Connecticut college was a little *too* delightful and easy for this born fighter. He accepted the call to Princeton, to which he moved with his wife and three little girls in June, little dreaming how big a fight awaited him.

Woodrow Wilson's classes at Princeton were the most popular ever known in the history of that university. And they were far from being snap courses. Four hundred students—almost the total number of Juniors and Seniors—attended his lectures. From Wesleyan too a colleague wrote: "I doubt whether any man in the faculty ever attained the same degree of popularity with the student body which fell to the lot of Professor Wilson." It is hard to reconcile this picture with the rigid, self-seeking, opinionated, and egotistical sort of person his enemies try to make of him. Boys are pretty shrewd judges of character, and pretty quick to quit a man if he is priggish or arrogant. The boys of Princeton flocked around Professor Wilson. They came to his house, drank tea with his wife, watched him on the football field helping young Captain Poe coach the team, and crammed his lecture room to the last chair. At Princeton the students vote each year for various popular personages. Year after year they voted Wilson the most popular professor.

"He radiated enthusiasm." "He was the most inspiring teacher I ever sat under." "He made everything he touched interesting" —these were some of the comments of his students, though he was lecturing on subjects usually considered abstruse and dull: international law and political economy. "But he made them so fascinating," one student said, "I could never stop to take notes."

He would first read three or four general statements which the students could take down and use as a reminder and outline of the lecture. With these as his text he then proceeded to develop his subject, using all his powers of description, characterization, wit, and imagery, and all his vivid "art of persuasion," so honestly acquired. He often commented on current politics and political leaders, putting the students on their honor not to report him—which they never did.

"There was about him an aliveness, an enthusiasm, an earnestness that was infectious," says one of his pupils; "every man in the room was inspired to do his very best." "I can see him now," says another, "with his hands forward, the tips of his fingers just touching the table, his face earnest and animated—many times illustrating an otherwise dry and tedious subject by his beautiful language and apt way of putting things."

Wilson put vast care and labor into his lectures. He exacted more of himself than of his students. If a lecture didn't go, he revised and improved it. "I must make them understand, get exactly what I have to give them." If he could not come before Congress and inspire statesmen as he had longed to do, here was a body of young men he could inspire, some of whom might go out and realize his own youthful ambition.

"His success, years later, as a political speaker . . . was no accident," says Mr. Ray Stannard Baker. "He had learned the art of clear and beautiful exposition of difficult subjects . . . learned by years of training in classrooms, in capturing the interest and firing the imagination of restless college students."

His influence over them was immense. One of his students, whom Wilson later appointed Ambassador to Japan—Roland Morris—tells of the remarkable first impression the future President made upon him at Lawrenceville Preparatory School when Morris was seventeen. "Mr. Wilson spoke at our chapel exercises one Sunday, his text: 'Whereupon, O King Agrippa, I was not disobedient unto the heavenly vision.' Well, you may imagine . . . ! I switched then and there from Yale where I was booked and decided to go to Princeton. I took every one of Wilson's courses and got more out of them than from anything at the University."

Another student, Raymond Fosdick, tells of the vivid impression made on a big class by Wilson's description of the scene in Greyfriars Churchyard, where (in February, 1638) the stern and determined citizens of Scotland declared their liberty of conscience and signed their name to the Covenant: a word and an act that evidently appealed strongly to the Scotch Presbyterian and future President. "Mr. Wilson was always at his best in the description of events like this," adds Fosdick; "we came away feeling that we had been in the presence of some Elisha upon whom the mantle of old prophets of liberty had fallen."

Always he was holding before them—as his father had held before him—the vision of society as a living organism; trying to imbue them with his own deep sense of the significance of political institutions in relation to that society, and their duty as individual citizens in the shaping and reform of those institutions. He had already begun his lifelong practice of appealing to the inherent idealism of the people.

He also became a powerful influence with the faculty, as with the student body. He had been at Princeton a very short time when indications appeared of the struggle that was to come later. The lethargic mental processes of some of the older men, their slowness to move, their tendency to let things drift, exasperated the vigorous and purposeful Wilson. He held earnest discussions among the younger men, he attended meetings on professorial porches, he incited to rebellion. One of his colleagues, Professor Bliss Perry, records that "it was admitted without question that Wilson was the most brilliant man among the younger faculty. He led us inevitably by his wit, his incisive questioning mind, his courage." He was a member of the faculty committee on outdoor sports, and of the committee on discipline.

As in his student days, he formed strong friendships: the Perrys, the Gilders, the McCormicks, the Finleys, the Fines, and especially the Hibbens, to whom Wilson was particularly devoted. Every Sunday afternoon for years an intimate little group met at the home of Mrs. Ricketts for tea and hours of animated talk.

During these years Wilson forged ahead with his writing and lecturing outside the university as well as at Princeton. Each spring he gave twenty-five lectures at Johns Hopkins; in 1892 he began lecturing at the New York Law School; every year he received many invitations to speak at other colleges. He began to think more specifically about problems of education and about his ideal university, and to speak and write about them. He addressed the American Bar Association on the subject, and an article which he wrote for the *Forum Magazine* on "University Training and Citizenship" drew special attention. Several of the policies he endeavored to carry out in later years were set forth in these early papers. They were remarkable productions, widely copied and commented upon. They established Wilson as an educational thinker and gave him such prestige that whenever a distinguished college post was vacant he was usually first choice to fill it. Within a few years he was offered the presidency of seven great universities—among them his beloved University of Virginia. By this time, however, he was referred to as "Princeton's biggest asset," and a group of Princeton friends prevailed upon him to enter into an agreement not to leave Princeton for a period of at least five years.

In October, 1896, came his great address at the Princeton Sesquicentennial. On this occasion the college officially changed its name from the College of New Jersey to Princeton University, and Wilson made the keynote speech. It was a memorable occasion, bringing distinguished visitors from European as well as American universities. "When Professor Wilson rose to speak," says the Memorial Book of the proceedings, "the members of the class of 1879 who were seated together stood up to greet him, but their cheers were drowned in those of the whole assembly. The oration was interrupted by applause at several points. . . . At its conclusion the cheering was general and long-continued."

Wilson's theme was "Princeton in the Nation's Service." For, he declared, education must not merely develop the individual but also serve the state. College instructors could "easily forget that they were training citizens as well as drilling pupils."

He saw danger that liberal education might be engulfed by the sweeping claims of the new scientific studies. "Science," he said, "has not made us less covetous or less ambitious or less self-indulgent. On the contrary, it may be suspected of having enhanced our passions by making wealth so quick to come, so fickle to stay. . . . It has wrought such incredible improvement in all the physical setting of our life that we have grown the more impatient of the unreformed conditions of the part it has not touched or bettered, and we want to get at our spirits and reconstruct them in like radical fashion by the processes of experiment."

He pleaded for the study of history and politics, of the ancient classics, and especially of religion, to balance the overscientific trend, and he closed his address with an eloquent description of the ideal of the university in modern life. His final challenging question asked: "Who shall show us the way to this place?"

From that moment increasing numbers of Princeton devotees

thought they knew. In 1902, when Dr. Patton announced his intention to retire, Woodrow Wilson was unanimously elected President of Princeton University.

II

BOTH Wilson and his university gained substantial prestige through his writings and addresses. The writings of most public men are elegant ornaments to their careers. Wilson's books were solid achievements, written with characteristic carefulness and beauty of expression at a time when he had determined to make writing and teaching his life work. He wrote all his books before he assumed executive office; when he believed that he had renounced an executive career.

"I can at least write," he said with some bitterness, after his futile efforts at the law and his failure to get a post in the State Department. Evidently the public, and some of the most exacting critics, agreed with him. While still in his early twenties he received acclaim which might well have turned the head of a mature author.

His works fall into three main categories: political, historical, and literary. The political works were the most important, since politics and government always remained his chief preoccupation. His first political book, *Congressional Government*, as we have seen, met with instant success and became a classic. To date it has run through twenty-nine editions. It won for Wilson his Ph.D. degree from Johns Hopkins and the John Marshall Prize given by that university.

In the early days of its success he arranged to write another political book, a textbook called *The State,* tracing government back to its origins and analyzing its ancient, medieval, and modern forms. This was a huge work, begun at Bryn Mawr, finished at Wesleyan: "a dull fact book" Wilson called it. He had to study German, improve his French, and do a colossal amount of reading and research. He spent three years of steady labor at it—but what a training for a future President, this comparative

The Story of Woodrow Wilson

study of the laws and governments of many different nations and epochs.

His third political volume, *Constitutional Government in the United States,* was published when he was a professor at Princeton. This brought together a set of lectures given at Columbia University, and other addresses and magazine articles on political questions. The conclusions of Wilson the scholar throw light on the subsequent acts of Wilson the President.

He always intended to write a fourth book on government, a great *Philosophy of Politics,* affectionately referred to by his family through the years as "Father's P.O.P." This was to be a *Novum Organum* of political science that would do for the world what Montesquieu did for France and what Burke and Adam Smith did for England. But destiny stepped in and called Wilson to play an active part upon the political world stage.

Congressional Government was his own favorite. "If ever any book was written with fullness and earnestness of conviction, that book was," he declared. Wilson wanted it to stand as "a permanent piece of constitutional criticism," though "its mission," he said, "was to *stir* thought and to carry irresistible practical suggestion. I carefully kept all advocacy of particular reforms out of it . . . but I hoped . . . that it might catch hold of its readers' convictions and set reform going in a very definite direction."

In it he showed the actual operations of our government, in contrast with what the early fathers intended. He also compared our government with other more "responsible" forms of democracy. Already, in his twenty-ninth year, he placed an unerring finger on our weakest points, and he kept calling attention to them and insisting on their reform until he died. They were indeed the cause of his death and of the American failure in time of crisis: in particular, the divided authority between the Senate and the Executive, and the highly undemocratic and hierarchical powers that some Congressional committees have gradually acquired.

When he wrote his bold analysis of the role of the Executive, he could not have foreseen the part that he himself would play.

Educator and Governor

One of his friends, Mrs. Toy, relates an amusing incident when she was visiting at the White House during the strenuous early war days. Wilson pulled his *Constitutional Government* down from one of the library shelves and said humorously, "Let's see what *this* says about the duties and prerogatives of the President!"

"And thus," says Mrs. Toy, "we had the piquant experience of hearing while the President of the United States read what was an ideal Executive, written by the President of a college when he had no idea what fate had in store for him."

Afterwards he commented that a man should look ahead and never write about an office he might one day be called upon to fill!

As an historian Wilson has been accorded less hearty praise than as a political scientist. His first historical book, *Division and Reunion,* is generally considered his best. This is an account of the Civil War period which he wrote by invitation for the "Epoch" Series edited by Professor Albert Bushnell Hart of Harvard University. Wilson was particularly pleased to be invited to write this book and told his publishers he hoped that his non-Southern parentage together with his strong affection and understanding for the South might make for an impartial and detached appraisal. Evidently he had his wish, for the book remains the best short account of that period and still has a wide textbook sale.

The critics were not so kind to his *History of the American People.* When a student at Princeton Wilson had been fascinated by Greene's *Short History of the English People.* He urged his friends and fellow-students to read it and made up his mind to write a similar history of America someday. This he did—years later, when he was a professor at Princeton—in his lively five-volume series: *A Short History of the American People.*

Historians say loftily that "Wilson was not really an historian," that "he had no claim to historical scholarship." Possibly. But he has succeeded, where ninety-nine out of a hundred historians fail, in making history readable. You actually read his book, enjoy it, and remember it. You do not skim through a few paragraphs and then put it down.

The Story of Woodrow Wilson

Wilson achieved his declared aim—to interest American people in their own history—perhaps because he was so interested in it himself. His *History of the American People* had a warm reception, first as a serial in *Harper's Magazine,* then in numerous editions as a book. It was translated into a number of foreign languages and, like *Division and Reunion* and his political volumes, is still a live and widely read book today. But his biography of *George Washington,* written at the suggestion of Henry Alden of *Harper's Magazine,* is considered over-eulogistic and less interesting than his other writings on great statesmen.

What he most enjoyed writing was literary essays. He had so much fun with these that he said he kept them for hours of relaxation. The volume entitled *Mere Literature* contains, besides three essays on the art of writing, pictures of some of his favorite political personalities to whom he gave so much time and study—Bagehot, in the essay titled "A Literary Politician," and Burke "The Interpreter of English Liberty." These, like his essays on John Bright and Gladstone, reveal the character and ideals of Woodrow Wilson quite as vividly as those of the men he is describing.

His "Calendar of Great Americans" gives a similarly striking set of characterizations of some of our own great men: Franklin, Clay, Jackson, Webster, Calhoun, and "the supreme American of our history," Abraham Lincoln. For all his Southern ties and sympathies, Wilson's admiration for Lincoln was immense. The greatness of both East and West—indeed, the greatness of the whole country, he said—was summed up in this "marvelous composite figure," and he "understood the South as no Northern man of his generation."

Another volume of essays under the title of *An Old Master* contains his paper on Adam Smith as well as several famous studies on political subjects. These essays are brilliantly, even, it has been said, too brilliantly, written. Wilson accused himself of too smooth and precious a style. "The phrasing is too elaborate . . . the sentences are too obviously wrought out," was his criticism of his own work. In his earlier days he was charged with overemphasis and overdecoration. His friend Professor Harper tells of his devotion to the older English writers, especially Charles Lamb (one of his favorites in his early reading with his father), and of his modeling of his style according to some of the quaint old prose writers of the seventeenth century. There are many passages in his books that remind one of Emerson, both in thought and in phraseology.

This passage from the essay "On Being Human" shows Wilson's literary style at its best:

> Who can doubt that man has grown more and more human with each step in that slow process which has brought him knowledge, self-restraint, the arts of intercourse, and the revelations of real joy? Man has more and more lived with his fellow-men, and it is society that has humanized him—the development of society into an infinitely various school of discipline and ordered skill. He has been made more human by schooling, by growing more self-possessed—less violent, less tumultuous; holding himself in hand, and moving always with a certain poise of spirit; not forever clapping his hand to the hilt of his sword but preferring, rather, to play with a subtler skill upon the springs of action. This is our conception of the truly human man: a man in whom there is a just balance of faculties, a catholic sympathy—no brawler, no fanatic, no pharisee; not too credulous in hope, not too desperate in purpose; warm, but not hasty; ardent and full of definite power, but not running about to be pleased and deceived by every new thing. . . .

> In a new age men must acquire a new capacity, must be men upon a new scale, and with added qualities. We shall need a new Renaissance, ushered in by a new "humanistic" movement, in which we shall add to our present minute introspective study of ourselves, our jails, our slums, our nerve-centers, our shifts to live, almost as morbid as medieval religion, a rediscovery of the round world, and of man's place in it, now that its face has changed.

The Story of Woodrow Wilson

We are renewed by learning in the sense that our minds are, as it were, brought back to the originals and first bases of thought, to direct communion with all that is primitive and permanent, and beyond analysis or conjecture: as our manners are renewed—that is simplified—when social convention and all mere fashion falls away in the presence of danger, of sincere unselfish love, and of all pure passion; as our lungs are renewed by the pure untainted air of free uplands or by the keen breath of the wind that comes out of the hills.

Learning has come into the world, not merely to clear men's eyes and give them mastery over nature and human circumstance, but also to keep them young, never staled, always new, like the stars and the hills and the vagrant winds, which make nothing of times or occasions, but live always in serene freedom from any touch of decay, the sources of their being some high law which we cannot disturb. . . .

I suppose that we can speak of our minds as indeed renewed when they are carried back in vivid consciousness to some first and primal standard of thought and duty; to images which seem to issue direct from the God and Father of our spirits, fresh with immediate creation, clear as if they had the light of the first morning upon them—as those who go back to the very springs of being. It is thus of necessity that our renewal comes through love, through pure motive, through intimate contact with whatever reminds us of *what is permanent and forever real*, whether we taste it at the fountains of learning, of friendship, or of divine example, the crown alike of friendship and of truth.

Wilson's earlier work contained a surplus of quotation—especially from favorites like Burke and Bagehot. Senator Lodge speaks contemptuously of the absence of classical quotations and classical references in Wilson's papers. The men closest to Wilson at Princeton thought that he quoted too much, both in his

Educator and Governor

conversation and in his books. Mr. Ray Stannard Baker notes quotations from twenty-five different authors in one essay alone (the essay on Burke) and a large number in Wilson's other writings.

These defects disappear, says Mr. Baker, when the man came "to grapple with the stark realities of a world crisis. In his greatest messages and public papers, when he was the accepted leader of world affairs, his style becomes lean, vigorous, scholarly." His idols are left behind. He stands upon his own two feet, in words as in ideas and policies. "Then came his highest triumph of style: one without superfluity, one that exactly hits the meaning he seeks to convey."

"It may now be said without any imputation of partisanship," wrote Professor Bliss Perry, "that Woodrow Wilson's greatest messages and speeches challenge in range of thought and beauty of expression the noblest utterances in the political history of our race."

"I have lately been reading, and I wish all of his countrymen might one day quietly read," said Dr. Edwin Alderman, "the thirty speeches made by the President on that fateful Western tour which he undertook in September, 1919, in order to secure from the American people the stamp of approval which he desired for his work in Europe, and which the American Senate was unwilling to give. There is no series of political speeches . . . in our annals attaining a higher level of oratory and exposition."

Some of Mr. Wilson's articles received as high praise and were accounted almost as important as his books. The article on "Cabinet Government in the United States," written in 1879 when he was a Princeton student, was the first of many outstanding articles on government. It was followed in 1884 by his article on "Committee or Cabinet Government" which appeared in the *Overland Monthly* while he was at Hopkins, an article on the "Character of Democracy in the United States" (*Atlantic Monthly*, 1889), and an article on "Political Contrasts" written while he was President of Princeton. He also wrote several articles on education—"The Ideal University" (which appeared in the *Delineator*), "What Is a College For?" (written for *Scribners* and his old friend Robert Bridges), and a number of articles on national problems, such as the tariff and the trusts.

His financial returns from his writings were higher than most authors' on such subjects. In the early days he was sometimes rejected. *Scribners* turned down "An Old Master," which they later published as first in his volume of essays under that title. He tried his hand at stories, with no success at all. He even had an ambition (unfulfilled) to write poetry. But his political and historical writings brought him a tidy revenue, and agreeably supplemented his salary as professor.

Mrs. Wilson, writing to a friend in December, 1896, said that "Mr. Wilson makes $1500 every year" on his lectures and articles, "and last year when we were building and he really tried himself, he made $4000 extra." With his *History of the American People* he had the delightful experience of being paid two thousand dollars for each of six installments of the serial—twelve thousand dollars all together—instead of the two thousand dollars he had expected for the whole thing. This was such a windfall that he took his family to Europe for a vacation.

His earnings had to meet not only the expenses of his own family of five; an additional five or six persons usually made up the Wilson household, and various relatives also looked to him and Mrs. Wilson for support. The Wilsons never owned an automobile. Neither Mrs. Wilson nor her daughters ever owned a piece of jewelry till they went to the White House. But there was always enough for everybody, and summer holidays and occasional outings, and a gay good time without parsimony or scrimping at home.

III

WILSON's home life through the years was very nearly ideal and, to a man of his temperament, a vital source of strength and inspiration. "People say a man is never a hero to

Educator and Governor

his valet or his family, but in all the years my father never disappointed me," Margaret Wilson once told the writer. "He was the most interesting and delightful person—I used to hang about 'eavesdropping,' always longing for more!"

"A deep, happy peace pervaded the household," says his daughter Eleanor; "a sort of quiet rhythm that attracted and held people." The key to this, of course, was the relation between the father and mother. They seemed to grow closer and more devoted with each year.

Wilson leaned upon his wife increasingly, turned to her constantly for counsel and sympathy. He read his speeches and articles to her, eagerly seeking her suggestions. When they were separated he wrote to her constantly—not hasty scrawls but long letters, love letters, in his beautiful script; pouring out his thoughts, sharing all his discouragements and his triumphs. More than twelve hundred of these letters still exist—letters like the one he sent her with the first copy of his first book:

> ... I took time only to write your name upon the fly-leaf. ... I had to refrain from putting anything more. ... I had to say everything or nothing—and what I wanted to put would have been out of place on the public face of a book. I *wanted* to say that everything in the book was yours already, having been written in the light and under the inspiration of your love; that every word of it was written as if to you, with thoughts of what you would think of it, and speculations as to your delight should it receive favor from the publishers and the public; that, as your love runs through this my first book, so it must be the enabling power in all that I may write hereafter, for without your entire love and faith and sympathy it must also be the *last* book into which I could put any of *myself*; that, in presenting it to you, I was presenting it to one whose praise and approval are a thousand times sweeter and more essential to me than the praise and approval of the whole world of critics and readers. In sending you my first book, darling, I renew the gift of myself. [January 24, 1885]

The Story of Woodrow Wilson

And this, when she was at home in Georgia on a visit:

> Have you gone any of the ways we went walking, or any
> of the ways we went driving together—and have they re-
> called anything? When you go to church (to-morrow after
> you get this letter) can't you sit near where you sat that first
> time I saw you—it was about where Uncle James Bones's
> pew used to be—and (will it be wrong in church?) think of
> me, of all the sweet things that that first glimpse of you
> made possible for both of us. . . . Forget all the suffering and
> hard work and anxiety, and think only of that which has
> illuminated and beautified everything, our perfect love for
> each other.
>
> I've been reading Herrick and here's a little poem entitled
> "Of Love—A Sonnet" which comes so near my present mood
> and meaning. . . . Though if I were *looking* for a poem to
> express what I felt when I first saw you and what all our
> subsequent life has shown me of yourself . . . I should adopt
> Wordsworth's "She was a phantom of delight," line for line,
> word for word, dropping not a syllable except to fit the
> color of your hair! That poem almost expresses both my
> mind's and my heart's judgment of you. . . .

That was written March 31, 1892—seven years after they had
been married! Their love seemed, like gold, more beautiful with
time. Stockton Axson, Mrs. Wilson's brother, said, "It's a plati-
tude seldom believed that 'there never was a cross word' between
people, but I saw them day after day for over thirty years and
honestly I never heard one."

It could not always have been easy. These were not milk and
sugar characters. Both were strong, with decided opinions which
they held to. "Once she has made up her mind, you'll never
change her," Wilson declared proudly. This was what he liked.
"Especially," he added, "where it's a question of principle."

They never deceived each other or held anything back. This
was part of a pact they made when they married, and they held

Educator and Governor

to it faithfully. They differed sometimes very definitely, but respected each other's opinions and simply continued to differ.

For their children they had a perennial fascination. "When we had finished our lessons in the evening we came down for a visit with Father and Mother," writes Eleanor. "Above everything else in the world we loved being with them, hearing them or listening to their conversation. Time after time when our playmates called to us to join in their games we huddled together and pretended not to hear." Not many a father and mother earn such a compliment!

It was a family of limited means and simple tastes. When the children were young—and even when they were older—"Mother" made all their clothes, delighting in the fact that "the entire family wardrobe cost less than Woodrow's books for the year" (as she triumphantly wrote to a cousin), planned and sometimes cooked their meals, and stretched the modest family budget to perform the almost incredible.

As soon as they had any extra space in the tiny house at Bryn Mawr, they took some of their poorer young Southern relatives to educate, and they kept this up at Wesleyan and Princeton in later years.

"I have often thought how hard it was for them never to have had their homes to themselves," said one cousin, Mary Hoyt, whom they helped in this way. "He would have liked it very much, just with Ellen, I think. Yet I cannot express to you the loveliness of life in that home. It was filled with so much kindness and courtesy, so much devotion between Ellen and Cousin Woodrow, that the air seemed to have a kind of sparkle."

Sometimes he would work at night in his study while Ellen sewed. When too tired to work he would read aloud or sing. He read *Richard II*, *She Stoops to Conquer*, and *Obiter Dicta*, which he especially liked. He walked every afternoon, generally alone, composing his lectures in shorthand as he went along and copying them later on his typewriter.

Mary Hoyt, Edward Axson, and half a dozen others owed their education and start in life to this generous couple. Older relatives also came for long visits. Grandfather Wilson—an old man

The Story of Woodrow Wilson

now, with a mop of white hair and a voice that thundered—spent his last days in his son's home at Princeton. Mrs. Wilson's younger sister, Margaret Axson—a young lady of uncertain punctuality but very certain attractiveness and dozens of beaux—was for years a member of the family. "Aunt Annie" (Wilson's sister) and her daughter "little Annie" were frequent visitors, as were various other cousins, uncles, and aunts.

Mrs. Wilson, sending a sample monthly budget to a professor contemplating a post at Princeton, explained that the item for "Food and Lights" ($100 a month, as she had listed it) would probably cost him less, "because our family usually averages ten persons, two of them being very large and hearty college boys!"

It must have taken some managing to keep any physical peace in such a household for a professor who loved and needed quiet for the books and lectures he was continually writing. His morning hours never were allowed to be disturbed. The steady click-click of the little typewriter went on quietly and efficiently in the book-lined study day after day. Evening was the time for relaxation. Then "Father" talked and read aloud and played with the rest of them—sang, danced a hornpipe, joined in whatever game or spontaneous bit of fun came along.

Wilson loved to act; he could have earned his living at it, his friends relate, and sometimes wished he had. He could do a drunken man, or the heavy Englishman with monocle and cane, to perfection. His Scotch burr and Irish brogue were equally good, and he could tell a story inimitably. Once he dressed up in a feather boa and, with a long velvet curtain trailing out behind, did a society woman greeting her friends at an afternoon party. "Come on, Nellie," he would say to his youngest daughter, who also liked dramatics, "let's run away and go on the stage. We could do a splendid father and daughter act!"

He was mad about ball games, especially baseball, and once scandalized a Southern relative whom he had escorted to a Princeton-Yale game by suddenly springing to his feet and yelling like a madman. "I beg your pardon, Cousin Mary," he apologized, "but that was a Princeton play!" According to his daughter Jessie he was "a curious mixture of dignity and almost wild gaiety"—the Celtic strain, maybe, or perhaps only the natural reaction of an intense and inwardly reserved nature.

He adored his daughters. The "little girls" grew into attractive young women, each with a very definite personality of her own, yet each seeming to embody some special, marked trait of her father. Margaret—strong, self-contained, intellectually independent—had a beautiful voice and was fond of singing. Jessie—deeply religious, poetic, imaginative—had a great love of beauty and was beautiful herself. Eleanor—gay and fun-loving—was fond of parties and games and acting.

They embodied much of their mother, too, as in their love of the artistic and in their practical common sense. She sympathized eagerly with their individual ambitions—Margaret's voice, Eleanor's art school, Jessie's social work and desire to be a missionary—though she was relieved when Jessie afterwards married Frank Sayre and went instead to be a professor's wife at Williams College. Mother was inclined to be strict, "but not too strict," the girls said. Once, when Margaret was about to depart for Europe to study singing, her mother, horrified, came upon this oldest daughter in her room, *smoking*.

"It's all over," Mother declared tragically to Father, "she can't go to Europe now. A girl who smokes will do *anything!*" Later she relented and let her go.

She was less strict than Father in some things: for example, the young men and the telephone, just then coming into use for social purposes and dating. Mr. Wilson detested this practice. "What's that young fool want around here?" he would growl testily when a young gentleman's name was announced as on the wire.

"Possibly to see your daughter," was his wife's calm reply.

"Let him come to the door, then, and ask properly!" The dignified professor of jurisprudence fumed with all an ordinary father's irritability, only to be subdued by Margaret Axson's soothing "Now, Brother Woodrow!"

It was a family of extraordinary unity and loyalty, revolving round its head day and night as a matter of course. Father was the natural center of the universe. They took his part passionately in his fights and struggles, defended him against all comers, found him always and completely right. He, on his part, told them everything, was always mindful of them, and always had a special radiant smile for his family when he was marching in a parade or making a speech in some vast hall. He never overlooked or ignored the children in his absorbing devotion for his wife but had a word or a glance of special recognition for each one of them.

There were illnesses, accidents, and sudden emergencies, as in all families; terrible moments, as when Father came home from a visit to the doctor in Philadelphia, condemned to no more work for six months, loss of his sight in one eye, separation from his loved ones, and a trip to England at once; or when Jessie was ill with diphtheria in Italy, on a pleasure trip, and when Nellie was rushed to the hospital for an operation that might cost her life. But on the whole it was a remarkably happy, spontaneous family group, absorbed in each other's joys and sorrows, ups and downs.

Families saw more of each other in those days; family ties were more intimate, more close-knit. Usually some older relative was living in the house, as well as the young students going to college. Older people were not shipped off to "homes." Life was simple, naïve, kindly, sometimes perhaps a little stodgy, but possessed of a certain roundness and wholeness—a substance—which it lacks now.

We have the picture of Mother and the girls rushing to meet Father, to make him comfortable and to hear everything after his return from the day's work; of Father going upstairs to sing with Grandfather after dinner, telling him every detail of his life and activity. "How Firm a Foundation," "Crown Him with Many Crowns," "A Mighty Fortress Is Our God": the old hymns, the grand old ideals, a sense of sturdiness and strength; a certain kind of provincial, but a good kind of provincial—the American provincial that made this country what it was and is.

When Father was elected President of Princeton, Grandfather, who was ill, sent for the three girls and stood them in a row at the foot of the bed. His deep-set old eyes seemed softer than usual. "Never forget what I tell you," he said. "Your father is the greatest man I have ever known."

"Oh, we know that, Grandfather!" said Margaret. Frowning at her, he continued: "I've lived a long time, Margaret, and I know what I'm talking about. This is just the beginning of a very great career."

On October 25, 1902, Wilson was inaugurated as President of Princeton, in "the most dignified and impressive celebration of its kind ever presented." A committee of alumni had worked for months on the program and arrangements, and as the day drew near town and college bustled with excitement. The crowds were so big and the social gatherings and reunions so many, we are told, that "extra carriages had to be imported from Trenton"!

Saturday the 25th dawned a dazzling autumn day. Princeton in gala attire welcomed her guests with flags flying and brilliant fall foliage to lend rich background for the sober dignity of academic caps and gowns.

"Father looked very impressive," writes one of the Wilson daughters, "in his black gown with velvet bands down the front and on the sleeves, his purple and orange hood, and the mortar board and tassel. Mother adjusted the hood" while admiring daughters looked on. He "went in to show Grandfather how he looked," then walked over alone to join the procession.

And a grand procession it was. America had never beheld so distinguished an assembly at a college ceremony. Dignitaries from Oxford and European universities were there, as well as from many American colleges; famous statesmen, captains of industry and finance too, and celebrated authors and notables from the world of education. Ex-President Grover Cleveland headed the procession, walking with Governor Murphy of New Jersey. Dr. Wilson came next, with the Chancellor of the State; then came the retiring President, Dr. Patton, and Dr. Henry van Dyke. Presidents of other great colleges followed—President Hadley of Yale, Butler of Columbia, Harper of Chicago, Remsen of Johns Hopkins, Professor Lowell of Harvard, and a number of women presidents and deans. Robert T. Lincoln was among the honored guests, as was Booker T. Washington, President of

The Story of Woodrow Wilson

Tuskegee. Thomas Reed, Speaker of the House of Representatives, drove over from Washington. J. Pierpont Morgan went down from New York in his special train, taking with him George Harvey, then editor of *Harper's Weekly*. William Dean Howells, Mark Twain, Clarence Stedman, Richard Watson Gilder were interesting visitors, and several of the men who were afterward to play a conspicuous part in Wilson's career: Walter Page, William McCombs, and William McAdoo.

Trustees, faculty, and alumni of Princeton University formed the bulk of the procession—conspicuous among these Wilson's class of '79, come to celebrate vociferously the "coronation of Tommy Wilson."

At the ceremonies the Governor of New Jersey presided— Grover Cleveland on his right, Woodrow Wilson on his left. Chancellor Magie administered the ancient and solemn oath. Wilson was presented with the historic Witherspoon key, and thus became the Thirteenth President of Princeton University. A number of notable speeches followed. Dr. Patton acquitted himself admirably, and Grover Cleveland surprised everybody with his ease on the subject of education. Finally came the great address of the newly inaugurated President: "Princeton for the Nation's Service." He developed his theme of the Sesquicentennial six years before—the university must serve the nation; the nation "needs efficient and enlightened men. The universities of the country must take part in supplying them. We must not lose sight of that fine conception of a general training which led our fathers in the days when men knew how to build great states, to build great colleges, also to sustain them."

It was one of Wilson's fine inspirational speeches, combining great vision with practical good sense, setting forth the creed of a dynamic, fearless leader.

"What do you think of the new President of Princeton?" George Harvey's son asked his father on his return home that evening.

"I think," said Mr. Harvey, "that he will make a very good President of the United States."

Educator and Governor

IV

H E HAD scarcely been inaugurated when everybody became aware that for good or ill Judgment Day had dawned for Princeton University!" Not that the new President rushed into things or attempted reforms without first carefully studying conditions. These, after twelve years on the spot, he already knew pretty thoroughly. He spent a year in his new position just looking around, getting his bearings. But when he did act he acted, as throughout his life, vigorously and boldly.

First, he would raise the standard of scholarship. Boasting fine scholars in its earlier days, Princeton later became known as a university for rich men's sons—"the most charming country club in America." Such studying as occurred was sporadic and incidental. Imagine the sensation, therefore, when the students discovered that now they had to go to work. Work was not "a Princeton tradition." Alumni were perturbed. Parents came down to investigate, almost tearfully. The new President announced that students must work or quit.

"But my Jim's such a fine boy. He's a great football player, and he has a wonderful personality." "I'm sorry, but he didn't pass the examination," the President would return quietly. Students who failed to pass their examinations—rich or poor, with or without social influence—were dropped. Work was absolutely demanded.

Dr. Wilson set up a committee on examinations and scholarship, headed by Professor (later Dean) Fine. A committee on the course of study was also appointed and reported the following year, when the real revolution in curriculum and general organization began. Heretofore a student had left college with a smattering of knowledge of various things but without a sound, systematic training in any one group of subjects that would fit him for life and for his chosen career. President Wilson's committee promulgated a new system of collegiate study, the "department system": the first attempt to bring college education into intelligent and systematic relationships as a body of discipline.

The Story of Woodrow Wilson

This system has prevailed at Princeton ever since, as well as in various colleges and universities that followed her example.

Next he introduced the preceptorial plan, which was equally revolutionary. Wilson believed that the university should no longer train its students merely through lectures and examinations. He thought that the life of the student outside the classroom—the place he lived in, his associates, the things he talked about, the books he read, the ideals held up before him—was quite as much a part of his "education" as the fifteen hours a week spent in the classroom.

His idea was to put the students in intimate association with a group of young instructors who were to offer the undergraduate friendly companionship and oversight. Formal recitations were largely abolished. Men studied subjects, rather than merely taking courses. Constant informal, personal contact between students and faculty was the keynote of the new plan. The cost of the preceptorial system came to approximately a hundred thousand dollars a year. Graduate classes contributed to the salaries of preceptors annually instead of raising capital for a foundation. Within a brief two years the system was established and became a distinctive feature of Princeton life, working a remarkable transformation.

The University—which, according to one of the Trustees, had been "threatened with extinction" when the last President resigned—was now pulsing with life and interest. Fine new scholarship standards, the preceptorial system working smoothly, students and alumni with a new pride in their college, other colleges hastening to copy it—most men would have been content to let it go at that.

"But Wilson never knew when to stop," as his friends averred more than once, ruefully. A ceaseless energy drove him on—and everyone in his vicinity—when one of his spirited crusades possessed him. His next reform carried him into much more dangerous territory: living arrangements and the social life of the institution.

His plan was to organize the University in a number of "colleges" or "quadrangles"—practically dormitories—each of which should house a certain number of men from every class, with a few of the younger professors. This was simply the natural culmination of the preceptorial plan. It was not a plan for dividing the teaching system of the university into colleges, as at Oxford and Cambridge. The "quads" were to be merely residence halls, each with its dining room and common room, and its own atmosphere as an individual social unit: in short, the home of the student while he was going to college. Wilson knew, both from observation and from his own experience as a student, how tremendously important this was. A committee of Trustees appointed to look into the matter reported favorably (June 16, 1907), giving their formal endorsement to Dr. Wilson's plan for the "social co-ordination of the University."

But another element was still to be heard from. Fraternities are forbidden in Princeton, but Prospect Avenue—a street unique in college towns—is the home of a dozen luxurious club-houses. The clubs originally started as eating associations; Wilson himself belonged to one when he was a student. Later certain clubs decided to perpetuate themselves, built their own houses, and eventually became a powerful aristocracy within the general democracy of the University. Membership in the clubs (confined to Junior and Senior classmen) is eagerly sought, parents and friends of a prospective student sometimes beginning a campaign in his interest long in advance; and the scholastic and social life of the underclassmen is seriously disrupted for two years by constant agitation and anxiety as to membership. Only about one third of the upperclassmen make a club. Often the unlucky ones who are not chosen leave Princeton for another college, or abandon their college career altogether.

Naturally, the snobbery and artificiality of this system was completely at variance with Wilson's ideas. He did not suggest abolishing the clubs. "Club life is based," he said, "upon social instincts and principles which are natural, but these instincts should express themselves in a different way." The social life must feed, not mar and cripple, the intellectual life. He would make the clubs the nuclei of the larger college units. So again Princeton would lead the way in this problem of social life and organization, which for a long time had troubled American educational leaders.

When Dr. Wilson first proposed these ideas, the Trustees received them with great interest and approved them almost unanimously. The evils of the club system had long been recognized, but nobody had been able to propose a remedy. At that June meeting the committee of members who had been appointed to study the question recommended "that the President of the University be authorized to take such steps as may seem wisest for maturing this general plan [of the quads] and for seeking the co-operation and counsel of the upper-class clubs in its elaboration." The Trustees approved this resolution 24 to 1. Dr. Jacobus, one of the Board, wrote Wilson on June 18 (1907) trusting that he was "getting some rest after the strain of Commencement Week and that you are gathering satisfaction from the remarkable triumph which you have won in gathering to your loyal support in your great plans for Princeton practically the entire Board of Trustees."

Wilson was indeed delighted. He went forward eagerly with his plans—too eagerly, perhaps, or at any rate with too little advance strategy and diplomatic overture in the direction of the club members. Princeton alumni come back at Commencement in large numbers, ready for a week's jollification. The clubhouses are the scene of gay reunions and hilarious good fun. In 1907 the festive spirit was considerably dampened when arriving alumni found Wilson's quad circular sitting on the doorstep. It was read by excited old grads and upperclassmen on the Friday night before Commencement. The proposal was instantly seen as a scheme for doing away with the clubs, however Wilson might deny it. Some even declared he meant to confiscate them. Angry graduates went home to spread stories of the attack on Princeton's traditional institutions and to rally former students to the defense.

The storm broke in the *Alumni Weekly* of June 12, when an avalanche of protest appeared in print. Old Princetonians wrote indignant letters to the *Weekly*, outraged that a Princeton President should so far forget himself as "to try to make a gentleman chum with a mucker." **They** wanted to know what the world was coming to.

"The fight for the quads is on," Wilson wrote a friend on July 1, "and must now be seen through to a finish." (Not that he ever minded a fight if it was fair and aboveboard.) Letters and personal interviews invaded his summer retreat in the Adirondacks; warm discussions with such old and prized friends as Jack Hibben and Dr. Henry Van Dyke, who disagreed with his policy. In the autumn the faculty divided itself into two camps —one strongly for, the other against the Wilson project; each began to hold meetings and plan strategy. At the October meeting of the Board of Trustees Wilson's long-time friend and supporter, Moses Taylor Pyne, introduced resolutions to the effect that "the Trustees do not deem it wise to adopt the recommendations of the President and the faculty committee for the social co-ordination of the University" and asking the President to withdraw the recommendations and to discharge the committee.

It was a tremendous shock to Wilson, after the wholehearted approval in June and with not only Pyne but his old friend Hibben lined up against him and (as Wilson considered) against the principles they had always believed in. The battle was carried into homes. Wives and friends took sides passionately. The whole community was split wide open.

The Trustees had some stout points on their side. It was the year of the 1907 money panic. They were worried about the financial status of the University: alumni contributions were of immense importance. Some of them felt that the President by his fight on the quads was alienating support vitally necessary to the institution. The President felt that the Trustees and the opposition among the faculty were sacrificing a vital principle to moneyed interests, allowing money to dominate the policy and conduct of the University.

Wilson withdrew his proposal as requested, but he did not abandon his fight. "You must keep right on," urged his friends, and leaders in other universities. "Your theory of quads seems to me more nearly to meet existing college requirements than anything else which has been advanced," wrote Charles Francis Adams. President Lowell and Albert Bushnell Hart at Harvard said the same. The President of the University of Wisconsin was about to put a similar plan in operation and had received a grant of a hundred thousand dollars for the purpose. In attempting to solve Princeton's problem, Wilson believed, he was helping to solve a national one.

He continued to expound his ideas on the subject of the social organization of the University when invited to do so at alumni meetings or when speaking in other colleges; but he made no aggressive campaign. The preceptorial system continued, in spite of the withdrawal of subscriptions by disgruntled club members; the necessary funds were voted by the Trustees.

Meantime, the prestige of the University, and Wilson's with it, increased as a result of his vigorous fight for "democracy in education." He was in demand everywhere for speeches and at distinguished gatherings. Several college presidencies were offered him. Nine honorary degrees had been bestowed upon him by leading American universities. The great newspapers were running admiring editorials. He was repeatedly spoken of for some major political post—even as a Presidential possibility.

George Harvey publicly nominated him for the Presidency at a Lotos Club dinner in New York in 1906, where Wilson was guest of honor. "Was Mr. Harvey joking?" asked Mrs. Wilson afterwards. "He didn't seem to be," said her husband.

Again in May, 1909, in the midst of the quad struggle Harvey wrote in *Harper's Weekly*: "We now expect to see Woodrow Wilson elected Governor of the State of New Jersey in 1910 and nominated for the Presidency in 1912." These predictions carried much more weight than the usual offhand political prophecy. Harvey was close to the men who ran the State of New Jersey; closer still to some of those who (it was alleged) ran the nation. A word may be interpolated, perhaps usefully, regarding this bizarre and brilliant individual who played such a significant part in Wilson's career.

A journalist by profession, Harvey had spent some time in New Jersey as representative of the New York *World*. His keen mind and social qualities attracted the attention of Governor Green, who made Harvey a "Colonel" on his staff. Later he was appointed Insurance Commissioner and thus came in contact with the political bosses of the State—Bob Davis, Jim Nugent, and the "Big Boss," Jim Smith. Still later came his association with Mr. Morgan, Mr. Ryan, the traction magnate, W. C. Whitney—and the appointment to edit *Harper's Weekly*.

A shrewd judge of men and of political "atmospheres," Harvey undoubtedly persuaded his wealthy friends that in Wilson the country would have a "safe" and able leader. Strongly impressed by Wilson's inaugural address at Princeton in 1902, Harvey kept him steadily before the public from that time forward: in 1906 the Lotos Club nomination; in 1907 he pushed Wilson's honorary nomination for Senator; in 1908 he was active in a movement to nominate Wilson as Vice-President on the Democratic ticket with Bryan. This Wilson refused.

When Dr. Wilson sailed in June, 1908, for a brief holiday in England, he left strict orders with his brother-in-law Stockton Axson that he was *not* a candidate for the Vice-Presidency. James Kern ran with Bryan; they were defeated. Mr. Taft was elected President, Mr. James Sherman, Vice-President. Wilson returned to his Presidency of Princeton in the autumn, much improved in health and spirits. But another and stiffer battle awaited him.

Some years before Wilson became President of Princeton a movement was begun to build up the graduate department. The Trustees appointed Professor Andrew West, a brilliant and ambitious member of the faculty, as Dean of the Graduate School with an appropriation to study the graduate systems in various universities. Dean West spent a year abroad in this study and on his return published a handsome little book giving his proposed scheme for a graduate college.

In December, 1906, Mrs. Thomson Swann had bequeathed to Princeton $250,000 for a graduate college, one of the conditions of the gift being that the college should be located on the grounds of the University. In the spring of 1909 Mr. William Procter, of the Procter and Gamble firm of Cincinnati, through the influence of Dean West offered the University $500,000 for the Graduate School on condition that another $500,000 be raised. Mr. Procter's letter on the subject implied that the money must be used in carrying out the scheme formulated by Dean West, and that the school must be built on one of two sites which alone would be acceptable to him. Each of these was at some distance from the University proper.

Great excitement naturally attended the receipt of such a gift. It is not often that a university gets a present of half a million dollars. But joy was mitigated by embarrassment over the conditions attached to the gift and to Dean West's scheme in general.

It was the story of the clubs and quads all over again. Dean West wanted a gorgeous building, elegantly remote from the undergraduate hurly-burly, where a group of specially chosen young men were to live a cloistered life of culture and seclusion. President Wilson wanted a graduate school in the heart of the University, to which the best type of graduate student would be attracted by highly competent instructors, fine laboratories, a splendid library, and the practical essentials of study rather than opulent buildings and fancy embroidery.

"The fact of the matter was," said a friend at the time, "he didn't want a hundred nice young gentlemen to come to Princeton and live apart pursuing the higher culture. His thought was aflame with the picture of a great democratic society of students in which undergraduates and postgraduates should meet and mingle—'with healthy clash of mind on mind, younger and older—no chasms, no divisions, a grand brotherhood of intellectual endeavor.' "

Above all he did not want, and most of the faculty emphatically did not want, to yield decisions regarding the conduct and buildings of the University to every rich donor who might be generously moved to make a gift to the University.

"I cannot accede," he wrote, "to the acceptance of gifts upon terms which take the educational policy of the University out of the hands of the Trustees and faculty and permit it to be determined by those who give money."

Mr. Procter withdrew his gift, thereupon calling down upon

Educator and Governor

President Wilson from furious alumni all the wrath not yet spent upon him. It was inconceivable to some of the Trustees, to a large number of alumni, and to a portion of the faculty that a gift of half a million dollars carrying with it the prospect of another half million (which had been nearly subscribed) could be rejected on any consideration whatsoever.

The Eastern alumni were the most hostile. They proposed to bring all possible pressure on the Board of Trustees to cause a renewal and acceptance of the Procter offer and to elect new members who would oppose Wilson. Adrian Joline, a well-known Princeton alumnus and corporation lawyer of New York, was their candidate. If Joline should be elected, he was to act as organizing leader of the opposition to effect Wilson's defeat. In that event Wilson possibly might decide to resign.

In the meantime he made a characteristic move, one that he was to make again and again in his life's struggle: he "went to the country." He would carry the fight to the alumni themselves, put his position before them, and let them judge. In March, 1910, he made a "swing-around," much like those of his political campaigns later, speaking to alumni audiences in Baltimore, Brooklyn, Jersey City, St. Louis, then back to New York and Pittsburgh. These speeches had an importance far greater than a single problem concerning a single American college. They dealt with an issue of vital significance to every American college and every phase of American life: the power of rich benefactors.

Wilson attacked in scathing terms the influences which really dominate the universities of America, the churches, and the nation behind them. He struck at the power of wealth and asked: Should it rule the country? Democracy was the real issue, and the statement covered an area far wider than Princeton.

Our colleges must be reconstructed from top to bottom. "The American college," he declared at his Pittsburgh meeting, "must become saturated in the same sympathies as the common people. . . . The American people will tolerate nothing that savors of political exclusiveness. Their political parties are going to pieces. Only those leaders who seem able to promise something of a

79

moral advance are able to secure a following. The people are tired of pretense and I ask you as Princeton men to heed what is going on."

This address caused a tremendous sensation. "That Pittsburgh Speech" was printed as a pamphlet and widely circulated. Wilson's enemies accused him of using it to curry political favor. Wilson never indulged in such cheap tactics. He was sincerely trying to save the university he loved from the dangers he saw threatening her.

But pressure was growing to make him accept political office. Another speech delivered at Elizabeth, New Jersey, on "The Living Principles of Democracy" also made a tremendous impression and was widely quoted. Lyman Abbott "wished the Democratic party would adopt as its platform" the program Wilson set forth therein. The editor of the leading Trenton newspaper wrote him on March 28th after reading it:

"More and more I am convinced that the Democracy of New Jersey *without any encouragement whatever from you* will turn to you for leadership in the coming campaign, and I do not believe you can resist such a call." He predicted Wilson's nomination for Governor in 1910 and for the Presidency in 1912.

No man could be insensible to such arguments—certainly not a man of Wilson's early dreams and ambitions. He had longed for active political leadership all his life. But he wanted to win the Princeton battle first; and it really seemed that he was winning. Plans were going ahead now for the development of the Graduate School along the lines originally intended, using the Swann bequest. At the June meeting of the Board, Joline was defeated. The Board again supported Wilson. He felt he could regain control and by powerful appeals to the alumni secure the ultimate recognition of his principles. He could then make Princeton the ideal university of which he dreamed.

But destiny willed otherwise. On May 18, 1910, at the height of the struggle, an old man died in Salem, Massachusetts: Isaac Wyman. He left his entire estate, almost five million dollars, to the Graduate School of Princeton University. Dean West and Wyman's counsel were named Trustees of the will

Educator and Governor

When the news came Mrs. Wilson heard her husband laughing in his study. She looked in and saw him reading a telegram. "See this—we have beaten the living, but we cannot fight the dead!" he said, handing her the fatal bit of paper.

Wilson took his defeat like a sportsman. The amount of the bequest made it possible to secure a great graduate faculty and thus attract large numbers of first-rate graduate students and house them in any way desirable. Wilson announced, therefore, that he would yield in the matter of locale on the golf links. Who could beat five million dollars? In June the Procter gift was renewed. And the Trustees ultimately wangled the proviso of the Swann bequest by declaring the newly acquired golf links part of the university grounds and that therefore Mrs. Swann's money could be used legitimately in that vicinity. Wilson considered it thoroughly illegitimate and unethical, but there was nothing he could do about it.

Should he give up and retire from Princeton? He did not like the idea of what might seem a petulant resignation. He played the game to the end. He went to a dinner at West's house to celebrate the Wyman bequest. He attended a ceremonial commemorating Moses Taylor Pyne's twenty-five years' service as Princeton Trustee and presented a silver cup to Mr. Pyne with a handsome speech. He observed all the amenities and went through all the courteous gestures. But the heart was gone out of him.

"The valedictorian of my class . . . pronounced Woodrow Wilson's valedictory, too," writes David Lawrence, who was graduated from Princeton that year. "The students gave him again and again that day in thunderous cheers a testimonial of their affection and esteem. They knew little of the Graduate School controversy. They knew only that he was a strong man and a capable teacher and an inspiration to them all."

The Graduate School struggle added enormously to his reputation—even more than had the fight over the quads. He was now under great pressure to consider the nomination for Governor of New Jersey. He consulted with some of his closest friends: Cleveland Dodge, David Jones, and others who had stood by him through thick and thin. Wilson hated to give up a job he had undertaken or to leave a great task uncompleted. Yet obviously his work at Princeton was finished. Under existing conditions he could never do what he wanted to do there. Ironically, his quad plan was being approved and introduced in a number of other universities, while repudiated by his own. His friends assured him he was under no obligation whatsoever, that he must do the thing that appealed to him personally.

George Harvey—after several consultations with "Big Jim" Smith, head of the Democratic organization of New Jersey, and other party chieftains—told Dr. Wilson he could have the Democratic nomination for Governor "on a silver platter" if he would take it: "no strings, no commitments, absolutely free as the air." It seemed a strange proposition in boss-ridden New Jersey, especially since Wilson flatly opposed Smith's re-election to the Senate and refused to run unless Smith withdrew. Harvey explained that the Democratic chiefs in the State understood that if they wanted to win the election they would have to change their type of leaders, and also, it was implied, their ways and methods.

On September 15, 1910, Wilson was unanimously nominated for the Governorship by the New Jersey Democratic State Convention.

So the famous "Princeton fight" came to an end—if it can be said really to have ended. The problems are still there, and to this day Princeton people take sides and seem unable to discuss either the clubs or Wilson calmly or with any degree of detachment. The dispassionate observer trying forty years later to arrive at an impartial judgment is struck with certain concrete facts: through both fights a substantial majority of the faculty stood with Wilson; the majority of the Trustees also; the overwhelming mass of the students—who had no voice in the matter but whose opinion was significant; even the majority of the alumni.

"There is no doubt about where the great mass of the alumni stand on this question," one alumnus, David Jones, wrote Wilson. "The obstruction narrows itself down to the clubmen who so largely contribute to the support of the University." It narrowed itself also to the wealthy alumni of the East as against the almost solid support of the alumni of West and South—just like the political alignments afterward.

In this fight we see every one of the elements of the larger fight of later years: great principles, passionate adherents; fierce and bitter opposition, chiefly on the part of conservative moneyed interests; Wilson's sharp criticism of those who differed with him, his biting tongue and sometimes lack of discretion in regard to attaining his own object—as with his famous remark about Grover Cleveland: "After all, what does *Cleveland* know about a university?" Such remarks, passed on, did not help him with reluctant adversaries. We behold the seeming triumph of these—the ultimate triumph of Wilson because his principles were true and presented the only true solution.

In 1917 President Hibben attacked the club abuses in terms almost identical with Wilson's. In 1924, shortly after Wilson's death, a committee appointed by Hibben made a report that reads like Wilson himself. It said in part:

"Our life here should and must be one complete whole, incapable of segregation into separate compartments. At the present time it is evident that the social life suffers by separation from the intellectual life and clearly the intellectual life suffers from a lack of spontaneous and wholehearted recognition of its worth in our clubs. Surely the social life cannot for all time be kept separate from the intellectual life. If it is so kept our intellectual life must suffer because of the inevitable over-emphasis of social distinctions.

"The present exaggerated emphasis upon false values and standards and the consequent divorce of our social from our academic life threatens, as we have already pointed out, our whole purpose and direction as an educational institution. There must be a fundamental change of viewpoint toward the whole social life of Princeton."

At present the problem remains still unsolved. But Wilson has a way of winning in the long run.

The Story of Woodrow Wilson

V

WILL Wilson make a good Governor?" somebody asked "Little Bob" Davis, one of Smith's henchmen in Jersey City.

"How the hell do I know whether he'll make a good Governor?" said Davis. "He'll make a good candidate, and that's the only thing that interests me!" And he certainly did make a good candidate—this staid "Presbyterian priest," as they called him; he made the best candidate that the State of New Jersey and the Democratic party, wandering in the wilderness lo these many years, had ever seen.

The whole story of Wilson's gubernatorial campaign is fantastic. The biggest boss of New Jersey sponsored him. At the convention the progressive Democrats of the State fought him furiously; among them was Joe Tumulty, who afterwards became his secretary and worshiper. The machine leaders, whom he had warned in advance he would attack without mercy if elected, steam-rollered him to victory. Judge Westcott, who nominated Wilson for the Presidency at both the 1912 and 1916 National Conventions, attacked the "immorality" of his forced nomination and the scandalous procedure of the pro-Wilson "railroaders." "Big Jim" Smith, whose re-election to the Senate Wilson uncompromisingly opposed, supported him unflaggingly if anxiously from first to last.

"Say," he told one of his lieutenants, "wish you'd find out where he stands on the liquor question. We've got to get the liquor interests behind the Doctor if we're going to elect him."

The son and grandson of a minister, and himself an Elder of the kirk! Wilson opposed prohibition; but he favored local option, which was anathema to the Jersey bosses. They shook their heads, but elected him anyway. For he turned out to be a candidate beyond their wildest dreams. His great acceptance speech after the nomination had won over his bitterest opponents. And now that summer vacation released him from academic restrictions he threw himself into political life with gusto. His speeches, far from being pedantic or top-lofty, pulled the country Assemblymen and the downtown wards right out of their seats.

The bosses feared his independence but remained entranced with the vision of victory. He was "a terrible man to manage," they said. Anyhow, the campaign soon outdistanced the organization. The young progressives of the State, Tumulty among them, had become vigorous Wilson campaigners, once they got to know the man. Funds came from Wilson's own friends and from many people not connected with politics but glad that a decent man had appeared upon the scene. Wilson was "the whole show," as one newspaper said. The bosses went through the motions of rounding up their voters, but no one paid much attention to them.

At every meeting right up to the end Wilson warned them. "If I am elected," he said at the final meeting at Newark three days before election, "I shall have been elected leader of my party and Governor of all the people of New Jersey to conduct government in their interest and in their interest only. . . . If the Democratic party does not understand it that way then I want to say to you very frankly that the Democratic party ought not to elect me Governor."

They elected him by a majority of 49,056—the next largest ever given a candidate for Governor up to that time. They also gave him a Democratic legislature—in a State that had gone Republican for seventeen years. Then came the "pay-off." Election over, Boss Smith's health miraculously improved; he decided he should "yield to the wishes of his friends" and consider re-election to the Senate. Wilson, indignant but standing firm on his pledges, opposed him in a series of public meetings and a State-wide campaign which attracted tremendous interest. Thanks to his efforts, James Martine—the people's choice by a large majority at the primaries—was elected. Smith was defeated, thus giving rise to charges of "disloyalty" and "ingratitude" on Wilson's part, and to the famous remark of arch-boss Richard Croker: "An ingrate in politics is no good."

The trouble was that nobody ever believed Wilson meant

what he said. He had been nominated because he was the only Democrat in the State who could get the votes. "So put him in and deal with his principles later," said the Old Guard. Principles . . . patriotism . . . "owe nothing to anybody"—it was good campaign stuff, "old talk"—but this was a new man speaking it. The incredible thing was that he did mean, and do, what he promised.

On October 20, 1910, Wilson resigned from the Presidency of Princeton University. Senator Lodge and other enemies having persistently written of "Wilson's forced resignation from Princeton," it may be well to record that the Board of Trustees, in accepting his resignation (November 3, 1910), after expressing "its high appreciation of his great services, both to Princeton and to higher education throughout America," resolved "that his salary be continued to the end of the year; that he be invited to continue to occupy the premises at Prospect and, if his duties would permit, to continue his present professorship of jurisprudence which he has made of such service to the student body." They also honored him with the degree of Doctor of Laws."

Wilson, however, refused to take any salary after the day on which he had resigned and soon moved with his family into very restricted quarters at the Princeton Inn. The State of New Jersey had a summer mansion for its Governor at Sea Girt but none at Trenton, so he now became a commuter, traveling back and forth between Princeton and Trenton each day. Living in three little rooms instead of the spacious residence he had enjoyed for so long, leaving the peace and beauty of his quiet library at Prospect—the lovely garden and stately old trees—he must sometimes have thought of the words of the Big Boss who had exclaimed: "Can you imagine anyone being damn fool enough to give up *this* for the heartaches of politics?"

Wilson's platform for Governor contained four main pledges: the direct primary, a corrupt practices election law, a public service commission with power to fix rates, and an employers' liability and workingmen's compensation law. Not a man in the

Educator and Governor

State except Wilson had expected to see that program go through. *But every item did go through*—and half a dozen more. The Governor's inaugural address revealed that he intended to fulfill his platform promises. He spoke of his program with confidence both in himself and in his colleagues.

"It is not the foolish ardor of too sanguine or too radical reform that I urge upon you but merely the tasks that are evident and pressing, the things we have knowledge and guidance enough to do, and to do with confidence and energy. I merely," he said, "point out the present business of progress and serviceable government."

Wilson attributed the growth of the boss system, with its corrupt unofficial leaders, largely to the scarcity of first-rate constitutional leaders in this country. He intended to be, as Governor, head of his party in the State. He had received a tremendous popular vote. He intended to see that the policies on which he was elected were promptly carried out in practical legislation.

He had a Democratic majority on joint ballot of the legislature; but the Senate—which had to concur before a bill became law—remained Republican, 12 to 9. The Democrats had a 42 to 18 majority in the Assembly, but many of them belonged to the old organization and resented the college President's victory. Imagine any New Jersey political organization voting for a direct primary bill to have all candidates for office nominated directly by the people; or a public service bill to have utility rates put under control of the people. The Governor hadn't a chance in a million, or so his friends in the party warned.

The Governor smiled genially and continued on his way. He intended to make his arguments for the bills so that the entire State should hear him (a lifelong Wilsonian technique), and he would oblige the opponents to state their objections publicly also. He consulted Democrats and Republicans alike, called them into his office, talked to them about the merits of the bills, and asked them to let him know where they stood. When the legislature opened on January 10, 1911, the Governor had trouble getting sponsors to introduce his bills. It was doubtful, he was told, if a single one of them could be put through before the end of the session. "Very well, then, we shall have to have a special session to do it," Governor Wilson coolly replied. "However, let us hope that won't be necessary."

First came the primary elections bill, or the Geran bill, as it was called. The bill, if passed, meant the end of the boss system —a death blow to corporation-controlled organizations. James Nugent, Smith's nephew, came down to lead the opposition. Smith had planned a coalition with the Republicans, whose organization was also in jeopardy. If the Republican majority in the Senate stood pat, the Geran bill would fail. But Nugent also wanted the Democratic Lower House to turn down the Governor's scheme. He was so sure this could be done that he arranged a caucus on the bill, which proved a fatal mistake.

The Governor heard of the caucus and pleasantly suggested that he be invited. They couldn't very well refuse him. The conference assembled in the Supreme Court Room of the State House. Picture the line-up of the hard-boiled Old Guard, confronting the equally determined Princeton Tiger. One Assemblyman challenged his presence, asking, "What constitutional right has the Governor to interfere in legislation?"

"If you appeal to the Constitution I can satisfy you," said the Governor. He drew from his pocket the Legislative Manual and read a clause which directed the Governor of New Jersey "to communicate to the legislature at such times as he might deem necessary such measures as he might deem expedient." "I am therefore," said Governor Wilson, "in pursuance of a constitutional duty to recommend a measure of that character."

And eloquently he proceeded to recommend it. He spoke for three hours, explaining the bill clause by clause, answering questions, parrying objections; showing a knowledge both of the law and of practical politics in various States that amazed his hearers. Finally with a rush of white-hot words he tried to show them the higher side of political duty and the great opportunity of the party in their State and in the whole country. The caucus called to repudiate the Geran bill voted to make it a party measure. One Assemblyman said afterward:

Educator and Governor

"We came out of that room with one conviction: that we had heard the most wonderful speech of our lives. Opposition melted away under the Governor's influence. That caucus settled the fate of the Geran bill as well as of the whole Democratic program."

Nugent then tried to get a Republican caucus to secure Republican unanimity against the bill, but so many Republicans refused in advance to be bound that the plan was abandoned. Various other maneuvers were tried, but when voting time came the Assembly passed the bill with a third more votes than it required. The Republican Senate accepted and passed it without a struggle.

The Governor's entire legislative program followed. New Jersey came then to have the most advanced and best-working primary law in the Union. It had a corrupt practices law of the sternest kind. Betting on elections was forbidden. Treating by candidates was forbidden. All campaign expenses must be published. Corporations might not contribute. The maximum amount to be spent by candidates for any office was fixed by law.

New Jersey had a public utilities commission with power to appraise property, fix rates, forbid discrimination, regulate finances, and control sales, mortgages, and leases in the case of railroads and trolleys, express companies, gas, light, heat, power, water, telephone, and telegraph, and half a dozen other services. It had an employers' liability law which gave an injured employee immediate automatic compensation, paid by the employer. The State decreed that such cities and towns as might desire to do so could adopt the Des Moines plan of the commission form of government, whereupon Trenton and eight other New Jersey towns attempted scientific municipal government. This extraordinary record of progressive legislation also included a statute regulating the cold storage of food, legislation establishing the indeterminate sentence in place of the old discredited fixed sentence, and the complete reorganization of the public school system.

By this time people had pretty well begun to find out who was running the State of New Jersey. As one contemporary put it, "The quiet gentleman just emerged from the tranquil groves of Princeton—the long-haired bookworm of a professor who just laid his spectacles on his dictionary—had come down to Trenton State House and licked the gang to a frazzle!"

The achievement, moreover, left the legislators in a surprisingly friendly frame of mind towards the Governor. They apparently liked to drop in for a visit at the Governor's office, where an agreeable reception and a lively story from the energetic man with the long jaw always awaited them. The Senators even found that the high tenor voice that had led two college glee clubs could lead the crowd delightfully at country club suppers; and on one occasion the Governor's long legs engaged in a cakewalk with one of the older Senators which won loud applause.

> The Legislature adjourned yesterday morning at three o'clock [Wilson wrote a friend]. . . . I got absolutely everything I strove for . . . as complete a victory as has ever been won . . . in the history of the country. . . . I have no doubt that a good deal of the result was due to the personal relations I established with the men in the Senate, the Republican Senate which, it was feared, might be the stumbling block. You remember . . . the supper at the Trenton country club which I described to you. . . . Since then the Republicans have resorted to my office for counsel and advice almost as freely as Democrats . . . and with several of them I have established relations almost of affection. Otherwise I do not believe that the extraordinary thing that happened could possibly have come about: for all four of the great "administration" measures passed the Senate *without a dissenting voice*. The newspaper men seem dazed. They do not understand how such things *could* happen.

Apparently there were some Republican Senators in this country who found Woodrow Wilson a man whom they could admire and follow, and who passed his administration measures without "reservations" or hostility.

Even after he reached the White House, Wilson kept a warm spot in his heart—and a watchful eye in his head—for the affairs

Educator and Governor

of New Jersey. When he resigned the Governorship his old enemies the bosses threatened some of the reforms to which the party was committed—notably jury reform. His friends sent Wilson an S.O.S. In the midst of his tariff fight and beset with Mexican, Japanese, and many other problems, he made a trip to New Jersey, "put on the war paint," and held some rousing meetings at Elizabeth, Newark, and Jersey City. When the vote came, the jury reform bill passed both houses of the legislature. "Magnificent fighting!" said the papers. "After New Jersey," said Wilson, "I am in training for almost anything!"

This whole New Jersey experience particularly pleased him because it confirmed his belief in the people: that they would uphold sound measures and insist upon the enforcement of good laws if only these were put to them clearly and reasonably.

The spring of 1911 brought a strong upsurge of the movement for Mr. Wilson's nomination for the Presidency. His defeat of the bosses had dramatized his ability for leadership. "He is being viewed as a national rather than a purely local figure," said the Washington *Post*. In all parts of the country people seemed to be increasingly aware that Wilson looked more like a great man than anyone who had come forward in a long time. Letters began arriving in Trenton and Princeton till they could no longer be read, much less answered. Invitations to speak also poured in.

A few friends clubbed together and raised a small fund for an informal sort of office and arranged an itinerary through some of the cities that wanted to see New Jersey's Governor and hear him speak. He set forth on May 3, 1911—after the adjournment of the legislature—with a journalist friend, Frank Stockbridge, and McKee Barclay, whom the Baltimore *Sun* sent along to report the meetings. Before he returned he had traveled eight thousand miles, made thirty-one speeches, and addressed thousands of people. Eight States had acclaimed him as the next President.

In January, 1912, at the Jackson Day dinner—where Presidential nominees are put through their paces—he made an address so commanding in power that he swept the eight hundred leaders off their feet and was declared by 32 out of the 51 National Committeemen as their preferred candidate for the Democratic nomination.

VI

MANY men have claimed credit for "making Woodrow Wilson President." No individual or group made Wilson. He made himself by his own work. For thirty years he had expressed himself vigorously on public questions in his books and speeches. His fight for democracy in education, and later his fight for clean government in New Jersey, had impressed the whole country. Many persons besides Harvey had proposed him for the Presidency; the Indianapolis *News* did so as early as May, 1902. He had refused a Senatorial and a Vice-Presidential nomination. He had been elected by a great popular majority Democratic Governor of a long-time Republican State; he had defeated some of the shrewdest bosses and put through some of the finest, most progressive legislation known to any State in the Union. The man made himself. And America has always loved a self-made man.

At the time that Wilson began to loom seriously as a Presidential possibility the United States was peculiarly ripe for such a leader. Muckraking writers had roused the country. People were up in arms against privilege and monopoly, though they were unconverted to the radicalism of Bryan and La Follette. Teddy Roosevelt, after his unexpected seven years of thundering and reforming, had departed; his successor—easygoing President Taft—proved himself no match for the powerful interests that dominated his Republican party. He yielded rather than challenged, and thoroughly disappointed the people as well as his sponsor, T. R. The elections of 1910 brought a Democratic landslide. But insurgent progressives had the upper hand in both parties. They were ready to ignore party lines and join forces in a new independent movement—if they could find a suitable leader.

Educator and Governor

Colonel Harvey and his wealthy backers, acutely aware of the situation and wishing to avoid a Bryan or La Follette regime at any cost, picked Wilson to head off the radicals. A man's party made no difference to them as long as his leadership was conservative. *Harper's Weekly* became almost embarrassing in its eulogies.

"It makes me smile," said Wilson, "to think that I should ever have been regarded as 'the Wall Street candidate' for the Presidency!" He refused, however, to ally himself with any coalition or third-party movement. "I must work through the party of which I am the accredited leader," he said. He had seen the failure of too many "independent" schemes.

But his position with the Democratic party was circumscribed. He had fought the Democratic organization in New Jersey. Tammany Hall, in control of New York, detested him. Bryan was the cherished leader of the West. The bankers and conservatives of the East, once they knew Wilson's real views, would certainly not support him. Where was his backing actually to come from?

It came, as might have been expected, from the rank and file of the people, in whom Wilson believed with all his heart. "If a man is right, the people will support him," he said. The trend to Wilson began to develop in January, 1911, after his defeat of Boss Smith. Quantities of letters from all over the country told him, "We want you to be our next President"—"Republicans as well as Democrats are with you." Some of the letters were signed by three Democrats and two Republicans, or vice versa.

His birthplace, Staunton, Virginia, organized the first "Woodrow Wilson for President" Club in November, 1910. Many Southerners rallied to him simply because he was a Southerner and could be counted on to understand their needs and forward their interests. The Pennsylvania group, with Roland Morris, Vance McCormick, and Mitchell Palmer, were early in the field, as were Thomas Love, Albert Burleson, T. W. Gregory, and other prominent Texans. Walter Page was an enthusiast from the first; so were Cleveland Dodge, Cyrus McCormick, and other Princeton friends.

The Story of Woodrow Wilson

McCombs, a New York lawyer, who eventually became Wilson's 1912 campaign manager, was especially eager to set up offices and an organization. Wilson hung back. He wanted to test his leadership in the South and West before making commitments or getting involved with organization. In the spring of 1911 he made a trip to Georgia, speaking in several cities and getting a great reception.

On March 9th he addressed the Southern Commercial Congress at Atlanta, where President Taft and Ex-President Theodore Roosevelt also spoke. Atlanta's Judge Hillyer, in introducing Wilson, said: "Last night we had here a man who has been President of the United States. This evening we shall hear a man who is President. . . . But we have with us this morning a man who is going to be President of the United States!" In Savannah he addressed eight thousand people and received an ovation. "Woodrow Wilson is coming at a rate which is a marvel of the politicians," said the Washington *Times*. "Governor Wilson made a tremendous impression in the South." Southern Congressmen returning to Washington began to discuss him seriously now as a Presidential candidate. If the West would receive him as cordially as the South had . . .

The West was Bryan's territory, and Bryan, in those early days, was Wilson's major problem. He had strongly opposed Bryan's free-silver campaign in 1896, regarding him for a while as a demagogue with dangerous oratorical powers. Later, after he heard him speak, he came to feel Bryan's sincerity but still doubted his intellect. He told Roland Morris, "It is a pity that a man with his power of leadership should have no mental rudder."

Nevertheless, the great Commoner had remained undisputed leader of the Democratic party for sixteen years. If a man expected to be elected President on the Democratic ticket he would have to make terms with Bryan. Mrs. Wilson—"a better politician than you are, Governor," Tumulty said—brought the two together for their first personal meeting. She heard that Bryan was to speak at the Theological School at Princeton and telegraphed her husband, in Atlanta, urging his prompt return. Wilson got back just in time to hear Bryan's speech (a fine one, on "Faith") and to take him home to the family dinner Mrs. Wilson had arranged.

It proved an agreeable and an important meeting. Politics was not mentioned. The two men swapped stories, enjoyed themselves, and established a real understanding. Both were idealists, both utterly sincere; each recognized and respected these traits in the other. Wilson wrote a friend that he was "completely captivated by Bryan's personal charm—I have a very different impression of him from that I had before." Bryan was equally pleased, having expected a somewhat dour Scotch professor. Tumulty exclaimed joyfully after Bryan had left: "You have nominated your husband, Mrs. Wilson!" "I? Why, I did nothing at all," said Mrs. Wilson with her quiet smile.

Three weeks later the two men appeared on the same platform at a big Democratic rally at Burlington, New Jersey. They met again at Indianapolis, where Woodrow Wilson as the guest of Governor Thomas Marshall of Indiana addressed the National League of Democratic Clubs. And when Wilson went to Nebraska, invading Bryan's home territory at the end of his speaking tour, the Bryan family gave him a royal welcome.

The tour was highly successful. He had visited Missouri, Colorado, California, Oregon, Washington, Minnesota, Iowa, Nebraska, meeting large and enthusiastic crowds everywhere. Wilson the scholar, the brilliant and delightful orator, was gratefully welcomed after the perpetual abuse and ranting of the radicals, the pomposity and flowery promises of the usual campaign speakers. He declared from the start his open war on "the interests" and special privilege, his absolute determination to reinstate government by the people; he offered no quick cure-alls or panaceas, but discussed the issues so clearly and simply and with such understanding of the everyday citizen and his needs that people trusted him and rallied to him instinctively. Here was the leader they had been waiting for: a common-sense, middle-of-the-road man.

"Wilsonism," said an Oregon paper after his visit, "is popular leadership with a safety valve . . . statesmanship without demagogy, and of caliber and character to match and master the gathering problems of our national life." "At the conclusion of his Western tour," said the New York *Times*, "Governor Wilson is a candidate in the fullest sense of the word."

Early in the campaign came his famous break with George Harvey. The story is well known. It added to the legend that Wilson was an ingrate in politics. On December 7, 1911, Wilson met Colonel Harvey and Colonel Watterson at the Manhattan Club in New York. The three discussed the political situation in Watterson's home state of Kentucky, and throughout the country. Just as Wilson rose to go, Harvey asked him: "Governor, is there anything left of that cheap talk about my advocating you on behalf of 'the interests'? Tell me frankly, is the support of *Harper's Weekly* embarrassing your campaign?"

"Colonel," said Wilson, "I am sorry you asked that question."

"That's all right—what's the answer?" said Harvey.

"Well, Colonel, I regret to be compelled to tell you that my friends in the West tell me it is." Some papers of the West had indeed suggested that Wilson was the candidate of the very "interests" he was supposed to be fighting.

Harvey replied, in a perfectly friendly way, "I thought you might feel that way about it. Then we shall have to soft-pedal for a bit."

"Yes, that's the only thing to do," said Watterson. "I myself shall not say a word."

On December 21st Harvey published a statement in *Harper's Weekly* announcing the withdrawal from its columns of Wilson's name as Presidential candidate "in accordance with his wishes and in consideration of our own self-respect," following a "statement made directly to us by Governor Wilson to the effect that our support was affecting his candidacy injuriously."

Then the floodgates were opened and the tides of criticism rolled in. Colonel Watterson said that Governor Wilson "without the least show of compunction" had permitted "Colonel Harvey to consider himself discharged from his position of trusted intimacy."

Wilson was both disillusioned and amazed. He had left the

conference with no idea of any break or of having offended Harvey. He had been asked a direct question; he had given a frank, direct answer, as one naturally would to a good friend. It did not occur to him to approach Harvey with kid gloves. But the best of friends has his vanity. Though Wilson had time and again expressed his gratitude in warm terms to Harvey, the latter still wanted truth and appreciation mixed. Wilson, eager to be clear on the main point, forgot, at that particular moment, the appreciation.

Several official "reconciliations" occurred after the historic episode, but the two men never really came together again. In any case the break was inevitable: an opportunist and an idealist cannot travel far in the same coach. For a time the incident seriously threatened Wilson's campaign, till an enterprising Washington correspondent wrote a story openly asserting that Harvey and Watterson represented "Wall Street interests" and that Wilson refused to be dominated by them. Then, by another twist of the political weather vane, the incident became a great asset in Wilson's favor.

Harvey's attitude to Wilson shifted many times during the next years, before it finally reached the blistering enmity of 1918. He expressed profound admiration for Wilson's currency reform, ardent enthusiasm (at first) for the Fourteen Points program, poetic eulogy for the famous Fourth of July address at Mt. Vernon a few months later. But he interspersed his praise with jeers and jibes, insult and ridicule on a variety of matters, until at last he gave the *coup de grâce* to Wilson's greatest project: the League of Nations.

Sometimes he appeared to speak out of his own conviction, sometimes "inspired" by his Wall Street friends and other backers, such as T. R., when they were running *Harvey's Weekly*. But a recurring and unquenchable admiration for Wilson seems to have possessed him, bubbling up spontaneously from time to time like a geyser that sputters for long periods in the mud, occasionally flashing a shining ribbon to the sky.

As one Colonel withdrew, another entered. Colonel Edward M. House, honored with his title in much the same way that

The Story of Woodrow Wilson

Harvey was honored by Governor Green, had for years been influential in Texas state politics. In 1911 he began interesting himself in national affairs, believing that the Democratic "day" was dawning. For months he had been looking for a possible Democratic leader. In Wilson he found his man.

Wilson—sore after the Harvey-Watterson break, following disappointments in his old friends at Princeton; profoundly hurt in his personal life while mounting to dizzy political heights—was inevitably attracted to the quiet, self-effacing Southerner who "wanted nothing but to be allowed to serve." The partnership was, one might almost say, predestined.

They met on November 24, 1911, at the Hotel Gotham in New York, and saw each other several times during the weeks that followed. The friendship progressed so rapidly that Wilson said, in one of his impulsive flashes: "My dear friend, we have known each other always!" House said: "We had a perfectly bully time. . . . Never before have I found both the man and the opportunity."

House, who at first favored Mayor Gaynor of New York as a Presidential candidate, now interested himself actively in Wilson's campaign and used all his influence to bring the Texas Democrats to his support. To what extent he was actually responsible for making Texas a strong Wilson State is a matter of dispute; House's account and the accounts of other Texans vary considerably on this point. House sailed for Europe two days before the Democratic convention opened. Strange how often he was away at a crucial moment.

A curious character, this soft-voiced Colonel; he grows on one in an odd fashion. At Wilson's inauguration again he was absent —preferring, as he tells his diary, "to loaf round at the Metropolitan Club" in Washington rather than look on while his "dearest friend" and political idol stood in the inaugural rostrum at the Capitol being sworn in for the highest office in the land. At the signing of the Federal Reserve Act, in which he was supposed to have taken special interest, once more he was absent. He "disliked such ceremonies," says his biographer. The ceremonies from which House absented himself were noticeably those where another man was receiving signal honor or where there was danger of failure on the part of someone with whom he had been prominently identified.

"I had no ambition to hold office," he says, "nor had I any ambition to speak, because I felt in both instances I would fall short of first place and nothing less than that would satisfy me." Yet he is not, he says, as people have supposed, without ambition. On the contrary, "my ambition has been so great it never seemed worth while to strive to satisfy it."

He satisfied it by attaching himself to the greatest man of his time and sticking closer to him than a brother—in the highest office of all, as personal adviser and confidant.

Harvey, House, Bryan: these three men had immense influence on Wilson's life; perhaps greater influence than anyone, except his wife. But Bryan, whom Wilson at first disdained, proved far and away the biggest.

As Wilson's prestige grew, his enemies made an organized attempt to destroy him. They exploited the fact that he had applied for a Carnegie pension—the prerogative of any scholar after twenty-five years' service in a university. They attempted to bring the Princeton controversies into politics, threatening to use a hitherto unpublished letter from Mr. Cleveland. Wilson was called "undependable, if not downright untruthful"; "selfish," "ambitious," "disloyal to his friends"—anything to blacken him with the public and the organization politicians. Finally, two days before the Jackson Day dinner and in order to alienate Bryan's friendship, the New York *Sun* published a private letter which Wilson years before had written to Adrian Joline saying, "Would that we could do something at once dignified and effective to knock Mr. Bryan into a cocked hat." Joline, now a bitter opponent of Wilson, was delighted to use this letter to make trouble.

Wilson's friends were greatly upset. But Bryan, asked for a statement, genially told the reporters: "You may say that if Mr. Wilson wants to knock me into a cocked hat he and the *Sun*

The Story of Woodrow Wilson

are on the same platform. That is what the *Sun* has been trying to do since 1896."

Democrats went to the Jackson Day dinner agog over the incident. This dinner—where the Presidential candidates are critically looked over—is an important milestone in the life of a candidate. On his way down to Washington for the occasion Wilson wrote one of his friends this description of the campaign against him: "A rain of small missiles . . . practically all supplied by the Princetonians who hate me. . . . But I go serenely on my way. I believe very profoundly in an overruling Providence, and do not fear that any real plans can be thrown off the track. It may not be intended that I shall be President,—but that would not break my heart and I am content to await the event—doing what I honorably can in the meantime to discomfit my enemies!"

In Washington he found his friends in a great state over the rumored displeasure also of Mr. William Randolph Hearst. Wilson was charged with having refused Hearst's invitation to dinner or to meet him in any way. Here Wilson was adamant. "I want the Democratic Presidential nomination," he said, "and I am going to do everything I can legitimately to get it, but if I am to grovel at Hearst's feet, I will never have it!" The bosses were right—he was a hard man to manage!

Dudley Malone went to see Bryan, to "sound out the land." Bryan was "very generous, indeed splendid," said Mr. Malone. "I believe," said Bryan, "that when Wilson wrote that letter to Mr. Joline, he believed it. It doesn't follow that he believes it now. If the big financial interests think that they are going to make a rift in the progressive ranks of the Democratic party they are mistaken."

At the dinner Bryan greeted Wilson cordially; he put his hand on Wilson's shoulder and talked with him for some minutes, with all eyes curiously upon them. When Wilson made his speech, later, he paid a glowing tribute to Bryan: "There has been one interesting fixed point in the history of the Democratic party [during the past sixteen years], and that fixed point has been the character and the devotion and the preachings of William Jennings Bryan."

Educator and Governor

"We have differed with Mr. Bryan on this occasion and that in regard to . . . specific things," but not, he implied, on major principles. Tonight, "we stand for setting the government of this country free and the business of this country free." The way to do that was "to keep a free and hopeful heart under every jacket. . . . When we die we shall look back and say 'Yes, from time to time we differed with each other but after all we followed the same vision . . . to a common purpose and a common ideal.' Let us apologize to each other that we ever suspected or antagonized one another; let us join hands once more around all the great circle of community of counsel and of interest . . . friends of our country and friends of mankind."

Bryan gazed steadily at Wilson throughout this address. He told a friend later that "it was the greatest speech in American political history." When it came his turn Bryan made what has been called his "speech of abdication." For sixteen years he had been leader of the party and three times its candidate for the Presidency. Now the time had come for new leaders, he declared. He was ready to fight in the ranks to secure victory for the principles to which they were all devoted. He sat down amid thunderous applause.

So the effort to alienate two big men failed—because of their bigness. The "rain of small missiles" was futile. Eventually the understanding cemented that night brought about Wilson's nomination and election, which in turn brought about Bryan's elevation to the distinguished post of Secretary of State: a higher position than he had ever attained through his own efforts as a political leader.

VII

I<small>T WAS</small> a strange campaign, run by "the oddest collection of amateurs that ever came together to elect a President," as one of them said. They had no money, no organization, no political experience, plus an erratic self-constituted campaign manager. Wilson won in spite of McCombs rather than because of him. They had an office with no name on the door, stationery with no letterhead, their equipment a borrowed desk and typewriter. At times there was not a dollar in the treasury. A few devoted friends kept them going—Cleveland Dodge, Henry Morgenthau, Frederick Penfield, Charles Crane. Many small contributors sent in modest sums.

Wilson's chances, seemingly so brilliant on Jackson Day, petered off during March and April. His enemies had gone to his books and dug up every sentence that could possibly be construed as against the Hungarians, Italians, Germans, Poles, woman suffrage, prohibition, or any other question that would influence votes. They used these with deadly effect, each in the quarters where it would do most damage. He went on a series of speaking tours during the spring months preceding the convention, campaigning in New England, the Southern States, Iowa and Illinois and Pennsylvania and meeting enthusiastic receptions everywhere. However, when the delegates began to be chosen he did not get them. The old organization leadership, resting comfortably on long-established relations and personal favors, generally held the field. Champ Clark of Missouri, Speaker of the House, Oscar Underwood, favorite son of Alabama, Governor Harmon of Ohio, and several lesser lights contended with Wilson for the nomination, but his chief rival was Champ Clark.

Clark was the regulation party man; solid with the organization party leaders with whom he had been on intimate terms for years. Hearst and his chain of newspapers backed Clark. Bryan insisted that the convention would be controlled by progressives; but the wise ones knew that Tammany Hall, the Martin Ryan machine of Virginia, and similar organizations really controlled the vote. McCombs urged Wilson to lose no time in coming to an understanding with Tammany—"Those ninety precious New York votes, Governor!"

Wilson steadily refused. He had a strong sense that the people were with him, in spite of official delegations apparently favoring other candidates. Bryan remained the great question mark. Nobody knew where he stood. Nebraska had come out for Clark, but Bryan personally had not declared himself. He sent Wilson a message a few days before the convention about the possibility of making Alton B. Parker, a dyed-in-the-wool reactionary, temporary chairman. The chairman delivers the keynote speech. Bryan of course wanted the chairman to be a progressive. He telegraphed Wilson and the other candidates asking them to state their position. McCombs counseled an evasive safe answer. But Wilson replied forthrightly that in his opinion the convention must have a progressive chairman and that he was sure his delegates would say the same. All the other candidates either opposed Bryan or avoided giving a direct answer.

The convention met on June 25th at Baltimore. The balloting lasted six days. On the first ballot Clark polled 440½ votes, Wilson 324. Harmon and Underwood came next, each with over a hundred votes. Favorite sons divided the rest. A private wire from the Wilson headquarters at the Emerson Hotel in Baltimore to the Governor's House at Sea Girt kept him informed of every development, and the newspapermen installed on the parade ground rushed in and out all day bringing the latest reports.

For three days very little change occurred in the voting. The Wilson family, at the other end of the line, were on tenterhooks. Wilson was the calmest of any of them. He played golf, read Morley's *Gladstone*, laughed at his daughters and Tumulty, who sat up most of the night discussing the situation in low tones or gazing bleakly into space, and himself went to bed and slept soundly. On the fourth day Boss Murphy of Tammany Hall startled the convention by rising slowly and delivering his entire delegation to Champ Clark. "The fight is over!" shouted a Clark devotee. Led by the Missouri delegation, a tremendous procession paraded jubilantly round the convention hall for over an hour. Everybody expected a stampede for Clark.

Early next morning McCombs, in a great state of mind, called the Governor on the phone, said that Clark's nomination was inevitable, and asked Wilson to send a telegram releasing his delegation and instructing them how to vote. Wilson went in to breakfast with his family looking very serious; he was on the verge of sending the telegram when again he was called to the telephone. This time it was McAdoo, furious with McCombs. "Your nomination is inevitable, Governor. Your delegates will stick if it takes all summer." McAdoo begged Wilson to call McCombs and tell him not to release the delegation. Another urgent call from Josephus Daniels clinched the matter. Wilson stuck.

And well he did, for on the fourteenth ballot Bryan rose in his seat and announced impressively: "Mr. Chairman, I wish to state that I cannot support a man who has received the votes of the Tammany delegation. I cast my vote for Nebraska's second choice—Governor Wilson!" Wilson's supporters went wild. Bryan's vast influence turned the tide. On the next ballot Nebraska voted 12 for Wilson, 4 for Clark. From that moment Clark began to lose, Wilson to gain, slowly but surely. "I've been figuring it out," he told his family: "if things go on as they are doing, I ought to be nominated on the 175th ballot!" He was nominated on the 46th. Little by little he began to creep up, till the thrilling moment on Monday, July 1, when the reporters tore up to the house yelling, "You've passed him, Governor, you've passed him!" On the 43rd ballot Roger Sullivan delivered Illinois's 58 votes to Wilson. On the 46th the delegates nominated Wilson by acclamation. He got 990 votes, Missouri alone loyally casting its last vote for Clark.

Tumulty, in a frenzy of joy, rushed out on the porch and began waving his arms in wild signals. From behind a clump of trees came a brass band blaring "Hail to the Chief" and "The Conquering Hero Comes." He had had them waiting there for six days! While the band played and the family and newspapermen congratulated him incoherently, the nominee himself remained strangely quiet.

"Governor, you don't seem a bit excited," said one of the reporters. "I can't effervesce in the face of responsibility," Wilson replied.

That night, his daughter says, "We all slept like the dead."

August 7 brought the formal notification ceremony. Senator Ollie James, chairman of the convention, made the delivery speech, in the presence of a large and enthusiastic throng of Democrats gathered on the lawn of the Governor's Sea Girt residence: "I hand you this formal letter of notification, signed by the members of the committee; I present to you a copy of the platform adopted there, and upon that platform I have the honor to request your acceptance of a tendered nomination and on behalf of the Democracy of the whole Republic, united, militant, I pledge you their hearty support, and may God lead you to a glorious victory in November."

Wilson's acceptance speech gave the keynote of his Presidential policy and of all the speeches of his campaign. The task was to restore to the people all the instrumentalities of their Government and of their life, the nation having lost for a time certain cherished liberties which must be recovered. "Every form of special privilege and private control" must go. This he applied to tariffs, trusts, labor problems, and other vital questions. The business of the Democratic party was not to catch votes but to serve the nation. "I feel that I am surrounded by men whose principles and ambitions are those of true servants of the people. I thank God and will take courage."

In October he was back at Princeton, in the little house on Cleveland Lane, engrossed in the problems of the election campaign. He disliked stumping, but his managers pleaded so strongly for a speaking campaign that he yielded. Taft and Roosevelt, the Republican and Progressive party nominees, were stumping extensively. Taft made no personal attack on Wilson, But Roosevelt never lost an opportunity. One of Governor Wilson's best imitations in the bosom of his family was T. R.'s famous "We stand at Armageddon and battle for the Lord." "Good old Teddy—what a help he is!" Wilson would laugh.

To him the great issues at stake in this fight completely dwarfed the personalities. His speeches were based on his political philosophy rather than on the usual pre-election promises. "How can anyone honestly present a definite plan?" he asked. "A sincere man can only explain the political philosophy which will apply to the problems when they present themselves. I do not want to promise heaven unless I can bring it to you. I can see only a little distance down the road." Such candor proved refreshing to a nation perennially skeptical of pre-election bombast and extravagant pledges. His managers had far more confidence in his election than Wilson himself. However, he wrote one of his friends with an odd detachment, "I have no deep stakes involved in this game."

Bryan, wholeheartedly supporting him, made a very effective speaking campaign. "Let me ask you to do twice as much for Wilson as you ever did for Bryan," he urged his followers. From the moment of his "abdication" he had shown never an atom of jealousy or repining; he slipped into second place graciously and without a murmur.

President Eliot of Harvard, Louis D. Brandeis, Samuel Gompers, and many other men of the first rank became devoted adherents, giving generously both of time and of money. Wilson was delighted when Henry Morgenthau (father of our recent Secretary of the Treasury) consented to act as Chairman of the Finance Committee. A large proportion of the gifts came, as Wilson had hoped, from small subscribers. There were 88,229 contributors of amounts less than $100; 1,625 of amounts over $100. When the campaign was over he could repeat what he had said at the beginning: "Nobody owns me."

The climax of the campaign was a great meeting at Madison Square Garden five days before election. A roaring mob of enthusiasts greeted him that evening, sixteen thousand people yelling, "Wilson! We Want Wilson!" at the top of their lungs. When Wilson appeared on the platform the cheering lasted an hour and five minutes before he could begin his address. He was deeply moved by a demonstration which "I realize is . . . for a cause and not for a man. All over this country from one ocean to another men are becoming more aware that in less than a week the common people of America will come into their own again. . . . What the Democratic party proposes to do is to go into power and do the things that the Republican party has been talking about doing for sixteen years!"

He spent Election Day quietly, going down early to vote at the little engine house with his neighbors. Afterwards he walked about the familiar town of Princeton with one or two friends, almost as if saying farewell. He had spent over twenty years of his life there, in addition to his student days. He stopped to point out the house where he had boarded when he entered the University, a raw young Freshman thirty-seven years before.

After supper he read aloud to the family and some close friends. Usually this was a great treat, especially when the chosen author was Browning. But nobody heard much Browning that night. Ears were straining to catch the tick-tick of the telegraph out in the hall. The room was still and tense as the beautifully modulated voice read steadily on. All at once a bell sounded: muffled at first, tentative, a bit uncertain; then loud and clear—the bell of Old Nassau Hall. In another minute it was ringing like mad. At the same moment the special operator came in and handed a telegram to Mrs. Wilson. She read it, went over and laid her hand on her husband's shoulder. For a moment neither of them said a word.

Half an hour later, at 10:30 P.M., McCombs wired the official confirmation: "My warmest congratulations to you, our next President. You have won a splendid and significant victory. At this hour you appear to have received the largest electoral vote ever given to a Presidential candidate. [It was Wilson 435, Roosevelt 88, Taft 8.] The indications are that your Administration will be supported by a Congress Democratic in both branches."

Then down the road came a swaying, jubilant procession of college boys, snake-dancing in triumph with their flags and torches. Wilson went out to meet them eagerly; there was no audience in the world he would so love at such an hour. With them came the townspeople—swarms of people, all at once surrounding the house, the garden, crowding round the porch. "Speech! Speech!" shouted the boys. Somebody brought a chair for him to stand on. He was silent for a moment, poised for a breathless second between one life and another. Then his voice rang out firmly: "I have no feeling of triumph tonight but a feeling of solemn responsibility. I know the very great task ahead of me, and the men associated with me. I look almost with pleading to you, the young men of America, to stand behind me, to support me in the new Administration. I know what you want and we will not accomplish it through a single man or a single session of Congress but by long processes running through the next generation."

From that moment there was no more privacy or peace for Woodrow Wilson. "The procession" had invaded his life for keeps: reporters, delegations, conferences, speeches. He escaped with his family to Bermuda for a few weeks' "vacation." Even there a gigantic correspondence pursued him, as pressing problems crowded his attention: Mexico, canal tolls, European relations, the composition of his Cabinet, the vast and difficult question of patronage. One of his interesting letters of this period went to Sun Yat-sen, congratulating him, as founder and first President of the new Republic of China, on "the liberty for which the Chinese people have so long been yearning."

Back home again, he faced an endless stream of visitors: Congressional leaders to be seen, legislation planned, strategy decided—and the legislative duties of Governor still to be discharged also. To the intense disappointment of the bosses, Wilson did not resign until March 1st, three days before he left for Washington. Men from Trenton as well as from Washington besieged him, State Senators and United States Senators, constantly coming and going. The little house on Cleveland Lane was in a tumult.

"A man *must* have time to think!" Wilson said despairingly.

During the last week of February the Librarian of Princeton University had a visitor making a rather unusual request, which was granted willingly. The visitor disappeared within the stacks. Here—well concealed in the only quiet spot he could find—the Princeton boy who had received his first great urge to statesmanship reading speeches of noted men in old South Hall of the library wrote the speech he was to deliver at his Presidential inauguration.

CHAPTER III

PRESIDENT

OF THE

UNITED

STATES

I

Mᴀʀᴄʜ 4, 1913: a sparkling winter's day in gala Washington; festooned balconies, soldiers, bands, and gay banners—Princeton's orange and black almost as much in evidence as the national red, white, and blue.

Vast crowds thronged the plaza around the Capitol and the inauguration platform: Justices in black robes, diplomats and generals in brilliant uniforms, a sea of faces, a great shout of welcome—all centering upon a straight, spare figure in the tribunal with bared head, book in hand, to whom the Chief Justice of the United States was administering the oath.

The Bible used, at the President-elect's request, was Mrs. Wilson's. Opened at random for him to kiss, his lips brushed these verses of the 119th Psalm:

And take not the word of truth utterly out of my mouth; for I have hoped in thy judgments.

So shall I keep thy law continually for ever and ever. And I will walk at liberty: for I seek thy precepts.

I will speak of thy testimonies also before kings and will not be ashamed.

At the beginning of the ceremonies, the President-elect, seeing that the people were crowded far back and that there was a large open space in front of the speaker's stand, called the guard and said: "Let the people come forward."

They came with a rush.

Someone else came forward also. Slipping quietly from her place, his wife moved over till she stood directly beneath him. There, oblivious of the watching crowds, she listened absorbedly to every word.

What thoughts must have crowded the man's mind as he ascended that platform and took that book in his hand! His father and mother . . . his old Grandfather Woodrow . . . the storm and stress of his childhood days . . . Ellen and he reading a chapter together during the difficult early time at Bryn Mawr. Princeton: the happy first years, the later time of bitter defeat; his stiff fight as Governor . . . the deep hurt of lost friendships, even in this moment of dazzling triumph. His children, sitting there gazing up at him. Ellen—in the end it was all centered and lost in that one face.

Without her, he had told her the very last thing that morning, "I should never be here."

He knew her thought was his in the words of his speech. He had read it to her in advance, as he did all his speeches. His

President of the United States

voice rang out clear but not in the least "oratorical" as he looked out over the heads of the tremendous crowd:

> My Fellow-Citizens: There has been a change of government. . . . It means much more than the mere success of the party. . . . We have been refreshed by a new insight into our lives.
>
> That life . . . is incomparably great in its material aspects . . . great also . . . in its moral force. . . . But evil has come with good. . . . With riches has come inexcusable waste. . . . The great Government we loved has too often been made use of for private and selfish purposes and those who used it had forgotten the people. . . . There has been something crude and heartless and unfeeling in our haste to succeed and be great. . . .
>
> We have come now to the sober second thought. . . . We have made up our minds to square every process of our national life again with the standards we so proudly set up at the beginning and have always carried at our hearts.

He spoke of some of the special things that needed to be changed: the tariff, credit facilities, an industrial system which exploits without renewing or conserving the natural resources of the country; agriculture and the farmer to be served scientifically. He spoke of his great aspiration "to lift everything that concerns our life as a nation to the light that shines from the hearthfire of every man's conscience and vision of the right."

> This is not a day of triumph, it is a day of dedication. Here muster not the forces of a party but the forces of humanity. Men's hearts wait upon us, men's lives hang in the balance; men's hopes call upon us to say what we will do.
>
> Who shall live up to that great trust? Who dares fail to try? I summon all honest men, all patriotic forward-looking men to my side. God helping me, I will not fail them if they will but counsel and sustain me.

The Story of Woodrow Wilson

It was the shortest Inaugural Address in years and one of the shortest in history—only fifteen hundred words; but it caught the imagination of the country.

"Not since Lincoln has there been a President so wonderfully gifted in the art of expression," said one paper. It was felt from the first that this President, risen from the quiet halls of philosophic thought and years of earnest reflection upon the problems of government and the good of the people, brought to the office the real pledge of "the new day" he so ardently prophesied. They trusted him, and let him know it—the crowd around the inaugural rostrum with a great roar of approval, papers and people throughout the country with multiple echoes of praise and hopefulness.

The usual inaugural parade followed that afternoon. There was no inaugural ball, much to the disappointment of commercial Washington. This was one of "Wilson's innovations." He believed in simplicity and said that these elaborate functions were not "in character" for himself and his family. The social functions of his first few days were confined to close friends and relatives, whose number seemed mysteriously to have increased since his election. There was a "Wilson dinner" and a "Woodrow luncheon," both very gay and full of amusing conversation and good stories.

Princeton also came in for its share. Nine cars of Princeton boys had accompanied their hero to Washington—his chosen guard of honor in place of the official military escorts. On the night before Inauguration eight hundred Princeton alumni gave him a dinner and a great ovation at the New Willard Hotel. On Inauguration night itself his old class of '79 held a dinner at the Hotel Shoreham, with their wives and children.

"Of course we had invited Woodrow," writes one of his classmates, Dr. A. J. McClure, "but we did not really expect him—because he had made his great speech at the Capitol, then stood in the reviewing stand for hours reviewing the Inaugural parade, and we felt sure he would be too tired to be present. But about the time we came to the dessert Woodrow turned up with Margaret."

President of the United States

He had stolen away from the gay family gathering at the White House, bringing one of his daughters with him to join the sons and daughters of his old friends. And now at the end of this tremendous day there he sat, with the fellows he loved best— with whom he had started out forty years before—beaming at him round the table. It must have been a moment of pure joy for Wilson. Princeton Trustees might triumph over him but with Princeton men he won a constant victory.

Beside him sat Charlie Talcott, now a Congressman, there to see the fulfilling of the "solemn covenant" they had made together years before. On his other side was Mahlon Pitney, now Justice of the Supreme Court; further along, Robert Bridges, Hiram Woods, and others of the old Witherspoon Gang.

" 'Course the Senate wasn't good enough for Tommy," they chuckled proudly. " 'When I meet you in the White House, sir,' it had to be for him!"

Pitney and Talcott and some of the others made little speeches. Then "a speech by Woodrow—a peach of a talk," says Dr. McClure. He said he had a curious feeling all the time that he was only a spectator, not really the person about whom everything during this day was centered. But he was sure he was only holding this position he had been elected to because he partly understood the will of the people.

He felt the great responsibility, he said—if he looked at all the things that had to be accomplished in four short years he would want to resign. But he would do the things as they came to his hand each day. That way he hoped that with their prayers and those of all the people he would get through.

That night he slept in Lincoln's bed. The young man who had tramped the streets seeking an appointment as humble assistant in the State Department—turned down all over Washington, advised to find some influential friend "to say a word for him"—had had one hundred million friends speak so loud that here he was: the leader and Chief Executive of the nation.

The Story of Woodrow Wilson

II

I T IS a good thing a President doesn't know in advance what it means, or we should never have any Presidents," said Mr. Wilson. "He needs to have the constitution of an athlete, the patience of a mother, the endurance of an early Christian."

First there is the elaborate system of checks upon his time and movements. Guards watch his room and the corridors leading to his room, all night. Secret-service men follow him about all day. Wilson, who loved to walk, avoided walking because he hated having his steps dogged, as of necessity they had to be.

During his 1912 campaign the attempted assassination of Theodore Roosevelt frightened the whole country for Mr. Wilson also. At that time Colonel House took matters into his own hands and wired an old Texas ranger friend of his, Captain Bill McDonald, these few brief words: "Come—and bring your artillery." To which Captain Bill replied still more concisely: "Coming."

When the stout fellow with his able six-shooter (and his immense scorn for the puny weapons of the secret-service men) had become Mr. Wilson's bodyguard, the Wilson family breathed more freely.

Then there is the vast and complicated matter of the President's engagements and visitors.

Wilson "wished I could just come in, hang up my hat, say 'Hello Bill,' and go to work."

It was not so simple as that. The first afternoon indeed, while the "Woodrow luncheon" was still sitting—the cohorts began to arrive: Congressmen, friends, constituents, and varied groups of admirers come to pay their respects.

The Congressman from Massachusetts brought two hundred; Representative Gallagher of Illinois brought a hundred and fifty of Chicago's Cook County democracy; Governor Fielder of New Jersey appeared with his entire staff; an editor from Atlanta, Georgia, came with one hundred and fifty newsboys "to shake the President's hand."

President of the United States

In the course of the afternoon the President received 1,123 guests. During those first days members of Congress had to be welcomed, with innumerable friends and followers; the Supreme Court called in a body; the diplomats one after the other were presented—first among them Wilson's old friend James Bryce, Ambassador from Great Britain. Many of the important Commissioners of the Government Civil Service, Interstate Commerce Commission members, and others appeared.

On top of all this an avalanche of correspondence, both official and personal: all the old friends wanting to tender congratulations, new ones wanting to greet him and be given a word of greeting in return; all eager to express their faith and belief in him, their high hopes for the country. And they all had to be answered.

Dinners and luncheons with official associates or eager friends taxed his strength further. And when all else was done his desk awaited him, piled high with reports, clippings, and envelopes marked *URGENT*.

Would you want it? Who would—except the man who was born to it, and whose natural destiny it was, as other men's is doctoring and lawyering, storekeeping and engineering.

Wilson had wanted it from the hour he was born, and he was equipped magnificently for it. But even he, at the end of four days' constant pressure, had to spend a day in bed on doctor's orders.

One of Wilson's first tasks was his Message to Congress. Again breaking precedents, he delivered it in person. John Adams was the last President to take advantage of this Constitutional right, 112 years before. When word came through that the new President intended to follow Adams's example, Congress was set by the ears. They were up all night up on the Hill looking up rules and procedure. But after the shock of the first time, they came to like it.

So the boy who had sat in old South Hall of the Princeton Library years ago, electrified by the great pronouncements of the English heads of state before their Parliament, came to stand before the lawmaking bodies of his own national Congress, gathered to hear him as their President.

He spoke for only ten minutes, centering his discussion on his first objectives, avoiding detail; telling of his pleasure in meeting them there face to face—"a human being trying to co-operate with other human beings in a common service, not a mere department of the Government sending messages from an isolated 'island of power.'"

Mrs. Wilson met her husband in the Speakers' Room afterward, and they drove back to the White House together.

"What wouldn't T. R. have given to have thought of that!" she said gleefully.

"Yes," smiled the President, "I think I put one over on Teddy."

The New York *Times* said: "The wonder is that in seven years Theodore Roosevelt never thought of that way of stamping his personality upon his age."

Next day came another innovation: Mr. Wilson motored to the Capitol to confer with the Senators. The last President to do that was Lincoln in time of war. Mr. Wilson wanted to confer with the Senate Finance Committee, which had charge of the new tariff bill. Its members cordially welcomed him, and he told newspaper correspondents afterward: "It is something that I hope the Senators will permit me to do very often."

Thus he swung into his stride.

The official diaries give some brief but interesting sidelights on the twenty-eighth President's calendar in those first days.

An early entry records that "a delegation of upstate New York Democrats headed by Franklin D. Roosevelt called at the White House and urged President Wilson not to recognize Tammany in his New York appointments."

Some days later: "Ex-Governor Glenn of North Carolina called on the President." No doubt to renew old times and to find his ex-ballplayer not so "damned lazy" as in the Davidson days.

On March 20th: "Justice Joseph Lamar [with whom Tommy Wilson had written the Constitution for the Lightfoot Club when they were boys of ten and eleven and for whom he got a bloody nose while saving him from a beating by his brother] called to pay his respects" to the Chief Executive.

Two separate diaries list the President's engagements and visitors—one kept in the executive office, the other by the chief usher of the White House. These give a fairly complete record of his daily life. We also have copies of all his letters and telegrams and even some records of important telephone conversations.

We find in his correspondence of those early days examples of the wide variety of subjects and personalities that come before a President, the enormous range of things he has to know about: livestock pens and astronomical laboratories, tomato raising, prison statutes, eyelets on shoes, forestation, salmon-canning in Oregon, labor conditions in maritime traffic, changes in the judicial department of Rochester, New York, game preserves in Alabama.

Wilson's own letters often show some of his outstanding characteristics—as, for example, a letter to Secretary of Commerce Redfield authorizing investigation of potteries making stoneware in Ohio, "in order that we may get the fullest possible information with regard to the industry and be guided in all our conclusions concerning it by official knowledge of the facts."

We also find letters on building a railroad to Alaska, on protection of bird life in the United States, on forms and procedure in connection with pardons; and in the midst of everything else a very characteristic message to a Princeton undergraduate, Charles Hendel, who had written an article in a Princeton magazine earnestly upholding Woodrow Wilson's views on education.

"My brother-in-law Professor Axson," wrote the President, "was kind enough to bring me a copy of *The Lit* containing your paper 'The Parting of the Ways.' I have, happily, had time to look through it and I want to send you at least this line of warm appreciation. It is delightful to find the men about whom I have thought so much and for whom I tried so hard to think right carrying forward the ideas which seem to me to underlie every enlightened plan for University education."

The young man replied a few days later: "I received your personal note with reference to my article in the *Nassau Lit* and want to tell you how sincerely grateful I am for this recognition and appreciation. There are quite a few of us students who feel deeply a lasting debt to you for just that *right thinking* and *hard effort* you devoted for our sakes. Believe me, I am not alone in this; the forces you set working here in the ideals of students continue to thrive. There *are* some who try to live out what you have taught us—and we regard your approval of any such effort as the inspiration of such living."

The care with which the President preserved this note showed how he treasured such expressions, even in the midst of crowding new preoccupations.

III

T HE question of appointments plagued Wilson's first days in office. From the moment of his election, every little out-of-the-way person who had helped elect him seemed to have sent a letter or telegram. "For the position at Jacksonville, Mr. President . . ." "In regard to the postmaster's place at Redlands . . . at Grand Rapids or Portland or Sioux Falls . . . you could get no finer Democrat, no more loyal supporter . . . A grand and loyal adherent who will call upon you personally, following this letter."

When the announcement came that he himself would not see applicants for office, some of them even wrote and asked to see Mrs. Wilson. They tried all kinds of tricks and maneuvers. Some of his worst trials came through requests of his own relatives.

"The matter of patronage is a thorny path, which makes me wish I had never been born," he remarked to a friend at this time. He had to write letters that cost him heartache, one of them beginning: "My dear Brother . . ."

He was determined to have the "right man for the right

place," regardless of Mr. Bryan's desire to reward "deserving Democrats." Wilson insisted on placing many hitherto appointive offices under the Civil Service. He tightened up the regulations and refused to dismiss men just because they were Republicans. In a number of cases in the Consular Service he actually promoted efficient Republicans to higher posts, thus bringing down upon his head acrid comment from the Democratic Old Guard.

When word of the President's new policy went round, consternation filled many hearts. The little leaders "back home" could not understand why they were not to be rewarded. They wrote Bryan in shoals, from West and South. One of the President's friends says they were not all so honest as the old politician down in Georgia who once wrote to a new Governor whom he had helped elect:

"My dear Sir: This will introduce my son John, who has as great desire and as little capacity for public office as anyone I have ever known. If you can do anything with him it will be greatly appreciated, as I have utterly failed."

Wilson wanted "the best men in the nation," genuine progressives not affiliated with private interest. Bryan—traditional leader of the Democratic party and faithful to party friends —remembered that Elmer Brown in Topeka had voted for him in 1896 and that Jim Johnson had done the same out in Seattle in 1900. He thought that "a good man" (i.e., one who had voted the Democratic ticket for the past twenty years) could fill any good place. He was even for "passing the offices around" by allowing each man to serve for a short time— "We have so many deserving Democrats and so few places to give."

Bridging the two extremes, and perhaps more realistic and common-sense than either, was the attitude of the man who had most to do with appointments, whose position has indeed become synonymous with patronage: the Postmaster-General.

Fifty-six thousand postmasters had to be chosen. It took two strong men to carry to the White House the vast collection of letters, documents, and recommendations which poured in from all over the country relating to the various candidates and favorite sons. And in their wake came the sturdy Postmaster-General himself, with his old-fashioned black clothes, shovel hat, and inseparable umbrella.

"Well, Burleson!" The President greeted him cordially, though with a certain guarded look in his eye. Burleson had served for twenty-four years in Congress and ran with the regulars.

It was their first official meeting, and a critical one.

Wilson announced forthrightly that he did not intend "to advise with reactionary or stand-pat Senators or Representatives in making these appointments." He was going to appoint forward-looking men and satisfy himself that they were honest and capable.

Burleson was equally forthright, indeed blunt.

"Mr. President," he said, "if you pursue this policy it means that your Administration is going to be a failure. It means the defeat of the measures of reform that you have next to your heart."

"How is that?" asked the President, a bit sharply.

"Mr. President," continued the seasoned old politician, "these little offices don't amount to anything. They are inconsequential. It doesn't amount to a damn who is postmaster of Paducah, Kentucky. But these little offices mean a great deal to the Senators and Representatives in Congress. If it goes out that the President has turned down Representative So-and-so or Senator So-and-so, it means that that member has bitter trouble at home. If you pursue the right policy you can make the Democratic party progressive, you can avoid rows in Congress, you do not need to yield your position. All you need to do is to adopt a policy of harmony and observe the laws of human nature."

Wilson, Burleson said later, was "absolutely ignorant" of that side of politics.

"As your Postmaster-General," Burleson went on, "I am going to make fifty-six thousand appointments. I will see honest and capable men in every office. But I will consult with the men on the Hill. I have been here a long time, Mr. President. I know these Congressmen and Senators. They are mostly good men. If they are turned down they will hate you and will not vote for anything you want. It is human nature. On the other hand, if you work with them and they recommend unsuitable men for the offices, I will keep on asking for other suggestions until I get good ones. In the end we shall secure as able men as we would in any other way and we will keep the leaders of the party with us."

It was sound advice. The President, canny Scot that he was, knew it. After a few days of consideration (the most anxious days, Burleson said, that *he* ever spent), Wilson accepted it. The appointment of postmasters from then on was left entirely in Burleson's hands. The President directed that no more papers be brought to him on the subject, and when the Postmaster brought him a list of appointments he would look up and say with a smile, "Well, Burleson, where do I sign?"

This marked the beginning of a staunch friendship which never faltered on either side throughout the Administration. It also opened up a closer and more helpful relationship between Wilson and the leaders on the Hill. Later on, after some of his hardest fights in Congress, where the President had come out triumphant in his big legislative reforms, he said to Burleson: "What you told me about the old stand-patters is true. They stand by the party and the Administration. I can rely on them better than on some of my own crowd."

The Cabinet offices had been settled before Inauguration, while he was in Bermuda and could think quietly, and after long consultation with Colonel House and other advisers. Bryan inevitably became Secretary of State; William G. McAdoo, energetic head of the Hudson tunnels enterprise and one of the staunchest supporters of Wilson's campaign, Secretary of the Treasury. Lindley M. Garrison, a Jersey City lawyer, was picked by New Jersey leaders for Secretary of War. Josephus Daniels, another strong Southern supporter, editor of the Raleigh *News and Observer*, became Secretary of the Navy.

For his Attorney-General Wilson chose J. C. McReynolds, a Tennessee lawyer who had been Theodore Roosevelt's Assistant

The Story of Woodrow Wilson

Attorney-General for four years. The stalwart Postmaster-General, as we have seen, was Albert S. Burleson, son of one of Texas' "fighting families" and longtime Congressman from the Austin district. Franklin K. Lane, genial head of the Interstate Commerce Commission, was appointed Secretary of the Interior; David F. Houston, Chancellor of Washington University in St. Louis, with a wide reputation as an economist, became Secretary of Agriculture. William C. Redfield, a Brooklyn businessman and Member of the 62nd Congress, received the appointment of Secretary of Commerce. William B. Wilson, a former coal-miner, later Congressman from Pennsylvania and the man largely responsible for the establishment of the Department of Labor, fittingly became its first Secretary.

Wilson wanted to give Louis D. Brandeis a Cabinet post, but was dissuaded by his advisers. He had followed Brandeis's writings and juristic feats in prosecuting New England trust cases, and admired him greatly. There was a bitter battle later when he appointed Brandeis Justice of the Supreme Court.

One of his most criticized appointments was that of his private secretary, Joseph P. Tumulty—the red-headed Irish Catholic who had been extremely useful to Wilson in his Governorship days and whom he brought with him from Trenton to Washington, in spite of the hundreds of objecting letters that poured in from all over the country. Wilson called the letters "asinine," said that Tumulty was a faithful public servant whose religion had nothing to do with his performance of his public duty, and kept him through eight years and two administrations, in spite of frequent and sometimes intense public disapproval.

The Ambassadors were his own private headache. The fact that the United States, the richest country in the world, paid its diplomatic representatives so badly made things twice as difficult. Several of his best men had to refuse because they could not meet the financial demands of the position. Others were subsidized by generous friends who were determined that the nation's miserliness should not interfere with its getting the finest type of public servant.

President of the United States

After weeks of corresponding, negotiating, and rearranging, Wilson's Ambassadorial roster stood as follows:

London	Walter Hines Page
Paris	Myron Herrick
Berlin	James W. Gerard
Rome	Thomas Nelson Page
Tokyo	William Guthrie
Austria-Hungary	Frederick C. Penfield
St. Petersburg	Henry M. Pindell
Constantinople	Henry Morgenthau
Madrid	Joseph E. Willard

Fifteen Ministers also had to be found for the smaller countries.

One of the most interesting appointments was that of Wilson's old playmate Pleasant Stovall, now a leading Southern editor, to the post of Minister to Switzerland. Brand Whitlock went to Belgium, Maurice F. Egan to Copenhagen.

The appointments naturally caused some private anguish. Paris was first offered to William McCombs, Wilson's campaign manager, who had wanted a Cabinet position and finally declined the Embassy—with considerable bitterness. Wilson had wanted his old friend Dr. Fine of Princeton for the post at Berlin, but Fine declined. Dr. Charles W. Eliot and Richard Olney also refused the Court of St. James.

Harry Lane Wilson was still in Mexico—unsatisfactory but unchanged. Most of the other South American appointments also stood. A chargé d'affaires remained in Berlin for an interval, till Gerard arrived.

The appointment of Dr. van Dyke as Minister to the Netherlands was unexpected—he had sided with the opposition at Princeton. He was astonished when the President's letter reached him and went down to Washington especially to thank him. He spoke to Mrs. Wilson of the appointment with tears in his eyes.

Morgenthau, Penfield, and Guthrie had been generous campaign contributors, in time and energy as well as money.

Perhaps the most dramatic of all the appointments was that

of Wilson's old friend Walter Page, who finally became his Ambassador to Great Britain. They must have thought back to the days in Atlanta long ago when, teetering back and forth on the hard chairs in the office of Renick and Wilson, they hotly discussed the affairs of the nation.

Even then Page had known that Wilson was great. After seeing him inaugurated (several weeks before any mention of the Ambassadorship) Page wrote:

"I have a stronger confidence in government now . . . than I have ever had before. I believe in Wilson very thoroughly."

IV

PRESIDENT WILSON's first official public act was a statement on relations with Latin America which also defined his foreign policy in general. He made this statement on March 12th, one week after his inauguration.

When Wilson came to office the Latin-American situation was seething. Two weeks before his inauguration President Madero of Mexico was murdered while in the custody of General Huerta's troops, under conditions that pointed to planned assassination. Harry Lane Wilson, our Ambassador in Mexico, and various Americans with Mexican concessions, urged the recognition of Huerta's Government. But President Taft preferred to leave this decision to the incoming President.

Panama and Nicaragua presented other urgent problems. Colombia, feeling that Theodore Roosevelt had unfairly seized the property on which the Panama Canal was built, had now bluntly refused a proposal looking to the settlement of Colombian rights on the Isthmus. In Nicaragua, where the United States was negotiating for exclusive rights for another canal route, a treaty which amounted to a protectorate over Nicaragua was signed a month before Wilson came in and would shortly come before the United States Senate.

The British introduced another complication. They demanded a reversal of the Panama Canal tolls regulation, arguing that foreign nations should use the canal on equal terms with the United States.

As Wilson came into power feeling on Latin America ran high, both in American business circles and in the Latin-American countries themselves. What, these countries were wondering, would the new President's policy be? Would he continue the cold-blooded business aggression and high-handed seizing of land which the Latin Americans had come to associate with the powerful Colossus of the North?

He soon let them know. Precisely one week after he had assumed office (and after a general discussion with his Cabinet) he issued a public statement. It began with a declaration that "one of the chief objects of his Administration would be to cultivate the friendship and deserve the confidence of our sister republics of Central and South America.

"We can have no sympathy," he said, "with those who seek to seize the power of government to advance their own personal interest or ambition [plain notice to Huerta]. We hold, as I am sure all thoughtful leaders of republican government everywhere hold, that just government rests always on the consent of the governed and that there can be no freedom without order based upon law, and upon the public conscience and approval."

Then came the bombshell, for the American businessmen: "The United States has nothing to seek in Central and South America except the lasting interests of the peoples of the two continents, the security of governments intended for the people and for no special group or interest, and the development of personal and trade relationships between the two continents which shall redound to the profit and advantage of both and interfere with the rights and liberties of neither."

This, said the Latin Americans bitterly, certainly *would* be a change from traditional American policy!

The statement caused a tremendous stir and met with wide approval. One week later came an announcement on the Far East—another blow to special privilege.

Four days after Mr. Wilson took office two members of the

banking house of J. P. Morgan and Company went to Washington and called on the Secretary of State. They wished to find out whether the new Administration intended to continue the Taft policy of government protection of private capital in foreign countries "to promote the national interests," the immediate question being the proposed Six-Power Loan to China.

Bryan called in Huntington Wilson and Chandler P. Anderson, Counselor of the State Department—both of them Taft appointees who upheld the Taft policy. Together with the Morgan representatives they frankly urged what had recently been christened "dollar diplomacy."

The matter was discussed at the Cabinet meetings of March 14 and 18. Bryan reported that the terms of the loan made it an out and out monopoly transaction, involving intervention by foreign officials in administering Chinese finances and even possibly the use of force in collection.

Again the President prepared a statement which he gave to the press on March 18 and which indicated a new and bold departure from former American foreign policy.

He said that the conditions of the proposed loan would "touch very nearly the administrative independence of China itself" and that the governmental responsibility involved "might conceivably go to the length . . . of forcible interference."

Participation in such an enterprise, he declared, was "obnoxious to the principles upon which the Government of our people rests." He said that the American Government would take all fair means of promoting its citizens' trade in China but that it would continue to stand for the Open Door—"the only door we care to enter."

The reverberation which followed this pronouncement, issued without any of the usual preliminary diplomatic consultations, was greater even than that roused by the Mexican statement. The President's procedure offended the bureaucracy of the State Department: Huntington Wilson, a supporter of the old policy, resigned. Business called the President "amateurish" and "sentimental." International loans had always been handled that way. Anything else was idealistic and impractical, "the ravings of an academic college professor."

But the people in general liked the President's boldness. His words were in keeping with American democratic tradition. Congratulatory letters and messages poured in.

The American group of bankers promptly announced its withdrawal from the Six-Power Consortium. The press called this a "knockout blow for Wall Street" by Wilson.

Thus early in the day he had taken his stand in defiance of powerful vested interests and established once and for all the principles which were to underlie his whole foreign policy. All through the years he maintained those principles and this keynote: "a new spirit in foreign relations based not upon material interests but upon mutual understanding and mutual service."

Eight years later, under Wilson's League of Nations, a new order of loans and financing came into being. Under negotiations conducted by the League Finance Committee seven countries bordering on financial ruin were put on their feet. They lost none of their independence; those who lent money gained no control. Sir Arthur Salter, one of the world's great economic and financial experts, became financial adviser to China. He helped survey the Chinese financial situation in the interests of the Chinese people themselves. The same expert paid two visits to India to advise on financial reconstruction there. Austria, Hungary, Greece, Rumania, Portugal, also received assistance. This kind of international financing led to lasting friendships between nations and statesmen; friendships which have continued through the years, to the general benefit.

It can be done if you really want to do it. The trouble with Wilson, and the reason he was so hated and feared, was that he *wasn't* academic. He insisted on translating his ideals into action immediately and concretely, which absolutely terrified the gentlemen who had been growing rich on the old system.

V

IMMEDIATELY after his inauguration, Wilson also faced the difficult question of land ownership by the Japanese in California.

Citizens of the Pacific Coast States were much wrought up over the increasing control that Japanese colonists had gained over their rich countryside. Legislative action had been proposed, which wounded the national pride of Japan. Ambassador Chinda therefore called on Wilson the day after inauguration to present the situation and express the acute concern of the Japanese Government.

The rights of the "sovereign states" serving their own necessities and the powers and privileges of the Federal Government in its constitutional control of foreign affairs presented a nice diplomatic puzzle. Wilson sympathized with the apprehensions of the Californians but believed they could achieve their ends by more tactful means. He urged that the pending bills be drawn on some other grounds than racial discrimination, anticipating that such discrimination would produce resentment from all Asiatics, including the Chinese and Indians. Bryan himself went to California to use his influence with the legislature. But both Houses of this legislature passed a law restricting the ownership of real property by aliens to those "eligible to citizenship."

The Japanese Government sent a note of violent protest, calling the law obnoxious, discriminatory, unfair, unfriendly, and in violation of the treaty. The Japanese asked the Federal Government to declare the California law invalid, which of course under our Constitution it could not do. A very tense situation developed, including even the possibility of war.

At an emergency Cabinet meeting Secretary Daniels gave his naval staff's analysis of the situation. It was their opinion that "the Japanese could take the Philippines, Hawaii, and Alaska, as we were not prepared." The President said that they might do so but that "they could not keep them—eventually," a verdict which the events of the past few years have dramatically vindi-

Flag Day Exercises, June 1914. At left, William Jennings Bryan and Josephus Daniels; at extreme right, Franklin Delano Roosevelt.

One of Wilson's precedent-breaking addresses to Congress. Not for over a hundred years had a Presider

peared before Congress to read his own message.
Photo: Harris & Ewing

Marching in Preparedness Parade in Washington, June 14, 1916. *Photo: Harris & Ewing*

cated. At the time, however, Wilson felt deep concern, but Bryan brought all his powers of persuasion to bear with Ambassador Chinda, and it was largely due to Bryan's efforts and his persistent tact and friendliness that eventually a less warlike message came from the Japanese.

Wilson's assurances that there would be no war proved correct. But the harassing negotiations continued for months until, like so many other diplomatic problems, they were lost in the general upheaval of the Great War.

In this instance at least the "amateurish" President succeeded in keeping a highly dangerous matter within diplomatic channels. But Japanese pride still nursed its sting. Later Wilson was to be faced by this same Ambassador Chinda over the peace table at Paris with another set of embarrassing demands for racial equality, growing no doubt in part out of the Japanese-American experiences at this earlier time.

VI

THE Mexican crisis, which confronted Wilson immediately upon his inauguration, was one of the most trying problems of his career and one which brought him loudest criticism. This happened because he held a "Quixotic sentiment" for the masses of the Mexican people, esteeming them more highly than he did American business interests or the Mexican overlords. "My passion is for the submerged 85 per cent of the people of the Republic who are now struggling towards liberty," he declared. And it was for them that he stood: the millions of downtrodden Mexicans seeking emancipation from the rich feudal class to which for generations they had been practically enslaved.

Shocked and indignant at the assassination of President Madero and Huerta's brigandish seizing of power, he flatly refused to recognize Huerta, or any other ruler in Mexico who had not been elected by constitutional methods and whom the majority of Mexican citizens did not accept. Many Mexicans felt deep indignation over the assassination of Madero, and

The Story of Woodrow Wilson

despised Huerta. Towards the end of March, Carranza, Governor of the northern State of Coahuila, led a revolt against him. Carranza's followers became known as the Carranzistas, or Constitutionalists.

The European nations had recognized Huerta immediately. They thought Wilson idealistic and naïve. They wanted a regime of "order" in Mexico so that they could go ahead, undisturbed, with their own highly profitable enterprises. They were ready to support any strong-armed ruler who would let them alone.

Our own businessmen in Mexico took much the same attitude. Some of the big companies sent an impressive statement to the President giving their view of the case and urging that Huerta be recognized on condition that he guarantee a fair election at any early date. Wilson studied this statement closely—together with hundreds of letters and demands from other businessmen; but he balked at recognition. Distrusting the reports of our Ambassador, Harry Lane Wilson—a friend of big business and of Huerta—the President sent his own emissaries (W. B. Hale and John Lind) to Mexico City to carry messages to Huerta and report direct to the White House. This antagonized both the Embassy and the State Department officials, and strengthened the resentment of the interests.

Indeed Wilson felt more and more that his real opponents were the oil men and other privileged concessionaires in Mexico. "Wherever I look," he said, "China, Mexico, Nicaragua, Santo Domingo—I see always the same enemy": vested interests working for the special profit and advantage of a privileged few, instead of for the general welfare of the many.

Huerta, getting all the financing and help he needed from Europe, paid little attention to the emissaries or to the President's demands. Marauding and bloodshed continued—it was alleged from both Huerta and Carranza forces, augmented later by those of a third and dashing bandit, Pancho Villa. Americans were attacked, American property destroyed. Criticism and complaint poured in to Congressmen. Some people began to regard the attitude of the President as weak-kneed. Jingo newspapers and some irate legislators loudly demanded intervention.

President of the United States

Finally, on August 27, 1913, Wilson laid the matter before Congress, urging that Mexico was engaged in a struggle for liberty like that of France in the eighteenth century and that this country should keep hands off and give her her chance. He believed that Carranza's Constitutionalists would triumph, if we had patience, and that the Mexicans themselves would oust Huerta. He urged all Americans to leave Mexico, thus removing danger to themselves and complications for their government; he announced a complete embargo on arms from the United States, so that neither side should have help from American supplies— and settled down to a policy of watchful waiting.

But "the old Indian" who had dug himself in down at Mexico City had no notion of being really dispossessed of power. The promised "constitutional" election was a farce. Huerta, having repeatedly declared that he was not a candidate, was nevertheless "elected." Thereupon the old Indian rose in Wilson himself. He sent an ultimatum to Huerta and also gave notice to foreign governments of his intentions, in no uncertain terms. He said he believed it "his immediate duty to require Huerta's retirement from the Mexican Government and that the Government of the United States must now proceed to employ such means as may be necessary to secure this result." Diplomats in Mexico City advised Huerta to yield. But Huerta remained obdurate. He was getting arms from Europe and evidently intended to establish himself as a permanent dictator. The Carranzistas had difficulty getting arms anywhere.

After consulting with the Senate Foreign Relations Committee, Wilson raised the arms embargo and began forthrightly to support Carranza. But this apparently served only to intensify civil warfare. For now the armies of all three chieftains were ravaging the distracted country and gradually destroying both the wealth of the people and the vast investments of foreigners. Daily outrages were reported. Senator Fall spoke in the Senate for three hours on the crimes committed against American citizens in Mexico.

Finally on April 9, 1914, came the inevitable explosion. The paymaster of the U.S.S. *Dolphin* was loading supplies at the

The Story of Woodrow Wilson

Tampico dock with seven of his men—none of them armed—when a Mexican officer and his soldiers, all of them armed, placed the Americans under arrest. Later a higher ranking officer released the Americans and the commandant of the Huerta forces at Tampico sent his regrets—stating that the officer who made the arrest was carrying out his instructions to permit no boats of any kind at the warehouse dock.

Admiral Mayo, the American commanding officer, ordered an investigation and then sent an ultimatum to the Huerta general demanding a formal apology, disavowal of the act, punishment of the officer responsible, and a twenty-one-gun salute to the American flag. He gave the general twenty-four hours, but the general did nothing. Wilson, having tried for months to avoid armed conflict, was exasperated when the news came. There was of course nothing for him to do but support Mayo—especially as several other provocative incidents occurred about the same time. The President ordered all available warships and a regiment of marines to proceed at once to Tampico. Huerta was notified of the very serious character of the situation. The country awoke to the fact that there might be war. Again the President went before Congress, which after considerable debate voted him the necessary authority for the employment of the armed forces of the United States to enforce Mayo's demands.

Senators Lodge and Root pressed for a substitute resolution giving the murder of American citizens and destruction of American property as the grounds for the action. Root in an eloquent speech stressed the "years of violence and anarchy in Mexico . . . hundreds of American lives sacrificed, millions of dollars' worth of American property destroyed"; but neglected to mention the ways in which that property had been acquired or seized—the point which always rendered such arguments invalid to Wilson.

Meanwhile news came through that the German steamer *Ypiranga* was arriving at Vera Cruz with a cargo of munitions for Huerta—perhaps in another day or two to be used for killing American boys. "I can wire Admiral Fletcher to prevent it and take the customs house," Secretary Daniels told the President. "I think that should be done."

After discussion with the Cabinet the President gave the order for the seizure. At 11:30 on the morning of April 21, 1914, marines and bluejackets landed at Vera Cruz, took possession of the cable office, the post and telegraph office, the customs house, and the railroad terminal. Mexican troops resisted, firing from the housetops and at the United States Consulate. Guns from the U.S.S. *Prairie* silenced naval resistance. Nineteen of our men were killed and a number wounded. Wilson had not anticipated any such serious opposition. The news that American soldiers and marines had gone to their deaths because of his orders "seemed to affect him like an ailment," said one of the newspapermen who interviewed him at the time; "he was positively shaken."

The next few hours brought serious developments. Huerta gave the American chargé his passports; the Mexican chargé at Washington demanded his. Word came that Huerta was preparing to destroy the railroad to Mexico City. Carranza sent word that he deplored the action of the American Government in landing forces at Vera Cruz. The South Americans believed that the United States intended to use this incident as a pretext for annexing Mexico and Central America, and that their turn would come next. Feeling in both North and South America ran high.

At the moment when things looked blackest, unexpected help came in the offer of mediation by the three largest South American States: Argentina, Brazil, and Chile. Wilson—with alacrity —accepted. Huerta accepted also—glad to extricate himself from an impossible situation. The settlement ultimately reached by the Mediation Conference, held at Niagara Falls, Canada, fell considerably short of Wilson's desires. It arranged for a provisional government established by agreement of all parties involved in the civil war—the United States to recognize this Government when constituted. There were no promises as to the ousting of Huerta, nor any mention of the salute demanded of him—which was never given. Nor did the Carranzistas sign the agreement.

The Story of Woodrow Wilson

However, several vital results were obtained. War had been averted. Huerta's fall was speeded. Soon after the Conference he resigned, and left Mexico. Carranza then came into power. All this Wilson profoundly desired. More than anything else, the co-operation of the United States with the A B C Powers and Wilson's positive assurance regarding the integrity of Mexican territory helped calm the fears of the Latin Americans and brought better relations among the nations of the Western hemisphere.

Many trying months lay ahead before peaceful conditions were actually established in Mexico. Civil strife between Carranza and other leaders continued for two years. Border attacks on American soldiers and civilians finally forced the President to send an expeditionary force into Mexico—for the sole purpose, he emphasized, "of the pursuit and capture of bandits who had been killing our people." Pershing and our troops did not leave Mexico until February, 1917, just as we were about to go to war with Germany. A Joint American-Mexican Commission ultimately recommended the recognition of the Carranza government as the least of many evils, and Wilson sent Ambassador Fletcher to Mexico City. But Mexico remained for years a troublesome problem that the President's opponents used to plague him at critical moments.

One thing people had to be convinced of: the honesty of the President's intention, his personal integrity and fairness of view. The most suspicious of the Central and South American States had to recognize that he was sincere in his expressions and was sincerely trying to do the just and right thing in regard to North American relations with those countries. He did not always succeed as completely as he wished; he had sometimes to make compromises, as he did later in Europe, which stuck in his throat and were even more distasteful to him than to the peoples involved. But that he was truly trying to work for the best interests of all the people the most grudging "suspicioner" could not deny. The sight of an honest man living up to his declared conviction was in itself a powerful stabilizer and a heartening vision for the world.

President of the United States

VII

OTHER Latin-American problems pressed for solution. Soon after Wilson's inauguration Colombia asked for a large indemnity and an apology from the United States for the "seizure" of the Panama Canal route in 1903. Wilson, recognizing the justice of the case, offered $20,000,000 "in full settlement." The Colombians demanded $50,000,000, boundary concessions, various privileges, and a formal expression of "regret." After a year of difficult negotiating, a compromise treaty was finally arranged. Colombia was to receive $25,000,000, along with the much-disputed word "regret."

America apologizing! The Republicans fought the treaty bitterly in the Senate, largely because of its obvious reflection on the Administration of Theodore Roosevelt, who declared, that "The payment of belated blackmail and the mere proposal to make it is an outrage on the honor and a blow to the interests of the American people. . . . An Administration that will conclude such a treaty as this treaty for the payment of blackmail to Colombia has forfeited all right to the respect of the people of the United States."

Wilson and Bryan had different ideas as to the honor of the United States and what besmirched it. "This nation," said Wilson, "can afford to be . . . generous in the settling of disputes, especially when by its generosity it can increase the friendliness of the many millions in Central and South America with whom our relations become daily more intimate."

The Colombian matter dragged on for years, Senator Stone publicly blaming the Republican Senators for preventing the necessary two-thirds vote. Not until Wilson had left office was the treaty finally ratified—without the desired apology.

Nicaragua presented another explosive situation. Americans had invested millions of dollars there—on the understanding, reached during the Taft and Roosevelt Administrations, that the Government would if necessary support them. There had been a bitter revolution in 1912 against the conservative President Diaz, with whom the bankers and the United States Government were sympathetic. Diaz had favored American business and capital and sought to promote economic stabilization.

President Taft interfered. He sent eight warships and a considerable body of marines to put down the insurgents and keep Diaz in power. The revolution left the Government almost bankrupt. The American bankers were willing to help it out but on terms which even the easygoing Diaz regarded as prohibitive.

Bryan and Wilson studied the situation with considerable indignation. They sympathized strongly with the Nicaraguans.

"It is pathetic," said Bryan, "to see Nicaragua struggling in the grip of an oppressive financial agreement [with American bankers as the extortionists!]. . . . No wonder the people of these little republics are roused to revolution by what they regard as a sacrifice of their interests." No wonder, too, that they came to hate the very name of the United States and to distrust every plan and proposal that emanated from that quarter.

Bryan did his best to get better terms from the bankers—but with little success. Finally a loan was arranged, stiff in terms but accepted by the Government of Nicaragua because of its needs, implacable circumstances forcing upon Wilson and Bryan an agreement highly distasteful to them.

Santo Domingo and Haiti were other little countries in turmoil, with constant insurrections and intermittent civil war. The Dominicans had had sixteen revolutions within forty years. In 1911, under Taft, had come armed intervention by the United States Government and from then on what amounted to financial and political control.

In Haiti a similar arrangement eventually came about.

Mexico, Colombia, Nicaragua, Haiti, Santo Domingo—through them all runs the same familiar pattern: rich countries, weak governments, development by outsiders—frequently the "Yanquis"—who obtained a strangle hold on the Government and thus came to control the lives and interests of the people. It is not a particularly glorious record for democratic, liberty-loving

President of the United States

America, especially with our marines and warships always in the background.

Wilson and Bryan fought this system with all their might, as fair-minded men devoted to a truly democratic policy. Sometimes they succeeded, sometimes they failed. Sometimes the dead weight of long-established habit and tradition—even the traditional domination of the hated Yankee—proved too much for them. But they tried, honestly and sincerely, and the country at large approved their trying and emphatically approved of Wilson's "new diplomacy."

The Philippines presented a brighter picture. Wilson believed that the Filipinos should have self-government but that "they must earn it as we earned our own liberty and independence" and that it would take time. The minute he assumed office well-meaning citizens and anti-imperialist Congressmen began besieging him with petitions to free the Filipinos immediately. Wilson, characteristically, wanted fuller information. He asked his old friend Professor Henry Jones Ford of Princeton to go to the Philippines as his special representative and make a complete survey. At the time when he sent out the new Governor-General, Francis Burton Harrison, he issued a public statement of general policy, casting the United States in the role of trustee: "Acting not for the advantage of the United States but for the benefit of the people of the Philippine Islands, every step we take will be taken with a view to the ultimate independence of the Islands and as a preparation for that independence and we hope to move towards that end as rapidly as the safety and the permanent interests of the Islands will permit."

One step, he announced, would be taken at once: native citizens would constitute a majority in the controlling commission and, ultimately, in the legislature. He hoped this would give "immediate proof" of the "political capacity of those native citizens who have already come forward to represent and lead their people in affairs."

Taft—first civil Governor of the Islands—and several members of Wilson's own Cabinet thought that he was going too fast.

But his message was hailed with great enthusiasm by the Filipinos, who regarded it as the turning point in their struggle for control of their own affairs.

VIII

So many thorny problems engaged Wilson's attention that he waited for almost a year before taking up the canal tolls question.

Work had begun on the Panama Canal in May, 1904, and it was supposed to be ready for traffic in 1914. The Panama Canal Act, passed during Mr. Taft's Administration, opened the canal to the ships of all nations but favored the United States in one respect: it exempted our ships engaged in coastwise traffic from payments of canal tolls. American ships engaged in foreign trade had to pay the same rates as all the others.

The British challenged this exemption for the coastwise vessels, declaring it to be in violation of the Hay-Pauncefote Treaty of 1901, which said: "The canal shall be free and open to the vessels of commerce and of war of all nations, observing these rules on terms of entire equality, so that there shall be no discrimination against any such nation or its citizens or subjects in respect of the conditions or charges of traffic or otherwise."

On December 9, 1912, Great Britain formally protested that any exemption of tolls whatsoever violated this provision, and urged repeal of the clause.

The Democratic platform of 1912 had approved the exemption. But Wilson, after studying the matter—and particularly after what he called a very "illuminating discussion" that he heard between Elihu Root, former Secretary of State, and Joseph H. Choate, former Ambassador to Great Britain—decided emphatically for repeal.

However, the President waited till other important legislation was out of the way before he embarked on what he knew would be a highly contentious issue. The time came when he could wait no longer. The canal was almost completed. Ambassador Page in

President of the United States

London was pressing for action. The British, he said, felt that we had acted dishonorably; and Page's letters showed that he agreed with them.

"We made a bargain—a solemn compact," he wrote, "and we have broken it. Whether it were a good bargain or a bad one, a silly one or a wise one; that's far from the point." We had made it; we should abide by our pledged word.

Many Americans agreed with him, among them leading internationalists like Andrew Carnegie and Oscar Straus. Others, including a substantial number of Senators and Congressmen of both parties, contended that "the Panama Canal, built and paid for by the American people, must be used primarily for their benefit"; that repeal was "bootlicking to Great Britain." It was evident from the start that a bitter struggle was brewing.

Early in 1914 Wilson called a conference of the Foreign Relations Committee of the Senate, inviting both Republicans and Democrats to meet with him at the White House, on January 26th. Among those present were Senators Lodge, Borah, Root, Stone, Bacon, Hitchcock, McCumber—names later to become famous in connection with another treaty. On this particular evening he met with more opposition from members of his own party, especially Irish Senator O'Gorman of New York, and Senators Newlands, Vardaman, and Bristow from West and South.

Early in March he formally demanded repeal in his message to Congress: "In my own judgment, very fully considered and maturely formed, that exemption constitutes a mistaken economic policy from every point of view, and is moreover in plain contravention of the treaty with Great Britain concerning the canal concluded on November 18, 1901. . . .

"The large thing to do," he said, "is the only thing we can afford to do, a voluntary withdrawal from a position everywhere questioned and misunderstood."

He decided not to waste time with temporary measures but to ask for outright repeal; and four days later Congressman Sims, backed by Adamson, introduced a bill for repeal. Then the battle began.

The Story of Woodrow Wilson

The Speaker of the House, Champ Clark, spoke vehemently against the bill, and Republicans vehemently cheered him. Congressman Adamson spoke eloquently for it. Many others joined what turned out to be one of the sharpest debates of Wilson's Administration. There were thirty-eight speeches in one day. The Senate left its own affairs and went over, almost in a body, to hear the debate in the House.

Once again Bryan threw his weight to the President. At a crucial moment he declared that "our country will not mar the glory of a great enterprise by doing anything that would raise a question as to the nation's honor in its dealings with foreign nations." His stand unquestionably influenced Democrats of both Houses.

Burleson and McAdoo also worked hard. Burleson spent the entire last day before the vote calling up members of the House —old friends, many of them—urging them to support the President's measure. When the final vote was taken the bill was passed, 247 to 162.

In the Senate too the fight was intense. All party lines were down. Lodge and Root supported the President strongly. O'Gorman and some of his own party as strongly opposed him. Wilson welcomed adherents from either side, and warmly expressed his appreciation.

"Mr. Wilson called me up on the telephone," writes Senator Lodge, ". . . and thanked me for my speech and for all that I had said in support of his position."

After weeks of debate the bill finally passed the Senate on June 11th, with a vote of 50 to 35, and on June 15th the President signed it. Meeting Burleson a day or two afterward, Wilson said: "Well, Burleson, it was a great fight!"

"It was a great victory for you," said Burleson.

"No," said the President, "it was a great victory for you."

To Congressman Adamson and others he wrote letters expressing his thanks and recognition of their efficient service.

The action brought approval throughout the country, though Theodore Roosevelt violently denounced the measure, disagreeing for once with his friend "Cabot."

From England came a chorus of approbation. Wilson had a letter of hearty congratulation from his old friend Lord Bryce. Sir Edward Grey made a speech in the House of Commons, hailing the act, and paying personal tribute to Wilson.

The conservative *Morning Post* of London said that Englishmen must pay "a tribute of respect to the statesman who did not hesitate to risk his personal popularity and political prestige in doing what he believed to be right and just."

Wilson himself considered the bill, because of the moral issue involved, as of the first importance. He said to his brother-in-law: "If everything else in connection with this Administration is forgotten, the action in regard to Panama will be remembered because it is a long forward step in putting the relationships of nations and the dealings of one nation with another on a par with the dealings of honorable men, one with another."

IX

THE three great domestic achievements of Wilson's early administration were tariff reform, currency reform, and anti-trust legislation. These were the issues on which he had been elected, the chief planks of his campaign platform. Directly he came into office he set about redeeming his pledges. He called a special session of Congress in April to consider tariff and currency reform in particular and made this the main theme of his much-discussed "in-person" message.

The tariff had been one of Wilson's chief preoccupations all his life, from the days when he used to orate on Cobden and Bright and the free-trade movement at Princeton and the University of Virginia, through the years of his professorship and executive activity in New Jersey, when he frequently spoke on the subject.

"Every business question in the country," he said, "comes back to the question of the tariff."

In an address in New York in 1908 he declared: "The old formula 'tariff for revenue only' has a barren sound . . . in existing circumstances. . . . The tariff as we now know it is not a system of taxation; it is rather a vast body of economic expedients which have been used, under the guise of taxation, for the purpose of building up various industries. . . ."

The Payne-Aldrich law, he declared, was wrong in detail and wrong in principle. It represented the entrenchments of special privilege—a method of granting favors—instead of regulating matters on a just basis.

The interest of the people versus the interest of special privilege: he had been arguing this since the day when he appeared as a raw young lawyer before the Congressional Tariff Commission at the Kimball House in Atlanta. Now he was to take his argument before the lawmaking bodies of the United States.

The law he sought to enact was not a free-trade measure but one that would reduce duties on over nine hundred articles, especially on primary necessities such as food and clothing. Wilson laid his plans astutely. Months before his inauguration he had begun his strategy, conferred with his coming Secretary of Commerce and Attorney-General, interviewed and corresponded with many economists and experts, called into conference Oscar Underwood—Chairman of the House Ways and Means Committee. He also made special efforts with difficult members, such as the Old Guard Senator Simmons of North Carolina and Representative Champ Clark, who might reasonably have been unfriendly after Wilson won the nomination from him at Baltimore.

The heaviest fight came on the wool and sugar schedules. Wilson favored bigger reductions on these than some of the men in his own party approved. There was fierce debate on both wool and sugar rates, and at one point the President threatened to go to the people if necessary.

On the other hand, he wrote conciliatory and friendly letters to members who he knew were under severe pressure from their constituents of the wool and sugar industry and whose views sincerely differed from his own.

The House passed the bill by a majority of 281 to 139. A much stiffer battle awaited it in the Senate. The debate lasted all summer—the President remaining at his post in the scorching Washington heat to see it through. He was constantly conferring with groups of Senators in his own office or at the Capitol. He had a special telephone put in so that he could speak directly to Senators from the White House.

All these patient efforts finally had their reward. A Democratic caucus declared the tariff bill a party measure, and the bill was formally laid before the Senate by Senator Simmons, the Old Guard man everybody had thought would be its worst enemy. On September 9 the victorious Democrats carried their measure in the Senate by a vote of 44 to 37, and on October 3rd the President signed the bill in the presence of some fifty of his delighted associates.

"I have had the accomplishment of something like this at heart ever since I was a boy," he said with a broad smile. "And I know men standing around me who can say the same thing."

Walter Page, who had sat in the Kimball House at Atlanta, sent an exultant message: "Score one! You have done a great historic deed and demonstrated and abundantly justified your leadership."

X

WHEN he signed the tariff bill Wilson said: "This is only half the journey. We are now about to take the second step in setting the business of this country free. This," he said, "is what we shall do in the bill for the reform of the currency."

He had long been interested in currency reform and had spoken and written on it before becoming President. He read everything he could find in connection with the monetary history of the United States, and carried on a considerable correspondence with bankers and financial experts, studying various forms of possible legislation.

Back in 1897 he had declared in a public address that "nothing but currency reform can touch the cause of the present discontents." In 1911, while Governor of New Jersey, he said in another

The Story of Woodrow Wilson

public statement: "The plain fact is that control of credit . . . is dangerously concentrated in this country. . . . The growth of the nation . . . and all our activities are in the hands of a few men . . . necessarily concentrated upon the great undertakings in which their own money is involved and who . . . by very reason of their own limitations, chill and check and destroy genuine economic freedom."

"The great monopoly in this country," he said, "is the money monopoly." And beyond all other questions waiting to be solved "lurks the great question of banking reform."

Certainly reform was needed. Since the Civil War the country had gone through five bank panics, which many experts declared to be wholly unnecessary: the fault lay in our "inelastic" and "unscientific" credit system. Congressional inquiries and attempted reform measures so far had resulted in nothing.

In 1908, under the Roosevelt Administration, the Republicans passed the Aldrich-Vreeland Currency Act, which provided for a great central bank owned and controlled by private banking institutions. It concentrated the control of credits in the hands of a small group of capitalists. Chairman Carter Glass of the House Banking Committee had a different program.

Two months before inauguration Wilson invited Glass and the committee banking expert, Dr. Willis, to Princeton for a conference. They talked for several hours, reviewing the memorandum of proposed legislation Glass brought with him. Glass's plan provided for the organization of regional reserve banks, to be under the control of the Comptroller of the Currency. Mr. Wilson thought that Glass and his colleagues were "on the right track," but the question of control troubled him. He then put forward his own scheme for "an altruistic Federal Reserve Board" at Washington. The other two men caught his enthusiasm. Glass gladly modified his plans and went to work wholeheartedly along the line suggested by the President. When the whole project had been carefully worked out by financial experts it resulted in the great Federal Reserve System.

This system provided for twelve Federal Reserve Banks in twelve different sections of the country. All national banks would be members. State banks and trust companies could join if they wished. A Federal Reserve Board at Washington was to supervise the whole system.

The member banks had to keep a certain percentage of cash reserves in the Reserve Banks, and the Government could deposit funds in these banks at the discretion of the Treasury. The Reserve Banks would issue currency as loans to the member banks against notes of their customers or against other securities acceptable under the Act.

Here was a system that could really provide a currency "elastically responsive to sound credit" and that could help the small businessman in a way that was impossible as long as he had to depend on the resources of small local banks or the favor of a few powerful New York banking houses.

Of course opposition developed. The minute the provisions of the new measure leaked out objections and criticisms poured in. Bryan and his radical followers feared too much banker power. The overconservative bankers feared they would not have enough. Currency reform had been the center of Bryan's interests since the free-silver days. Certain provisions of the bill worried him, and he opposed dealing with the currency question till the tariff legislation was out of the way.

Wilson had a difficult course to steer, with radical Congressmen attacking the bill as "a Wall Street measure," the bankers attacking it as "Socialism," and his own Secretary of State possibly opposing one of his major pieces of legislation. Bryan wanted the President to appoint the whole board. Glass favored giving the banks some voice. Senator Owen, head of the Senate Finance Committee, sided with Bryan. So did Louis Brandeis, whose opinion rated high with Mr. Wilson. McAdoo agreed with Glass, though he later proposed a compromise.

The President, after listening to all the arguments, decided against any banking representation whatever. It must be a government board. It was a question of a basic principle: "the deep-seated progressive principle that the Government, not private interests, must be supreme."

The decision, as Glass had predicted, brought a storm of protest from the bankers. Glass himself accompanied a delegation to the White House to convince the President that he was wrong. They descended on him in a body—some of the foremost bankers of the nation, from the liberal Midwestern as well as the conservative Eastern group. Mr. Glass describes the scene in his book, *An Adventure in Constructive Finance*:

"These great bankers, arbiters for years of the country's credit, were grouped about the President's desk in the executive office adjoining the Cabinet room. . . . President Wilson faced the group across the desk . . . as these men drove home what seemed to me good reason after good reason for banker representation on the central board. When they had ended . . . Mr. Wilson asked quietly:

" 'Will one of you gentlemen tell me in what civilized country of the earth there are important government boards of control on which private interests are represented?' "

There was a painful silence. Before it was broken Mr. Wilson further inquired:

" 'Which of you gentlemen thinks the railroads should select members of the Interstate Commerce Commission?' "

No reply could be made to this question either. The bankers, despairing of the main point of their visit, turned the discussion to other phases of the bill. Later a desperate effort was made in the Senate to give the banks minority representation on the Reserve Board. The proposition did not prevail. Wilson's arguments silenced the bankers. They also entirely convinced Mr. Glass that "Mr. Wilson knew more about these matters than I did." From that time forward Glass became a vigorous defender of a change that he had at first opposed.

He had to swallow another hard dose when it came to the President's decision on the issuance of currency. The Bryan element held that "power to issue currency should be vested exclusively in government officials." The President also favored this government issuance.

Glass was horrified. "There is not in truth any government obligation here, Mr. President. It would be a pretense on its face. The suggested government obligation is so remote it could never be discerned."

"Exactly so, Glass," said the President. "Every word you say is true; the government liability is a mere thought. And so, if we can hold to the substance of the thing and give the other fellow the shadow—why not do it, if thereby we may save our bill?"

Glass yielded, most reluctantly.

Wilson's astuteness was quickly proved. For Bryan now came to the support of the bill with real enthusiasm, expressing the opinion that "the bill in its final form would be acceptable to the party and that its immediate introduction would no longer menace the tariff bill."

In a statement to the press he praised "the wise, steady, unrelenting leadership of the President, without which a satisfactory Federal Reserve Act would not have become a reality." As a final tactical move Wilson invited the entire Banking and Currency Committee to a White House conference. Here he vigorously presented the various provisions of the bill and urged strong and united support for it.

On June 23rd, 1913, he presented his currency reform to Congress, stating that "it is absolutely imperative that we should give the businessmen of this country a banking and currency system by means of which they can make use of the freedom of enterprise and individual initiative which we are about to bestow upon them" (with the tariff revisions).

Three days later the currency bill was introduced in both Houses of Congress and a six months' battle began. Wilson's strategy in these great pieces of legislation reveals his qualities as a leader and as a man. He brought constant, steady pressure to bear on friend and foe alike. He invited his radical opponents—especially Congressmen Henry and Wingo—to the White House for conferences, in which he persuasively explained the objects of the bill. He welcomed letters from doubtful Congressmen and answered them carefully and with keen appreciation. He received delegations of bankers from the South and West, trying to allay their doubts and fears. He stood behind Glass with unfailing support, and at one point kept him from resigning. "Damn it, old fellow, don't resign. Outvote them!" said Wilson.

The sweltering hot summer was a trying time for him personally. Huerta in Mexico, a coal strike in Colorado, the wool and sugar contests over the tariff were also giving him acute concern. His family at his insistence were away in New Hampshire.

"I could not have been easy about them had they not gone," he wrote a friend. But, he had to admit, "it makes the situation complete. . . . These are stern days, and this all but empty house fits well with them. . . .

"I play golf every afternoon because while you are playing golf you *cannot* worry and be preoccupied with affairs. . . . I, of course, find a real zest in it all. Hard as it is to nurse Congress along and stand ready to play a part of guidance in anything that turns up, it is all part of something infinitely great and worth while, and I am content to labor at it to the finish."

By early September the long battle over the tariff left Congress exhausted. It wanted to recess. But Wilson came out flatly against any recess of more than three days. Amendments—a word for which he was to come to have a great distaste—were now being proposed. He announced that he would not budge, as to either the bill or the calendar. This resulted in a charge, later to become very familiar, that "we have a dictator in the White House."

The bill went through a stormy attack in the Democratic caucus, but it finally triumphed under strong pressure from Bryan and on September 18th passed the House by the handsome vote of 287 to 85. Forty-eight Republicans voted for it, and only three Democrats opposed it.

The fight in the Senate was far more serious. Here conservative interests dominated. The bankers asked for hearings and got them. Lobbying became intense.

Almost all the great bankers opposed the President's legislation. They lined up solidly behind the Aldrich plan. The American Bankers Association as a body denounced Wilson's bill and induced the United States Chamber of Commerce and hundreds of local chambers to do the same. On September 30th Representative Stevens wrote the President:

> I am informed by a banker in my district that the big banks have their agents out ostensibly soliciting business but as a matter of fact spreading poison against the currency bill. I have no doubt they are doing the same thing all over the country. Put this action with the attitude of the subsidized press of the country and the various repetitions of the action of the American Bankers Association by the State bankers associations and we have before us clear as day the propaganda of the money trust to so amend our bill as to legalize the strangle hold the money trust now has upon the country.

For a while it seemed as though the measure might actually be defeated, or modified to such an extent as to make it ineffective. The bankers even went so far as to present an entirely new bill of their own to the Senate Committee, urging its substitution for the Owen-Glass Act. Wilson refused to countenance this, or to see the bankers who had brought it to Washington.

Another revolt, led by a group of insurgent Senators, also ended in fiasco, with the November elections showing a strong trend to Wilson's leadership and policies.

Finally Christmas loomed—and surely even legislators could be allowed to go home for Christmas! The majority the President could count on in the Senate was so small, he dared not risk delaying action. He announced that he would not consent to a recess under any circumstances until the vote had been taken. "It was the last necessary exhibition of that firmness and inflexibility on the part of the Executive," says Dr. Willis, "which was so primarily responsible for the adoption of the Federal Reserve Act."

On December 19th the vote was finally taken, and the Senate passed the bill, 54 to 43. Differences between the two Houses were speedily settled, and on December 23rd a jubilant group of "happy warriors" gathered in the Executive Office at the White House to watch the President affix his signature: Glass, Owen,

McAdoo, the members of the Cabinet and the two committees.

"I'm drawing on the gold reserve," Wilson said with a smile, as he used four pens one after the other.

Now he could go off for a happy holiday with his own family, warmed by a vast chorus of approval. "The greatest financial reform in one hundred years," said a leading Republican newspaper. The law is so important in the country's financial history, writes Mr. A. D. Noyes, in *The War Period of American Finance*, that "it is difficult to construct an imaginary picture of what that history would have been without it."

Once the Act was successfully passed, all the former opponents wanted to climb on the band wagon. Seven hundred and sixty-seven banks applied for entry during the first week after the bill was signed. The Republicans announced that it was simply a natural outgrowth of the Aldrich plan. Telegrams and congratulations flowed in from officials and everyday citizens all over the country.

It was a triumph for Wilson even greater than the triumph of the tariff bill. Characteristically, while he signed it he was planning new activities. The Federal Reserve Act, he said, was "only the first of a series of constructive measures by which we are going to seek more and more to serve the country."

He cast an eager look ahead to "other and greater labors, new victories in the reconstruction of American economic life."

Success for Wilson invariably meant "What next?"

XI

THE backlog of both tariff and currency reform, Wilson felt, was anti-trust legislation.

In his acceptance speech after the nomination of 1912 he declared that the "vast confederacies . . . of banks, railways, express companies, insurance companies, manufacturing corporations, mining corporations, power and development companies" having become a menace to our civilization. Laws must be created to control the situation "without destroying or seriously embarrassing any sound or legitimate business undertaking. . . ."

He realized, he said in a speech in 1912, that modern business could not be handled by old-fashioned methods. The day of individual competition had no doubt gone by. We would do business in the future by means of corporations. But such corporations must not restrain trade or establish monopoly. Directly Wilson came into office, he asked the Attorney-General and the Secretary of Commerce to make organized inquiries as to possible violation of the anti-trust law by some of the big corporations and the degree of influence they exerted in various industries.

All through his arduous work on the tariff and currency bills Wilson was steadily laying the ground for his trust legislation. He consulted Chairman Clayton of the Judiciary Committee, who would be the man to guide the legislation in the House, going over with him the sort of anti-trust laws he had launched in New Jersey. He corresponded with other Congressmen and Senators. He read Mr. Brandeis's writings and exchanged further letters with him on the subject.

Some of the President's closest advisers, including members of the Cabinet, again urged him not to go too fast. They felt it would be wise to let the country get its breath and make the necessary adjustments after the new currency and tariff legislation.

Wilson forged straight ahead, as usual. He spent much of his time during the holiday at Pass Christian, as he wrote a friend, in "careful study of the wise course to pursue in the matter of the trusts."

His daughter Eleanor recounts that he wrote four hundred letters during the three weeks of this "holiday." "But he managed also to rest and relax, playing golf, riding horseback, and loafing on the water in a little slow-moving launch."

On the twenty-eighth of December he celebrated his fifty-seventh birthday and looked, his daughter says, "amazingly young" as he unwrapped his presents, "carefully untying the ribbons and folding the paper." He had gone through a grueling

summer and terrific strain, but was well and vigorous and looking forward with undiminished eagerness to the next step in his
program: trust legislation, a wisely planned budget system, and
framing his next message to Congress.

In the midst of these labors came an unexpected bombshell
from big business. On January 3, 1914, J. Pierpont Morgan,
George F. Baker, and other leading financiers announced their
intention of withdrawing from the directorates of various corporations with which they were affiliated. Mr. Morgan stated:
"An apparent change in public sentiment in regard to director-
ships seems now to warrant us in seeking to resign from some of
these connections. Indeed it may be, in view of the change in
sentiment upon this subject, that we shall be in a better position
to serve such properties and their security holders if we are not
directors."

The House of Morgan filed notice of its withdrawal from a
number of railroads, trust companies, and wealthy corporations.
This created a sensation throughout the country. It was declared
"a surrender of the Money Trust," the "beginning of a new era
in American finance," "a great victory for President Wilson and
his Administration."

In his message to Congress on January 20th Wilson acknowledged it handsomely: "The antagonism between business and
government is over," he said. "The Government and businessmen are ready to meet each other halfway in common effort to
square their methods with both public opinion and the law."

However, if the Wall Street move had been calculated to sidetrack the President's legislation it was not successful. For he
then went on to propose precisely the legislation he had planned
all along: laws to prohibit interlocking directorates; laws giving
the Interstate Commerce Commission greater power over the
railroads; a law to create a Federal Trade Commission with
large powers of investigation; swift and sure penalties for trans-
gressors.

Long and heated discussion took place in both Houses, but the
program finally took shape in several notable bills: the Clayton
Anti-Trust bill, the Federal Trade Commission bill (both passed

in 1914), and the Rayburn bill giving the Interstate Commerce Commission power to pass upon the stocks and bonds of railroads and common carriers. The Clayton bill contained the provision for prohibiting interlocking directorates, also an important provision that "labor organizations shall not be held or construed to be illegal combinations or conspiracies in restricting trade." This, with the much-discussed Sundry Civil Service bill rider and other acts of his early administration, marked Wilson as the friend of labor.

Three great pieces of legislation were put through in a bare eighteen months: the Tariff bill, the Federal Reserve Act, and now the Anti-Trust laws. "Never in the history of the country has a party and its President so dramatically and thoroughly executed its platform and redeemed its pledges," said one commentator.

"A year of achievement for which there are few if any parallels in American history," the New York *World* called it.

"The man who was regarded as a pedagogue, a theorist, is accomplishing the most astonishing practical results," said the veteran Republican Chauncey Depew, at a New York dinner in contrast with the long-ago occasion when he poked fun at the "over-serious" young professor.

"The whole country is proud of Wilson," declared a former opponent, Thomas Fortune Ryan. "He is a great man and a great President."

Wilson, much moved by the tributes that poured in upon him, wrote to Representative Underwood just after the signing of the Clayton bill: "I wish I could speak by name of the many men who have so honorably shared in these distinguished labors. I doubt if there has ever been a finer exhibition of teamwork. . . ."

The Trade Commission and the Clayton bill, he said, should make men in small business as free to succeed as the big business tycoons. He felt that "the new constitution of peace" and the "new freedom" were in large part accomplished, that the little fellow's opportunity was now really assured him.

Alas for the hopes of earnest men! A long arm reached out from three thousand miles away to wreck Wilson's cherished plans and those of millions of other men and women.

The Story of Woodrow Wilson

On June 28th a shot rang out that shook the world. The Archduke Franz Ferdinand and his wife were assassinated at Sarajevo. The first week of August brought what Wilson had never believed possible: a general declaration of war in Europe.

It also brought the greatest tragedy of his personal life: the death of his wife, Ellen Axson Wilson.

XII

I DISTRUST success," Wilson had said.

During the first eighteen months of his Presidency his achievements mounted steadily to a peak; he had one triumph after the other. The summer of 1914 brought the first sharp down-beat.

Even before the European war there were ominous rumblings. Business, made unmistakably nervous by some of Wilson's innovations, suffered a severe depression, which Wilson declared had been artificially created by a conspiracy of his enemies. In the spring and summer of 1914 he had to call out Federal troops, in connection with the very serious Colorado coal strikes, which lasted over a year. Thus he had both capital and labor to reckon with—the big businessmen, whom he had chastened, declaring in the words of the New York *Times*: "Let the President beware of the 'conspiracy' of the next Election Day!"

There was, mercifully, a let-up in Mexico, following the mediation agreement. Huerta resigned and fled the country. Wilson's favorite, Carranza, was elected President, and the Wilsonian policy seemed vindicated at last.

But the cloud that had long been gathering over Europe broke with the assassination of the Archduke. Austria presented an ultimatim to Serbia; the reply was considered unsatisfactory; diplomatic relations were broken off; on July 28th came the formal declaration of war.

The President was immediately faced with grave decisions. How would a European war affect America? Would not such a conflict almost inevitably draw in every great nation? What could he do—could he do anything—at this eleventh hour to stem the torrent which apparently threatened to engulf the whole world? During those last days of July and the early days of August his public duties grew daily more complex. Conflicting anxieties tore at his mind. As he sat at his desk surrounded by dispatches and bulletins hourly bringing him the latest events in the swiftly moving world drama, on an upper floor of the White House another drama approached its climax.

In March Mrs. Wilson fell, in her bedroom, stricken with the disease from which she died and which, her physicians tried to make the President understand, would inevitably prove fatal. But he obstinately refused to believe them.

"Mrs. Wilson is gaining—slowly, oh so slowly, but still gaining," he wrote to their close friends. And again: "Ellen has been suffering from a painful fall . . . but . . . is at last getting over the soreness and shock. She will presently be free to take her needed rest without pain and get her tone and elasticity back again."

He took her to White Sulphur Springs, firmly asserting that it had done her good, that she was better. In May of 1914 came their daughter Eleanor's marriage to Mr. McAdoo. "After that she can get rested." But she did not get rested. She got worse. Dr. Grayson moved to the White House and was in constant attendance. "Her case was hopeless from the beginning," said the Doctor, "but the President would not admit it."

His devotion, Dr. Grayson said, was such as he had never seen in the course of a long practice. Wilson would rush from a Cabinet meeting to sit by his wife's bedside. He would get up at three in the morning and go in to cheer her up. He would take his notebook and compose his messages and memoranda by her side, while she slept, not even knowing he was with her.

Tremendous problems confronted the President. There was an acute financial crisis, with foreign exchanges falling and a serious panic looming at home. Ships had to be found to carry our produce. Americans stranded in Europe were besieging our embassies and consulates, trying to get help and return passage. The press had to be met and advised more carefully than usual.

The Story of Woodrow Wilson

Interviews with Cabinet Ministers and Congressmen crowded one upon the other in the harassed President's office.

By the first of August Germany had declared war on Russia; by the third, on France; by the fourth Germany had crossed the Belgian frontier. And that night Great Britain, her ultimatum to Germany disregarded, made formal announcement that she had entered the conflict.

In Washington, in the oppressive August heat, the President sat at his desk trying to chart his path in this maze of complexities, while upstairs the life dearest to him in the world was slipping away. "I carry lead in my heart all the time," he told his friend Mary Hulburt. It must have added to his grief that during that terribly crowded year, working under pressure, he had had so little time to spend with his wife, either at Cornish in the summer or in the White House at Washington.

All the family had been summoned. At five o'clock in the afternoon of August 6th Mrs. Wilson died, clasping hands with the man at whose side she had trod the years so gallantly and for whom she had been "the most perfect wife and helpmeet."

It was a relief to remember in the days that followed that she had died without knowing the terrible cataclysm that had occurred. "I cannot help feeling that she was taken in order to be spared that dreadful spectacle," said the fatalistic President.

Ellen Wilson was a woman of talent in many directions, but her real genius lay in her ability to make an ideal home. Wherever she went—from the first tiny rooms at Bryn Mawr to her last days in the White House—she was known for her joyous and overflowing hospitality. She could make a festive party out of nothing; under her touch even state dinners and huge receptions became easy and delightful. "Isn't it strange," writes one of her cousins, "we said to each other after our first visit to the White House, that Ellen's homes no matter where they are always have the same feeling?"

When she went to Washington and to that "big garish White House" she took with her many of the familiar things. "We found our own rugs, our desks, our chintzes and curtains," says one of her daughters. "In a few days Mother had the furniture rearranged, the bookcases filled with our favorite books, and our piano near the windows [of the first stiff and unlived-in Oval Room]. Even though it was the White House, it was *home*."

How much she imbued her husband with this feeling is shown in his own spontaneous cordiality, the dozens of letters and messages sent to old friends urging them to "come and stay with us whenever you can."

One of the most delightful letters of all the hundreds of the President's that this writer has examined was carefully preserved by an old friend to whom Mr. Wilson wrote on the handsome stationery of the Executive Mansion:

"Of course you must stay with us when you come to Washington. Come right up to the house as soon as you arrive—you and Agnes. We won't take no for an answer!"

The man who had been drafting currency bills and tariff reforms and who was to write a constitution for the peace of the world—"*Come right up to the house!*" And they did.

Another, who had been invited with his wife and son to spend a week end, writes:

> It was just like the old times in Princeton. After dinner we drew up our chairs round a fire in the drawing room and talked about books. Mr. Wilson stretched himself out on the hearth rug and recited poetry, as we had often heard him do. There was not a single interruption . . . the whole evening. The scene was just a bit of Princeton in a somewhat larger and less plainly furnished room. . . . The President of the United States rocked back and forth in the firelight, with his knees clasped between his hands, declaiming sonnets, while his face glowed with affection. I have never heard a man address a woman with a more perfect blending of love and respect than was present in the word "Ellen" when Mr. Wilson addressed his wife.

When the daughters were married Mrs. Wilson "made one feel that the stately surroundings simply added a tone of dignity to a function that would not have been very different if she had still been the wife of a college professor. They were all present—

her friends and her father's friends, and members of the family who had not seen one another for years, gathered in corners talking of old times."

A little more gold lace and scarlet coats and fanfare; slightly larger chandeliers; the Marine band instead of the old church organ. Otherwise it was much the same.

Mrs. Wilson had a good share of her husband's crusading spirit. Three weeks after inauguration, she accompanied a group of public-spirited Washington women on a visit to some of the unsavory back yards and hidden alleys of beautiful Washington. Housing conditions among the city's ninety-six thousand Negroes were scandalous, and she was determined to do something about them.

On the second visit she induced some Congressmen to come along too. A sum of fifty-four thousand dollars was raised to help in these poor districts, Mrs. Wilson's one hundred dollars starting the subscription. Eventually through her efforts a bill was introduced into Congress to abolish the unhygienic dwelling places and build better ones. When she was dying she "wished she could know that her bill was passed." Congress was notified and acted quickly. She received the good news shortly before she lost consciousness for the last time.

Ellen Wilson seemed devoid of personal ambition or any thought at all for herself.

> She did not care a penny about being the wife of the President [said her brother]. But she cared far more than for her own life that he should be President because he wanted to be and was big enough for the job.
>
> When he was meditating entering practical politics I questioned his physical capacity to meet the strain—I feared it would kill him quickly. She answered: "We must not think about that. He is greatly fitted for it and wants it, and we must do all we can to help him get it. There is no limit to his capacities and nothing must thwart such a career."
>
> His fighting career shortened her own life but she would not have had her life prolonged on other terms and she was

at his side fighting. . . . Mrs. Wilson was as uncompromising as he.

He often said she had the clearest judgment and firmest tenacity of anyone he knew. In her relationship with her husband she could upon occasion be a valiant critic—one of the few real critics he had among his intimate friends.

"I fancy few wives as devoted as she, as submerged in the life and career of her husband, could so firmly oppose his views at times, argue so persistently and yet so without heat," said Dr. Axson. ". . . I never heard an irascible conversation between them; but I often heard them differ . . . about a contemplated project—and differ without capitulation."

It is reported that when Wilson selected his Cabinet he was closeted long and often with Mrs. Wilson. Also, he never prepared a really important speech without reading it first to her and getting her criticism. She would usually suggest some one change—"and it was just that passage," he told Dr. Grayson, "that would make the strongest impression in the whole speech."

"We who knew her," he said, "knew what a warrior she was and what a mind she had"—and then he added, "Wasn't she the most *radiant* person you ever knew?"

XIII

RETURNING from his sorrowful funeral journey to Georgia, the President sat alone for hours on the observation platform of his private car, trying to gather up the broken threads of his personal life and to grasp the full significance of the awful calamity that had come upon the world. Well he understood the dislocating tragedy of war.

"Every reform we have won will be lost if we get into this," he told one of his Cabinet officers. "We have just got our new tariff and currency and trust legislation . . . we don't know yet how they will work. War means autocracy. The people we have unhorsed will inevitably come into control of the country again

The Story of Woodrow Wilson

—for we should be dependent upon the steel, oil, and financial magnates. They would run the nation!"

Everything must be done to avoid involvement. Practical measures must be taken to protect American trade, American property, and the lives of American citizens. Continued efforts must be maintained to bring about a peaceful adjustment for all.

Wilson did not share the convictions many people held on the question of actual war guilt. Germany had taken the first step; in the immediate responsibility for opening hostilities the Central Powers appeared the aggressors. But for the real cause— economic rivalries and international jealousies—everybody was responsible, including the United States. Nothing could solve the complicated questions created by those rivalries except a permanent organization for the maintenance of peace. Economic and political problems must be settled at the council table, not on the battlefield. These subjects had long engrossed Wilson's mind. Coming back from Georgia he began discussing definite plans with Mrs. Wilson's brother, Stockton Axson.

In the meantime a neutral country had certain immediate duties to perform. On August 3 the President had issued the formal proclamation of neutrality between the United States and the warring nations. Sitting by his wife's deathbed, he had, as a last desperate move, written a message tendering his good offices to the governments about to open hostilities:

> As official head of one of the powers signatory to the Hague Convention, I feel it to be my privilege and my duty under article three of that Convention to say to you in a spirit of most earnest friendship that I should welcome an opportunity to act in the interest of European peace, either now or at any other time that might be thought more suitable, as an occasion to serve you and all concerned in a way that would afford me lasting cause for gratitude and happiness.

This document went to each of the belligerent governments. No one of them accepted. All argued that they were entirely in the right, the Kaiser, through Ambassador Gerard, sending the

President of the United States

most elaborate statement. The only thing left for the United States to do was to perform such friendly services as a neutral nation could—always with the thought of being, as Mr. Bryan said, "in a better position to exert our influence for peace when the time came."

Naturally, people at once began to take sides. The President made a powerful appeal to the American people to be neutral in fact as well as in name—to keep at peace among themselves, to look ahead to the great work of establishing permanent peace in the world when the moment might come for "impartial mediation."

This address met with general approval. At that time even Senator Lodge and Theodore Roosevelt declared that it was "our duty to remain entirely neutral with all with whom we are at peace," though later they violently criticized the President's demand for neutrality as "unsound" and "impractical."

Mr. Wilson then turned his attention to the great economic problems into which the war had plunged America. The crisis came just at harvest-time, when farmers awaited the yearly payments that settled their debts. Now, with no carriers for their produce, with belligerent and neutral vessels afraid to leave port, that produce lay rotting in freight cars and warehouses. Freight and insurance rates soared. Simultaneously prices went tobogganing. By the middle of August cotton dropped from thirteen to six cents a pound. Farmers, banks, and railroads all faced ruin.

At the same time returns from tariffs and other taxes showed a decrease of ten and a half million dollars compared with August, 1913. A continued reduction on such a scale would mean a total loss of seventy-five or a hundred million dollars.

In those hectic days the nation fortunately had strong leadership in the Treasury as well as in the White House. Mr. McAdoo gives this interesting bit of the story in his book *Crowded Years*:

About nine-thirty on Friday morning July 31st, J. P. Morgan of New York called me on the telephone. He said that in view of the demoralized condition of the market the

The Story of Woodrow Wilson

Governors of the New York Stock Exchange would meet at ten o'clock that morning to consider . . . closing . . . the Exchange. He went on to say that they would be glad to have my advice as to whether or not this should be done. . . .

I did not relish the thought of assuming any part of the responsibility, but after some reflection I said, "If you really want my judgment it is to close the Exchange." He said it would be done, and it was done that day.

McAdoo went to New York that week end to consult with the bankers. He was met at Pennsylvania Station by some of the most important financiers in New York.

"I was startled by their white faces and trembling voices," says Mrs. McAdoo, who accompanied her husband. "Were these America's 'Great Men'?"

The Secretary greeted them cheerfully, took his wife to the hotel, told her not to worry—he had already deposited fifty million dollars of emergency currency in the Sub-Treasury in New York—and departed for the conference. After midnight he returned and told her what had happened.

The bankers had asked for emergency currency and were enormously relieved when he told them it was there already. But such currency could be issued only to national banks. McAdoo paced up and down the hotel room. "My God, why couldn't this have happened a little later? Just a few months and the Federal Reserve system would have been in operation and taking care of a situation like this!"

There was only one thing to do: go back at once to Washington and get Congress to pass an amendment immediately giving him the right to issue currency to any bank or trust company that had "signified its intention to join the Federal Reserve system and could deposit satisfactory collateral."

"I wondered if even Father and Mac could get Congress to pass anything immediately," Mrs. McAdoo comments. But they hurried back to Washington, and in twenty-four hours it was done and panic was averted. During the next three months the Treasury advanced about $370,000,000 to the banks throughout the nation, all of which was eventually retired without the loss of a single dollar by the Government.

Next to money the thing most needed was ships. Indeed, the farmer couldn't sell his goods and get his money unless he had ships to transport the goods. In his acceptance speech of 1912 Wilson had begun urging a strong merchant marine for America: "Merchants who must depend upon the carriers of rival mercantile nations to carry their goods to market," he said then, "are at a disadvantage in international trade too manifest to need to be pointed out." His farsightedness now became uncomfortably evident.

Soon after the outbreak he called leaders of the House and Senate and told them he was depending on them to get ships to carry our commerce wherever our merchants needed to send it. An emergency measure was put through both Houses providing for the transfer of foreign ships to American registry under certain conditions. But the transfers proved pitifully few. Shipping interests hesitated to take the risk of purchasing idle German ships—especially after France and England had strongly protested and threatened to fire upon and sink all such vessels. The Allies did not want the Central Powers to receive American money for their ships or the American goods that these ships might bring.

Again the Government came forward. McAdoo worked out a scheme for a Government-owned corporation to buy or build ships. He warned the President that it would probably be attacked as socialistic. The President studied the plan, then asked, "We'll have to fight for it, won't we?"

"We certainly shall," said McAdoo.

"Well then," said the other Scotsman tersely, "let's fight!"

On August 24 Congressman Alexander introduced a bill for an appropriation of thirty million dollars for the Government to build or purchase the necessary ships.

Then came one of the greatest battles of partisan politics that even Washington ever had seen—and for the usual reason. The proposal interfered with an immensely profitable private interest.

The Story of Woodrow Wilson

Since the outbreak of war the shipowners could and did charge anything they liked to transport goods. "In the course of a year an ocean-going freighter," said Mr. McAdoo, "would bring in a net return . . . of three to five hundred per cent on the money invested." Private capital would not take risks but wanted to reap rich returns.

Again Mr. Morgan called on Mr. McAdoo—this time to protest the purchase or construction of ships by the Government. He said government entrance into the field would be considered "a menace." He also produced a letter from his firm in London which asserted that the British would not hesitate to capture ships purchased from the Germans even if they sailed under the American flag. This highhanded communication the President turned over to the State Department.

The French and British opposed Wilson from one side, business interests and Congress from the other. Lobbyists poured into Washington in greater numbers than in the tariff and currency days. As on so many occasions, the Republican opposition and the "interests" stood solidly together. Senators Lodge and Root attacked the bill as a radical departure from American tradition, with the Government actually proposing to compete with private enterprise. The President came back at this with a plea for emergency necessities, asserting that private capital refused to take the risks and that the Government would withdraw the minute private shipowners would serve the country's needs and provide vessels at fair and just rates.

Unable to defeat the bill directly, the Senate filibustered. Senator Smoot talked for eleven and a half hours, Senator Burton for thirteen. One session lasted fifty-five hours, another thirty-seven. The nation was treated to the spectacle of its most dignified body of legislators sleeping on cots in their cloakrooms and talking gibberish for hours like silly schoolboys in order to prevent by delay what they could not prevent in an immediate showdown.

Finally Wilson called the leaders of the House together. "I am tired of this obstruction," he said. "We need the ships. I want the House for the moral effect of it to pass the bill."

President of the United States

A Democratic caucus whipped the party into line. On February 16th the House passed the bill 215 to 121. But the Senate remained obdurate. Congress adjourned on March 4th with nothing done in the matter of ships. Producers and shippers had to adjust themselves as best they could to an intolerable situation.

On January 31, 1916, a new shipping bill came before Congress proposing a shipping board "for the purpose of encouraging, developing, and creating a naval auxiliary and naval reserve and a merchant marine." More debate and opposition. But both Houses finally passed the bill, which became law in September. It had taken two years for the President to win through and for Congress to admit that the situation could be met only by government operation of shipping. The delay had proved ruinously expensive.

The President, laying down the pen with which he had signed the bill, said to his Secretary of the Treasury with a smile, "Well, we won!"

"Yes—but at what a price!" said McAdoo ruefully. "The ships we could have bought in 1914 for forty dollars a ton now bring anywhere from one hundred and fifty to three hundred!" Partisan politics once more cost the country fabulous sums.

More lay behind this fight than the matter of ships. The time had come, the conservative Republicans felt, to curb the rising power of Woodrow Wilson. Republican prestige was being challenged as it had not been for years. A concerted revolt gathered strength against "executive domination" in general and against Wilson in particular: the fight now began that later became so bitter. Senator Lodge made a long and clever attack on the President's Mexican policy, though that issue was not then to the fore. Wide difference of opinion also developed between Congress and the President on the immigration bill, which he later vetoed.

The Republican leaders, reinforced by more or less open assistance from certain unsympathetic Democrats, were out to stop Wilson. The President, entirely aware of all this, hit back vigorously in his 1915 Jackson Day address at Indianapolis.

The Story of Woodrow Wilson

> These self-styled friends of business [he declared], these
> men who say that the Democratic party does not know what
> to do for business, are saying that the Democrats shall do
> nothing for business. I challenge them to show their right
> to stand in the way of the release of American products to
> the rest of the world! . . .

> You know it is the peculiarity of that great body [the
> Senate] that it has rules of procedure which make it pos-
> sible for a minority to defy the nation; and these gentlemen
> are now seeking to defy the nation and prevent the release
> of American products to the suffering world which needs
> them more than it ever needed them before.

He lapsed into occasional colloquialisms of the stump and bits
of personal facetiousness which were sharply criticized, even by
some of his closest friends. To one of these, Mrs. Toy, the wife
of a Harvard professor, he wrote on January 31:

> Of course you did not like the Indianapolis speech. . . .
> But I cannot fight rottenness with rose-water. . . . There is
> a real fight on. . . . You cannot know to what lengths men
> like Root and Lodge are going, who I once thought had
> consciences but now know have none. . . .

> I have no serene confidence in my own judgment and
> discretion: but of one thing I am resolved, to break the
> control of special interests over this Government and over
> this people.

Being human and fallible, he did not always choose the best
means for accomplishing his great purposes. The Jackson Day
speech did not do him any good. He used overstrong words and
overharsh references.

"The Republican party has not had a new idea for thirty
years . . . the Republican party is still a covert and refuge for
those who are afraid, for those who want to consult their grand-
fathers about everything. . . .

"Jackson," he said, "used to think that everybody who disagreed with him was an enemy of the country." It was what Wil-

son himself tended to do. Sometimes he showed some of the strong partisan bias he criticized in his opponents.

But there was one unforgettable difference between them: Mr. Wilson was genuinely and sincerely out to serve the interests of the people. The men who opposed him so bitterly were, as events proved again and again, quite definitely out to serve their own.

Meantime the difficulties of neutrality became more complex every day. The myth of American "isolation" fast exploded. With our economic life hopelessly enmeshed with that of countries in all parts of the world, it was senseless to suppose that we could remain unentangled politically. Part of the strategy of the belligerents was to win American assistance by stirring American sympathy. The war had scarcely started before each side was bitterly protesting to the President about the military methods and barbarities of the other: aerial bombardment of towns, use of dumdum bullets (alleged by both sides), the destruction of great libraries and works of art (as at Rheims and Louvain), the British blockade and the suffering of the children among the Central Powers, wanton killing and maiming of Belgian children by the Germans. On and on it went, organized propaganda agencies on both sides stimulating hatreds and traditional prejudices in our melting pot and raising American emotions sometimes to fever point.

Wilson, determined to keep the country out of war and understanding the seriousness of these emotional upheavals, did his utmost to hold the people steady. Lacking at that time the priceless medium of the radio, he made frequent press statements and personal addresses. He warned his ambassadors in both England and Germany against showing any partiality and also sent a special warning to American military and naval officers.

He had his own thorny problems with both sets of belligerents. Britain gave notice that she intended very literally to rule the seas and early declared certain articles contraband, for neutrals as well as enemies. At the beginning of the war the United States, standing on the 1909 naval conference Declaration of London, asserted its right to loan money and sell any commodities it pleased to any belligerent power. But Britain saw to it that the Central Powers actually received very little from American markets. Shipments of copper and cotton met with constant interference. British officers searched American vessels; instead of being searched at sea, ships were detained in port. Cargoes of foodstuffs were also held up and sometimes confiscated. Shippers complained that all these delays caused their products to deteriorate and sometimes to become completely valueless.

Bitterness increased as some people suspected an organized British effort to benefit empire trade at the expense of American shippers. Mails also were held up, and the British were charged with using information thus obtained to gain advantage over their American competitors. "Probably true," said the British Ministers barefacedly when Wilson protested. "And why not?" What was the loss of a few American dollars or the ruin of a few American merchants when they were fighting for their very existence?

In spite of his English ancestry and temperamental sympathies, Wilson became sorely tried with the British as months went on and the inconveniences and injustices to American commerce increased. At times it looked as though history might repeat itself and the American people find themselves forced into war with England for the same reasons that they were in 1812.

The situation with Germany was still more serious. The Germans protested bitterly against the sale of munitions to their adversaries by a "neutral" nation while that nation permitted the embargo on food and materials which those adversaries forced upon the Central Powers. If Germany's enemies continued to cut off her supplies while they themselves received all they needed, including the very means of warfare, that country would be reduced to starvation and possibly to defeat. The German Navy could not break the blockade, but it had in the submarine a means of preventing the Allies from getting what they needed, and Germany had perfected this new weapon to a higher degree than any other nation.

Thus began the series of systematic ship sinkings, with their inevitable menace to American life and property, which became for the President a never-ending nightmare. "The last two weeks have been like a fever," he wrote to a friend on February 14, 1915. "No one who did not sit daily here with me, each anxious twenty-four hours through, could possibly realize the constant strain," entailed, he said, both by Congress and in the war area.

"Together England and Germany are likely to drive us crazy. . . . I go to bed every night absolutely exhausted . . . with all my nerves deadened, my own individuality . . . blotted out. . . . I never knew before that it was possible . . . for a man to lose his own personal existence . . . to have no individual life apart from his official duties. . . . But it is possible. It has happened. . . ."

Perhaps the most dangerous factor of all was the degree to which the economic fortunes of this country had become involved with the Allied cause. On the one hand we had lost our normal foreign trade; on the other we had built up a huge business making war munitions for the Allies. There was only one solution for all these problems, only one hope: a speedy termination of the conflict. Several tentative moves towards mediation had been made since August, 1914, but with no result. Meanwhile the war thundered on, and reports from the battle line grew hourly more serious. It was not surprising that after various abortive attempts the harassed President turned a receptive ear to the proposal of his friend Colonel House that he personally should go on a special mission to the belligerents to sound out peace terms.

XIV

VOLUMES have been written and a score of theories advanced about "the strangest friendship in history"—the friendship of President Wilson and Colonel House. Some people think that the Colonel was a very shrewd politician secretly avid for power which he enjoyed through his unique position with the President, but that the clever diplomats of Europe wound him round their fingers by outward deference and playing up to his prestige. Some think that he—consciously or unconsciously—sold out the

The Story of Woodrow Wilson

President at the Peace Conference, while Wilson was away for some weeks on what proved to be a costly absence. Still others think that "House was the best thing that ever happened to Wilson" and that "if only the President had listened to him" the outcome of the peace of 1919 would have been different.

Certain points arrest the attention of the dispassionate observer coming cold to the question after the passing of the years; certain phrases and adjectives in the letters and books of the men who knew the Colonel best and saw him and the President most frequently, certain statements repeated again and again:

"Nice fellow . . . quiet, tactful . . . very ingratiating . . . brought the President a lot of useful information . . . never differed with the President . . . greatest yes man in history . . . changed after the Paris conference . . . succumbed to flattery . . ."

The similarity of these views coming from men of exceedingly varied backgrounds, tastes, and temperaments—their almost identical observations recorded at different times and under many different circumstances—cannot but strike the objective inquirer as rather remarkable. The close associates of President Wilson differed on many matters; they seem to have agreed to a man on Colonel House.

Especially are they agreed on two things. First, "House had a habit of finding out what was in the President's mind and then suggesting that very thing to him. This made the President think they were of one mind and extraordinarily one in their views and outlook.

"He would come to Washington and call on the President's friends and say 'What's up? What is the President thinking these days?' Then when he had got the opinion of some of the men who were close to Wilson he would go along to his call at the White House."

"Again and again," says one Cabinet member, "after I had given House certain information I would hear a day or two later Wilson himself telling me that House said so and so—that House concurred with him on this or that. House was always advising him what he had already found out that Wilson believed."

President of the United States

Second, House gave the impression that many plans and proposals originated with him which actually originated with the President or others.

"It was always House who gave the ideas and great schemes to the other fellow—according to House."

"Now," said one of the Texans, "we have all known House since he was a boy, and we all like him. But he never would have accomplished anything of his own initiative. He was no great figure till Wilson took him up—yet to hear House you would think he made Wilson!"

There is no doubt that House gave Wilson real assistance in the early days, before and just after his election. Wilson was new to politics and inexperienced. House knew everybody, proved very helpful with Bryan, with the choice of a Cabinet, and in his advice on early tactics. He refused a Cabinet post for himself. He told Wilson when he first met him: "I want nothing for myself—all I want is to be of help." ("Of course nothing House could have said would have made him more solid with Wilson!" observes one of Wilson's associates.)

In the first months of the Administration the Colonel contented himself with the role of silent messenger. Every now and then he would appear in Washington, bring the President a tidy little batch of information, stay a few days, have some pleasant chats with important personages, and disappear again.

"Eminence Grise," the French called him. And indeed this title, first bestowed upon Cardinal Richelieu, fitted the soft-spoken, gray-haired Colonel excellently. He might well have been one of the suave, smooth Cardinals of old, gliding in and out, standing behind the King, finger on lips, a discreet word here, a low-toned suggestion there. Boundless influence. Little that was certain or definite. "Colonel House—tiptoeing about, apparently vested with very large powers of a very vague sort," as one Washington man well put it.

House had a bland and innocent confidence in himself, a fashion of talking with perfect assurance about matters of which he knew little, or even nothing, but of which he was always serenely certain that he knew much. In his own eyes he was responsible for shaping some of the President's most important measures—the tariff, for instance. House reports several times setting straight Wilson—who had studied the tariff for a lifetime! Again, he fancied himself a guiding power in connection with the currency bill—evoking from Carter Glass, who engineered the bill, some decidedly caustic comment. He "determined" Secretary Daniels's naval program—which Daniels vigorously denied. He "made some important moves" in regard to the Mexican situation and Sir William Tyrrell's visit.

In the wake of this came the Colonel's first big opportunity: his mission to Europe in the summer of 1914.

Ambassador Page in London and "His Eminence" at home had undertaken some friendly plotting to help the cause of international relations and bring glory to their Chief and his Administration. At the time many people had apprehensions about the possibility of a big-scale war. House and Page felt that the best chance for peace lay in an Anglo-German agreement to limit naval armaments, that the United States might give a friendly push in this direction, and that wider international agreements might follow.

When Tyrrell came to Washington in December, 1913, to confer with the President about Mexico, House brought up the subject. Winston Churchill had recently proposed a "naval holiday" for England and Germany. House suggested to Wilson and Tyrrell that America use her influence to bring about an all-round reduction of armaments. He would be willing, if the President and their English friends approved, to do a bit of preliminary scouting. Tyrrell favored the idea and encouraged House to undertake a secret mission as "the power behind the throne" in Washington. Wilson seemed pleased—"I might almost say enthusiastic," says House—and thought there might also be a chance of reducing the American naval program if the European States reduced theirs. It was decided that House should go to Berlin and sound out the Kaiser as soon as practicable.

On this mission the Colonel had no formal credentials. He carried only a personal letter from Wilson referring to House as his "friend and spokesman." House was not attached to the State Department or responsible to anybody but the President himself. He sailed the middle of May, 1914, went directly to Germany, and on June 1st he had a conversation with the Kaiser in Berlin. The two men met in the gardens at Potsdam, and after a "delicious" lunch House discussed Germany's naval-building program. He spoke of the community of interests among England, Germany, and the United States, and suggested that "the President and I thought perhaps an American might be able to . . . compose the difficulties here" better than the Europeans who distrusted and feared one another.

The Kaiser—puzzled, no doubt, as Europeans increasingly were, by this "unofficial spokesman" with so much power and so little—"concurred . . . in my suggestion that whatever program America, England, and Germany agreed to would be successful. I made it plain, however," House wrote Wilson, "that it was the policy of our government to have no alliances of any character, but we were more than willing to do our share towards promoting international peace." In other words, he outlined to the Kaiser the virtues of a triangular entente while at the same time telling him that America could under no circumstances enter one.

From Berlin he went on to Paris, where he saw only American Ambassador Herrick. Again he wrote Wilson telling him with great confidence that "the French think" this and that—in particular that French statesmen "dream no longer of revenge and the recovery of Alsace-Lorraine." Very few Frenchmen at that time dreamed of anything else.

Then on to England and Sir Edward Grey—whom he found "a willing listener, very frank and sympathetic." After two hours' preliminary exploring they agreed to adjourn to a later meeting. "In the meantime the general idea was accepted that a frank and open policy should be pursued by all the parties at interest." With regard to what, the letter does not say.

Many of House's letters—and some of Page's—give an impression of extraordinary ingenuousness, of broad statements with very little behind them. Americans at international meetings during the early part of the century frequently gave that impression: great good will, eagerness to assist in putting through some big general scheme for world welfare—"Outlawry of War," "Moral Disarmament"—but with no basic understanding of political fact or of essential political machinery. Colonel House seemed to Europeans the very embodiment of the traditional "American." His heart was big, his knowledge negligible, his political experience outside his own country nil. Yet he aspired to remake the world. Magnificent—ridiculous—and more than a little touching.

True, the Colonel had one specific plan which he proposed to the Kaiser and to Lord Grey and which he hoped "may have your [the President's] approval: I have suggested that America, England, France, Germany, and the other money-lending and developing nations have some sort of tentative understanding among themselves for the purpose of establishing a plan by which investors on the one hand may be encouraged to lend money at reasonable rates and to develop, under favorable terms, the waste places of the earth, and on the other hand to bring about conditions by which such loans may be reasonably safe."

Here is a plan indeed! He tells the President that he "touched lightly on this with the Kaiser and feels sure he too will approve"! He also discussed the plan with Tyrrell, Spring-Rice, Thomas Nelson Page, our Ambassador to Italy, and Walter Hines Page, our Ambassador to England—all of whom Colonel House entertained at a luncheon conference on July 3rd in London. They agreed to meet again for further discussion, the Englishmen evidently wondering how far Wilson was committed to such an idea.

But the plan died in embryo. The assassin's bullet at Sarajevo put an end to all such projects. House's delightful suggestion that he and Grey meet the Kaiser at the Kiel regatta "for the purpose of the three of us getting together so there may be no go-betweens and no misunderstandings" never came off. He wrote one more letter to the Kaiser. By that time the Kaiser was otherwise engaged.

President of the United States

Thus ended Mission Number One. House returned to his beautiful Massachusetts summer home, "kept in touch," tried to help in his characteristic way. When the cool weather arrived he swung into his winter schedule; flitted to Washington for occasional very private conversations with Ambassadors and bigwigs, wrote insistent little notes to the President about not allowing Bryan, the Secretary of State, to "interfere" by speaking on foreign policy; strongly urged the President not to try to mediate the European war in November (which House afterwards contradictorily said was the logical time to have mediated); and finally, as the situation grew daily more impossible and the President's burdens fairly crushed him, suggested that he himself be allowed "to go along with the peace negotiations." To which the President wearily replied, "Think there can be no harm in your going on."

Wilson was pretty well discouraged with his own peace efforts. His first offer of mediation had yielded nothing. Neither had a move initiated by Oscar Straus and Count von Bernstorff in September. Weeks rolled on, and the war brought no decision. The Germans had the advantage on land, the British on the sea. Some of the President's most trusted counselors—Ambassador Herrick, Lord Bryce, Ambassador Page, and House—had advised holding off on further offers. Page reported that he had confidential information from British officers that in all probability there would be a "drawn war" in the summer.

"Then a great revulsion will come," said Page. ". . . The President of the United States will be called on to mediate" and to lay down the broad principles on which the struggle may be ended. Naturally, that appealed greatly to Wilson.

In November some of the South American and other neutral nations suffering from the obstructions of the war urged a concerted effort for mediation, with the United States in a leading part. Wilson felt disinclined to join an enterprise for which we would bear the chief responsibility but which might be hampered by other nations' dissimilar views. Peace organizations and prominent individuals continued to urge some positive move for mediation. And now came Colonel House persuasively sug-

175

gesting secret negotiations, conducted by himself. Again, as in the case of House's earlier mission, the overburdened President seems not to have given any detailed thought to the matter, simply trusting his friend "to see what could be done."

House sailed in late January, 1915. This time he carried a letter of credentials specifically defining—and limiting—his powers:

> It gives me peculiar pleasure [wrote the President] to give you my commission to go, as my personal representative, on the mission you are now so generously undertaking. . . . It is altogether right and fortunate that you are to act only as my private friend and spokesman, without official standing or authority; for that will relieve both you and those with whom you confer from any embarrassment.
>
> It is my desire . . . to supply through you a channel of confidential communication through which the nations now at war . . . may [decide to] have a preliminary exchange of views with regard to the terms upon which the present conflict may be brought to an end and future conflicts rendered less likely.

The President accompanied his friend to the station. Their parting was full of affection.

"There is not much for us to talk over," said the President, "for the reason that we are both of the same mind and it is not necessary to go into details with you."

There lay the weakness of the whole relationship: they were *not* of the same mind, nor (what was almost equally important) of at all the same training. Wilson knew political matters from long years of study, painstaking reflection, quiet intelligent appraisal. He knew what he thought, and it was clear, definite, unchanging. House had no disciplined mind, no intellectual training. He did not even complete the four years' college course. His viewpoint changed with each visitor. Wilson was thorough, exact, carefully documented on any subject he tackled. House had no systematized knowledge; his mind was frequently foggy.

It seems a strange, almost incomprehensible association. It can be explained only by Wilson's passionate need for friendship, his profound hunger for the affection he was generally too reserved to attract, his utter loyalty and devotion once he thought he had found it.

"Up to his neck" in a maze of problems, he trusted House implicitly. He felt, very naturally after the impression had been steadily built up for two years, that House's mind worked just as his own did and that under any given circumstances his friend would proceed exactly as he, Wilson, would. When they finally sat at the conference table in Paris, working side by side, the President had some surprises.

Naturally the reports of another secret foreign mission for the President's confidential adviser caused wide speculation, though nothing definite could be learned about it. House sailed on January 30, 1915, in what one writer calls "a blaze of mystery." He landed in England on the sixth of February.

By what seemed almost a stroke of Providence, this happened to coincide with a real desire on the part of Germany to discuss peace proposals. A confidential letter from Ambassador Gerard to the President shows this. The Germans' ambitious first scheme had failed: they had not been able to take Paris in six weeks and then blaze on to Russia as they had intended. There were now strong indications that Italy would join the Allies. Allied control of the sea became increasingly important. Two alternatives presented themselves: peace, or a much more intensive and terrible submarine warfare.

On February 10th Gerard wrote the President from Berlin urging the advisability of "getting an intimation to the Allies . . . that if certain proposals were made there was a disposition here to accept them." Gerard also wrote House in London that German Foreign Secretary Zimmermann "told me he had written to you saying they would be glad to see you. . . . I am sure if a reasonable peace is proposed *now* it would be accepted." The President, eager to seize the opportunity, sent word to House that "I will do whatever I can to stimulate the interest of Germany from this end through Bernstorff." On February 12th House received the expected invitation to visit Germany.

On February 13th he lunched alone with Grey. Ah, those intimate, delightful luncheons!

House went to the meeting, he writes in his diary, with "a feeling that the sooner I went [to Germany] the better." Grey told him quietly and very confidentially—and very flatteringly—the British plans, intimating, House records, that "he did not think it wise for me to undertake a peace mission to Germany until after there had been further military developments."

On that same day Wilson had cabled House quoting Gerard: " 'It is my belief that if you seize the present opportunity you will be the instrument of bringing about the greatest peace which has ever been signed. But it will be fatal to hesitate . . . success is dependent on immediate action.' Have you had the invitation from Berlin?" Wilson asked his special messenger anxiously.

House had the invitation from Berlin in his pocket at that moment. "The greatest peace which has ever been signed" was the possible prize. House went round again to consult Grey.

On February 18 an urgent letter came from Gerard saying that peace proposals were a matter of days and even of hours. "The submarine blockade once begun, a feeling will arise which may make it impossible until another phase of the war. If House could get the desired intimation from the Allies and then come here peace proposals would go over, to the best of my belief." But House did not budge. On February 19th House wrote Gerard that Grey found it "utterly impossible to make any such hasty proposal," that he (House) could not get to Berlin soon, and that "we will have to let the situation drift till another period of deadlock ensues."

On February 20 Wilson sent a decidedly sharp cable reminding his friend that "if the impression were to be created in Berlin that you were to come only when the British Government thought it the opportune time for you to come you might be regarded when you reached there as their spokesman rather than as mine. . . .

"The whole atmosphere may change at any moment," the President urged. "We are sending today identical notes to the

President of the United States

British and German Governments. Please say to Page that he cannot emphasize too much ... to Grey the favorable opinion which would be created in this country if the British Government could see its way to adopt the suggestions made here."

House replied: "We must be patient."

On the 22nd the President sent another urgent cablegram. On the 23rd House wrote Wilson a letter explaining the delays and saying that "the time was not opportune for peace proposals."

Imagine what might have been the outcome had there been in London at this time a man like Wilson: forceful, strong, and definite with the British; not pliant, yielding, and susceptible to pleasant luncheons. History might have been different. Two million American men might never have gone to France. A hundred and twenty-five thousand Americans might not have been killed or wounded. Wilson's collective security plans might have gone through then. There might never have been a second World War. All this is doubtful, but it is possible. In any case, Colonel House must have gone to sleep nights with the knowledge of that one chance in a hundred, that he missed.

Finally House wrote that he had "persuaded Grey" that it was time for him to go on to Germany. He arrived in Berlin four weeks after Gerard had warned that peace proposals were a matter of hours. The Germans had now begun their campaign in the East. The submarine zone order had gone into effect. The President's peace messenger arrived too late. The unavoidable impression, Mr. Baker notes, is that House, like Page, fell completely under the spell of British diplomacy throughout this period—particularly the potent spell of Sir Edward Grey.

The President apparently gave up hope of any immediate opening for peace. The tone of his letters to House changed. They became more general and impersonal. Evidently he had stopped expecting anything from that quarter and was now concentrating on urgent domestic problems.

House returned to England, after nine days in Germany and a brief formal visit to the French Foreign Office in Paris. Still a third time, in early 1916, he was to travel about Europe on one

179

of these curious unproductive "peace missions." None of his journeys achieved any practical results.

In 1915 House quickly found his way back to London and settled down again at those cosy British firesides. During the next two months three ships were attacked by the Germans—the *Falaba,* the *Cushing,* the *Gulflight*—with the loss of several American lives. "I would welcome any advice you may have to give as to the best way of handling the matter of the sinking of the American oil boat," Wilson cabled his friend.

On May 5th the President sent a curt message, which he asked House to transmit to Grey, protesting once more against the continued British obstruction of American cargoes and emphasizing the increasing resentment in America of these tactics. On May 7th the sinking of the *Lusitania* put an end to thoughts of peace.

XV

A STUNNED president received the news just at the close of a Cabinet meeting. The *Lusitania* had been torpedoed off the coast of Ireland; 1100 persons were lost (almost her entire passenger list), including 112 Americans. By nightfall the press blazed with charges of "piracy" and "murder." A flood of furious letters and telegrams poured into the White House demanding action.

The tragedy came as a tremendous shock to the American people. This was the first time any large number of their own citizens had been killed during the war. It was, most people considered, a flagrant defiance of the rules of international law to fire upon civilians—to fire upon any boat without warning and search for contraband. The loss of American lives profoundly stirred public emotion. Retaliation, even war, was demanded if necessary to avenge the national honor.

But the picture had another side. The *Lusitania* was loaded with war materials. British ships had prevented supplies and food from reaching Germany, and Germany needed these things as much as Britain did. The British had simply counted on the presence of passengers to enable this and other vessels similarly loaded to get that cargo through. They illegally flew the American flag on the *Lusitania* and on other boats that they wished to protect.

American passengers had been repeatedly warned not to sail on these ships. Congress had considered taking action to prevent such sailings. The German Embassy had issued a special warning just before the *Lusitania* departed. Embarking passengers considered this "impertinent" and treated the matter lightly or contemptuously. This is not to justify firing on civilians in wartime, but can the honest student make a completely clear case for Britain and a completely damaging case against Germany?

Wilson had all these facts in mind as he sat thinking out his message of protest to the German Government after the *Lusitania* tragedy. He said to Tumulty: "I am bound to consider all the facts and circumstances. I am not going to be carried away into radical action based upon the present emotionalism of the people." Tears stood in his eyes as he listened to the details that kept coming in through the press. "If I let myself listen to my own heart, I should see red," he said.

An excited contingent of the people clamored for immediate war on Germany. Congress undoubtedly would support him if he called for war. What then?

It was very easy to shout war and to declare war. But when a nation was plunged into the "horror and bloody aftermath," when people were poring over casualty lists, and when fathers and mothers with boys overseas turned pale each time the doorbell rang, what would people say? Wouldn't they ask: "Why did Wilson move so fast in this matter? Why didn't he try to settle this question peacefully with Germany? Why couldn't he have waited a little longer?"

Wilson could well endure Theodore Roosevelt's charge of poltroonery, the contemptuous accusations in the pro-Allied newspapers about "Wilson's weakness," "Wilson's procrastination"—if only he could succeed in his consuming longing to avoid the loss of thousands of American boys' lives. The gentlemen shrieking for revenge because a hundred lives had been lost seemed to give little thought to the prospective loss of thousands.

Harrowing incidents of the *Lusitania* disaster came in every hour during the days that followed. In the midst of drafting his note to Germany the President had to go to Philadelphia to make an address before a big meeting of newly naturalized American citizens. Every American should read that speech at least once a year, for in it Wilson told what America should mean —to the new citizen, to all citizens:

> A great ideal, a great body of principles, a great hope for the human race. . . .
>
> You cannot become thorough Americans if you think of yourselves in groups [as so many excited war partisans at that moment were doing]. . . . This great country was called the "United" States . . . and the man who seeks to divide man from man, group from group, interest from interest . . . is striking at its very heart. . . .
>
> The example of America must be a special example. The example of America must be the example not merely of peace because it will not fight but of peace because peace is the healing and elevating influence of the world where strife is not. There is such a thing as a nation being too proud to fight. There is such a thing as a nation being so right that it does not need to convince others by force that it is right.

Hardly had the words left his lips than they appeared in the headlines of every newspaper, not only in America but in England, where they were bitterly featured: "TOO PROUD TO FIGHT"—a mockery, it was felt, by those who were fighting for their very existence.

The President perceived too late that he had perhaps chosen an unfortunate phrase to convey a true and lofty idea. But how could a man with the weight of the world literally on his shoulders, confronted with a swirling kaleidoscope of problems changing every hour, consider every single phrase in every speech and message of the day? Immense mischief has been made again and again for Wilson, as for other public men, by some such lifting of one clause from the full content of a speech.

In any case, the bulk of the country supported his stand on Germany. The Philadelphia speech showed that he intended not to rush the country into war, that he felt the limit of forbearance had not yet been reached, that Germany must have every possible chance to make amends for what she had done and give assurance against its repetition.

In the meantime Germany had declared that attacks on neutral ships were contrary to orders and that she would at once tender regrets and compensation for such incidents if the facts clearly warranted such action. The Germans offered preliminary explanation in the *Gulflight* case, and their Ambassador called at the State Department to express his Government's "deep regret that the events of the war had cost the loss of so many American lives." This seemed to show at least that Germany was not trying to provoke a break with America.

Wilson's note was stern. It stated that the American Government "confidently expects, therefore, that the imperial German Government will disavow the acts of which the Government of the United States complains, that they will make reparation as far as reparation is possible for injuries which are without measure, and that they will take immediate steps to prevent the recurrence of anything so obviously subversive of the principle of warfare for which the imperial German Government have in the past so wisely and so firmly contended."

The Cabinet on the whole approved the note, though some members questioned the results which might follow. Suppose Germany refused to comply with the demands—would that not inevitably mean war?

Bryan in particular was deeply troubled. He argued that we were condemning Germany for illegal actions while tolerating other "illegal actions on the part of Great Britain." He thought we should "protest against the objectionable conduct of the Allies also and show that we are defending our rights from aggression from both sides." Wilson opposed this.

On May 13th the note went to Germany virtually as the President drafted it. It met with nation-wide approval. Ex-President Taft publicly endorsed it. On May 14th, when Mr. Wilson went to New York to review the Atlantic Fleet, he received a great welcome. President Eliot of Harvard wrote: "Your message to Germany is adequate and altogether admirable. Come peace, come war, you have the American people at your back."

But the reply from Germany doubled Bryan's anxiety. This time the Germans showed more defiance and disposition to argue. They refused to admit that the *Lusitania* sinking was entirely without excuse and implied that submarine warfare would continue, neutrals having to take their chances and settle their claims according to each individual case.

The President at once drafted a strong answer. Bryan again pleaded for a note to be sent at the same time to Great Britain. The President and other Cabinet members opposed him, and a heated argument ensued. After the meeting Bryan told the President he thought it unfair to all concerned for him to remain in the Cabinet. He was, of course, almost fanatically for peace, and he believed that the President's second note would probably mean war. The President tried to show him he was wrong and to persuade him to remain. "Your fears are exaggerated," said Wilson, "and your resigning at such a time will only increase the dangers and difficulties of the situation." Bryan was greatly perturbed, but he too stood firm. On June 8th he sent his resignation to the White House.

Much speculation followed in the press and elsewhere as to the "real reasons." But they were exactly as stated. There was no petty irritation or personal resentment on either side; two earnest men, equally desirous of keeping out of war, sincerely disagreed. Wilson's letter and Bryan's resignation show that their mutual regard had grown steadily during their years of association. It was, indeed, rather remarkable how they maintained this tone to the end.

The note did not produce the results Bryan had feared. Germany let it ride and did nothing. At home the press and public approved the second message as cordially as they had approved the first. Bryan subsided, and the President asked Robert Lan-

sing to become the new Secretary of State. "He was the best material at hand, he could put diplomatic notes into proper form
and advise on international law, and the President," says his
son-in-law Mr. McAdoo, "had determined for the future to be
practically his own Secretary of State." "What he wanted," said
another member of the Cabinet, "was really a high-class clerk!"

Thus what had been from the first a main weakness of Wilson's Administration remained. And the day was to come when
the President would need a strong Secretary of State for his life's
sake.

XVI

N O SOONER could one draw a breath regarding one belligerent than the other posed a fresh problem. As the year of
1915 wore on, the Allied governments were running short of
money. Foreign exchange was dropping steadily. McAdoo told
the President that unless large American credits could be obtained, British and French purchases in this country would be
drastically cut, and American industry would seriously suffer. In
short, we had to finance loans to the Allies to pay for goods they
were ordering from us—otherwise our own economic structure
would collapse. It was "absolutely imperative," McAdoo said,
that England establish at once credits of "at least $500,000,000"
in this country.

The embarrassing part of it was that Bryan in August, 1914,
with the President's approval, had made a statement that "in
the judgment of this Government loans by American bankers to
any foreign nation at war are inconsistent with the spirit of
neutrality." McAdoo complained, "We approve and encourage
sales of supplies, but we disapprove the creation of credit balances here to finance the purchases." He pointed out that during
the spring of 1915, the German Government had floated in
Philadelphia and New York ten million dollars' worth of short-
term bonds. McAdoo urged that the Allies at least receive the
same privilege.

The Story of Woodrow Wilson

Wilson of course saw that such loans would involve us still further in the Allied cause. He delayed decision. But he could not delay long, for Lord Reading was en route from England with a British commission to confer with New York bankers and discuss possible terms for a loan. Lansing joined his arguments to McAdoo's. On September 7th Wilson talked with them both at the White House. After three hours' earnest discussion Wilson's arguments went down, before implacable economic necessity.

First our goods; then our ships; then our credit; finally our lives. Where and what was "neutrality"? What had become of American "isolation" and "detachment"? Is there such a thing in wartime—or at any other time—actually?

The contract for the loan was signed on October 15, 1915. On October 21st Wilson sent a stiff note to the British Government regarding the blockade: a formal indictment of the entire British policy. This was a *quid* for the loan *quo*; it preserved the illusion of impartiality. The British were annoyed but gave no sign of relaxing the blockade. On the contrary, they threatened to put cotton on the contraband list. Excited mass meetings were held in New York, and protests came flooding into the White House from many cotton centers of the South. When Congress met in December it passed resolutions condemning both the British and the Germans.

However, it became evident in the late summer and early fall of 1915 that the President and the country were changing their attitudes. While Wilson's purpose remained the same—to keep America out of war—he found it more and more difficult to remain neutral either in thought or in action. His letters showed that he was beginning to distrust everything the Germans did.

"Apparently they do not know how to keep faith with anybody and we are walking on quicksand!" he wrote a friend.

During the latter months of 1915 the country showed increasing hostility toward the Germans. Spies, sabotage, rumors of underground preparations for outbreaks here in America stirred the people. Foreign Secretary Zimmermann actually informed Gerard that in case of trouble "five hundred thousand trained Germans in America would join the Irish and start a revolution"! German agents were everywhere, and German diplomatic representatives abused their official privileges. These included Captain von Papen, who later became Chancellor of Germany and Hitler's Ambassador to Austria and Turkey. A Federal Grand Jury indicted both von Papen and Boy-Ed, the military and naval attachés of the German Embassy in Washington, for plotting to blow up the Welland Canal in Canada. They were also connected with the famous Black Tom explosion in New Jersey. Letters discovered among the papers of Dr. Dumba of the Austrian Embassy showed that Dumba too had plotted to cripple our munitions factories, and Dr. Dumba admitted his complicity. These three diplomats were recalled at the request of the United States Government. But a network of German agents continued subversive activities.

All these happenings, together with the repeated ship-sinkings by German submarines, the execution of Nurse Cavell, and other atrocities, were building a hostile as well as a distinctly nervous feeling in America. Urgent demands reached the White House for military and naval safeguarding of the country. The word "neutrality" was less and less heard. It had given way to a new and more insistent word: "preparedness"—for the United States of America.

XVII

SECRETARY of War Garrison had long been agitating for reorganization of the Army. He regarded our military force as utterly inadequate. When we read that the authorized strength of the Army at that time was one hundred thousand men, we are inclined to agree with him. During the note-writing period of 1914 and 1915 many leading Americans had insisted that we should be in a position to back up these notes with physical force if necessary. We should not, as Mr. Root said, shake our fist first only to wag our finger later, if it came to a showdown.

In his passionate determination to keep us out of war and to avoid anything that might foster the war spirit, Wilson at first discouraged such agitation. In his 1914 message he pointed out that we had never had a large standing army; all American tradition was against it. A powerful navy was our natural means of defense. The National Guard, he said at that time, should be strengthened, we should be ready to defend ourselves, citizens who wished to volunteer should receive military training. But we should "not turn America into a military camp" or "ask our young men to spend the best years of their lives making soldiers of themselves." We were at peace with all the world, we did not dread any other nation, and so on.

After the sinking of the *Lusitania* his attitude changed. Another such incident might force us into war at any moment. The time had come for positive action. On July 21, 1915, he wrote both Garrison and Daniels asking them to submit programs for the proper development of the Army and Navy. He intended to present a preparedness program to Congress in his next message and characteristically wished to have his facts in good order: he asked Garrison for "a succinct plan with figures, costs, and all other details." He wrote to leaders of the Military and Naval Affairs Committees of both Houses, starting with Chairman Hay of the House Committee, and began with his usual thoroughness to lay his strategy.

Throughout his preparedness campaign the President was caught between two sets of extremists: the pacifists on the one hand, the militant preparationists on the other. For several years —until America actually entered the war—these two groups gave him a lively existence. Theodore Roosevelt and Leonard Wood led the militant group, with Roosevelt loud in his condemnation of "college sissies" and "elocution as a substitute for action." Bryan, Henry Ford, Jane Addams, Oswald Villard, and some of the most intelligent and liberal-thinking people in the country headed the pacifists, with vast numbers of lesser lights behind them. Wilson kept steadily to his middle-of-the-road course, good-humoredly listening to both sides, spending endless hours in interviews and reception of delegations; patiently trying to explain his position, keeping his temper when he was—as it often seemed, deliberately—misquoted and misunderstood.

President of the United States

At a great meeting in New York on November 4th the President put his preparedness program before the people: four hundred thousand soldier citizens to be developed within the next three years, with the National Guard used as part of the training force; our Navy speeded up and made the chief line of defense. Daniels called for a five-year building program involving the then sensational figure of $502,482,214. Today this seems ridiculous—a "shadow program," as Theodore Roosevelt called it—no preparedness at all. To millions of Americans in Wilson's time it was revolutionary. Congressman Kitchin, one of the foremost Democratic leaders, called the program "stupendous" and said that it would "shock the civilized world"!

The militarists immediately clamored for a much bigger force than that proposed by the President; compulsory military service, a fleet the equal of Great Britain's. The antipreparationists considered that the President's plan turned the country into a "militaristic nation" comparable with Germany, held mass meetings, and sent petitions from all over the country, one of them fifteen miles long. [On December 4th the Ford Peace Ship sailed for Europe confidently expecting "to have the boys out of the trenches by Christmas!"] On December 7th the President delivered his preparedness address before Congress. He asked the members to accept without curtailment the measures recommended by the Secretary of the Navy and the Secretary of War. "We cannot do less," he urged. Stony faces greeted him. Some of his listeners sincerely disagreed. To others, the 1916 Presidential campaign loomed large. Every means from now on must be used to "stop Wilson!"

Disharmony emanated from the War Department itself; Secretary Garrison differed radically from both the President and Congressman Hay on certain parts of the program. In the spring of 1916 he resigned, and Newton Baker succeeded him; but through the winter Garrison remained, pursuing a set of tactics defiantly at variance with the President's.

Pacifists—preparationists; warring powers—warring Cabinet officials; disapproving Republicans—disaffected Democrats; demands of the industrial East, growing rich on munition-making

—demands of the impoverished West and South, bitter over the throttling blockade: it was a trying and difficult period, after the Administration's brilliantly triumphant first year.

German-sympathizing Congressmen tried to stop the sale of munitions to the English. English-sympathizing Walter Page cried that we were doing "shamefully little." Hugo Münsterberg and other prominent German-born residents accused the President of partiality to the Allies, while House informed him that in France and also in England "you are accused of being definitely pro-German." And the whole country cried: "Be firm— but keep us out of war!" There was no pleasing anybody, and sometimes even Wilson's patience broke and he grew mighty tired of it all.

The months of grueling work and strain were harder because of the emptiness and desolation of the President's personal existence. "It is no exaggeration to say that he was the loneliest man in all the world," said the cousin, Helen Bones, who was with him.

"I can see the lonely figure of the President now, walking down the long hallway," says another relative, "the hair so much whitened in the last few months. . . ."

"There was an evening on the south porch when his few broken words to me about his unbearable suffering, the bleakness of his life, made me sick at heart," writes a third.

"The best thing possible for me is to stick to my task—turn my attention elsewhere," he wrote to Colonel House. And to another friend: "Every night finds me exhausted—dead in heart and body, weighed down by a leaden indifference and despair (as far as everything concerning myself is concerned). . . . God helping me, I shall regain command of myself and be fit for my duties again. For a little while it must be only a matter of exhausting will power."

Two of his daughters were married and gone to homes of their own. His eldest daughter and "Cousin Helen," who had lived with the family for several years, did their best to cheer him. But the mainspring of the home and of his life was broken.

President of the United States

Miss Bones records that she thinks he "couldn't have lived without some companion." He had few resources outside his own family. He was never a man for clubs, and though he enjoyed meeting friends who came to his home he never learned the art of meeting them outside. It was always Mrs. Wilson who, thinking they were "good for him," brought people to dinner and into the picture. He always enjoyed them after they were there.

During the long evenings after the return from Georgia he would sit on the porch of the White House with Dr. Axson, talking over his memories, recalling incidents of the early days and the happiness and struggle he and Ellen had shared together. He saw the old friends as much as he could, but the heart had gone out of him. Intensely reserved, yet intensely hungry for affection —needing it as he needed his daily food—he was like a man toiling up a steep mountain with an insufficient supply of oxygen. "Cousin Helen" herself was so much alone that Dr. Grayson worried about her also, and one day he introduced her into the home of a friend of his, Mrs. Norman Galt.

Mrs. Galt, a beautiful and highly intelligent woman, was the widow of a Washington jeweler who had been dead for about eight years, leaving her to handle his extensive business. A Virginian by birth, she had rare charm and many interests, and proved in many ways "kin" to the President's little cousin. The two became friends. Miss Bones went two or three times a week to Mrs. Galt's house during that lonely spring of 1915. They took drives together in Rock Creek Park and the lovely country around Washington.

After several months Miss Bones declared that this "one-sided hospitality" must cease. She insisted that Mrs. Galt return to the White House with her for tea one day after one of their drives. "I always come to you," she said—"you *must* come to me just this once. I assure you we shall be quite alone."

Just as they entered the White House elevator to go upstairs for their tea, the President and Dr. Grayson arrived from a round of golf. "I think you might ask us, too," said the President, reproachfully. Thus began a friendship which developed rapidly through that spring and summer, with Mrs. Galt win-

191

The Story of Woodrow Wilson

ning an ever-stronger place in the affections of the entire family. It was the President's daughters, his brother-in-law (the first Mrs. Wilson's brother, Dr. Axson), and the close friends and cousins who were keenest in encouraging the new attachment.

Early in their acquaintance the President began to send Mrs. Galt books—Wordsworth, Shelley, and his favorites Bryce and Bagehot. Soon he began to talk to her about some of the heavy problems he was facing, and to ask her opinion, which she gave very candidly. She was a businesswoman with common sense and a well-trained mind as well as an attractive personality. The President found her stimulating, "vivid," "an absolute tonic" in his lonely house. After several months of urgent pleading on his part, they became engaged.

> Something very delightful has happened to me [he wrote to Mrs. Reid on October 5, 1915]. The last fourteen months have seemed for me, in a world upset, like fourteen years. It is not the same world in which my dear Ellen lived; and one of the very last things she said to me was that she hoped that what has happened now would happen. It seemed to me incredible then, and would, I think, have continued to seem so if I had not been brought into contact with Mrs. Galt. She seemed to come into our life like a special gift from heaven, and I have found a sweet companion who will soon make me forget the intolerable loneliness and isolation of the weary months since this terrible war began.

They were married on the eighteenth of December—"barely sixteen months after his first wife's death!" barked the old ladies of both sexes.

"What'll this do to the election next November?" asked his political friends anxiously.

"Poppycock! Didn't cost him five thousand votes in the whole country," said Burleson, reminiscing after it was all over. "Didn't cost him a thousand!"

The war invaded even Wilson's honeymoon—spent at Hot Springs, Virginia. Here the President and Mrs. Wilson took long tramps in the hills and had a few days of blissful seclusion. Only a few. On December 30, 1915, the British liner *Persia* was sunk, with appalling casualties. Lansing telegraphed, "Very much alarmed." The President returned at once to Washington, faced with a serious crisis.

The entire country was on tenterhooks about the war, anxious and uncertain about the President's policy. A year ago he had assured the people that America would not become involved in the conflict. Now he was warning them to prepare for any eventuality. Senators and representatives came back to Washington that winter reflecting the nervous state of their constituents. They were disturbed about many things: the *Lusitania* case still unsettled, other ship-sinkings—half a dozen of them; the British still interfering with our commerce. The tragedy of the *Persia* put the finishing touch to this piled-up exasperation.

On January 5, 1916, an open fight was launched in the Senate, threatening Wilson's leadership. Senator Gore introduced a bill "to prohibit issuance of passports for use on the vessels of a belligerent country"—it being well known that the President opposed such a measure. Senators Lodge and Fall attacked his policy in Mexico, and some Senators demanded armed intervention—another course Wilson intensely disapproved. Finally a large number of Congressional leaders backed a motion by Representative McLemore, "virtually serving notice on the President that unless within forty-eight hours he agreed to warn American citizens that they must not take passage on belligerent armed merchant ships, the House by an overwhelming majority would issue the warning in the form of a resolution." Here was a challenge both of the President's prerogative in foreign policy, and of his very leadership of the Democratic party!

The President met the attack boldly. He wrote to the ranking member of the House Committee on Rules requesting an early vote on the Gore and McLemore resolutions so that our foreign relations might be "once more cleared of damaging misunderstandings." He had let it be known in a conference with the committees on foreign affairs of both houses that "if a German war vessel should fire upon an armed merchant vessel of the enemy on which American citizens were passengers he would

consider it his duty to hold Germany to strict accountability."
Secretary Lansing was working on a proposal for mutual concessions by the British and the Germans, involving the possible
disarmament of merchant vessels. This was a matter for diplomacy (as Senator Williams of Mississippi eloquently urged in a
stirring speech), not for hasty or clumsy legislation.

The revolt collapsed as swiftly as it began. Gore's resolution
was tabled on March 3, McLemore's on March 7. A large majority
of Democrats supported the Administration; the Republicans
divided about equally. The President triumphed. A highly successful swing-around speech-making tour had also increased his
confidence and that of Congress and the country in him. His
leadership was now secure. Preparedness legislation went steadily
ahead. On March 23rd the House passed the Hay army bill but
the National Defense Act did not go through until June.

Meantime, on March 25th came a major crisis—the torpedoing
without warning of the *Sussex*, a cross-channel ferry-boat carrying no guns. A large number of passengers lost their lives.
Lansing and House immediately urged that this should mean
war. They wanted the President to break off diplomatic relations
with Germany at once.

Wilson refused. He steadily maintained his course—to keep
the country out of war at all hazards, and give Germany one
more chance to change her tactics. But he informed Germany
that unless the Imperial German Government immediately
declares that it abandons its present method of submarine warfare against passenger and freight-carrying vessels, the Government of the United States can have no other choice but to sever
diplomatic relations with the German Empire.

On April 19th he went before Congress to ask approval of his
action. It was a moment of utmost gravity; the nation was so
close to war that it "held its breath." Hearty applause greeted
the President. A gratifying majority of Senators and Representatives supported him. From the country at large came vociferous
approval.

On April 28th Ambassador Gerard visited the Kaiser at his
field headquarters and discussed the entire war situation with

him and with the Chancellor. The Germans asked: "If we accede to your demands will the American government bring pressure to bear on Great Britain in regard to the blockade? Further, will America try to bring peace if we assent?" Gerard replied reassuringly.

Germany's final answer was terse and to the point. She agreed in future to give warning and protect lives, provided the ships did not "attempt to escape or offer resistance." She hoped that the United States would now also insist that Britain alter her blockade policy, to comply with international law. If this were not done, "the German government would then be facing a new situation in which it must reserve for itself complete liberty of decision."

The President's reply was equally blunt. He accepted the main concession—abandonment of illegal submarine policy—while asserting that the United States "could not entertain any suggestion that American rights should in any way . . . be made contingent upon the attitude or action of any other government." By this clever stroke he placed the Germans in the position of unconditional acceptance of his demands. Technically he won the victory, but the situation remained precarious.

XVIII

His mind somewhat relieved by the German pledge, Wilson now moved definitely toward the objective so dear to his heart: some international association to guarantee permanent peace for the world. Many problems pressed for his attention: shipping, defense, the Tariff Commission, conservation. Mexican relations had reached a very critical point, and the Pan-American Pact was having an uphill time. The Democratic convention—which presumably would renominate him—was barely a month away.

But more important than anything, to his mind, was this problem of a permanent international organization to keep the peace. Two years before he had said to Dr. Axson that after the war "all nations must be absorbed into some great association of nations whereby all shall guarantee the integrity of each so that any one nation violating an agreement between all of them shall bring punishment on itself automatically." In line with this conclusion and his wish to admit the Latin-American republics to partnership in the Monroe Doctrine, the President proposed to them during the period of American neutrality a draft treaty that "the High Contracting Parties to this solemn covenant and agreement do hereby join one another in common and mutual guarantees of territorial integrity and of political independence under Republican forms of government." Meanwhile Ex-President Taft and Ex-President Lowell of Harvard had been working on a scheme to extend this principle in an agreement by all the nations.

In October, 1914, Mr. Taft, speaking to a group at the Century Club in New York, declared: "The time has come when the peace-loving nations of the world should organize themselves into some sort of society in which they should agree to settle their own disputes by amiable methods and say to any nation that started to go to war, 'You have got to keep the peace or have all the rest of us against you!'"

Many other thoughtful Americans had reached this same conclusion. The movement took concrete form in a great meeting at Independence Hall in Philadelphia, June 17, 1915, where the League to Enforce Peace was organized, with over a thousand distinguished citizens and leaders from all walks of life.

Mr. Taft was elected President of the new organization, and Mr. Lowell Chairman of the Executive Committee; Mr. Theodore Marburg, Herbert Houston, Hamilton Holt, and Professor Irving Fisher took a very active part. Within a few months it had established branches all over the country. The organization did yeoman's service in the League fight for the next three years. Its platform ran as follows:

The United States should join a league of nations binding the signatories: (1) to submit all justiciable questions to an international court of justice both upon the merits and upon any issue as to its jurisdiction of the question; (2) to submit all other questions to a council of conciliation for hearing, consideration, and recommendation, and (3) jointly to use forthwith both their economic and their military forces against any member committing acts of hostility against another before submitting to arbitration or conciliation; and (4) to hold periodic conferences to formulate and codify international law.

Ex-President Roosevelt and other statesmen had been thinking along the same line. Theodore Roosevelt wrote as follows in the *Independent* on January 4, 1915:

"My proposal is that the efficient civilized nations—those that are efficient in war as well as in peace—shall join in a world league for the peace of righteousness . . . that they shall agree that all . . . questions arising between them shall be submitted to a court of arbitration and that they shall also agree to act with combined military strength of all of them against any recalcitrant nation."

A letter from Sir Edward Grey to Colonel House on the subject particularly impressed Mr. Wilson:

"My own mind," wrote the British Foreign Secretary on August 10, 1915, "revolves more and more about the point that the refusal of a Conference was the fatal step that decided peace or war last year and . . . that the pearl of great price if it can be found would be some League of Nations that could be relied on to insist that disputes between any two nations must be settled by the arbitration, mediation, or conference of others." The Powers must bind themselves, he said, to give a sanction to international law.

In another letter two weeks later Grey bluntly asked: "How much is the United States prepared to do in this direction?" Wilson answered that tremendous question at a meeting of the League to Enforce Peace, where he had agreed to speak on May 27, 1916.

On May 18th Wilson had written House, "I am thinking a great deal about the speech I am to make on the twenty-seventh. . . . I realize it may be one of the most important I shall ever be called upon to make."

It is interesting to follow the President in the preparation of one of his great speeches. He kept his notes, clippings, corre-spondence, and all related papers on each subject in confidential folders in his own study; no secretary and no member of his family was allowed to touch them. Now after almost thirty years we find them neatly filed away: for the May 27th speech, clip-pings from addresses by some of the English statesmen—Grey, Asquith, Lloyd George; editorials from American papers; ex-cerpts from an article by James Bryce in the *New Republic*: "America's Traditional Isolation"; and a specially marked edi-torial from the Baltimore *Sun* urging a conference of neutrals to offer a peace program that would, by requiring the surrender of a little independence by the great world powers, guarantee an international system of keeping the peace.

We can see him very plainly at his writing table studying these papers, setting down his thoughts first in rapid shorthand notes, then tapping these out swiftly on his typewriter. He seldom changed a word once he had written a speech. His method was to think out very clearly beforehand what he had to say and not waste time in doing any job twice over.

He believed that the American people were ready for the proposition he was about to put before them: that the experi-ences of the past two years—their hardships as neutrals, their acute fear of being forced into war now—had brought them to the point where they were ready to hear the pronouncement he had to make. He believed it represented their own deepest thought and conviction. The time had come to put much fine talk and general resolutions into political proposals for practical consideration by statesmen. Thus the great speech of May 27th came into being.

The meeting was held at the New Willard Hotel in Washing-ton, where an audience of some two thousand outstanding Americans had assembled from all over the country. Senator Lodge, at that time a strong believer in a league of nations, directly preceded the President. Lodge had spoken at various colleges and public meetings in favor of such a league, giving it as his conviction that "if we are to promote international peace at the end of the present war, if we are to restore international law as it must be restored, we must find some way in which the united forces of the nations could be put behind the cause of peace and law."

"No one can, I think, feel more deeply than I do the difficulties which confront us in the work," he said in his address at the New Willard meeting, "but the difficulties cannot be overcome unless we try to overcome them. I believe much can be done. . . . The limit of voluntary arbitration has, I think, been reached . . . the next step is . . . to put force behind international peace. . . . I do not believe that when Washington warned us against entangling alliances he meant for one moment that we should not join with other civilized nations of the world if a method could be found to diminish war and encourage peace."

The Senator little realized what trouble he was storing up for himself in the days ahead when the League of Nations was to become a partisan issue and Henry Cabot Lodge its bitterest opponent!

The President directed his talk at once to the supreme question. He was there, he said, not to discuss the program of the League to Enforce Peace but "because the desire of the whole world now turns . . . more and more eagerly towards the hope of peace, and there is just reason why we should take our part in counsel upon this great theme. . . ." As "spokesman of the United States Government" he assumed that he was expected to state that government's position.

The war in its various phases "has affected us very profoundly. . . . With its causes and its objects we are not concerned"—another unfortunate phrase which Wilson meant in a different sense from the way it was taken abroad. It was plain, however,

> that this war could have come only as it did—suddenly and out of secret counsels, without warning to the world, without discussion. . . . It is probable that if it had been foreseen just what would happen . . . those who brought the great contest on would have been glad to substitute conference for force. . . . If we ourselves had been afforded some

opportunity to apprise the belligerents of the attitude which it would be our duty to take, of the policies and practices against which we would feel bound to use all our moral and economic strength, and in certain circumstances even our physical strength also, our own contribution to the counsel which might have averted the struggle would have been considered worth weighing. . . .

The peace of the world must henceforth depend upon a new and more wholesome diplomacy. Only when the great nations of the world have reached some sort of agreement as to what they hold to be fundamental to their common interest, and as to some feasible method of acting in concert when any nation or group of nations seeks to disturb those fundamental things, can we feel that civilization is at last . . . finally established.

Leading statesmen of the world had repeatedly endorsed the necessity for such an agreement. "The nations of the world have become each other's neighbors," said the President, twenty-eight years before Dumbarton Oaks; ". . . they should agree to cooperate in a common cause." What should be the basis of this general agreement? As for America:

We believe these fundamental things: First, that every people has a right to choose the sovereignty under which they shall live. . . . Second, that the small states of the world have a right to enjoy the same respect for their sovereignty and for their territorial integrity that great and powerful nations . . . insist upon. And third, that the world has a right to be free from every disturbance of its peace that has its origin in aggression and disregard of the rights of peoples and nations.

Then comes the great declaration:

So sincerely do we believe these things that I am sure I speak the mind and wish of the people of America when I say that the United States is willing to become a partner in any feasible association of nations formed in order to realize these objects and make them secure against violation.

Applying these principles to the immediate moment:

If it should ever be our privilege to suggest or initiate a movement for peace among the nations now at war I am sure that the people of the United States would wish their government to move along these lines:

First, such a settlement with regard to their own immediate interests as the belligerents may agree upon. . . . Second, an universal association of the nations to maintain the inviolate security of the highway of the seas for the common and individual use of all the nations of the world—and to prevent any war begun either contrary to treaty covenants or without warning and full submission of the causes to the opinion of the world—a virtual guarantee of territorial integrity and political independence. . . .

God grant that the dawn of that day of frank dealing and of settled peace, concord, and co-operation may be near at hand!

The immense significance of this address was at once understood in America. According to one paper, it marked "the opening of a new period in our history and the ending of our deepest tradition. There was, of course, vigorous opposition, based on Washington's historic warning against entangling alliances. To this Wilson replied in an address delivered at Arlington on May 30, 1916:

"I shall never myself consent to an entangling alliance but I would gladly assent to a disentangling alliance—an alliance which would disentangle the peoples of the world from those combinations in which they seek their own separate . . . interests and unite the people of the world to preserve the peace of the world upon a basis of common right and justice."

American leaders had hoped European leaders would make a sympathetic response to the speech. But in Europe battle followed battle, and to peoples engrossed in the daily turmoil of war's awful events Wilson's "rhetoric" and "incredible phrases" struck an unreal, even a repellent, note.

On July 8th House wrote to Grey that "there was nothing for us to do . . . if the Allies preferred to gamble for military victory rather than accept Wilson's mediation on the basis of a league." Grey now proved curiously unresponsive. In the face of grim reality peace again seemed a far-off dream.

XIX

WHILE intent on world peace and great projects for international organization, Wilson never for an instant neglected domestic affairs or forgot the interests of the everyday man here at home. An impressive list of measures stands proof: the Rural Credits Bill, the Farm Loan Act, the Child Labor Bill, various conservation measures, the Workmen's Compensation Act, and the Adamson Act giving railroad workers an eight-hour day.

The President was always working to improve the lot of the farmer, trying to get him better prices, better interest rates, better roads and warehouses. The Farm Loan Act provided twelve land banks which reduced the cost of handling farm loans and served the farmer in a number of ways. The Agricultural Educational Extension Act brought scientific help to his farm door.

The highly controversial Adamson Act reached its climax in August, 1916, in the midst of Wilson's campaign for re-election. His chances were seriously jeopardized by the anger of the business interests because he came out with all his strength for the principle of the eight-hour day. For a time campaign contributions virtually ceased. A railroad strike threatened to tie up 250,000 miles of track and 400,000 men and dislocate the whole commercial activity of the country. The President went before Congress asking for the immediate establishment of the eight-hour day (which the men were demanding), not merely as an emergency measure "but as a permanent and necessary addition to the law of the land." The result was the Adamson bill—passed by both houses just before the strike was to begin. It was one of the most courageous acts of Wilson's career.

His veto of the Burnett immigration bill gave further proof of Wilson's fight for the common man. He believed that the tests for good citizenship should be character, industry, and natural capacity, rather than the ability to read and write a language, as the bill proposed. The bill, he said, did not take into consideration personal quality or personal fitness but merely penalized lack of opportunity, a most un-American procedure. He vetoed it twice—in 1915 and 1917—but it was finally passed over his veto.

In his work for conservation he also tried to protect the people, making many efforts to get a slow-moving Congress to act on water-power and leasing bills. Attempts to conserve the nation's oil involved another clash with powerful financial interests, and sharp disagreements within his own Cabinet. Daniels and Gregory wanted to keep the Naval Oil Reserves entirely for naval uses. Lane—hailing from California, where oil interests were powerful—favored a more lenient attitude toward private operators. He sent the President many leases of oil lands to private companies, but Wilson steadily refused to sign them. This finally (in 1920) brought about Lane's resignation, but other members of Wilson's Cabinet were profoundly grateful for this sample of the Chief's obstinacy when the Teapot Dome scandal, involving some of these very leases, broke during Harding's Administration.

With these manifold cares and problems crowding in upon him from all directions, one element in the President's life helped and inspired him: his marriage and the buoyant new companionship that came with it. The dark depression and tragic sense of loneliness which dominated him from August, 1914, until the autumn of 1915, when he became engaged, had completely vanished. A new exhilaration, a new power of concentrated effort appeared. Edith Galt brought into his life effervescent good spirits, radiance, and humor, as well as steady sympathy and devoted help with his daily work.

They rode and drove and played golf together. She went with

him on all his trips. He discussed every public question with her. Night after night she worked by his side in the White House, poring over papers, laboriously coding or decoding important messages.

The desk in the President's study contained a compartment which any woman might have considered her mortal enemy and which Mrs. Wilson has described graphically as "The Drawer." Everything for the President's immediate attention went into this drawer, and he never entered or left the room without looking into it. "Many a time when we had planned a free evening together," writes Mrs. Wilson, " 'The Drawer,' with all the problems sealed in big linen envelopes bearing an ominous red square in the corner . . . *Immediate and Important*,' would end all hope and we would settle down to work instead of to rest and read as we had hoped."

The desk in that room was a present to our Government from Queen Victoria. On it stood the green-shaded student lamp which Mr. Wilson used when he studied law at the University of Virginia. He loved to work under it.

The State Department sent over all the important reports in the form of flimsies, and the President examined every one of them, keeping a small burner at his side in which he dropped them as fast as he had finished reading. Many were the secret documents which had to be promptly destroyed. When change and relaxation were demanded he could "turn off his mind" even when heavily burdened, go to the theater, enjoy it greatly, then go back and work sometimes for hours more.

His trips on the *Mayflower* helped too. The President and Mrs. Wilson would leave Washington Friday evening or Saturday afternoon and drive down to the Navy Yard, where the yacht was always in readiness. In half an hour they were gliding smoothly down the Potomac River.

The President counted on these quiet hours on the boat to think out his most perplexing problems, and to write some of his important messages and speeches.

The daily motor ride through the country around Washington also enabled him to get away from his daily task. On these drives some friend often sat with Mrs. Wilson on the back seat while the President sat with the driver and carried on no conversation whatever, but enjoyed complete rest and relaxation. Mrs. Wilson said she never knew anyone who could drop off to sleep so quickly as the President. She firmly believes that he was able to return the salutes of passers-by without waking!

It was a mercy that he had these avenues of refreshment and escape during that strenuous spring and summer of 1916, when he carried such burdens: strikes, trouble in Mexico, battles with Congress on preparedness, the problems of the Great War, and the re-election campaign.

Wilson had not visualized a second term. "It would be a delightful relief," he told Colonel House in May, "if I could conscientiously retire." But he knew that this was impossible. "You wanted to be elected in 1912," said Burleson, "and you needed the party to nominate you. This time the party and the country need you."

Could they elect him? Wilson's spectacular record of progressive legislation, so enthusiastically approved by his own party, had roused the bitter animosity of many businessmen—especially in the East, where conservative moneyed interests felt their power challenged and their profits threatened. They disapproved his "radical" legislation only slightly more than they disliked his "patient" attitude toward the war. The tariff, the Currency Act, antitrust laws, Canal tolls repeal, the eight-hour day—all these stacked up on the debit side of the sheet with big business.

Henry Morgenthau, Sr., returning to Washington for a visit, was shocked by what seemed the very dubious prospect.

"It will take strong leadership to re-elect him," said Secretary Lane.

XX

WILSON never liked the slogan "He Kept Us Out of War." "Why at any moment," he remarked to one of his aides, "some little German lieutenant may do something that will force me to lead the nation to war!" Wilson wanted the keynote of the 1916 convention and the Democratic platform to be "Americanism," with special emphasis on the need for unity. Wilson himself wrote the platform and Newton Baker took it to the Democratic convention at St. Louis. But at the opening session Martin Glynn made an eloquent and dramatic speech stressing the theme "He Kept Us Out of War"; and Senator Ollie James, chairman of the convention, followed it with more on the same line. The Resolutions and Publicity Committees took it up and featured it. Wilson was nominated by acclamation, in a wild burst of enthusiasm.

The slogan was seized upon and very effectively promoted, but the first publicity disturbed some leading Democrats. Lansing went to the campaign manager, McCormick, in a great state of mind, remarking that if another American ship should be sunk by the Germans we might be rushed into war at any time, "and here we are declaring that Wilson has kept us out of it!"

"That does not disturb me in the least," said McCormick. "If Wilson has to declare war between now and November he will certainly be elected. Nothing can more nearly assure him the election than that."

McCormick, whom Wilson called "a steam engine in boots," was a first-rate manager and the campaign was marked by unity and harmony throughout. Naturally, it was an easier campaign in many respects than that of 1912. The party rested on the Administration's achievements. Wilson's great program of domestic legislation had been completed; his preparedness program was under way; his ideals for the peace of America and of the world were now clearly defined.

The hard-pressed Republicans nominated Charles Evans Hughes, called by some "a whiskered Wilson," by others "a pale edition of Wilson." Mr. Hughes went about the country making campaign speeches with as much of the Wilsonian "idealism" as he could muster. The Democrats had an unusually strong campaign organization that year, especially in their publicity. Robert Woolley, an old Princeton man, had charge, with George Creel a dynamic second. A Democratic victory hinged on Wilson's ability to attract the Progressive and Independent vote. This came about through the co-operation of some former Progressive leaders, notably Bainbridge Colby, who felt intense disappointment when Colonel Roosevelt abandoned the 1916 Progressive convention.

The men who had organized that party, out of their great admiration and devotion for Theodore Roosevelt and their desire to see him continue in office, could not believe their senses when it became evident at the convention that Mr. Roosevelt (in Colby's words) was "using the party as a stalking horse for his personal ambitions with the Republicans."

"It was not Colonel Roosevelt's intention really to run as a candidate for the Progessive party," said Mr. Colby. "He was to be nominated and given a chance to develop his full strength in the Republican convention—as part of his private understanding with the Republican managers."

As the developments of the two conventions forced this bitter truth upon Colonel Roosevelt's faithful friends, the disillusion became complete. It changed Mr. Colby from an ardent Roosevelt supporter to a Wilson man. He now said publicly:

> The record of the President is a veritable claim upon all sincere Progressives which the latter cannot consistently ignore or deny. Particularly is this true since the opposition to the President proceeds from an unregenerate Republicanism which has now weathered the danger of reform, reabsorbed its most vociferous critic [Theodore Roosevelt], and abandoned itself again to rancid reaction.
>
> There they all are—the "Old Guard." See for yourself—count them: Cannon and Penrose, Smoot and Gallinger, Jim Watson, Joe Kealing, Estabrook, Rodenburg, McKinley of Illinois, Hert, McGraw, Hemenway, Crane—not to speak of others too numerous to mention; all friends of the tariff and among those "fit to govern." What business has a Progressive in such company?
>
> They are the pickets and mentors of privilege. Hughes is only their decoy and retriever. If he were elected they would

rope him and tie him as they did when he was Governor at Albany, reducing him to pliant futility.

Colby took the stump for Wilson in an intensive tour of the Western States, covering key towns in Michigan, Iowa, Nebraska, and along the Pacific Coast, giving a succession of effective speeches. The election returns indicated that the Progressive vote in the Middle and Far Western States had turned the tide. As a New York *Times* headline of November 11th put it: "Progressives Cost Hughes Election."

It was rather ironic that T. R., who hated Wilson so bitterly, should have been the one whose action swung the vote that actually elected him: a bit of unexpected humor which the former Progressive leader could scarcely be expected to enjoy. He lost all round, for in the end the Republican party turned him down hard, turned down his friends Leonard Wood and Cabot Lodge also, and nominated Hughes.

Hughes did an immense amount of campaigning. Wilson was opposed to doing much, if any. He thought he should stay at his work in Washington. "The people want the President at a time like this to stay on his job," he told McCormick. "Let Hughes run about the country making speeches if he wishes to."

Wilson finally agreed, however, to speak at Omaha, Chicago, and three or four other cities. His growth in power and leadership during those turbulent four years in office made a deep impression on the people. Tempestuous applause greeted him wherever he went. As Thomas Edison said, "if he has blundered, he usually blundered *forward*."

The Republicans were hard put to it to meet all this Democratic prestige. Since they had so few real issues, they fell back on that familiar last resort—a whispering campaign against the President's private life. Certain women in Chicago would call other women on the telephone and repeat stories about Wilson's old friend Mrs. Peck, later Mrs. Hulburt, whom the entire Wilson family had visited for a month at Bermuda and who had several times visited them. The slander-spreading was all done secretly and anonymously and could not be met in the open.

One of the best answers to Mr. Wilson's attackers came from a newspaper reporter and staunch friend of the President's who made this quiet reply to the scurrilous charges launched at one dinner table: "If you can furnish proof of the statement you have just made, sir, surely you are wasting your time to make it here. Mr. William Randolph Hearst and half a dozen other people would gladly pay you twenty-five thousand dollars for proof of the charge you have just proffered." Needless to say, a sudden silence followed. Proof was never forthcoming because there was no proof.

Possibly the best answers of all appear in the letters that passed between the President and his friend Mrs. Peck, bubbling over with adoration of his wife and family, showing his complete absorption in them and dependence on them.

"There is nothing in any letters I ever wrote," said the President, "that I am ashamed to have published."

Wilson liked brilliant women, enjoyed and depended on their friendship. His letters to Mrs. Reid and Mrs. Bird, Baltimore friends of his Johns Hopkins days, and to Mrs. Toy all show this same kind of dependence. His daughters tell of it. He relied on friendship more than most men; craved the understanding ear, the sympathetic response to his eager outflow of ideas, as a person with great powers of expression naturally does. Writing letters to a friend was his greatest source of relaxation and pleasure. He wrote thousands of them, many to women. Furtiveness, underhandedness, intrigue of any sort was simply not in the nature of the man. "Ask anyone who knows me," was his sole reply to the scandalmongers. Even his old enemies at Princeton, some of the men who had opposed him most bitterly, called those stories about Wilson "ridiculous."

Toward the end of the campaign attacks of every sort became more virulent. Many powerful papers supported Mr. Wilson. Many outstanding personalities had come out in his favor—Ida Tarbell, Jane Addams, Samuel Gompers, Thomas Edison. But his chances of election were by no means sure. The opposition was powerful—and rich. Contributions of the Republican campaign fund totaled $2,445,421. The Democratic campaign fund totaled $1,564,549. It was "anything to beat Wilson." The betting in Wall Street was 10 to 8½ in favor of Hughes.

As the day of decision drew near and things looked exceedingly uncertain, Wilson took a step unique in American history. Before going off to Princeton to vote he sent a letter to Secretary Lansing. If Hughes should be elected Wilson proposed to resign immediately. "I would ask your permission to invite Mr. Hughes to become Secretary of State," he wrote Lansing, "and would then join the Vice-President in resigning," thus opening to Mr. Hughes the immediate succession to the Presidency. The new regime could then at once take over leadership in the field of foreign affairs.

"The choice of policy in respect of our foreign relations," wrote the President, "rests with the Executive. No such critical circumstances in regard to our foreign relations have ever before existed. It would be my duty to step aside so that there would be no doubt in any quarter how that policy was to be directed." This from the man who, Senator Lodge tells us, "thought only of himself," who was "first, last, and always *for Wilson*." Lansing, who was no great Wilson devotee, says in his *Memoirs*: "The letter shows very clearly that Woodrow Wilson had first in mind the welfare of the United States and the purpose to conform to the will of the American people at once without waiting for his presidential term to expire. He did not think of himself but of his country. . . ."

When Election Day came Wilson was the calmest, least concerned person in the land. He played golf after voting, joked and talked nonsense with his worried family. At night, when the whole nation was tense and doubtful about the outcome, he went to bed at ten o'clock and slept soundly.

Some of the family stayed up all night to get the returns, keeping watch with a profoundly gloomy Tumulty. In the morning reports came that Wilson was defeated. It seemed not to disturb him a particle. He went about his tasks for the day, discussed all the things he had wanted to do for a long time, as soon as he should be "a free man" again—that is, out of the Presidency. He was by far the most cheerful person in the house.

That night he and Mrs. Wilson were going to Williamstown for the christening of the President's second grandchild. They took the yacht to Rhinecliff, New York, rising early next morning to change to a train. In the meantime the California returns turned the tide in favor of Mr. Wilson. They were both surprised when the trainmen rushed up to congratulate him on the platform.

"But why do you congratulate a defeated man?" asked the President.

"You are not defeated, you are elected," said the trainmen.

Thus Wilson learned of his election to a second term in the Presidency.

XXI

THE re-election seems . . . to impose an additional responsibility upon me and I am not at all sure I can rise to it. I only know I shall try with all my might." Thus wrote Wilson to a member of his family on November 16, 1916.

He returned directly from Williamstown to Washington, arriving on the evening of November 12th. The excitement and strain of the campaign over, the President now turned to a mass of accumulated affairs. Many important matters awaited his attention: correspondence, new appointments, diplomats to be received, the preparation of his annual message to Congress.

"I have piles of papers around me so high that I am invisible below the eyes," he wrote to Senator Stone.

He had hoped that when the election had given him his new "mandate from the people" his worries in regard to the war would be considerably lighter. But these hopes did not materialize. The Germans in evident preparation to renew their submarine warfare had sunk two more ships. The overthrow of the Asquith Government and the coming to power of Lloyd

George had committed Britain to the policy of the "knockout blow." America clearly was headed for more serious trouble unless the President could win some response for his peace efforts.

Wilson was convinced that he must launch a powerful new peace move. His proposals for a league of nations were too vague—too much in the future. Something more specific for the immediate situation was necessary. He began to work on a note to the belligerent powers.

Meantime a new financial crisis with the Allies was developing. They had already liquidated two billion dollars' worth of their American securities in our country. During two years we had accumulated one third of the entire supply of gold in the world—and the trend continued sharply upward. In November the British were reaching the end of their ready resources. Early that month Lloyd George had written a memorandum stating that the British would need to spend nearly ten million dollars a day for every working day of their purchases in America. They now asked for an unsecured loan—backed by government credit only.

New York bankers looked askance at such loans, but they knew that if the British were not thus financed their purchases in America would swiftly decline—with demoralizing effects on American industry. Our economy was now much more deeply enmeshed with Allied expenditures than during the similar crisis of the previous year.

The house of Morgan drew up a plan for "renewable short-term treasury notes" for the British and French governments. This did not please the Federal Reserve Board because, being renewable, the notes were not really short-term; and being treasury notes they were not really secured. Wilson conferred with W. P. G. Harding, Governor of the Board, and agreed that our bankers and private investors must be warned against investing in such unsecured loans. If the Allies wanted loans they must put up for collateral the "hundreds of millions of our own and foreign securities which they still held." American finance must remain strong to meet the needs of the world after the war, and the needs of our own people.

President of the United States

The British then altered their request. They asked that no treasury notes be issued, and agreed to ship gold to pay for their purchases and to borrow on secured loans only. But this solved the problem only temporarily. The British could not go on indefinitely spending $10,000,000 a day for American goods. What would happen when their gold and securities were gone? What would happen to the economic structure of the United States—grown so dependent on their purchases?

Our own people might go bankrupt in large numbers unless peace came quickly, or unless America entered the war. Wilson fought both the emotional and the economic pressures which seemed to be driving us relentlessly in that direction.

He worked early and late on his note—in its original form one of the strongest documents he ever wrote. After conferences with House and Lansing he toned it down—perceiving that if he asked for too much probably he would get nothing. In the midst of his labors the arrival of an unexpected peace proposal from Germany herself caused him some embarrassment. The German generals had won some victories and manoeuvred their side into a good position; now they wanted to talk peace. They indicated some of their conditions in a characteristic note—tactless, truculent. Wilson transmitted the note with the best grace he could to the Allies—who rejected it furiously. On December 18th he finally dispatched his own note to the Powers.

He pointed out that "the objects which the statesmen of the belligerents on both sides have in mind in this war are virtually the same, as stated in general terms to their own people and to the world. Each desires to make the rights and privileges of weak peoples . . . secure against aggression. . . . Each wishes itself to be made secure in the future, along with all other nations and peoples against the recurrence of wars like this. . . . Each is ready to consider the formation of a league of nations to insure peace and justice throughout the world."

He said he was not offering mediation or proposing peace, but hoped his communication might bring about an exchange of views which then might lead to a conference. He "would be happy himself to serve or even to take the initiative in its accomplishment." The United States, he stressed, had "a vital interest" in the ending of the war, "lest the situation . . . be rendered altogether intolerable"—that is, lest she herself be forced to enter the conflict.

The note was not too cordially received in Europe. British statesmen could not understand the President's attitude. Could it be possible that he still did not understand what the war was being fought for? To France, with the enemy fighting and looting on her own soil, talk of peace was anathema and Wilson a visionary dreamer. The Germans with a sanguine Admiralty painting rosy pictures of an early victory via the submarine, tended more and more to snap their fingers at "Wilson's ridiculous peace proposals."

Christmas that year brought a happy family day for the President—carols, presents, relatives gathered together—good talk, games. His 60th birthday followed three days later. It found him in a not particularly cheerful frame of mind.

On December 27th came the German reply to his note requesting peace terms—arrogant and discouraging. It was only "after the present conflict was ended by victorious Germany and her enemies that the Imperial German Government would be willing to cooperate with the United States in the sublime task of preventing future wars."

The Allied reply had not yet appeared. Every day the prospect for realizing his hope for peace diminished. His heart was heavy as he approached a New Year shrouded in threatening storm clouds.

XXII

WHEN everything else failed Wilson appealed to the people. Again and again during his life he tried this method. He believed profoundly in everyday men and women, in their natural instinct for what was right and just. He believed that if they could be informed they would understand his purpose and stand behind him. And almost invariably they did. He went to them in that January of 1917 when all other efforts seemed futile.

The results of his last public address had not been reassuring. Theodore Roosevelt was attacking him violently in magazine articles and climbing down from his former support of a league of nations. Lodge echoed Roosevelt. In the Senate a fierce debate had developed, following a resolution by Senator Hitchcock to back the President's peace note. The fight foreshadowed the greater struggle to come.

Wilson's proposal for a league "to insure peace and justice throughout the world" roused hot controversy: the idea of America entering a world alliance for collective security! Senator Lodge declared that the Hitchcock resolution "projects Congress into the field of European politics and involves us in the affairs of Europe." Borah contended that it would put the American Army and Navy behind every small European nation, "placing us in the storm-center of European politics"; the advice of Washington and Jefferson would be abandoned and the Monroe Doctrine destroyed.

The vote on Senator Hitchcock's thrice-amended resolution revealed a formidable opposition to the President's peace policy. The final resolution approved only that part of Wilson's note which requested discussion of peace terms.

On January 10th came the Allied reply to the note. It was no more encouraging than that of the Germans, though it was more explicit as to terms. Both belligerents scorned negotiations. Both insisted on victory and a dictated peace. All the more reason why the President determined to come before the people of the world. If he could not make the governments understand his arguments perhaps the people would.

The result of this decision was an address which the British philosopher Lowes Dickinson called "perhaps the most important international document of all history" and of which Dr. Edwin Alderman, President of the University of Virginia, said: "No greater state paper . . . exists in the records of modern states."

The President made this address before the Senate on January 22, 1917, at one o'clock in the afternoon, confronting men of two camps—the one strongly for, the other powerfully against, his peace policies.

"On the eighteenth of December last," he reminded them, "I addressed an identic note to the Governments of the Nations now at war," speaking "on behalf of humanity and of the rights of all neutral nations" and requesting them to state their peace terms. The replies of the Powers had brought us "that much nearer the discussion of the international concert which must thereafter hold the world at peace."

> In every discussion of the peace that must end this war it is taken for granted that that peace must be followed by some definite concert of power which will make it virtually impossible that any such catastrophe should ever overwhelm us again. . . . It is inconceivable that the people of the United States should play no part in that great enterprise. . . . It is right that . . . this Government should frankly formulate the conditions upon which it would feel justified in asking our people to approve its formal and solemn adherence to a League for Peace. I am here to state those conditions. . . .
>
> It will be absolutely necessary that a force be created as a guarantor of the permanency of the settlement so much greater than the force of any nation now engaged or any alliance hitherto formed or projected that no nation, no probable combination of nations could . . . withstand it. If the peace presently to be made is to endure it must be a peace made secure by the organized major force of mankind. . . .
>
> Only a tranquil Europe can be a stable Europe. There must be, not a balance of power but a community of power; not organized rivalries, but an organized common peace.
>
> The statesmen of both . . . groups of nations . . . have said . . . that it was no part of the purpose they had in mind . . . to crush their antagonists.

This implies, continued the President, "a peace without victory," which, he admitted, was "not pleasant to say." But "victory

would mean peace forced upon the loser . . . accepted under
duress," leaving "a bitter memory upon which terms of peace
would rest not permanently but only as upon quicksand."

The right state of mind, the right feeling between nations,
is as necessary for lasting peace as is the just settlement of
vexed questions of territory. . . .

The guarantees exchanged must neither recognize nor
imply a difference between big nations and small, between
those that are powerful and those that are weak. Right
must be based upon the common strength, not upon the individual strength of the nations upon whose concert peace
will depend.

No peace can last . . . which does not recognize and
accept the principle that governments derive all their just
powers from the consent of the governed, and that no right
anywhere exists to hand peoples about from sovereignty to
sovereignty as if they were property. . . .

Every great people . . . should be assured of a direct outlet to the great highways of the sea . . . no nation need be
shut away from free access to the open paths of the world's
commerce. . . .

It is a problem closely connected with the limitation of
naval armaments and the limitation of armies and of all
programs of military preparation. Difficult and delicate as
these questions are, they must be faced with the utmost
candor and decided in a spirit of real accommodation if
peace is to come . . . and come to stay. . . .

It is clear to every man who can think that there is in this
promise no breach in either our traditions or our policy as a
nation, but a fulfillment, rather, of all that we have professed or striven for.

I am proposing, as it were, that the nations adopt the
doctrine of President Monroe as the doctrine of the world:
that no nation should seek to extend its polity over any
other nation or people, but that every people should be
left free to determine its own polity, its own way of de-

velopment, unhindered, unthreatened, unafraid, the little along with the great and powerful.

I am proposing that all nations henceforth avoid entangling alliances which would draw them into competitions of power. . . . There is no entangling alliance in a concert of power. . . .

I am proposing government by the consent of the governed . . . freedom of the seas . . . and that moderation of armaments which makes of armies and navies a power for order merely, not an instrument of aggression or of selfish violence.

These are American principles, American policies. . . . They are the principles of mankind and must prevail.

This address gave Woodrow Wilson moral leadership of the world. Here as in many of his great public utterances he seemed to have reflected the mind of the masses and uttered the thoughts and deepest inarticulate longings of the people themselves. "I would fain believe," he himself declared, "that I am speaking for the silent mass of mankind everywhere who have as yet had no place or opportunity to speak their real hearts out concerning the death and ruin they see to have come already upon the persons and the homes they hold most dear. . . . I hope and believe that I am speaking for liberals and friends of humanity in every nation."

European governments received the address with small enthusiasm. That phrase "peace without victory"—what an idea to fling before nations who for two and a half agonizing years had poured out their blood and treasure, given the flower of their young manhood, to win a victory! Some liberals in England sympathized; so did a certain section of the French Socialists, and the Russian Foreign Office. But most government officials abroad felt deep resentment.

Germany considered the speech "no step in the direction of a peace acceptable to us." "The British," wrote House, "consider it inconsistent for us to want to let Germany go free from punishment for breaking the very rules we wish to lay down for the future."

Letters and telegrams poured in from every corner of America —some faultfinding, most of them enthusiastic. Wilson took both the praise and the blame calmly. "I think it ought to have been said, no matter what comes of it," was his own final summing up.

He had directed his address to the peoples of the countries at war. He hoped that a great body of public opinion would form behind it, but he did not want any particular plan formulated at that time. "I have purposely put forth only the idea, the principle, with the feeling that it could be best advanced by leaving the whole question of organization and detail to the international conference which I hope will someday meet to determine the ways and means of concerted action in the support of peace. If we leave this field clear we can hope for such an ultimate acceptance of the idea as will create the most favorable possible atmosphere."

Meanwhile the German Government had taken a decision spelling failure for every peace effort. On January 31st, nine days after Wilson's appeal, Germany's formal answer was received: a declaration of unrestricted submarine warfare.

XXIII

THE President was writing in his office when the first news came, in the form of an Associated Press bulletin over the telephone. His secretary took it to him immediately.

As he read, Mr. Tumulty said, you could see in his face first amazement, then incredulity, finally gravity and sternness— "compression of the lips, locking of the jaw, which always meant with him supreme resolution."

Later in the day the German Ambassador presented the official communication at the State Department, but the worst shock came with that first reading of the message: "Germany will meet the illegal measures of her enemies by forcibly preventing after

The Story of Woodrow Wilson

February 1, 1917, in a zone around Great Britain, France, Italy, and Eastern Mediterranean all navigation, that of neutrals included. . . . All ships met within that zone will be sunk."

The President looked up from the ominous bit of paper.

"This," he said heavily, "means war!"

The break he had tried so hard to prevent had come, barely a week after his passionate appeal to the people. But the decision had actually been made at German military headquarters three weeks before. Bernstorff had pleaded with his Government that war would be unavoidable if such a course were followed. But the German leaders scorned American military power and went ahead.

Admiral von Capelle said: "I consider . . . the assistance of the United States in the war on the side of our enemies will amount to nothing." He thought his people could win the war with their submarines before America could muster sufficient strength to become of any consequence. With all their cleverness and efficiency, the Germans in both their recent wars were wrong on the crucial item—on several crucial items.

In their note they stated that one ship per week would be permitted to sail from America to Falmouth under strict regulations as to insignia and rulings laid down by them—an additional piece of insolence calculated to infuriate the usually easy-going and peaceably-minded Americans.

Lansing favored an immediate break—indeed, a formal declaration of war. But the President, though smarting too at Germany's impudence, was thinking of what was best for the country and the world. One could fight any time.

He tried every possible loophole for avoiding war: a separate peace with Austria, which he tried without success to arrange, a joint declaration with the neutral nations, but the neutral nations refused.

He sent for the Swiss Minister, Mr. Ritter, asking whether his Government still adhered to the suggestion made on January 9th that all neutrals unite to assert their rights and lay down the basis of the peace which they were ready to support. He received an encouraging reply.

He drafted the "Bases of Peace" as a foundation for the discussion: a remarkable document, really the first outline of a league of nations constitution, with clear and definite statements on territorial guarantees, limitation of armaments, political independence, joint economic action, and so on; only to find that Herr Ritter was on close terms with von Bernstorff and that nothing constructive could be expected from that quarter.

The failure of these various moves was disheartening. The Cabinet meeting of February 2nd found Wilson still in great uncertainty of mind.

The Cabinet unanimously favored breaking relations with Germany. Even then Wilson did not finally give up. After the Cabinet meeting the President—who, according to legend, "would never confer with Senators"—went to the Senate building for a long conference with Senator Stone of the Foreign Relations Committee and with other Senators, following his custom on any grave decision. Most of the Senators favored breaking relations and believed their constituents would approve.

He reached the final decision in the quiet of his own room that evening.

On February 3rd, at two o'clock in the afternoon, the President appeared before Congress to deliver his message recommending the breaking of relations with Germany. In the same hour the German Ambassador and his staff were handed their passports.

"I refuse to believe," said the President before a tense and hushed Congress, "that it is the intention of the German authorities to do in fact what they have warned us they will feel at liberty to do. Only actual overt acts on their part can make me believe it even now." If such acts were committed in violation of law and humanity, "I shall take the liberty of coming again before the Congress, to ask that authority be given me to use any means that may be necessary for the protection of our seamen and our people."

His speech was approved throughout the country. The Senate

sanctioned it by a resolution endorsing his action; the vote was 78 to 5. The nation was in a state of tense excitement. In some cities long lines of young men already waited to enlist. The people expected war to follow at once.

Wilson held back as long and as hard as he could. The thing he had predicted happened almost immediately: the rise of the "interests." There were overtures from the United States Steel Corporation, Remington Arms, Bethlehem Steel, some of the big banking houses. Overtures from the Republicans for a "coalition government" deceived him not a particle.

He wrote Colonel House about these "Junkers of America," "trying to get in under cover of the patriotic feeling of the moment. They will not get in. . . . The nominal coalition in England is nothing but a Tory Cabinet such as they are eager to get a footing for here."

While he was casting about for some eleventh-hour solution he received a cable from Ambassador Gerard: "Suggest if you decide to make any threats, threaten war. Germans not afraid of break of diplomatic relations which simply means they can go ahead and do what they please and attack us if they win. Chancellor spoke of the great hatred the military and naval people have for America. Even if there is war German military calculate they can starve England before America can do anything. These people have only one God—Force. Gerard."

The Germans haven't changed much in twenty-five years, either in their God or in their faulty calculations about England and America.

Feeling rose throughout the country during the month of March. Germany sank 781,500 tons of vessels in February, including two American ships (with warning) and the British liner Laconia, carrying Americans—sunk without warning. Evidence of a secretly planned land attack by the Germans, plus news of subversive activities in the United States, fanned the feeling of the people to new intensity.

The press, the clergy, labor, and Socialist leaders exhibited a steadily mounting crescendo of indignation—especially the clergy.

President of the United States

"Have our ministers gone mad?" asked the President in amazement. No pagan gods were ever invoked with greater passion and fury.

Groups of all sorts were coming out for war, defense committees organizing all over the country. A few voices still called for peace, but they were a tiny minority compared with the vast volume of clamor from the other side. The majority of Congress wanted war. The dominant conviction among the people was that war was imminent, and at last desirable.

"If Germany wants war with us, she shall have it!" said the Boston *Globe*, expressing the general decision.

On February 26th, in another solemn address the President asked Congress to arm merchant ships to safeguard our rights at sea. The Republican leaders, already desiring an extra session in order not to leave a Democratic President in charge during the next critical nine months, seized the opportunity. The House voted for the bill 403 to 14. But the Senate filibustered. In that time of gravest danger to the nation, a handful of Senators rendered action impossible. Pacifists La Follette and Norris joined hands with Republican die-hards and certain disaffected Democrats within Mr. Wilson's own party.

After one of the bitterest fights in parliamentary history, seventy-five Senators signed a manifesto stating that they favored the armed ship bill but were prevented by a small minority— twelve votes—from expressing their support of the measure.

A hard-pushed President spoke sharply: "The Congress," he said, "has been unable to act either to safeguard the country or to vindicate the elementary rights of its citizens. A little group of willful men representing no opinion but their own have rendered the great Government of the United States helpless and contemptible." He declared that a special session of Congress would be useless unless the rules were so changed that vital measures might be passed.

The country was in an uproar. The "willful men" were bitterly criticized. Hot words and accusations rained from both sides. And there were darker dangers: the President received letters that threatened his life.

He rode to his second inauguration surrounded by a heavy guard of regular troops and secret-service men.

The inauguration ceremonies were of the simplest. The immediate crisis absorbed the country. People gave only cursory attention to the Inaugural Address, one of Mr. Wilson's masterpieces.

On March 12th the President gave the order to arm the ships—"all American ships sailing through barred areas." He had the power, according to the Attorney General's ruling, but, as he said in his address, would have preferred to have Congress share with him so grave a decision.

War now looked almost more certain than before.

XXIV

WILSON was by no means a pacifist, as many people charged. War in his opinion was "a crude instrument" to which nations might sometimes have to resort. Roosevelt clamored for it, Bryan opposed it. Wilson agreed with neither. One question always lay uppermost in his mind: What is the right thing to do? What action shall America take that in the long run will be best for the world and for civilization?

Many factors pressed varied claims upon him. German triumphs in the field were daily increasing. In that month of March, 1917, German victory looked very likely. If Germany won and German aggression dominated the world and the peace-making—which would mean surely another speedy war to follow —what hope was there for the just and permanent peace Wilson longed for? Might not America's immediate entrance into the war perhaps actually be the means of saving civilization?

Wilson's longing that America should make a great positive contribution towards a real and permanent peace had for a long time dominated his thinking. Lloyd George played upon this adroitly when he told Ambassador Page of his hope that America would play a leading role at the Peace Conference— where, he said, "your President's cool and patient and humane counsel will be wholesome for us all."

President of the United States

Wilson was greatly attracted by such arguments, as the canny Welshman well knew. These considerations were strongly in his mind during March as Germany's successes continued. The threat of German victory loomed large, on the one hand; his terrible responsibility for the lives of American young men, on the other.

"He said," records Lansing, "that he would be willing to bear all criticism and abuse which would surely follow [our failure to declare war] . . . that contempt was nothing unless it impaired future usefulness, and that nothing would induce him to act unless he was convinced that it was the wisest thing to do." This from the man Lodge called "timid—furtive—and out for himself alone!"

Early in March the President received via Mr. Page and the British Secret-Service Intelligence a sensational communication. The British had intercepted a note from German Foreign Minister Zimmermann to the Government of Mexico, offering in case of war with the United States to make an alliance with Mexico with "an understanding on the part of the German Government that Mexico is to reconquer Texas, New Mexico, and other territory." Japan also was asked to join the pact.

This note, which Zimmermann openly admitted to be authentic, completed the President's disillusionment. He now saw the German Government's real sentiments and intentions towards this country and began to realize, however reluctantly, that there was probably no escape from war.

March 15th brought another astounding piece of news: the abdication of the Czar and the "bloodless revolution" in Russia. This was hailed in America as a tremendous event—the abolishing of the only autocratic government among the Allies. There was now a clear road ahead for the democracies to pull together for a real new order. Wilson gave orders at once to recognize the new democracy—America being the first nation to do so. This of course laid him open to the charge of being a "Redsympathizer." Charges were plentiful just then.

Since the Zimmermann note people were clamoring for action

on the part of our Government. The President shut himself up in his room for days to battle it out with his stern Scot's conscience. While others glibly declared that "we should go in at once—teach those Huns a lesson—American honor must be avenged," he could not get those lines of uniformed young men out of his head. The White House diaries record again and again of this period: "The President remained alone in his room."

His advisers awaited with anxiety the outcome of these lonely vigils. On Tuesday, March 20th, the Cabinet met for a three-hour discussion. Each member declared his conviction that war was inevitable and each thought that Congress should be convened before April 16th. Cabinet officials left the meeting with solemn faces.

On March 21st the President summoned Congress to meet in extra session on April 2nd, "to consider grave questions of national policy."

Even after he had completed his war message he was so overwhelmed that he sent for Frank Cobb of the New York *World,* a trusted friend of honest mind and shrewd judgment with whom he could talk. Cobb reached the White House at one o'clock in the morning. He records:

> The "old man" was waiting for me, sitting with his typewriter on his table where he used to type his own messages. I'd never seen him so worn down. He looked as if he hadn't slept, and he said he hadn't. He said he was probably going before Congress the next day to ask a declaration of war, and he'd never been so uncertain about anything in his life as about that decision.
>
> He said he'd been lying awake nights going over the whole situation—he said he couldn't see any alternative, that he had tried in every way he knew to avoid war.
>
> "I think I know what war means," he said. "Is there anything else I can do?"
>
> I told him his hand had been forced by Germany—that so far as I could see we couldn't keep out.

"Yes, but do you know what that means?" he asked.

He said war would overturn the world we had known—that so long as we remained out there was a preponderance of neutrality but that if we joined with the Allies the world would be off the peace basis and onto a war basis.

He said when a war got going it was just war and there weren't two kinds of it. . . . To fight you must be brutal and ruthless, and the spirit of ruthless brutality will enter into the very fibre of our national life. . . .

W. W. was uncanny that night. He had the whole panorama in his mind. He said that so far as he knew he had "considered every loophole of escape and as fast as they were discovered Germany deliberately blocked them with some new outrage. . . .

"If there's any alternative, for God's sake, let's take it!" he exclaimed.

Cobb couldn't see any and told him so. The fateful day of April 2nd was even then dawning.

The President delivered his message to Congress at eight-thirty in the evening. Dense crowds greeted him as he reached the Capitol. Troops were standing on guard round the entire building, which stood out white and majestic in the indirect lighting, used on this eventful night for the first time.

The House of Representatives was packed to capacity. Every seat in the galleries was taken, but the crowd was so still you could almost hear them breathing. In the front seats on the floor sat the Vice-President and the Cabinet, the Justices of the Supreme Court in their black gowns, and to one side the diplomatic corps; behind them the Senators and Representatives of the people. Mrs. Wilson and the ladies of the Cabinet were among the throng in the galleries. Everyone waited, tense and hushed.

Then the announcement that brought all to their feet: "The President of the United States!"

The applause as he entered was the greatest Wilson had ever received in that historic room.

The Story of Woodrow Wilson

He took his place at the rostrum, grave and very pale. His voice was low and showed his emotion, as he began sternly to outline the solemn crisis that confronted the nation. The simple record was indictment enough of German brutality: unarmed ships sent to the bottom without warning, and with no mercy for civilian passengers; "even hospital ships and ships carrying relief to the sorely bereaved and stricken people of Belgium."

"German submarine warfare . . . is a warfare against . . . all nations. The challenge is to all mankind. Each nation must decide for itself how it will meet it. We must put excited feeling away. Our motive will not be revenge."

But "there is one choice," declared the President, "we cannot make, we are incapable of making: we will not choose the path of submission and suffer the most sacred rights of our nation and our people to be ignored or violated."

At this point Chief Justice White—an old Confederate soldier —rose to his feet and cheered. House, Senate, and galleries followed him with a unanimous roar. Wilson's voice grew clearer now and more firm.

> With a profound sense of the solemn and even tragical character of the step I am taking and of the grave responsibilities which it involves . . . I advise that the Congress declare the recent course of the Imperial German Government to be in fact nothing less than war against the Government and people of the United States; that it formally accept the status of belligerent which has thus been thrust upon it; and that it take immediate steps not only to put the country in a more thorough state of defense but also to exert all its power and employ all its resources to bring the Government of the German Empire to terms and to end the war. . . .

> Our object . . . is to vindicate the principles of peace and justice in the life of the world as against selfish and autocratic power and to set up amongst the really free and self-governed peoples of the world such a concert of pur-

pose and of action as will henceforth ensure the observance of those principles. . . . We are at the beginning of an age in which it will be insisted that the same standards of conduct and of responsibility for wrong done shall be observed among nations as are observed among the individual citizens of civilized states."

We had no quarrel with the German people. But the present German government—the Prussian autocracy—had proved a foe to liberty and to the United States. Its members showed by their continued plots and subversive efforts that they meant to act against our peace and security. The whole force of the nation, if necessary, must be spent to check them.

We are glad, now that we see the facts with no veil of false pretense about them, to fight thus for the ultimate peace of the world and for the liberation of its peoples, the German peoples included; for the rights of nations great and small, and the privilege of men everywhere to choose their way of life and of obedience. The world must be made safe for democracy. Its peace must be planted upon the tested foundations of political liberty.

Finally came the irrevocable moment. His voice took on a deeper solemnity:

It is a fearful thing to lead this great peaceful people into war, into the most terrible and disastrous of all wars, civilization itself seeming to be in the balance.

But the right is more precious than peace, and we shall fight for the things which we have always carried nearest to our hearts,—for democracy, for the right of those who submit to authority to have a voice in their own Governments, for the rights and liberties of small nations, for a universal dominion of right by such a concert of free peoples as shall bring peace and safety to all nations, and make the world itself at last free.

The Story of Woodrow Wilson

To such a task we can dedicate our lives and our fortunes, everything that we are and everything that we have, with the pride of those who know that the day has come when America is privileged to spend her blood and her might for the principles that gave her birth and happiness and the peace which she has treasured. God helping her, she can do no other!

CHAPTER IV

WAR

LEADER

I

ONCE war was actually declared, the whole country—Republicans, political opponents, even Senator Lodge—rallied solidly behind the President. The nation confronted a stupendous task. Today we have become accustomed to thinking in world terms, to moving and planning on a world scale. In those days it was something entirely new.

"The enterprise," said one of the President's oldest friends, Dr. Edwin Alderman, "of converting American energies into war energies, the transforming of the American spirit and philosophy into a war spirit and philosophy, the actual throwing across three thousand miles of sea resources, men, money, and resolution, takes rank among the greatest practical enterprises of mankind."

It can be done expertly now because it was done so well then—and for the first time.

For months the President had been studying potential organization for this emergency. War changed the normal processes of democratic government. If he were to place the control of industries in the hands of Cabinet officers the normal affairs of the Government would be overwhelmed by war activities and at the close of the war it would be difficult to deflate them properly. He had noticed, he said to one Cabinet member dryly, "an extreme reluctance on the part of government departments to relinquish any powers which had once been granted them!" But temporary outside organizations could be abolished immediately at the war's end without interfering with the normal functioning of democratic processes.

Wilson accordingly created four new agencies to meet four essential demands: Food, Fuel, Shipping, War Industries. Mr. Bernard M. Baruch was made head of the War Industries Board, "to act as the general eye of all supply departments in the field of industry"; Edward M. Hurley was made head of the Shipping Board; Herbert Hoover headed the Food Commission; Harry Garfield, son of the former President, the Commission on Fuel. These men rapidly organized their several departments and attained a high degree of efficiency in an amazingly short time. "Dollar-a-year men"—also called into service now for the first time—dropped everything and came on call from all over the land.

The President's own duties were doubled. With the country at war, avalanches of people descended upon the White House, each one with an apparently good and legitimate reason for seeing him. Delegations and special bodies of all sorts clamored for "just a few moments" of his time. Complicated new problems had to be worked out: the draft, conscientious objectors, financial questions, transport and servicing.

The formidable array of foreign Commissioners began to arrive, each with his special problems and demands. First to come was British Commissioner Mr. Balfour. Next, Marshal Joffre and Mr. Viviani of France. The Italian, Belgian, Russian, and Japanese missions followed.

Most of these people had endured years of hardship in a war which they were threatened with losing. But the entrance of the United States, with its great reserve of men and supplies, gave them new hope. The President and Mrs. Wilson felt it an important part of their own work to see and encourage the Commissioners as much as they could, at private meetings at the White House as well as in public.

The most acute early problem of the war was Colonel Roosevelt. On February 2nd—two months before America entered the war, but when the break with Germany made war almost inevitable—Mr. Roosevelt wrote the Secretary of War requesting permission to raise a division of infantry and a divisional brigade of cavalry, which he would command in France. Mr. Baker replied, pointing out that the enlistment of such divisions was expressly prohibited by Congress unless directly sanctioned and stated that "a plan for a very much larger army than the force suggested by your telegram has been proposed for the action of Congress whenever requested."

The plan referred to, of course, was the project for compulsory military service and the Selective Draft. The President, Mr. Baker, the entire Cabinet, and the General Staff were firmly resolved that the wastes and inefficiencies of the volunteer system should not be permitted to diminish America's fighting strength. Strong resistance to the draft developed in Congress, which urged that the volunteer system be given a fair test before the introduction of conscription as a last measure. The President and the General Staff held firm. On April 29th the selective service bill passed the House, after bitter debate.

On April 11th, Mr. Roosevelt went to Washington and saw the President personally, to urge acceptance of his project. Here was a dramatic moment—the dynamic and virile Rough Rider who had occupied that Executive Chair himself, coming back to his onetime office to face across his onetime desk the quiet but in his way equally dynamic ex-President of Princeton, and victor over the New Jersey bosses. It seemed not to trouble Mr. Roosevelt in the least that he had for the past five years scathingly attacked the man of whom he now asked a favor. He emerged from the interview in high good humor and told newspaper reporters that the President had received him with utmost courtesy and consideration. Would that Mr. Roosevelt had taken a leaf from the President's book.

The President had great personal sympathy with Mr. Roosevelt's desire to lead some divisions to France. He expressed to several friends and relatives the sincere wish that he might grant the request and allow him to go. But several considerations, in addition to the projected Draft, compelled him to decide otherwise.

The battle over the Draft had now moved to the Senate Chamber. Here, Lodge, Harding, Penrose, and Weeks succeeded in putting through an amendment to give Mr. Roosevelt the right to raise four volunteer divisions. The House refused to concur in the amendment, a deadlock resulted, and for two weeks this single question paralyzed the war effort of the nation. On May 15th a compromise was reached. The Senate agreed to make it optional with the President to accept or reject the four volunteer divisions offered by Mr. Roosevelt. This of course put the President in a very difficult position. If he refused he would be accused of partisan politics and lack of personal magnanimity. If he consented he would seriously embarrass his generals in the field.

The final decision rested with Secretary Baker. He believed that it would be a tragic mistake to entrust the lives of American soldiers to a man as unqualified as Colonel Roosevelt. The latter's experience had been in an old-fashioned war of twenty years before—child's play compared with the highly technical, scientific warfare of 1917. He would constantly have embarrassed General Pershing, not only by his personal characteristics but by his actual lack of knowledge. It would have caused no end of embarrassment to have an ex-President in the capacity of subordinate commander—particularly an ex-President with the explosive temperament of Mr. Roosevelt. His offer was refused, and he became more rabidly anti-Wilson than ever.

An interesting story in connection with this drama has come from an eminent American artist via several people to whom he told it. This artist was a great friend of Roosevelt's. He had spent a large part of his life in France, where he had become a close friend of one of the members of the Joffre Commission, which had come on a visit to President Wilson. Roosevelt talked over his project with this friend and got him to act as a kind of private ambassador to raise the issue with the French Commissioners.

The artist took up the matter with the Frenchmen and was astonished to find that they were all intensely opposed to it. They said the French would consider it a mere political gesture —a "flash in the pan." What they wanted was not a few regiments but a part of the American Army in Paris, indicating the serious determination of the American Government to come to the support of the Allied cause. This message, brought back to Colonel Roosevelt, did not improve his wounded ego or soften his mounting rancor towards the President.

The matter of General Leonard Wood's not being sent to France also produced intense bitterness in Rooseveltian and Republican circles and was laid at the President's door. Actually, the military men themselves made that decision.

II

THE Wilson family joined in all the wartime activities and voluntary sacrifices of the rest of the nation. Mrs. Wilson got out her sewing machine, which the girls had teased her about taking to the White House, and she and her secretary and the President's Cousin Helen made one of the thousands of Red Cross units daily doing their stint of sewing and bandage-rolling. The White House observed meatless days and wheatless days like everybody else. Early in the war Mrs. Wilson and the wives of Cabinet members set themselves a pledge "to reduce living to its simplest form . . . to omit the usual entertaining . . . to enable us to give more time and money to . . . preparedness and relief work, to buy simple clothing and food . . . and to do everything in our power . . . to hasten the end of the struggle and win the war." They asked all the women of the nation to join with them.

The Story of Woodrow Wilson

Many people started wartime gardens, the Government giving and plowing the ground for any citizen who volunteered to grow vegetables. The Potomac Drive in those days proudly displayed not cherry blossoms but a huge truck garden. Man power was a crucial factor, so to release the White House gardeners the Wilsons bought eight sheep to eat the grass. The sheep prospered and multiplied, and when shearingtime came their wool was given to the Red Cross and auctioned off as "White House wool" to the different States. It brought the Red Cross nearly one hundred thousand dollars.

On September 1st a request from the Fuel Administrator to conserve gasoline brought a Presidential plea for gasless Sundays. The following Sunday the President and his wife set forth to church, Mrs. Wilson records, "in an ancient victoria found in the White House stables and hastily polished up. For the Secret Service an old-time surrey with fringe around the top was discovered. The two smartly uniformed motorcycle policemen who since the war had been detailed to escort the President were mounted on bicycles." Churchgoers stared at the quaint procession weaving through the streets of Washington, then when they saw who it was greeted them with warm enthusiasm.

Both President and people settled down to the wartime schedule with amazing ease and rapidity. The weekly meetings of the War Cabinet resembled conferences of executives of large corporations reporting on the progress of their work to their President and submitting ways and means of carrying on. Several of the members said that they had never seen a group that worked together so harmoniously and effectively.

Each man had a supertask to perform: War—Navy—Finance —Industries—Food—Fuel—Ships: all interwoven with each other and directly affecting the daily lives of our people at home as well as the people in most of the countries of Europe. According to the men who took part in these meetings, the President always acted promptly; he never hesitated to assume full responsibility in any matter on which he was asked for an opinion. "He showed remarkable knowledge of American business problems," said one of the businessmen on the War Cabinet, "making valuable suggestions that were most helpful."

And Mr. Edward Hurley said that in the course of thirty years' business experience he had never met a man with more acute business sense and practical knowledge than President Wilson.

He seemed also to have an uncanny grasp of what the people of the country would think of each new war policy in which he had to ask them to make personal sacrifices; and whenever he made an appeal for their support they confirmed his faith in them. No doubt this led to his strong confidence in them for support in his League of Nations plans later.

One advantage of the American system of government, though it came in for a good deal of criticism during Mr. Wilson's life, was the unified command under one leader for the war's duration. "When we take into consideration the frequent changes in administrations and war officials by Great Britain and France and the other Allies during the war," says one of President Wilson's associates, "and the trying times they experienced in struggling to create a permanent constructive and workable war organization, I believe that our strength was in having a centralized control under one Commander-in-Chief. Individually we made many mistakes under war pressure, but with the counsel and co-operation of the War Cabinet under the leadership of President Wilson we were prevented from making very serious ones."

Mr. Hurley has given a picturesque account of these weekly War Cabinet meetings. The President met his War Cabinet in his study. It was formerly the room where Lincoln, Grant, Cleveland, and McKinley held their regular Cabinet meetings before President Theodore Roosevelt built the Executive Office Building and the new Cabinet Room. "We generally met in the Red Room a few minutes before two-thirty and when all the members had arrived we went upstairs. The President stood just inside the door and shook hands with each member as he entered—greeting us in the most cordial manner. 'How are you, McAdoo? Hello, Baruch! Glad to see you, Mr. Secretary!'"

Sometimes he referred to a letter he had received that day

The Story of Woodrow Wilson

from one of the members, or to some outstanding report or bit of work one of them had produced, which particularly pleased him.

The first thing the President did was to remove the flowers from his desk and put them in some out-of-the-way place so that he could see each one of the board. Then he would pass the cigars around and ask if the chairs were comfortable. Often he would tell some amusing story before commencing the business of the day. These pleasant little preliminaries and the President's warm and hospitable manner reminded the Irish Mr. Hurley of their common heritage.

> When a person crosses the threshold of an Irishman's cottage [says Mr. Hurley] he receives a hearty handshake of welcome. The first thing his host does is to get the poker, stir the grate or the kitchen fire, and put on a bit of coal or peat. Until the fire is burning brightly he feels there is a lack of cheer and that you have not received a real welcome suitable to the honor you have paid him in visiting him in his humble home.
>
> I have often watched the President on these occasions with pleasing interest—feeling that while he had no fire or poker he demonstrated his warm hospitality in making us all feel at home and that this cordial characteristic was proof of his Irish ancestry.

The writer has gone through hundreds of personal records and accounts by men associated with Mr. Wilson during the eight years of his Administration and has never found one that mentions his being cold or hard to work with. On the contrary, his associates again and again refer to his "courtesy" and "cordiality," his "great kindness" and "personal charm." Even his arch-enemy Senator Lodge records: "He was always courteous and pleasant with me."

He was exacting, but agreeably so. Mr. Joseph E. Davies records that in every situation that confronted him the President demanded "the *facts*." It was always "the facts—the facts" which he required. He made special use of the Federal Trade Commission for this purpose.

Mr. Davies, who was President of the Commission at the time, recalls an occasion just after we entered the war, when

> the President walked over to the offices of the F.T.C. and came in upon us unexpectedly one afternoon. I immediately called the Commission together and he sat down with us and stated that the purpose of his visit was to find out whether we could procure for him the costs of steel plates, shapes, and so on which went into the fabrication of ships.
>
> Rather jocularly he stated that he had been confronted in conference with the statements of two very able but differing gentlemen, Mr. Denman, a member of the Shipping Board, and General Goethals—whose statements were diametrically opposed to each other on the facts in connection with the controversy over the construction of wooden ships. He wanted the facts obtained for him as speedily as possible. We undertook the work and put on a large body of expert accountants and were able to procure for him within a few weeks the costs of approximately 95 per cent of the production of the steel industry of the United States.

Apparently the Commission, first suggested by the astute Justice Brandeis, was proving its usefulness in many ways.

One envelope from the President to Mr. Davies contained a memorandum from one of the commercial agents abroad describing the German dye cartel and certain developments in the international dyestuff situation which threatened American oil concerns. The President was intensely interested in all the scientific and inventive aspects of the war. Secretary of Commerce Redfield in his records emphasizes that one of the things not sufficiently stressed regarding Wilson's Administration was his interest in scientific research. "He understood the value of it without argument," says the Secretary, "and encouraged it in every line."

In December, 1917, Mr. Redfield and Mr. Stratton of the

Bureau of Standards worked out a memorandum showing the great wartime need for additional equipment and laboratories. They prepared a statement with great care. At first they estimated that a few hundred thousand dollars would serve their purpose, but before they appeared at the White House their figures had gone beyond the million mark. Redfield said that Wilson listened intently to their presentation of the subject and decided on the spot to give them what they needed, appropriating it from the President's fund. This enabled the Bureau of Research to double its laboratory space and to perform valuable investigations, notably in the construction of airplane motors.

Several members of the Cabinet speak of the President's familiarity with the Civil War period and other historic times. "Wilson profited enormously by Lincoln's problems. He was the quickest man to benefit by historical example that I ever saw," said Newton Baker.

Joseph Tumulty, the President's secretary, tells a story that reveals another side of Wilson's character. One day during the most critical period of the war, when Wilson was closeted with his Cabinet in one of their long meetings, an old Southern gentleman appeared at the White House asking to see him.

"Dressed in an old frock coat and a frayed but tolerably respectable high hat, he was the essence of refinement and culture and seemed to bring with him a breath of the old Southland from which he had come. In the most courteous way he addressed me saying:

" 'Mr. Secretary, I am an old friend of the President's father, Dr. Wilson, and I want to see Woodrow. I have not seen the boy since the old days in Georgia, and I have come all the way up here to shake him by the hand!"

Tumulty was used to such requests all day long, and in the midst of the heavy burdens of the war he tried to spare the President all he could. But this old gentleman captivated him. Besides, the old man told a story about Wilson's father that was one of the President's favorites. So the Secretary excused himself and tiptoed up to the Cabinet Room, whispered to the President, and added: "He told me the old horse story, the one that you have often told me about your father."

One of the passions of the President's life was his love for his father. Turning to the members of the Cabinet, he said, "Gentlemen, will you please excuse me for a few minutes?"

"When I told the fine old chap that the President would see him at once, he almost collapsed. Then, fixing himself up, rearranging his frock coat, taking his high hat in his hand, and striking a statesmanlike posture, he walked into the President's office. No words passed between the two men for a few seconds. The old man looked silently at the President, with pride and admiration plainly visible in his eyes, and then walked slowly toward the President and took both his hands. Releasing them, he put one of his arms round the President's shoulder and, looking straight into the President's eyes, said: "Woodrow, my boy, your old father was a great friend of mine and he was mighty proud of you. He often told me that some day you would be a great man and that you might even become President."

"While the old man was addressing him the President stood like a big bashful schoolboy, and I could see that the old man touched . . . memories that were very sweet and dear to the President." Removing his arm from the President's shoulder the old man said, "Well, well, Woodrow, what shall I say to you?" Then, answering his own question, "I shall say to you what your dear old father would have said were he here: 'Be a good boy, my son, and may God bless you and take care of you.'"

"The President said nothing but I could see that his lips were quivering. For a moment he stood still, in his eyes the expression of one who remembers things of long ago and sacred. Then he seemed as with an effort to summon himself and his thoughts back to the present and I saw him walk slowly toward the door of the Cabinet Room, place one hand on the knob, with the other brush his handkerchief across his eyes. I saw him throw back his shoulders, and grow erect again as he opened the door . . . and said in quiet steady tones, 'I hope you will pardon the interruption, gentlemen!'"

III

SOON after the war declaration partisan politics reappeared. An effort was made in early summer to create a joint committee of both Houses of Congress to "assist" the President. It resembled the attempt to fasten Congressional control on Lincoln during the Civil War. Then in September, came a sustained campaign, led by Colonel Roosevelt, to create a War Cabinet to conduct the war. The Colonel, wounded in his ego and fuming for an outlet for his superabundant energies, was determined to play a leading role of some sort. He first attacked the President bitterly in magazine articles, declaring that "we did not go to war to make democracy safe" and referring to Wilson as "a combination of glib sophistry and feeble sham amiability."

Then, taking the stump, he spoke in Chicago, Detroit, New York, and other great cities. He denounced the idea of a "Wilsonian soft peace" and went so far as to compare Wilson to the German rulers themselves. Mr. Roosevelt had a great personal following. Many members of Congress decided that nothing less than a coalition cabinet with Roosevelt in charge as munitions head would meet the situation. Senator Chamberlain, the Democratic Chairman of the Military Affairs Committee, joined the movement. It culminated in a great luncheon of nineteen hundred people in New York on January 19, 1918, in honor of Senator Chamberlain and Representative Kahn of California.

At the luncheon Senator Chamberlain declared that "the military establishment of America has fallen down through wholesale inefficiency. There is no use to be optimistic about a thing that does not exist." A few days later he introduced bills creating a Munitions Department and a War Cabinet of three men. Mr. Roosevelt went to Washington to take personal charge of the campaign. For a time things looked serious, but the President met the challenge boldly. He publicly branded Senator Chamberlain's criticism of the War Department as "an astounding and absolutely unjustifiable distortion of the truth," saying that "as a matter of fact the War Department has performed a task of unparalleled magnitude with extraordinary promptness and efficiency."

He wrote Senator Martin, majority Democratic leader, that "such activities on the part of a particular committee" as Senator Chamberlain's resolution called for "would constitute an attempt to take over the conduct of the war so as to interfere in the most serious way with the Executive" and asked "that every Senator who intends to support the present Administration vote against it." Finally Wilson asked for himself greater powers than the committee had demanded and got them, in spite of the opposition plus certain Senators of his own party.

The New York *Times,* supporting the President, said in an editorial on January 21st that "the country agreed with his stand against the Chamberlain Resolution. . . . Whatever confusion may exist anywhere would be intensified a hundredfold if Congress tried to take over the executive business or superintend it or overhaul it or meddle with it. It is not what Congress is for, and the Congress which did try to exercise such functions in Lincoln's time, although headed by much abler men than most of those at the head of this Congress, only succeeded in interfering with the nation's war activities and making bad matters worse."

The President got the vote of confidence he asked for. He invited Mr. Edward L. Stettinius to go to Washington as a kind of Munitions Minister to help straighten out the cross-purposes of some of the departments. Another victory for Wilson. But each additional triumph increased the jealousy of his opponents and fed the mounting fire of hatred.

Wilson had tried to handle the matter peaceably. He wrote a long letter to Senator Chamberlain, following a personal interview, and explained why he could not favor the War Cabinet bill. But the Senator disregarded the letter and presented his resolution. Political history consists in large part of the vanities of frustrated men. Senator Chamberlain was called a "disaffected" Democrat. It was said that he coveted the post of Secretary of War when Mr. Garrison resigned, and that he had it in for Baker, who got the appointment, although Baker himself doubted his own fitness and would have preferred not to take the job.

"Are you ready to be sworn in?" was the President's only reply to Baker's resistance.

Mr. Wilson had the highest regard for his Secretary of War and said in his own protest on the Chamberlain statement: "My association and constant conference with the Secretary of War have taught me to regard him as one of the ablest public officials I have ever known."

Baker stood five foot six and weighed one hundred and twenty-five pounds. If he had stood six feet and had weighed two hundred he might have assumed more heroic proportions in the country's war councils. In any case, after the Roosevelt and Leonard Wood decisions he came in for bitter attack and criticism, especially by Senator Chamberlain and some of the chronic soreheads among the retired army crowd in Washington.

The country at large, impatient of delays and ignorant of issues, unconsciously played into the hands of the opposition. During 1917 Baker's unpopularity increased daily. Colonel Roosevelt went so far as to applaud from the gallery of the Senate one of Senator Chamberlain's most violent anti-Baker speeches.

One day while the Congressional critics were still peppering away, the Secretary heard a familiar tap-tap coming down the hall toward his office. He recognized the umbrella of the Postmaster-General. Burleson went in quietly, looked all around to see if they were alone, came up to the desk, and said softly:

"They're after you, Baker!"

"Are they, Albert?" said the Secretary, smiling.

"Yes. But never mind," Burleson chuckled, "I'm going to put them after me presently."

He meant that he intended to take over the telephones and telegraphs and expected a storm of criticism to fall on his own head from the Congressional hecklers—as of course it did. Burleson left Baker's office still chuckling and waving a friendly hand.

Baker took the criticism philosophically; he told the President it was inevitable. Congress had no real comprehension of the size of the war, the magnitude of the undertaking in which the country and especially the War Department was involved. The people, typically American, wanted to do things in a big way. They did not know everything that was really being done. The War Department permitted and even encouraged some of the misinformation. We preferred not to let the Germans know what was going on or the actual strength of our war machine. But in January, 1918, the Secretary decided that the time had come to make a reply to the attacks and a report to the nation. With the President's consent he demanded the right to answer from the floor of the Senate the charges made against him. This was refused, but he did get a hearing before the Military Affairs Committee.

He told the newspapermen that he intended to make an important statement. When the time came for him to speak a large crowd had assembled and the Committee moved to a larger room. The war work had advanced so far now that there seemed no danger in letting people know just what had been accomplished. So Baker started in and let them have it.

He spoke for five hours—three in the morning, two in the afternoon. He outlined all that had been accomplished, explained and exploded the charges of wanton neglect that the Committee had sought to bring against his Department. At the noon recess huge Senator Ollie James—who had listened intently in the front row all morning, head bowed upon his cane—jumped in a cab and hurried to the White House. "You ought to see that little old Baker!" he cried, rushing into the President's room—"he's down there eating 'em up!"

When the afternoon session began the Senator was back in his place, ready for the next round.

This speech gave the country its first assurance as to what had really been achieved in the war effort. The newspapers gave it great publicity, Baker received barrels of complimentary letters, and the spirit towards the War Department changed decidedly. From then on, he had little trouble.

IV

Less than a month after the declaration of war the Selective Service Act was passed. Registration machinery was introduced on a nation-wide scale, and on June 5th more than ten million men were registered, quickly and without difficulty.

No doubt one reason why the draft worked so well was because the Government held back from entering the war until we were provoked into it and the people felt we had to go in. Also, the draft was administered in democratic fashion by boards made up of civilians from the communities where the draftees lived. This idea was conceived by Secretary Baker.

Thirty-two encampments, each one a city able to accommodate forty thousand men, were built in ninety days—supposedly an impossible achievement. In June, 1917, two months after the war declaration, General Pershing and his staff arrived in France. Throughout that month four groups of transports were continually landing American fighting men on French soil. On October 10th our men had reached the firing line.

Because of overpressure on French railroads and supplies, the Americans had to build their own debarkation systems, provide housing, transportation, hospitals, and ordnance bases, and keep the necessary supplies of all sorts coming steadily across the Atlantic. The writer saw a substantial part of it being done at her post in the largest American hospital center in France.

The problem of shipping required the revival of America's shipbuilding industry. Workmen had to be trained and yards built. This work went forward with such speed and efficiency that by November 11, 1918, the transport service of the Army alone numbered 431 ships, totalling over three million deadweight tons.

In June, 1917, 2,261 troops and 2,798 marines were embarked. In December embarkations had risen to fifty thousand a month; in March, 1918, to eighty-four thousand. Then came what Europe called "America's transport miracle." In April the embarkations were 118,637; in May, 245,950; in June, 278,756; in July, 306,185.

At the time of the Armistice the total embarkations amounted to 2,045,169 soldiers and 30,665 marines.

The first shipment of supplies totaled about sixteen thousand tons and went out in July, 1917. By October we were shipping 750,000 tons a month. All together we shipped 5,153,000 tons of supplies to our soldiers in France, 95 per cent of it carried in American vessels. Ships had to be altered to carry the 1,145 locomotives we sent. A cross-Channel fleet had to be assembled—not slowly and gradually but immediately, at top speed. "It can't be done!" would have been the natural response of engineers and construction men and workmen, faced with such a problem. "It can be done because it's *got* to be done!" said America. And done it was.

The Navy of the United States, whose Secretary was held up to derision also, proved an invincible first line of defense. Our Navy guarded 2,079,888 men sent overseas, and not a single soldier on any American troopship lost his life on the way to France, in spite of the perpetual prowling of Germany's submarines.

Before the declaration of war the Navy had prepared by increasing its enlistments to eighty-seven thousand and then raising its numbers to 533,000 officers and men during the war. From April 6, 1917, till the Armistice two thousand new naval vessels went into service, and every one of them had officers and men ready to take it over immediately. "We fully realize," said General Pershing, "that had it not been for the Navy who kept watch and guard night and day over our transport fleet the American effort in France would never have been successful." The efforts and devotion of Secretary Josephus Daniels played a large part in this achievement.

Of 227 encounters with U-boats, 193 were successfully combated. Forty-four were surface engagements, some with long-continued gunfire contests. At the time of America's entrance into the war the German submarine campaign had brought the Allies "to the borderline of starvation," according to distinguished Allied representatives before the Senate. It was our vigorous and instant co-operation that crushed the U-boat menace.

The story of the Air Arm of the services is a war epic all by itself. On April 6th, 1917, the United States had three small aviation fields, fifty-five training planes, only four of which were in use, and an air personnel of sixty-five officers and 1,120 men. By the time of the Armistice, eighteen months later, we had thirty-four aviation fields, and our aviation training schools had graduated 8,602 men from the elementary courses and 4,028 from advanced courses. More than five thousand pilots and observers were sent overseas. This in the days when aviation was in its infancy.

From June 24, 1917, when the appropriation was made, until the time of the Armistice, the United States produced more than eight thousand training planes and more than sixteen thousand training engines. The Allies, after three years of war, had developed only one machine gun that could be successfully synchronized to fire through a revolving airplane propeller. In twelve months we produced two, both susceptible to quantity production.

We gave to the world the greatest airplane engine—the Liberty engine. We produced typical American machines that were acknowledged to be superior to Europe's best. We invented new airplane cameras, electric-heated clothing for aviators in high-altitude work, and the oxygen mask equipped with telephone connections that enable the flier to endure any altitude without losing speaking contact with his fellows. We developed the military parachute to a degree of safety undreamed of by the Europeans. During the entire war there was not one casualty due to parachute failure. We developed in quantity the wireless telephone that placed the flier in easy and constant communication with his ground station and his commander in the air.

The story of our aircraft is the story of the whole war—and the story of the tough, ambitious, indomitable American-mechanic character. The American people wanted to become the world's greatest airplane power overnight; the Army and Navy Technical Board caught the spirit. So did every smallest workman and mechanic along the line. "And by golly it was done!" Even the order for forty thousand planes in one year did not satisfy some enthusiasts. They demanded—Admiral Peary among them—that America have fifty thousand planes in the air at one time, and never became reconciled to any smaller figure. If we have over two hundred thousand planes today, that is due in no small measure to the magnificent spirit and effort of the pioneers of 1917 and 1918.

Raising the money for all this was a war achievement of major dimensions. Billions were needed—thirty-seven billion dollars, to be exact—and Secretary McAdoo met the emergency with his usual astuteness and clever inspiration: short-time certificates of indebtedness followed immediately by the announcement of a bond issue. The financiers of the country assumed that these issues would be floated through the banks on the usual commission basis. But Secretary McAdoo had the courage and vision to conceive a plan that would save money even as it manufactured war spirit. Coining the name "Liberty Loan," he went straight to the people, and, although the idea met bitter opposition from the bankers, each of five bond issues was oversubscribed. It was likewise the genius of McAdoo that conceived the idea of War Savings and Thrift Stamps, a plan that made the smallest child a partner of the Government in winning the war.

And there was the War Risk Insurance—also conceived and administered by Secretary McAdoo—giving a helping hand to the wives and children of the fighting men. And—greatest pride of all—the care of the men themselves. No paper-soled shoes or fever camps, no embalmed beef such as shamed the Spanish war and brought grief into thousands of American homes. The American soldier in 1918 as in the 1940s had the best medical care of any army in the world, the best food, the best clothing. The death rate per thousand during the war with Spain was 26. The death rate in World War I was 6.4 in the United States and 4.7 in the American Expeditionary Forces. And even these percentages were made much larger by the influenza epidemic that swept the country at that time. A wonderful achievement, this first World War record, whether taken as a whole or in piece-by-piece analysis.

The committee appointed by President McKinley to examine the conduct of the war with Spain prefaced its report by asking the people to remember that the task of mobilizing, training, and equipping 275,000 men was of such massive proportions that all the criticisms and comments that were made with regard to it "must be read with regard to the size of the task." Only nineteen years later America mobilized, trained, equipped, and maintained an army of five million and sent two million of them across the ocean, without one of the scandals or failures that shamed the records of 1898 and of the Civil War. The successful struggle of today—the equipment, training, and efficiency of our men, our ultimate victory—all rests upon that great struggle and effort of twenty-five years ago, under the leadership of Commander-in-Chief Woodrow Wilson.

V

PERSHING arrived in France on June 13, 1917. On October 22nd American troops entered the trenches for the final phase of their training. They were greeted warmly by the French; each man was shaken by the hand, some were even hugged and kissed on both cheeks. In England there had been a "tremendous demonstration" when United States troops marched through the streets of London, escorted by the famous bands of the Guards, to be reviewed by the King at Buckingham Palace.

The lift to Allied morale was needed sorely. If the year 1916 had been bad, 1917 was calamitous. Russia's "bloodless revolution" had been succeeded by a counterrevolution disastrous to the Allies. The Bolsheviks ousted the Kerensky Government and called upon all belligerents to begin negotiations for an immediate peace without annexations or indemnities. Two million soldiers lost to the Allied forces, and the whole Eastern front thrown wide open to the enemy! The Russian breakdown, the terrible reverses in Italy (where Germans and Austrians took

250,000 prisoners in a single week), the mortal weariness of the English Army after the terrific effort of the past summer, with reports from the Flanders front daily growing worse—all combined to end the year in an atmosphere of heavy gloom.

Colonel House, returning from two months with the American War Mission to the Inter-Allied Council, wrote the President on December 15, 1917: "Unless a change for the better comes, the Allies cannot win, and Germany may. For six months or more the ground has been steadily slipping away from the Allies."

General Bliss was even more explicit. In his report from the Supreme War Council he declared that "a military crisis is to be apprehended culminating not later than the end of next spring [1918] in which, without great assistance from the United States, the advantage will probably lie with the Central Powers. This crisis is largely due to the collapse of Russia as a military factor and to the recent disaster in Italy. But it is also largely due to lack of military co-ordination, lack of unity of control on the part of the Allied forces in the field. National jealousies and suspicions must be put aside in favor of unified control," he said—even, if necessary, to the extent of accepting a unified command. "We must send to France as early in the year 1918 as possible the maximum number of troops that we can send. There may be no campaign of 1919 unless we do our best to make the campaign of 1918 the last."

Early 1918 looked unencouraging. German planes bombed London and the southern English counties. There were air raids in France too, and Paris was bombed by long-range guns from Chaulgny, seventy-five miles away. On March 26th General Foch was appointed Supreme Commander to co-ordinate the operations of the Allied Armies. On March 28th General Pershing tendered the entire American force to General Foch, giving up the plan of building a distinct American force in Lorraine. Pershing had vigorously opposed the incorporation of American forces with British and French fighting units, but when necessity compelled he yielded like a good sportsman and gallant soldier.

"Pershing had the largest vision of any man, civil or military," said Secretary Baker, reviewing World War I and its problems after it was over. The Secretary "had talked with practically every important civil and military man of the Allied countries," and no one of them saw the war in its true terms as Pershing did. "He has imagination and daring," said Mr. Baker—"two great qualifications for military leadership."

General Scott, General Harbord, Generals Summerall, Hines, and Liggett all "performed fine service and deserve to be ranked high on the list of American commanders." On one of the very few occasions when the President made a suggestion to Secretary Baker regarding War Department matters, he ventured to hope that "that very gallant officer [General Harbord] was going to receive a citation for his extraordinary bravery at Château-Thierry." Baker assured him this was already arranged.

The Secretary believed that the army men of this country are "a fine upstanding body of men who can hold their own with the fighting men of any country," frequently surpassing the "professional militarists" in ingenuity and strategy. Pershing, he pointed out, saw that the war must be won on the Western front and held to this conviction while others were frittering away time and strength in petty conflicts on a number of secondary fronts. Wilson and Baker also favored this course.

The President steadily refrained from interfering with General Pershing in his activities and problems in Europe. He knew that the General was too far away and that conditions were changing too rapidly to permit of suggestion or interference. Characteristically, having given command to a man, he trusted him implicitly. He confined his communications to Pershing largely to brief messages of appreciation:

It was thoughtful of you to send me the photographs which have just come to me this morning of the American troops in action in the attack at Cantigny. It gives me an opportunity I had not had before of visualizing the circumstances of an attack like that. But I am writing not merely to thank you for the photographs. I want also to say how very proud we are of the record our men have been making under you in the recent fighting at the front. It has given a deep sort of pride and joy to the whole country, and my sincere congratulations go out to you and to the immediate commanders of the men who have been rendering so fine an account of themselves.

One of the strongest influences in Wilson's life, after he had taken the nation into war, was his sense of responsibility to the American soldier—his acute and constant consciousness of the debt of every one of us to "those boys." In every major crisis of his life after that—his bitter defeat at the hands of Senator Lodge and his associates, his deep disappointment in his trusted friend Colonel House on his return to the Paris conference, in the discussion of the Treaty and every war and postwar problem—Wilson's first thoughts and first words always concerned "those boys whom I sent into all this, to whom I am responsible." Whatever happened, he mustn't fail them.

In order not to fail them he set out on the journey that cost his dearest hopes and in the end, his life. He did as much as he had asked of them—gave everything in the line of duty. They were constantly before him in his journeys on the *George Washington*, when he spent hours every day in their company. A party for them at the White House—where he did K.P. and served them himself—was his last public social act.

Early in the war the President had publicly urged our troops to keep alive their faith in God and to feel that they were crusaders in a just and holy cause. On one occasion he received a company of soldiers at the White House and talked to them along the same line.

One man spoke up: "You wouldn't promise us to read a chapter in the Bible every day, no matter how busy you are, would you?"

"I will, with all my heart!" the President replied.

"Well," said the boy, "I know it will make it a lot easier for us to do it if we can count on you."

The President had a Y.M.C.A. pocket Bible bound in khaki

and sent him by a soldier. No matter how late the hour or how weary his brain, he never slept until he had kept his promise and read his chapter. And he kept this up to the end of his life.

VI

WHILE the great war machine was being built up and affairs in Europe demanded 100 per cent of Wilson's thought and energies, another series of major problems presented itself at home. Strikes of various sorts threatened the war effort: coal strikes, carpenters' strikes, shipbuilding troubles on the West Coast, and troubles with the railroads—which the Government eventually took over on December 26, 1917. The race problem sprang up, ugly and threatening, with riots in Philadelphia and St. Louis similar to those in Harlem and Detroit twenty-five years later. The problem of religious intolerance arose also: anti-Catholic feeling and hatred between Catholics and Jews was persistently fomented by certain political interests and the fifth column of that day. The President received hundreds of indignant letters for keeping his Catholic secretary.

Then there was the continual problem of the "hyphenated groups"—German-American, Irish-American, and Italian-American. Political factions kept playing up to special prejudices for their own purposes and to interfere with the Administration. Finally there was the American attitude to Russia. What was this country going to do in regard to the bewildering events in that great nation? Were the Soviets anti-Christs and devils, as some Americans maintained, or were they liberators and redeemers, as others insisted? Headlines of the day read: "Wilson faces Bolshevism." "Wilson studies relationships with Great Britain." "England worried about our shipping competition after the war." "Wilson meets conflicting attitudes on punishment of German people." . . .

Woman suffrage was a burning issue in 1917-18. The Federal amendment to give women the vote was up for hot discussion. Wilson, once an "anti" but converted by his own daughters, pursued a vigorous campaign with Senators and Congressmen. He went before the Senate and urged the amendment in these words:

> I tell you plainly that this measure . . . is vital to the winning of the war. . . . And not . . . of the war only. It is vital to the right solution of the great principles which we must settle . . . when the war is over. We shall need them in our vision of affairs as we have never needed them before, the sympathy and insight and clear moral instinct of the women of the world. The problems of that [postwar] time will strike to the root of many things that we have not hitherto questioned, and I for one believe that our safety in these questioning days as well as our comprehension of matters that touch society to the quick will depend upon the direct and authoritative participation of women in our counsels.

The amendment granting suffrage to women passed the House by a vote of 274 to 136. Mrs. George Bass, leader of the Democratic women, wrote the President: "It could not have passed but for you."

With all these matters at home and abroad pressing for attention, the President had also to perform his regulation official duties: open Liberty Loan drives, address the American Federation of Labor at Buffalo, the Annapolis Naval Academy graduating class, attend the Memorial Day celebration at Arlington and the Fourth of July ceremonies at Mt. Vernon, confer with ambassadors and generals and scores of other dignitaries on imperative questions—plus his daily round of appointments on routine Congressional affairs. Complaints and investigations took up no small part of his time. There were indignant protests over Mr. Garfield's coal order, for "heatless Mondays" and theater closings—a highly judicious move which in two months saved the nation's coal supply and averted the crippling of war industries; complaints against Burleson for refusing the mails to "seditious" papers and magazines, and stalwart replies from the Postmaster-General, who "would be glad to offer his resignation" but would not relax his patriotic vigilance; a general complaint against "Socialism" and "Communism," alleged to be threatening the whole country as a result of the government action regarding the cables and railroads.

In short, there was all the fuss and pother that goes with running a democracy whose citizens are on the job twenty-four hours a day. Wilson never complained of their interest or questionings. He answered them courteously, reasonably, and went straight ahead with his duties. "I think you have misinterpreted the purpose of the Postmaster-General . . . he is as anxious as I am to see that freedom of criticism is permitted. . . ." "Mr. Garfield's order saved the country millions of tons of coal and enabled the war industries to go forward 100 per cent instead of seriously hampered." "Had it not been for Mr. Hoover's vigorous move on wheat we should not have had sufficient to feed our fighting men" . . . and so on.

In these strenuous weeks the President was saved by what he called his one-track mind. He could get off the official track and onto the personal track at a moment's notice. When he closed the door of his office he apparently closed that door in his brain too and was ready to play, with the abandon of a boy. "Frequently at night," his wife says, "he would go into the Oval Room after dinner, put on a victrola record, and say 'now I'll show you a good jig step.' He was very light on his feet and often said he envied Primrose the minstrel dancer and wished he could exchange jobs."

Mr. Wilson loved the theater and went every week to a vaudeville show. He said it rested him to see lighthearted people who "took on no more at their hearts than they could kick off at their heels." He was a great baseball fan all his life and during the war often went to ball games and concerts for the benefit of the Red Cross.

Every afternoon Mrs. Wilson served with a canteen at the old B. and O. railroad station, where thousands of troops passed and usually stopped for a few minutes on their way through Washington. Part of her duty was to censor postcards which the boys bought at the canteen and wrote to their friends at home—particularly lest any hints should go through regarding embarkation plans or possible destination.

The boys liked to give the home folks a thrill. Underneath a picture showing one of the White House rooms they would write: "Got to Washington this A.M. Drove to White House where we shook hands with the Old Man. This is a picture of the room he was in. Feeling fine. Love. Joe."

The boys could not believe their eyes when some sharp lad would discover the President's wife among the canteen workers and pass the word along. Sometimes the President would come for Mrs. Wilson just before dinner. He was delighted when a train was in and he could really see the boys. He liked to shake hands with each one. If there wasn't time for that he would wave them farewell and good luck, and as the train pulled out a great cheer would go up for him.

On the seventh of August of the steaming summer of 1918 Alice Wilson, the President's niece, was married from the White House. Her family lived in an apartment in Baltimore, and a wedding at home in midsummer would have been difficult for them. Mrs. Wilson hospitably suggested the White House. Other members of the family demurred, thinking it would be too much for the President with all he had on his mind. But Mr. Wilson "wanted Alice to have a nice wedding" and one that she would always remember; so in the middle of August in the full heat of a Washington summer the President and Mrs. Wilson saw to it that she had one.

The correspondence of the President during these wartime days forms an important and revealing part of his life. He still wrote letters—hundreds of them—on his own typewriter, in addition to the thousands that he dictated. We find a letter to a mother who had given six sons to the armed forces; letters to several who had lost sons; a letter to Huston Thompson following his operation for appendicitis—"I have just heard of it, in this crisis nobody tells me anything!"; a letter to Senator Thomas Walsh of Montana expressing "great distress" regarding Mrs. Walsh's illness; a letter to Douglas Fairbanks thanking him for a book, *Laugh and Live*; also thanks to Harnell Vreeland for a book on Grotius, and to Secretary Baker for a copy of Conrad's *Typhoon*—"which I am looking forward to reading—*sometime!*"

There is a letter to his cousin Jessie about a bird cage which her old playmate had difficulty in procuring in wartime even in Washington—this on the same date as a grave labor telegram and one of his important notes to Germany; a letter to the widow of Charlie Mitchell, one of the old Witherspoon Gang; letters to some of the fellows about Charlie; a letter to Bobby Bridges, as warmly affectionate after six years of the Presidency as in the old days; a letter to his Southern "Cousin Lucy" full of news tidbits and family gossip; a letter to "Aunt Felie," Uncle James Woodrow's wife, who still lived in Columbia, South Carolina. She had written:

"My dear Tommie, Not a letter but just a line to let you know that I am thinking of you, and that my daily prayer for you is 'As thy days so shall thy strength be.' " The President, on December 31, 1917, replied:

"My dear Aunt Felie, Your little note gave me the greatest pleasure and cheer, and I want to send you in return for myself and from all my little household the warmest and most affectionate greetings of the New Year. I wish I had time for a real letter but you will know how much this message means even though it is short. Affectionately yours, Woodrow Wilson."

One of the most interesting of the President's wartime letters came from the Assistant Secretary of the Navy, Franklin D. Roosevelt, as the latter was about to depart for an inspection tour in France. It had to do with certain proposals in connection with young Mr. Roosevelt's political career—proposals he strongly disapproved.

My dear Mr. President,
I entirely forgot on Sunday evening to speak to you of a personal matter which might come up during my absence —the question of my nomination for the Governorship of

New York. I have tried in every way to stop it, but some of your friends and mine have talked of the possibility of forcing this while I am away and of asking you to encourage me to accept it.

I sincerely hope the matter will not come up. I have made my position entirely clear—that my duty lies in my present work, not only my duty to you and to the country but my duty to myself. If I were at any time to leave the Assistant Secretaryship it could only be for active service.

Furthermore, may I say to you that I am very certain that it would be a grave mistake for either you or any member of the Administration to ask that I give up war work for what is frankly very much of a local political job in these times. I cannot accept such a nomination at this time either with honesty or honor to myself. I think I have put off all danger of it, but in case you are appealed to I want you to know what I feel—and I know that you will understand and that you will not listen to the appeal.

Faithfully yours,

July 8, 1918   Franklin D. Roosevelt

The tone of this letter is extraordinary; the author writes like an equal rather than as a subordinate making a respectful request to a superior—and that superior the President of the United States. Mr. Roosevelt doesn't ask the President what he thinks of the matter, or say "of course I would be guided by your judgment," or any of the natural conventional phrases. He says very decisively what he will and will not do—and the matter of his own political advancement is evidently of not the slightest consequence. At that time Mr. Roosevelt urged New York leaders to nominate Alfred E. Smith, then President of the New York City Board of Aldermen, for the Governorship—and Smith received the nomination, almost unanimously.

The thing that worried President Wilson, and the other Allied leaders, most of all during this period was the Russian question. A once powerful ally had become a questionable and highly dangerous factor in the war game, played upon with skill by a clever and unscrupulous enemy. Wilson, wanting to help the Russian people in their struggle to achieve democracy, was handicapped by confused and sometimes long-delayed news reports and troubled by stories of fighting and atrocities under the new regime similar to those of the tyrants it had supplanted. It was hard to know how to act or what to believe.

On November 22, 1917, Trotsky suggested an armistice on all fronts and the opening of peace negotiations. The allied representatives by unanimous agreement took no notice of this proposal. They would not recognize the Bolshevik Government "until it can show some authority from the people." The United States did not finally recognize it until November 16, 1933.

Trotsky made some very forthright statements regarding the capitalist powers. The Bolsheviks began to release many of the secret treaties made under the Czarist Government and gave notice that they intended to publish them all. Certain American newspapers called this "an act of dishonor" and showed decided hostility to the new Russian regime. Colonel House telegraphed that such criticism should be suppressed, as "it will throw Russia into the lap of Germany if the Allies and ourselves express such views at this time." Wilson and Lansing—in a very trying position, with news coming through piecemeal and in highly contradictory reports—made a statement on December 1, 1917, that Russia was going through a very difficult time, had suffered severely through German intrigue, and that every effort was being made to assist the Russian people in working out the salvation of the country.

On December 17th a seventeen-day armistice went into effect between Russia and the Central Powers, and on December 22nd discussion of peace terms began at Brest Litovsk, with Austrian Foreign Minister Count Czernin acting as spokesman. On December 29th Trotsky made a public address to the peoples and governments of the Allied countries inviting them to share in peace negotiations. The program proposed by Germany, he said, was "profoundly inconsistent—an unprincipled compromise between the pretentions of imperialisms and the oppositions of the laboring democracy." (What it boiled down to was that Germany refused to give up one foot of occupied territory or to recognize Russian claims or Russian sovereignty.) But, he added, "the very fact of the presentation of the program is an enormous step forward." Once more he urged the Allies to state their aims. Importunate messages came through from our military and commercial attachés at Petrograd urging that the United States should not desert Russia in the crisis and that the Allies should restate their objects.

Colonel House, reporting back from the Inter-Allied War Conference at Paris, told of his unsuccessful effort to persuade the Allies to join in formulating a broad declaration of their war aims which, he believed, "would not only help to a solution of the Russian problem but would knit together the best and most unselfish opinions of the world" and show the world united against Germany.

VII

For months the President had been trying to get the Allies to join in a statement of war aims. He wanted a diplomatic offensive to arouse liberal leaders in enemy countries and pave the way for a just peace. In view of the failure of these efforts and the urgency of the Russian situation, he decided to undertake the task himself. He went to work with Colonel House as his only confidant. The result was the famous Fourteen Points address.

The President delivered this address before the two Houses of Congress at twelve-thirty on January 8, 1918. Only a small audience was present, since the occasion had not been made known in advance. Colonel House wanted it announced that the President was about to state American war aims, but Wilson feared newspaper speculation and interference in relation to this extremely delicate subject. He had communicated with Mr. Balfour and arranged his paper in consultation with the Allied chiefs—considerably in advance of Mr. Lloyd George's speech to the Trade Unions of Britain, which Mr. Wilson is often accused of having copied. When Wilson came before the Congress of the United States on that January morning, he spoke with more than his usual gravity and forcefulness.

Gentlemen of the Congress, once more . . . the spokesmen of the Central Empires have indicated their desire to discuss the objects of the war and the possible bases of a general peace. . . . Whatever their confusion of counsel and of purpose [in the parleys at Brest Litovsk], the spokesmen have again attempted to acquaint the world with their objects in the war and have again challenged their adversaries to say what their objects are and what sort of settlement they would deem just and satisfactory. That challenge should be responded to . . . and with the utmost candor. . . .

Within the last week Mr. Lloyd George has spoken with admirable candor and in admirable spirit for the people and Government of Great Britain. There is, moreover, a voice calling for these definitions of principle and of purpose: the voice of the Russian people . . . prostrate and all but helpless . . . before the grim power of Germany which has hitherto known no relenting and no pity. They [the Russians] call on us to say what it is that we desire—I believe that the people of the United States would wish me to respond with utter simplicity and frankness.

We entered this war because violations of right had occurred which touched us to the quick and made the life of our people impossible. . . . What we demand in this war, therefore, is . . . that the world be made fit and safe to live in; and particularly that it be made safe for every peace-loving nation which, like our own, wishes to live its own life, determine its own institutions, be assured of justice and fair dealing by the other peoples of the world as against force and selfish aggression. All the peoples of the world are in effect partners in this interest, and for our own part we see very clearly that unless justice be done to others it will not be done to us. The program of the world's peace, therefore, is our program; and that program, the only possible program as we see it, is this:

Here followed the Fourteen Points. They are particularly interesting to us today in relation to the Eight Points of the Atlantic Charter,* several of which they resemble and for which they substantially paved the way.

1. Open covenants of peace openly arrived at.
2. Absolute freedom of navigation upon the seas.
3. The removal, so far as possible, of all economic trade barriers.
4. Adequate guarantees for reduction of national armaments.
5. A free, open-minded, and impartial adjustment of colonial claims.
6. The evacuation of all Russian territory and settlement of all questions affecting Russia, to obtain for her unhampered and unembarrassed opportunity for her political development.
7. Belgium must be evacuated and restored.
8. All French territory must be freed and the invaded portions restored and the wrong done in Alsace-Lorraine righted.
9. A readjustment of the frontiers of Italy along recognizable lines of nationality.
10. The peoples of Austria-Hungary should be accorded autonomous development.
11. Rumania, Serbia, and Montenegro should be evacuated, relations of the several Balkan States determined by friendly counsel along historic established lines of allegiance and nationality.
12. An independent Polish State should be erected.
13. The Turkish portions of the present Ottoman Empire

* See appendix for the complete text of the Fourteen Points and the Atlantic Charter.

should be assured secure sovereignty, the Dardanelles opened as a free passage to the ships of all nations under international guarantees.

14. A general association of nations must be formed under specific covenants, affording mutual guarantees of political independence and territorial integrity to great and small States alike.

"For such arrangements and covenants," declared the President, "we are willing to fight—and to continue to fight until they are achieved. We do not wish to fight her [Germany]," he added, "if she is willing to associate herself with us and the other peace-loving nations . . . in covenants of justice and fair-dealing. We wish her only to accept a place of equality among the peoples of the world instead of a place of mastery."

Thunderous applause followed the reading of this program. When the President read Point 8—that French territory and Alsace-Lorraine should be returned to France—Congress rose as one man and cheered. The galleries forgot all rules and clapped and shouted, wild with enthusiasm for France and for the President.

Within an hour the speech was flashed to every country of the world. And it "swept" the world—both friends and adversaries. "No public utterance Mr. Wilson ever made was received with such general acclaim," said the New York *Times*. "One of the great documents of American history," observed the New York *Tribune*. Even Theodore Roosevelt and Mr. Lodge at the time praised it. The President's old enemy George Harvey said: "Mr. Wilson's declaration was a veritable masterpiece. He has never done and we doubt if anybody could have done better." The New York *Tribune*, often critical of Wilson, added: "The President's words are the words of a hundred million. To-day as never before the whole nation marches with the President, certain alike of the leader and the cause." Not only this nation—all the nations. His words were caught up by exhausted millions, worn out from the struggle of four agonizing years, and eagerly welcomed as the basis of a new standard, a new conception of life.

The President was surprised but naturally greatly pleased with the reception his address evoked. Congratulatory letters and telegrams poured into the White House: messages from Thomas Lamont, Rabbi Wise, Dr. Eliot, Paderewski. Perhaps the tribute that secretly pleased him most was one which he acknowledged in a letter to his old friend Dr. Hibben. The letter expressed the President's "warm appreciation of the message of the Trustees of Princeton University and my hope that the address to Congress which it so generously supports may bear some substantial fruit in the year which has just opened."

The response from Capitol Hill gratified him too. "Your speech was clear as crystal," wrote Speaker Clark. "Anybody who can't understand it . . . is an incorrigible fool!" "It is one of the greatest state papers the President ever delivered," said Senator Chamberlain—at that time a bitter opponent on the War Cabinet matter. The impression on the majority of Congress was excellent.

European comment varied, each nation considering the Fourteen Points with a wary eye to its own future. British officials, while politely applauding President Wilson's "idealism," gazed apprehensively at Point 2—the poignant question of the freedom of the seas. France was joyful over the Alsace-Lorraine declaration, though some French officials grumbled at Wilson's taking such a firm directing hand in European affairs. The Italian Government feared that certain of the Fourteen Points threatened its interests in the Adriatic and jeopardized some of the prizes promised Italy under the Treaty of London. "The people of Italy, however, are tremendously impressed and encouraged," wrote our Ambassador, Thomas Nelson Page.

It was extraordinary how swiftly the special interests of each nation, which afterwards dominated the Peace Conference, rose to the surface. Less than twenty-four hours after Wilson's statement was off the press, the counterattack began. Indeed, this first clear-cut formulation of war and peace aims divided the friends and foes of the President's policies into two clearly defined camps, and the cleavage became more evident with every subsequent public pronouncement. Liberals, labor organizations, the mass of the people lined up solidly behind him, and remained behind him, the world over. Reactionaries—the old-time politicians of Europe as well as the Old Guard at home —were natural antagonists and skeptics.

Recognition of the moral quality of the man also became increasingly evident from this time on. Lloyd George and others were making similar statements, but, it was said, "in an apparently different spirit." The Germans questioned the sincerity of most of the Allied leaders. They never questioned Wilson. They might hate him, fear him, ridicule him; but they were completely convinced of his sincerity and integrity. The German Chancellor, reviewing both speeches before the Reichstag on January 24th, saw "no serious will for peace in Mr. Lloyd George's speech," but the Fourteen Points of the President he examined respectfully and with care. With some of the Points he declared he agreed: with the League of Nations he was definitely "in sympathy." Of course, German integrity and various other matters were to be taken care of. "Let the Entente bring new proposals," he concluded. "We shall seriously study them." The Foreign Minister of Austria-Hungary announced that he was in accord with many of President Wilson's views.

So the boy brought up in a little Southern town, who never got much nearer the great world than the ships at the docks, wove that world into the shining web of his thought, felt and communicated the sense of unity and brotherhood that was so deep in his own heart and, as he often recognized, "so deeply embedded in the hearts of all men." "Thought is the great amalgam," he declared. And feeling too. The secret of Wilson's power was not only his clear thinking, it was his passionate, white-hot feeling which struck sparks in far-off lands and fired the souls and the imaginations of millions of beings whom he never had seen.

During the last year of the war, says Dr. D. F. Fleming, Wilson's words spread everywhere. His speeches, distributed in great quantities among the people of the Central Powers, were one of the chief causes of the breakdown of morale which preceded the military collapse of the Teutonic Alliance. Among Allied and neutral nations their influence was even greater. Travelers from remote regions of the earth began to send in reports showing the extent of the President's influence. A mission superintendent from Meerut, India, sent word that "somehow these people have heard extracts of what President Wilson has said and it has gripped their hearts as nothing else since the war began."

Walter Lowrie wrote the President from Italy: "Today in this little Alpine village the local deputy of Parliament gathered the people in the village square to hear from him a patriotic speech. He had much to say about . . . America and about the clear words of President Wilson. The enclosed translation of your Decoration Day speech was then distributed to his electors." Dr. William Ellis wrote as follows: "I think it is true that no other mortal man has ever attained so nearly . . . universal fame as President Wilson. . . . The illiterate millions of the backward continents know nothing of the men ordinarily called famous in civilized lands, but because of his magic appeal to the deepest sensibilities of all human life . . . the Wilson principles quickly spread to the uttermost parts of the earth. There the innate vitality of the ideals caused them to take root and to grow. As no other . . . man has ever done before, Woodrow Wilson voiced the basic instincts and desires of the race."

VIII

THREE great addresses completed the "moral offensive" led by the President, which, complementing the crushing blows of Allied forces in the field, consolidated public opinion in both Allied and enemy countries and helped bring about the final surrender of the Germans in the autumn of 1918.

He made these great speeches on February 11th, July 4th, and September 27th—rounding out the group of war papers of which several famous contemporaries said, "There is not their equal in modern history." In the February speech—a direct reply to the war-aims address of Hertling and Czernin—he enlarged upon his speech of January 8th and gave four supplementary points which clarified and explained the Fourteen.

"I would have given a year of my life to have made the last half of that speech," Lord Reading told Colonel House afterward.

Of the July 4th speech hostile George Harvey said: "No such Fourth of July speech ever has or probably ever again will be heard in the country's history. . . . A masterpiece . . . flawless in style and virile substance." Here Wilson drew a dramatic picture of the two line-ups—"on one side the peoples of the world"; on the other "an isolated friendless group of governments who seek no common purposes but only selfish ambitions . . . governments clothed with strange trappings and the primitive authority" of "an alien and hostile age. . . . The Past and Present in deadly grapple."

In the address of September 27th the President outlined the principles of what he specifically now called a League of Nations, and spoke in definite terms of what the American nation and the Allies were ready to pay as the price of peace. They intended to fight on until their aims were accomplished.

Hard upon the ringing phrases of this September 27th pronouncement came the first German note requesting peace.

While these moral and psychological assaults were hammering the enemy's psychological resistance, smashing victories in the field were breaking his military resistance at Château-Thierry, Saint-Mihiel, and the Argonne. Germany began to go to pieces on the inside, with the Socialists and various workers' unions leading a revolt movement while Ludendorff and Hindenburg warned the Kaiser that it would probably be necessary to seek an armistice.

The President was in New York when the news first came, just after the Liberty Day festivities of October 12th. In the afternoon he had led a mammoth Liberty Day parade, "receiving an ovation such as no President has ever before encountered in this city," according to the *Times*. In the evening, as he sat at dinner with a party at the Waldorf Hotel, Tumulty hurried in with the word about Germany, telephoned from the Military Intelligence Bureau at Washington. House whispered it to the President, whose face beamed with delight. He wrote on a card. "Tell Mrs. W."

The moment for which he had waited four long years.

On the morning of October 14th the German note was formally presented by the Swiss chargé d'affaires at Washington. That note is worth studying. Its brief phrases tell the whole 1918 peace story. The Germans did not say, "We accept the peace terms as stated by the Allied nations." They did not say, "We agree to the peace terms outlined by the United States Government." They said—and let every American remember it and ponder it for all that it signifies—"The German Government has accepted the terms laid down by President Wilson in his address of January 8 and in his subsequent addresses as the foundation of a permanent peace of justice."

The note from Austria, received a week later, was of almost identical wording.

The leadership of the Allies and the leadership of the world was openly declared and candidly ascribed to the man to whom it belonged: *the terms laid down by President Wilson.*" This is probably the only time in modern history when capitulation of a group of nations has been made to a man rather than to a government. It is something to remember while the books with their condescending discussion of "Wilson's failures" and "Wilson's blunders" and "what Wilson should have done" come rolling off the presses.

The President had a first draft of his reply to Germany ready that same evening of October 14th. He discussed it with Colonel House and the Secretary of State until after midnight. The Cabinet next morning approved it *in toto*. These were the terms: The conditions of an armistice must be arranged by the military advisers of the Allied nations. No arrangements could be accepted that did not provide "absolutely satisfactory safeguards and guarantees of the maintenance of the present military supremacy of the armies of the United States and the Allies in the field." No armistice would be considered until all U-boat warfare ceased. He also called for the cessation of "the wanton destruction by the German Army" and in plain terms for the abdication of the Kaiser. This message, warmly applauded by the American press, fell like a bombshell in Germany. The Kaiser and the Imperial Government had been all-powerful for so long that their passing could hardly be conceived of.

The Senate and the House—even Senator Lodge—approved the President's terms. On October 17th Colonel House sailed for France to represent Wilson at the scene of action. The Supreme War Council and the Prime Ministers of other Allied countries had already gathered at Paris. Tension increased as they felt the end drawing near. On October 19th came the Austrian note. On October 20th Germany accepted all the requirements laid down by the President. On October 23rd Wilson laid his final word to the Germans before the Cabinet. He informed the Germans that he had sent the correspondence to the Allied Powers with the suggestion that if they were disposed to effect the peace upon the terms and principles indicated they would ask their military advisers to draw up an armistice of such a character as to "ensure to the associated governments the unrestricted power to safeguard and enforce the details of the peace to which the German Government has agreed." He gave final notice that their "monarchical autocrats" and "military overlords" must go. The Allied Powers must know with whom they were dealing, and must be able to trust the German representatives as they were not able to trust those who had hitherto been in power.

The Cabinet changed not a word of this message. When it reached Germany, the Social Democrats—the strongest political force in the country—were convinced that the Imperial Government must abdicate. The Emperor indignantly refused. But on November 9th the Chancellor, Prince Max of Baden, on his own authority declared that the Emperor intended to renounce the throne. The Kaiser fled to Holland, and Friedrich Ebert, Socialist leader, succeeded Prince Max as Chancellor of the

German Provisional Government. The final German note accepted Wilson's terms. For the first time in history a civilian ruler had sealed the doom of an empire and his ideals were accepted as the terms of surrender by the military chieftains.

Late in the evening of November 10th the German delegates waiting with the French Commissioners in the forest of Compiègne received authorization from their new Government to sign the armistice. Wilson got the news at 3 A.M. He stood in silence—unable, he said, really to grasp the full significance of the words.

IX

IN FRANCE the war was ending. In America war was just beginning. More formidable than the Kaiser and the Junkers of Germany—for Wilson's plans—were the traditional ruling class of the United States and their representatives: the leaders of the Republican party. These forces, representing the great industrial wealth of the East and North, had held power, almost without interruption, since the Civil War. They believed that they alone were capable of governing. The verdict at the polls in 1912 had been bad enough; that of 1916 was unendurable.

As Dr. Randolph Adams, of the University of Michigan, wittily records: "Jealousy was a predominant Republican emotion from 1912 to 1920. Fussy old gentlemen sitting in Union League Clubs in America never could and never would be able to reconcile themselves to the fact that at the greatest moment in world history the Presidential chair was occupied . . . by a Democrat and the son of a Rebel."

The Democrats were traditionally "inept" and "provincial." Wilson was an interloper. His legislation had upset the whole accustomed scheme of things for the "governing class"; the new tariff, the banking system, and worst of all the innovations of the income tax, affected their interests profoundly. Wilson's conduct of the war, in which with his "weak" Democratic aides he had ably managed the greatest effort in our history, disturbed them still more. And now all this talk about a new world order—a new order in which we "would never again seek any selfish interest of our own"; an order in which there would certainly be attempts at tariff-lowering and menacing tendencies towards free trade!

The time had come to call a halt. The result of the War Cabinet contest had thoroughly alarmed the Republican forces. Control of Congress must be regained. Wilson and the farmers of the South and West had won four straight elections. Their power must be broken or they would be in indefinitely.

A major party struggle was on for the autumn of 1918. A Republican Congress was an absolute necessity. First came the reconciliation between Taft and Roosevelt, for the past eight years bitter political enemies. They met in the dining room of the Blackstone Hotel at Chicago in May, 1918, publicly made up, and a few weeks later addressed an unofficial Republican State convention together at Saratoga. Both urged a Republican Congress "to stimulate the President to victory and to control reconstruction after it." This convention also adopted a plank for the creation of a league of nations to establish, and from time to time modify and enforce, the rules of international law and conduct.

In August Roosevelt and Albert J. Beveridge conferred with George Harvey at Beverly Farms, Massachusetts, and arranged for the publication and support of *Harvey's Weekly*. T. R. and Beveridge, it was reported, guaranteed that they would furnish Harvey twenty thousand subscribers a year for the next two years. Harvey was to attack Wilson as strongly as possible and on every occasion. Roosevelt himself constantly wrote vehement attacks which increased in virulence as the autumn elections approached.

During summer and early fall popular interest centered on the war and the victorious march of the Allied armies, which resulted early in October in the first moves for peace, by Austria. On October 14th came the German note. Directly after the receipt of this news Colonel Roosevelt issued a statement in which he denounced the President for entering into negotiations. He urged that the Senate "emphatically repudiate the so-called Fourteen Points and the various similar utterances of the President."

Again on October 24th, immediately after Wilson's final and most important message to the Germans, Roosevelt sent a long public telegram to Lodge and several other Senators saying: "I most earnestly hope that . . . the Senate will take affirmative action against a negotiated peace with Germany. . . . I also earnestly hope that on behalf of the American people it will declare against the adoption in their entirety of the Fourteen Points and of the President's address of last January as offering a basis for a peace satisfactory to the United States." This telegram was published while the newspapers were full of dispatches from Allied capitals expressing warm approval of the President's conduct of negotiations with the enemy powers.

On October 26th Secretary Baker wrote the President: "Should you not take some occasion to point out that your Fourteen Point address was made on January 8 and that it is scandalous for Mr. Roosevelt to remain silent about it for nine months until our Allies rely upon it, our own country approves it, our enemies in professed good faith accept it—until our national good faith is pledged to it as a statement of our war aims—and then seek to repudiate it by writing to Republican Senators in an effort to make a partisan row?"

"Roosevelt's ill-advised and most untimely attempt to stir up partisan strife against the President" was sharply criticized by the New York *Times* and other papers. The Colonel—now more bloodthirsty than the generals in the field—declared that, "far from negotiating for peace, we ought to declare war on Turkey without an hour's delay." Marshal Foch himself said that, "our aims being accomplished, no one has the right to shed another drop of blood." But this did not satisfy Roosevelt.

Spurning the idea of a peace conference led by Wilson, he summoned both the Senate and the people to turn their backs upon the President's peace program—which the whole nation, with our Allies, had accepted and fought for up to that time. He declared that he intended to make his appeal "to representatives of the American people from one ocean to the other." In short, he announced on the very eve of the election, that if the Republicans regained control of the Senate the chief Republican leader would see to it that the President's program should be completely scrapped.

Wilson, in the midst of his delicate and difficult peace negotiations with Germany, hit back with what is generally considered the most unfortunate act of his political career: his famous "appeal for a Democratic Congress." In this appeal he told the people that unity of command was as necessary in civil action as it was on the field of battle, at such a time; that the Republican leaders had sought to block his efforts and to take the control out of his hands straight through the war. He warned that they would certainly persist in this course if they gained a majority in Congress. "If it is your wish to sustain me with undivided minds," he said, "I beg that you will say so in a way which it will be impossible to misunderstand."

There was plenty of precedent for his action: Hayes, Garfield, McKinley, all had made similar appeals. Wilson himself, in response to urgent requests, had also appealed for the support of Democratic candidates in two previous elections as a matter of ordinary political routine. But a storm of protest greeted the present message. It bitterly offended the Republicans, especially those who had supported the President in many of the main issues; it troubled and upset a good many Democrats. Everybody denied responsibility for having advised the President and blamed somebody else. The disastrous result remained the same.

The election returns gave the Republicans a majority in both Houses—with control of the Senate and the powerful Foreign Relations Committee, which one year later wrecked Wilson's cherished plans.

War Leader

X

HUMAN relations, not legislatures, write history; and the relations between Woodrow Wilson and Theodore Roosevelt, George Harvey and Henry Cabot Lodge wrote the history of the peace of 1919. The destinies of nations, the lives of thousands of soldiers, the happiness of millions of human beings, were determined by the relations between these four men. And especially by the vanity and frustration of three of them.

Lodge and Roosevelt had been friends for many years. They conducted a lengthy correspondence which Senator Lodge published in two volumes totaling some thousand pages. The letters during Mr. Wilson's era consist largely of withering comment on the Administration and highly complimentary comment on each other.

"Upon my word," T. R. writes to Senator Lodge on December 8, 1914, "Wilson and Bryan are the very worst men we have ever had in their positions." He declared again, "They are worse than Jefferson and Madison."

In the early days this correspondence had largely to do with their own affairs and political projects. They were very frank in regard to their personal aims and ambitions. Roosevelt wrote to Lodge on December 14, 1899: "Of all things I should like to be Secretary of War—if Root should decide to take the Vice-Presidency." And again in March, 1917: "Dear Cabot, I shall be back on the evening of April 2nd. Do see that no army legislation is so framed as to leave me out." Strange advice from an ex-President to a lawmaking representative of the people!

As good Republicans the two were united in their dislike of Wilson's policies. At first their attacks were comparatively mild: disapproval of his Mexican policy, criticism of his "unpreparedness," occasional disapproval of his legislation—though Lodge supported him on the canal tolls and later on the armed ship bill and certain other pieces of legislation. It was after the affront to each man's personal pride that each grew bitter.

The Story of Woodrow Wilson

Roosevelt especially resented Wilson's re-election in 1916 and his own failure the next year to secure a command in France or to attain power in a War Cabinet. Lodge especially resented his exclusion from the Peace Conference.

A very bitter attack comes from Roosevelt in May, 1917, just after his failure to "land" the French command: "The one real arch offender is Wilson. . . . If our people were awake he would be impeached tomorrow." Strong words. A young man in the District Attorney's office sent Mr. Wilson statements of certain Senators about Lincoln very much like them.

"I regard Wilson as far more blameworthy than the 'wilful' Senators," Roosevelt said again. "To think of the folly of having cursed this country with the really hideous misfortune of four years more of Wilson in this great and terrible world crisis."

"It is dreadful to think that some millions of Americans will vote for Wilson—including men like President Eliot," he wrote in July, 1916. "They can't so vote without incurring moral degradation."

"This last submarine threat has made all Wilson's League to Enforce Peace talk go glimmering down into the waste and futile spaces of dead rhetoric. What an exhibition he has made of himself, and unfortunately of the country also. . . .

"He is responsible for the existence of the very Peace Party which he brings forward as an excuse when he ought to act boldly."

This is all rather sad when we remember that Mr. Roosevelt in his own term as President had done such fine work for the cause of peace and had expressed himself so vigorously in favor of the very aims and specific objects the President was now sponsoring. For Theodore Roosevelt had received the Nobel prize in 1910, after his successful attempts to bring about peace between Russia and Japan. He also played a major part in negotiations at the Algeciras Conference and the settlement of the first Moroccan crisis between Germany and the Allied Powers. In his Nobel address in May, 1910, he suggested further development of arbitration and the Hague Court and said:

Finally it would be a master stroke if those great Powers honestly bent on peace would form a League of peace, not only to keep the peace among themselves, but to prevent, by force if necessary, its being broken by others. . . .

"The combination," Mr. Roosevelt continued, "might at first be only to secure peace within certain definite limits and certain definite conditions," but "the ruler or statesman who should bring about such a combination would have earned his place in history for all time and his title to the gratitude of mankind."

Evidently, in the Colonel's mind, Woodrow Wilson was not to be allowed at any price to be that man.

Lodge, speaking at the New Willard meeting in 1916, at Union College, and in various other places, endorsed with equal vigor the immediate necessity of a league to enforce peace. "I know the difficulties which this league . . . undertakes but . . . I believe much can be done. Probably it will be impossible to stop all wars but it certainly will be possible to stop some wars and thus diminish their number. The way in which this problem must be worked out must be left to this league and to those who are giving this great subject the study which it deserves."

Yet in December, 1918, we find both Lodge and Roosevelt vehemently opposing the very same sort of league, proposed by Wilson almost word for word in the terms which they themselves used, and rounding up the cohorts to crush it.

Roosevelt's campaign of depreciation and "repudiation" during the German negotiations has already been seen. As soon as the Armistice celebrations had ended, the fight began on a wider scale. Senators Knox and Poindexter attacked the League proposal, declaring it would mean an abrogation of the Monroe Doctrine and revision of the Constitution. Senator Reed, a Democratic opponent of the President's, also spoke against it. On December 3rd Senator Knox introduced a resolution to the effect that "our purposes in the Peace Conference should be confined to the aforesaid aims [to vindicate the ancient rights of navigation as established under international law and in order to remove forever the German menace to our peace]; (2) that for the safeguarding of those aims . . . there shall be the same complete accord and co-operation with our chief co-belligerents, and (3) that any project for any general league of nations or for any sweeping changes in the ancient laws of the sea should be postponed for separate consideration . . . at some future time when general conferences on those subjects might be deemed useful."

About this same time Senator Albert J. Beveridge delivered an address before the Massachusetts Bar Association in which he took up almost every objection to a league of nations that could possibly be conceived. Other Senators spoke on the Senate floor, from both sides, and with heat.

The Boston Evening *Transcript* of December 18th announced: "One of the greatest debates in the history of popular government is about to begin in the Senate of the United States. . . . It will afford our Allies a barometer of sentiment in the place and among the men who under the Constitution have the power from the people to veto even the words and wishes of the President of the United States, whether his name be Washington or Wilson." Coming from the leading conservative paper of Senator Lodge's home city, this pronouncement had an ominous significance.

A determined drive to prevent the creation of a league of nations had evidently begun.

On November 26th Lodge wrote Roosevelt of "this dangerous idea of a league of nations"—it had become dangerous because Wilson sponsored it and because of its alarming possibilities in relation to the next Presidential election—and spoke of his great desire "to have a long talk" with the Colonel. On December 17th at Roosevelt's urgent request Lodge went to see him at the Roosevelt Hospital in New York, where the Colonel was lying ill, and the two spent some time taking counsel together. Mr. Roosevelt's sister Mrs. Robinson gives the following account of that meeting in her book, *My Brother Theodore Roosevelt*:

"The Senator spent two days with me, and of those two days two whole mornings were spent in Colonel's room at the hospital.

War Leader

I was with them the first morning when they discussed the tentative league of nations—parts of which in problematical form were already known to the public [through Mr. Wilson's speeches and diplomatic papers]. The different reservations insisted upon later by Senator Lodge when the League in its eventual form was presented to the United States were tentatively formulated at the bedside of the Colonel." And all this two months before a constitution of the League existed or the final terms and organization of the League were known.

"Senator Lodge and my brother went over every one of the reservations during a session of three hours," says Mrs. Robinson, "changing and deciding upon this one and that and finally every one of them was O.K.'d by Theodore Roosevelt."

The two top-ranking leaders of the Republican party thus planned—seven months before the League and the Treaty ever came before the United States Senate—the precise terms and reservations and amendments by which it should be defeated. "The decision at that December war council was very evidently," says Dr. D. F. Fleming, "to attack whatever League proposals the President might bring home by the amendments and reservations agreed upon in advance—so many amendments and reservations that participation by the United States on the terms agreed on by the President with other Powers would be effectively blocked."

This fact makes farcical all the subsequent arguments—"if Wilson had only taken Lodge to Paris," Lodge's "genuine support" for the Treaty with reservations and "belief that these reservations made the League safe for the United States," that "with these reservations the Treaty would go through," et cetera, et cetera. The League and the Treaty were defeated long before they reached the Senate. The decision had been taken—and the League doomed—before ever the Peace Conference began.

CHAPTER V

PEACE-
MAKER

I

ON DECEMBER 4, 1918—three weeks after the signing of the Armistice—President Wilson sailed for France and the Peace Conference: flags flying, whistles blowing, crowds cheering, the guns booming an historic salute as his ship with its accompanying escort of warships left the harbor. Never before had a President of the United States set sail for foreign shores while in office.

In his address to Congress, three days before, Mr. Wilson had set forth his reasons:

The peace settlements which are now to be agreed upon are of transcendent importance both to us and to the rest of the world, and I know of no business or interest which should take precedence of them. The gallant men of our armed forces on land and sea have consciously fought for the ideals which they knew to be the ideals of their country;

280

Peace-Maker

I have sought to express those ideals; they have accepted
my statements of them as the substance of their own thought
and purpose, as the associated governments have accepted
them; I owe it to them to see to it, so far as in me lies, that
no false or mistaken interpretation is put on them, and no
possible effort omitted to realize them. It is now my duty
to play my full part in making good what they offered their
life's blood to obtain. I can think of no call to service
which would transcend this.

Of course there was an outcry from his political opponents
and others who loudly defended the tradition that the President
should never leave the country. But Wilson had no intention of
conducting negotiations at the end of a cable, three thousand
miles from the scene of action; and at that time the entire
world was so much with him that even this unprecedented move
was regarded with special leniency by most Americans. Today,
with our Presidents flying back and forth between Casablanca,
Hawaii, Yalta, and Berlin, it seems strange to think that the
question should once have roused such passionate controversy.

On the boat—in the blessed nine-day respite for recuperation
and marshaling his forces—Wilson began to realize the im-
mensity of the task before him. His cabin desk was piled with
perhaps the most extraordinary collection of documents a statesman ever contemplated: the Koreans were pleading to be free
of Japan, the Armenians wanting to be free of the Turks; the
Persians fearing Russian and British encroachments; the Rumanians appealing for their compatriots in Hungary, the Jews for
the future of Palestine. All these peoples seemed to believe that
if President Wilson would just say the word he could bring
justice, heal old wrongs all over the world—even to the return
of islands and the restoring of plundered art treasures.

"We come therefore to you, sir," wrote the Albanians, "as the
respected chief of the most powerful democracy, as to the man
who has placed the sentiment of justice above all other interests. . . . Today Albania is struggling painfully in the hands of
those who wish once more to dismember her and who wish

to take possession of territories which do not belong to them and which never have belonged to them. . . . Albania, a poor country, found no advocate in Europe to take her part. . . ."

Wilson was to be the advocate for them all. There were reports too from other heads of States and from anxious relief workers; reports about the millions of homeless and destitute wandering over Europe, memoranda about the starving Russians, about the starving Germans—the aged, the orphaned, the expatriated, the diseased.

In those papers was poured out before him all the misery, the longing, the anguished hope of the world. He tended to agree with Homer Cummings, who said as the Armistice bells rang out, "You know, Mr. President, I have a feeling our troubles are just beginning!"

Wilson was under no illusions as to the fight ahead of him. The world wanted a new order—or it had, up to the Armistice. The difficulties of getting that new order and getting it running would be enormous. But they must be faced and conquered. "If it won't work it must be made to work," said Wilson. The Conference confronted a terrific task; only a terrific good intent and a patience which never faltered could accomplish it.

When he spoke of "a new order" he meant two things: first, *self-determination*, the right of peoples to choose their own government and have a say in it themselves; and, second, *a world association* of nations in which all should co-operate for mutual aid and protection—his League of Nations. These two principles, like all of Wilson's program, were fundamentally American and had been expressed straight through our history in the balancing ideas of States' rights and the power of the Federal Government.

Wilson had put a wealth of thought and devotion into preparing for this peace. A whole year before the Armistice he had directed Colonel House to organize, under the immediate headship of House's brother-in-law Dr. Mezes, a group of experts and research workers known as "The Inquiry." The group included some of the most brilliant political scientists, economists, historians, and specialists of various kinds in the country. These men worked singly and together for a year before their studies were called for. Many of them accompanied Wilson to the Peace Conference. Their task was to study every phase of the intricate problems that would come up before the Conference, the history of those problems in the different countries, the special points to be borne in mind regarding the relation of different peoples to the problems and to each other.

Among the members of the Inquiry were: Professor Charles Haskins, Dean of the Graduate School of Harvard, Dr. Isaiah Bowman, Director of the American Geographical Society, a general territorial specialist; Professor Allyn A. Young, head of the Department of Economics at Cornell; George Louis Beer, formerly of Columbia, an authority on colonial possessions; Professor W. L. Westermann, head of the History Department of the University of Wisconsin and specialist on Turkey; R. H. Lord, professor of history at Harvard, specialist on Russia and Poland; Roland B. Dixon, professor of ethnography at Harvard; Professor Clive Day, head of the Economics Department at Yale, specialist on the Balkans; W. E. Lunt, professor of history at Haverford College, specialist on northern Italy; Charles Seymour, professor of history at Yale, specialist on Austria-Hungary; Mark Jefferson, professor of geography at Michigan State Normal School, and James Shotwell, professor of history at Columbia.

The President himself attended to the major problem of preparing a draft-constitution and plan for his cherished world association. Studies on this had been going forward for months. Wilson began his own concrete written work on it in June, 1918, with Colonel House acting as scout and assistant. The Colonel conferred with Elihu Root, Ex-President Taft, Dr. Lowell of Harvard, and other distinguished authorities, and in Europe with Lord Cecil and Lord Bryce. House embodied all the various ideas and suggestions in a rough draft for a covenant which he sent Mr. Wilson in July, 1918. The President proceeded then to make his own first draft, which was to undergo many changes before it finally came to the consideration of the Peace Conference. But it was begun, as we see, well ahead of time.

The Story of Woodrow Wilson

Then there was the matter of the choice of personnel for the American delegation. Thousands of words in hundreds of books have been written on this—how the President should have selected stronger men to advise with him at such a time, how he should have taken several leading Republicans, how his League would probably have gone through had he done this—et cetera. The practical question is: What Republicans? Whom should he have taken? The leaders of the Republican party at that moment were Henry Cabot Lodge, whose views on the League and whose ruthless peace demands were hardly reassuring, aside from his personal animosity to the President; Boies Penrose, notorious political boss; Senator Knox, reactionary imperialist par excellence; Senator Borah, who detested the very idea of international co-operation. Whom should he have taken?

Mr. Taft and Mr. Root were the only real possibilities. There was awkwardness about the presence of Mr. Taft—a former President—and he divided his allegiance between his desire for a league of nations and his desire for the dominance of the Republican party. Mr. Root was a "hard-shell conservative" who worked very closely with Mr. Lodge and whom Mr. Wilson had come to distrust in the shipping bill days. He did not believe that either Root or Taft would stand up under pressure. Nor did they when pressure came regarding the League, later.

The Republican Mr. Wilson did take to Paris—Mr. Henry White—was a diplomat who had been American Ambassador to France and Italy, well acquainted with European procedure and European personalities, sympathetic with Wilson's program, and sufficiently popular with his own party leaders for Theodore Roosevelt to write to Senator Lodge, "I am overjoyed that Harry White is going to the Peace Conference." During his own Presidency T. R. had declared White "the most useful man in the entire diplomatic service" and entrusted him with his most important diplomatic tasks. White had headed the American delegation at the last great international conference at Algeciras, where he put through Roosevelt's important strategy in bringing about an agreement between Germany and the Entente Powers on Morocco. Lodge also was pleased by

White's appointment to the Paris Conference. White did not accept the appointment till he had talked with both Lodge and Roosevelt on the telephone and was sure they approved his going.

The other members of the American Commission were the Secretary of State, Mr. Lansing; the President's personal adviser, Colonel House; and the very able and well-liked General Tasker Bliss (also a Republican), who had been sitting on the Supreme War Council and thoroughly understood European leaders and problems. In addition to the five Commissioners, Mr. David Hunter Miller and Dr. James Brown Scott joined the American delegation as advisers on international law, Admiral W. S. Benson as Naval Adviser, Major-General F. C. Kernan as adviser on Military Affairs. Mr. Joseph Grew was General Secretary and Supervising Director of the American Commission. Dr. Edwin Gay served as Director of the technical bureau known as "Washington Central."—or the "Central Bureau of Planning and Statistics"—which had to do with food, shipping, war trade, raw materials, finance, tariffs, and other vital technical questions. Mr. Norman Davis, Mr. Herbert Hoover, Mr. Thomas Lamont, Mr. Vance McCormick, and Mr. Bernard Baruch represented America on the Supreme Economic Council later.

Fifty-eight Technical Commissions of experts completed the roster of Conference members in addition to the controlling body, which was generally known as the Council of Ten, and the League of Nations Commission presided over by President Wilson. Each country had, of course, its own group of specialists and secretaries, military and naval representatives, as well as its official Commissioners. The British delegation alone filled five hotels. Including its elaborate secretarial and executive services, the American delegation numbered more than thirteen hundred persons. They were housed, most of them, at the Hôtel Crillon, which became the American Foreign Office and official headquarters.

To understand the complex series of meetings and issues that were to occupy the attention of the President and of the world during those crucial months, one must have some idea of the background, both physical and psychological, of the Conference. At the beginning of the year 1919 eight million men lay dead in Europe. Twenty million more had been wounded. The people who had been fighting for four years faced the future in an atmosphere of ruined cities, wrecked factories, crushing debts. For four years Allied leaders had worked constantly to instill the military spirit in these people, building up a war psychology of hate. Now in a few weeks Wilson and his colleagues were expected to build an elaborate strategy of peace.

In late 1918 and early 1919, when the Peace Conference convened, no less than fourteen "small wars" were still sputtering in Europe and Asia. This meant that even after the war was officially ended war strategy still went on. The military men, whose leadership supposedly ceased when the Peace Council came in, kept turning up at odd times throughout the Conference, still trying to insist on military viewpoints and methods. Sometimes they tried to influence political and economic decisions too. Foch, for example, exercised a powerful influence on Clemenceau.

But the real struggle at Paris was between the diplomacy of the Old and of the New Order. These were President Wilson's terms to describe the contending forces: they corresponded, roughly, with the ambitions and training of the Old World and the New.

At a traditional peace-making of the Old Order half a dozen diplomats, each representing the special interests of a single nation, came together in a series of secret meetings and after days of fencing and maneuvering, of private deals and understandings, finally reached a settlement—which was then maintained by treaties and military force, upholding certain traditional balances of power.

The general public had nothing to do with this old-style peace. It was engineered behind closed doors by a handful of the governing class of each country. They arranged their settlements according to numbers of population and the military power of the nations concerned. When it was all over they announced what had been done—or as much as they cared to reveal; for many of these treaties and settlements were secret. This traditional "peace" and traditional diplomacy of the Old Order had existed for centuries. The old-time leaders had no idea of really giving it up.

The New Order of peace-making, inaugurated by President Wilson, involved an entirely different attitude as well as method. It was first of all a people's peace. It began with certain general principles laid down in the Fourteen Points, approved by the people and accepted by the nations of the world. These principles were then applied to various specific problems—not by self-interested politicians but by impartial scientists, geographers, statisticians, and economists who had made protracted studies of those problems and whose one desire was the best possible solution, on the basis of the greatest good for the greatest number. The members of the Inquiry who accompanied the President to Paris took with them the masses of material which they had assembled over the year and with a lifetime background of specialized knowledge. The President consulted these specialists constantly. They sat near him at every meeting; it was their dictum he trusted as to facts, his own as to principle.

It is often said that Mr. Wilson would take no opinion but his own on important matters. Mr. Thomas Lamont, commenting on the President's procedure at Paris, said, "I never saw a man more ready or anxious to consult than he." Over and again in the meetings he would say to Lloyd George or Clemenceau, "You will have to argue that out with my expert Mr. So-and-so. He is my brain on this question."

The French and the British too had their staffs of experts and scientific consultants, but the Americans were able to use this method more effectively because they had fewer material interests to serve.

To the diplomats of the Old Order "peace after victory" meant the "plums" promised by secret treaties. It meant mines, colonies, oil wells, huge indemnities, new frontiers, guaranteed by a complex system of ententes and alliances. Wilson's plan involved a complete change of system: the coalition not of a few countries in competitive alliances but of all countries for an efficiently organized world. The object of this co-operation was not material booty but permanent peace and justice for all nations, the weakest as well as the strongest, guaranteed by one overwhelmingly powerful body—so strong that no lone aggressor would dare to challenge it. This single body, the League, was to be the trustee and protector of the peace for the whole world.

It was a staggering idea for the diplomatists of the Old Order. They accepted it for a while because they must—because America was powerful and they needed her, and Wilson was her leader, a man of force and vast influence. But directly the danger had passed and their worst fears were calmed, they reverted to the habitual policies. A different note was noticeable even a week after the Armistice. Once the cheering was over, Wilson's all-powerfulness passed too. The minute people were no longer frightened—so frightened that they had to stick together or go under—all the old greeds and hates and grabbings began. "New claims and new interests are being presented of which we know little," wrote Colonel House's aide, Colonel Bonsal, from Paris at the time, "and of which the powers we have brought to victory think we should know nothing at all. Some of our people are beginning to say that Wilson should have made hard and fast agreements with the Powers while the eventual issues still hung in the balance."

Even before the Armistice attacks on the President's policy began to appear in the Paris press. "The Allies are bound by nothing that Mr. Wilson wrote or even typed on his famous typewriter," announced the French writer Pertinax. On the eve of the President's departure for Paris Theodore Roosevelt in a damning public statement announced: "Our allies and our enemies and Mr. Wilson himself should understand that Mr. Wilson has no authority to speak for the American people at this time"—at this time, when world peace was to be made and Mr. Wilson's Fourteen Points had been accepted as the basis for that peace by all nations including his own. When the American people themselves scorn their President and hold him up before the world as an object of contempt and insult what can be expected from outsiders? Senator Lodge added to Roosevelt's statement: "We are abundantly able to make our opinions known not only to the President but to the Allies, who have a very clear and even acute idea of the power of the Senate with regard to treaties." Lodge accompanied this with a private memorandum to Henry White which he asked the latter to show—behind the back of his President—to Mr. Balfour and the Allied chiefs at the Peace Conference.

Colonel House, engaged in negotiations towards an Armistice in Paris, found himself confronted with a group of war-weary and naturally skeptical Premiers who asked dubiously: "Are we really now expected to negotiate on the basis of the Fourteen Points? If we agree to this Armistice does it mean we are accepting Wilson's terms?"

"It certainly does—you certainly are," said House. How quickly they forgot that it was on those terms that the enemy had sought an armistice, and that the speeches of the man they now shied away from had brought about the breakdown from within as his soldiers had brought about the physical defeat of the enemy. The Fourteen Points were reviewed and discussed there in the Colonel's apartment during that portentous first week of November. Differences among the leaders were so great that for a time there was actually threat of a separate peace.

Finally Colonel House said he intended to advise the President to lay before Congress the peace terms he had approved—and that the Supreme War Council of the Allies had approved—together with the peace terms England, France, and Italy now apparently insisted upon, and ask for a decision. Germany had accepted our terms. If now, after all previous understandings, our allies did not choose to accept them. . . . On November 3rd the President sent a very stern cable showing that he did not intend to budge from his Fourteen Points. The situation was so grave that the French and British yielded, making only one or two minor reservations, which the President let pass. It was a triumph for Wilson but not a very cheering prelude to the Peace Conference.

The Story of Woodrow Wilson

As significant as the program and atmosphere of the Conference were the dominating personalities behind it. We have heard many times of their individual special traits: Clemenceau, "the avowed cynic," with his yellow eyes and huge mustaches, his hard (but never thick) skull under its little cap; Lloyd George, the political weather vane, shifting with every wind that affected his personal fortunes; Orlando, with his crown of silver hair and his alternately childlike and very shrewd approach; the "bland and inscrutable Japanese" of tradition, Baron Makino, Viscount Chinda—very quiet, very discreet, saying little, noting everything; and Wilson, standing practically alone, with House engaged in his pleasant personal meanderings, and Lansing, who had gone to the Peace Conference, as he himself records, hostile to the President's principles.

At first the President hoped for powerful support from Lloyd George, but this hope soon vanished. For Clemenceau Wilson's regard steadily increased. The two had few points of agreement, but each recognized the sincerity of the other and saw in the other a foeman worthy of his steel. The old Tiger came to have a genuine respect and liking for the man whom he had at first considered "a dreaming schoolmaster."

Wilson liked Clemenceau because he was frank, blunt, and you always knew where you were with him. With the changeable and erratic Lloyd George, you never knew. He might agree to something one day and say the exact opposite tomorrow. Bourgeois, second French delegate, was a long-time worker for peace, a former Premier, and a natural for Wilson's ideas, though an opponent on the question of armed force behind the new peace organization. Pichon and Larnaude, the two other members of the French delegation, embodied all that was conservative, traditional, and old-French.

The British delegation presented a curious bundle of contrasts: the dynamic opportunist Lloyd George flanked by the urbane and philosophic Balfour—witty, detached, with an almost ironic attitude toward the great events in which he was, somewhat wearily, engaged. Cecil was idealistic as Wilson in many ways, essentially "British" and worldly in others. Standing alone and perhaps the greatest figure of the entire British Commonwealth group was Smuts, who has stayed great through the twenty-five years that have followed. He towered above the other Dominions Ministers—Hughes of Australia, Massey of New Zealand, and Borden of Canada.

Another attractive figure was our American General Bliss, a robust old soldier "with the finest intellect in the Army," says Newton Baker. An extraordinary character, this grizzled old general—a great linguist and student of Latin, a learned geologist and Oriental botanist, a student of folklore of people all over the world. "He was a statesman as well as a military man, broad-gauged, farsighted, and astute," said his War Department chief. For months he had held the Supreme War Council together, the only man looked to by all of them in the final settlement of disputes, and he was as eminently fitted for peace-making as for his work in the conduct of the war. "He commanded the respect and trust of the President from beginning to end," said one of the American delegation, "and, oh, he could swear beautifully!"

A word may be added about Henry White, who had considerably greater force of character and general worth than was generally realized. White was loyal, tactful, self-effacing; too self-effacing, perhaps. Had he been more aggressive, forced his views and knowledge on the President a bit more, it might have worked out to our advantage. He never showed Lodge's memorandum to the Allied leaders or engaged in any behind-the-scenes private negotiations or partisan intrigues. He tried to help the President and the peace cause with all his might.

Other distinguished men at the Conference were Hymans, Premier of Belgium; Reis, the profoundly religious Ambassador who represented Portugal; Dr. Beneš from the new Republic of Czechoslovakia; Mr. Wellington Koo, able Chinese Ambassador to the United States.

Into this maze of motives, plans, and personalities came the Presbyterian Covenanter and former Governor, toughened by his preliminary bouts with the New Jersey bosses and six years of lively encounters with rebellious Congressmen. "A prophet and a dreamer" they called him—before they had come upon his highly capable fist in the ring. Then their voices took on a new respect.

II

ON DECEMBER 14th the President landed at Brest and proceeded to the great ovation that awaited him in Paris. "No Louis in splendor, no Napoleon in the gaudy glamour of conquest, no revolutionary with a new vision of happiness . . . had ever drawn so great a reception from this people who above all others appreciated splendor and glamour, dreams and visions," writes David Loth. It was a revelation even to Clemenceau, who said, "I do not believe there has been anything like it in the history of the world."

Fifty thousand people jammed the Place de la Concorde. The throngs gathering since daybreak packed the four miles of procession route thirty feet deep. Cheering, shouting humanity filled every inch of space. "We grew giddy," says Mrs. Wilson, "trying to respond to the bursts of welcome. Flowers rained upon us till we were nearly buried." "The tribute which Paris paid to Wilson," wrote Dr. Shotwell, who witnessed it, "was one that I never saw the like of and shall never see again. It was heartfelt . . . the populace of Paris turning out to see the man who is in their eyes and in the eyes of most of the oppressed of Europe the first moral force in the world today."

The triumphal drive proceeded down the Champs Elysées and across the Place de la Concorde, with fountains playing, troops at attention, and people cheering; then into the Rue Royale past the classically beautiful Church of the Madeleine and on to the Rue de Monceau and the palace of Prince Murat, which was to be the Paris home of the President and Mrs. Wilson. The President of France entertained them at luncheon at the Elysée Palace that same day, with the War Generals Joffre, Foch, Pershing, Bliss, the French Cabinet Ministers, and other officials. Next day the city of Paris honored them with a ceremony at the Hôtel de Ville, where the President received the freedom of the city and a gold pen "with which to sign a just, humane, and durable peace."

Processions, functions, and honors occupied the first few days. The President met his colleagues in the Supreme War Council and the three other members of the inner Council of Four— Lloyd George, Clemenceau, and Orlando. Then the organization of the Conference began. Wilson, of course, wanted to start at once, but here he met his first disappointment. The English thought it impossible to open the Conference till after their General Election. Mr. Lloyd George's political fortunes were in the balance, and he said that he had to go home. Both the British and the Italians felt that personal visits from the President to their countries would do much towards smoothing out domestic differences and making things easier for their representatives at the Peace Conference. Mr. Wilson was urged to visit London and Rome at once; the King of Italy even went to Paris to deliver his invitation in person. There was nothing to do but to accept. It was agreed that directly after Christmas the President and Mrs. Wilson would go to England and from there to Rome.

They spent Christmas with the American troops near General Pershing's headquarters. Tired, badly needing some rest and relaxation, the President insisted on this way of spending his holiday. He and Mrs. Wilson took an ice-cold train from Paris at midnight on Christmas Eve and reached their destination at seven on Christmas morning. It was snowing hard when they left their train and started on the long drive with General Pershing and his aides. They spent the whole day visiting and talking with the boys in their billets—sometimes in barns where the mud was deep, sometimes in cellars or in lofts reached by a ladder. In one place there was a cantonment, with temporary shacks for barracks, and a canteen. The boys had tried to make some Christmas decorations with sprays of green and bits of red paper.

"Some faithful American women were there to look after them," says Mrs. Wilson, "but they were all so brave and things were so lonely and uncomfortable that they brought tears to our eyes despite their efforts to pretend they were full of Christmas cheer."

Later in the day there were maneuvers of cavalry and infantry, in full marching equipment; the infantry kept "a well-formed line and spirited marching in spite of the appalling mud underfoot." The President and General Pershing addressed the troops, and the chaplain said a prayer. Then the party went back to the automobiles and drove to the nearest mess and a big Christmas dinner. It was a gay meal, with officers and men in high spirit. The President told some good stories, and everybody was sorry when he had to leave.

The writer particularly appreciates this story as she spent that Christmas in the largest American Hospital Center in France, trying to get supplies and Christmas decorations for twenty-six thousand wounded men. The mud came over our knees; we were in hip rubber boots all day. Our boys were greatly pleased when they heard that the President had left his grand palace and gone down to spend Christmas with some of their buddies.

The day after Christmas the President and Mrs. Wilson crossed the Channel to be the guests of the King of England. King George and Queen Mary, together with the Princess Mary and various dignitaries and imposing masses of troops, met them at Charing Cross Station. Traditional English coaches drawn by four horses drove them down the Mall to Buckingham Palace, and the man who as a boy modeled his life on Gladstone and John Bright and his early speeches on English Parliamentary debate, was cheered to the echo by vast throngs of British citizens within the very shadow of that great golden-brown Parliament he once worshiped from afar. They gave him a welcome such as staid old London had never seen. At the top of Marlborough House steps a tall gray-haired lady waved an American flag and cheered with the rest. "Why, it's Grandmamma!" cried Princess Mary, waving back enthusiastically to Queen Alexandra as the procession rolled past.

A crowded three days followed: the grand luncheon given by the Lord Mayor, another with Lloyd George to meet the British party leaders; an address to the labor crowds at Manchester—not so warmly smiled upon by Mr. L. G.; the "pilgrimage of the heart" to his mother's home in Carlisle; the state dinner at Buckingham Palace with the gold dinner service and the blazing jewels and Orders, following the more appealing first evening when the two heads of state and their wives dined alone and Queen Mary took Mrs. Wilson through her own apartments afterwards and showed her her treasures—"while our husbands talk over their affairs"—as women have done since time immemorial.

Another gala three days in Italy, with wildly cheering Italians in place of cheering Britishers, and a gorgeous special performance at La Scala Opera House in Milan following a second series of royal entertainments at the palace of King Victor Emmanuel. And so finally back to Paris, the impatient President at last buckling down to the work of the Peace Conference and the duties for which he had crossed the ocean.

One thing stood out vividly in his mind as this tour ended: the people were with him—far too much with him to suit some of their leaders. On several occasions local authorities had deliberately kept him from contact with the people. In Rome a huge crowd waiting for him to make a speech to them after his audience at the Vatican had been dispersed as "disorderly." In Paris the working people and the soldiers were repeatedly prevented from seeing him or demonstrating in any impressive numbers their belief in his principles.

"The French Government does not want the people brought too closely in contact with Wilson's ideas," was the shrewd popular reaction conveyed to him again and again. "A reactionary press will also try to defeat you. But have no fear, Mr. President —we the people of the world are with you!" How many times have I read that line in the masses of letters, cables, and telegrams sent to Mr. Wilson from all over the earth. *The people of the world are with you.* The governments and old-time political leaders are not." Which will win out? This was the great question on the eve of the opening of the long-awaited Peace Conference.

The Story of Woodrow Wilson

III

ON JANUARY 18, 1919, the President of France formally opened the Peace Conference. The splendid Council Room of the French Foreign Office had seen many remarkable gatherings but none like this: the first world conference to fix not only the immediate war settlements but to draw up a permanent organization to maintain an enduring international peace. Twenty-seven nations were represented.

Early in the day crowds began to throng the Quai d'Orsay. French troops took their positions fronting the Palais Bourbon, with a guard of honor drawn up in the court through which the delegates must pass. As each group arrived they were greeted with a fanfare of trumpets and military honors. The Japanese came first, followed by the Siamese and the East Indians in their picturesque turbans. President Wilson's arrival brought an enthusiastic demonstration from the crowd. Monsieur Pichon, the French Foreign Minister, met the President and conducted him to the Council Room, already crowded with delegates who greeted Mr. Wilson warmly as he passed toward the table of honor.

The sumptuous Room of the Clock, with its white and gold decorations, gorgeous chandeliers, and beautiful frescoes, presented a magnificent spectacle. The first thing that met the eye of the delegates was a marble statue of Peace holding up the torch of Civilization. This stood directly behind the chair assigned to Premier Clemenceau. In front of the statue was spread the huge horseshoe council table, covered with the traditional diplomatic green baize and with seventy-two seats around it for the opening session, including the nine places of honor at the head of the table.

Precisely at three o'clock a ruffle of drums and blare of trumpets announced the arrival of President Poincaré. The Premiers of other States accompanied him to the council table. A hush fell upon the gathering as the great moment arrived for the opening of the Congress. The entire assembly rose and stood while the French President spoke. He made only a brief address of welcome, then shook by the hand the Ministers and plenipotentiaries of twenty-six nations—and President Wilson. The tragedy for the Conference was that Wilson was *not* a plenipotentiary. Under our system of divided authority the President of the United States lacks the full powers of negotiation possessed by the heads of other States.

After the opening ceremonies President Wilson proposed Premier Clemenceau as permanent Chairman of the Conference and Clemenceau was unanimously elected. In his eloquent little speech of acceptance the old Tiger spoke of the stern duty before them: "It is not merely to establish a peace in terms of continents that we have come together. We meet here to establish for all time peace among the peoples of the earth. . . . The achievement of our purpose is not possible unless we remain firmly united. Here we have met as friends, from here we must go as brothers. . . . Our program speaks for itself. I shall not add a superfluous word. Let us work speedily and well. Gentlemen, to our task!"

The vital issue of the early days of the Conference—and one which aroused much controversy at home—was Wilson's determination to make the League of Nations an integral part of the peace treaty. This was no sudden "idealistic" whim on his part but a reasoned decision evolved from three years' hard practical thinking. An association of nations appeared in every one of the President's discussions of his peace terms. Without it, how guarantee the peace our soldiers had fought for—how protect the people of the world against future aggressors and outlaws?

After he went to Europe, faced the bedlam of greedy interests and demands, saw the overwhelming problems, he believed the League was more than ever needed, to adjust many differences, regulate many matters that could not wisely be dealt with so soon after the passions and bitterness of the quarrel. He also felt for the first time the reluctance of some of the Powers to enter into a collective peace organization and knew that if they did not do so now under compulsion the chances at some vague future conference were very slim.

The European countries and Japan wanted military and economic settlements made first and a general adherence to the old secret treaties—peace based on the necessities, interests, and fears of the great nations—the League to come afterwards if at all. Wilson wanted the American principles and program, which had been accepted at the Armistice, applied now to all issues of the settlement. The League of Nations was the cornerstone of that program. He therefore insisted on the League now, and knit into every part of the settlement.

On the first day the French offered their plan of procedure, which put consideration of the League of Nations last. On the next day President Wilson introduced his "List of Subjects," which gave the League first consideration. He wished it discussed by the Council of Ten at once and its principles worked out by the States as the basis of settlement. His List of Subjects was accepted. The French and the British tried to sidetrack the League by referring it to a special committee. The President's proposals in the Covenant for cutting down armaments and mandatory control of colonies terrified the European diplomats. They began to perceive for the first time the revolutionary changes his scheme portended.

Nevertheless, on January 22nd the President's proposal that "this League shall be created as an integral part of the general treaty of peace" was adopted. The very next day Lloyd George precipitated the attempt to divide up the German colonies among the British Dominions and the French and the Japanese —to get a division of the spoils *before* the discussion of the League and the new order, on the basis of the old secret treaties and in spite of the fact that the President's List with the League first had been accepted.

Mr. Lloyd George staged a dramatic scene in which he brought all the Prime Ministers of the British Dominions into the Council Room in a body to state their claims. Australia wanted New Guinea and other islands. New Zealand wanted Samoa. South Africa wanted German Southwest Africa. All were frankly for complete annexation. France presented an equally frank demand for the annexation of Togoland and the Cameroons. The Belgians expected a piece of German East Africa, and Italy had certain other provisional claims based upon the secret Treaty of London.

The President saw that he had a major battle on his hands, and shrewd and powerful antagonists to deal with. The whole foundation of his peace was at stake. They were willing to let him have his principles and his League *after* they had annexed the colonies they wanted. But they had reckoned without their opponent.

He reminded them of the fifth of the Fourteen Points, which had been accepted by all at the Armistice as the basis of the peace. That point proposed: *"A free, open-minded, and absolutely impartial adjustment of all colonial claims, based upon a strict observance of the principle that in determining all questions of sovereignty the interests of the populations concerned must have equal weight with the equitable claims of the government whose title is to be determined."* In the present discussion, said Mr. Wilson, it would appear that the claims were based primarily upon the security and interest of the great governments, not upon the principle that "the interest of the weakest is as sacred as the interest of the strongest."

He spoke his mind very candidly there in the Council, his steady gaze first on Lloyd George, then on Clemenceau. If their proposals were carried out, he contended, the world would say that the Great Powers first portioned out the helpless parts of the world and then formed a League of Nations. The crude fact was that each of these parts of the world had been assigned to one of the Great Powers. He wished to point out in all frankness that the world would not accept such action. It would make the League of Nations impossible, and we should have to return to the system of competitive armaments with accumulating debts and the burden of great armies. Thus the principle he urged was economical as well as moral.

Prime Minister Hughes of Australia strongly—even, at times, angrily—opposed the President; the Ministers from New Zealand

and South Africa less violently. The fight raged for an entire
week and developed considerable bitterness. On January 30th
there was threat of an open rupture. Mr. Wilson bluntly asked
Mr. Hughes if he intended to leave the Conference if his claims
were not satisfied? Lloyd George saved the day by introducing a
resolution which both Wilson and the Dominions Ministers
provisionally accepted, but which actually awarded the palm to
the President's principle. At the end of that week there was no
doubt in anyone's mind as to the quality of Wilson. He had come
through the first big battle victorious over the masters of the old
regime. The fight was bitter, but he carried his point. That is
the thing to remember—and we shall note how many times this
was said of President Wilson at this often belligerent Peace
Conference: "He had a hard battle—*but he carried it through!*"

On January 25th, at the second plenary session of the Confer-
ence, the League project was presented in a draft resolution.
Wilson in a powerful speech drove home his contention that the
League was the foundation of the whole program of the peace:

> We have assembled for two purposes: to make the present
> settlements which have been rendered necessary by this war,
> and also to secure the peace of the world. . . . The League
> of Nations seems to me . . . necessary for both of these
> purposes. . . .
>
> It will not suffice to satisfy government circles anywhere.
> It is necessary that we should satisfy the opinion of man-
> kind. The burdens of this war have fallen in an unusual
> degree upon the whole population of the countries involved
> . . . upon the older men . . . the women . . . the children,
> upon the homes of the civilized world . . . the real strain
> of the war has come where the eye of government could not
> reach but where the heart of humanity beats. We are bidden
> by these people to see that this strain does not come upon
> them again, and I venture to say that it has been possible
> for them to bear this strain because they hoped that those
> who represented them could get together after this war and

make such another sacrifice unnecessary. It is a solemn obligation on our part, therefore, to make permanent arrangements that justice shall be rendered and peace maintained.

Everywhere he had been, he said—in Italy, France, and England as well as at home—the people made it clear to him that their hope was in this project of the League of Nations. The representatives of the United States "regard it as the keystone of the whole program which expressed our purposes and ideals in this war." The idea of the United States in entering the war was not that of "intervening in the politics of Europe or Asia. . . . Her thought was that there was a single cause which turned upon the issues of this war. That was the cause of justice and liberty for men of every kind and place. Therefore the United States should feel that its part had been played in vain if there ensued . . . merely a body of European settlements. It would feel that it could not take part in guaranteeing those European settlements unless that guarantee involved the continuous superintendence of the peace of the world by the Associated Nations of the world."

The United States, of course, was not alone in this matter, for there are champions of this cause on every hand. "I have only tried in what I have said to give you the fountains of the enthusiasm which is within us for this thing, for those fountains spring, it seems to me, from the ancient wrongs and sympathies of mankind, and the very pulse of the world seems to beat to the surface in this enterprise."

It was a moving plea, which affected all present. Tears were in the eyes of Mr. Léon Bourgeois, who had fought so long and so gallantly for peace at The Hague and other conferences. Mr. Lloyd George rose "to second this resolution" and to make on his part a moving reference to the devastated regions of France which he had just visited. Mr. Orlando and others followed.

The resolution was unanimously adopted. Clemenceau, who had sat with closed eyes during the President's address, immediately set in motion the necessary machinery for implementing the project. A League of Nations Commission was appointed with the President as Chairman. Thus early in the Conference Wilson had brought his plan strongly into the foreground and was himself head of the Commission which was to prepare a constitution for it. He had also secured the reluctant acceptance of the second main plank of his program: that this League should be organized "as an integral part of the peace treaty." He had now to proceed as quickly as possible with the actual business of the League organization.

IV

OH, BUT you know President Wilson didn't really originate the League of Nations. Why, my cousin knows the man who . . ." "No—it was Briand, wasn't it? Oh—Sir George Paish!" "Why, President Taft had been working on it for years. My brother-in-law has a copy of the authentic first draft!"

The idea of an association of nations for the purpose of maintaining world peace and adjusting common problems had been in men's minds for centuries. Seneca, the great Oriental sages, William Penn and his Quakers, the Spaniard Vitoria in the fifteenth century, the Abbé de Saint-Pierre whose *Plan for Perpetual Peace* was published in Utrecht in 1728, and within our own time Czar Nicholas II and the members of the Hague Conference—these are only a few of the scores of eminent men and women who have worked for this grand ideal throughout the centuries. Mr. Wilson made no claim to originating it.

What President Wilson did was to give political reality to the ideal that had heretofore been simply a dream, by incorporating it as a specific proposal in this peace program. Many had dreamed of it. Wilson—"the academic, the visionary"—gave the dream practical shape. He had studied the idea all his life. One of his earliest magazine articles, written in 1887, referred to it. Shortly after the outbreak of the war in 1914 he talked with his brother-in-law Stockton Axson, setting forth some specific suggestions. He kept in touch with the League of Nations Society in England and the League to Enforce Peace in the United States—the two chief organizations actively promoting such a movement. During all the harassing efforts at mediation in Europe it was always in the foreground of his mind, the center and object of first consideration, in relation to which all his peace thinking proceeded. He made it the last and most impressive of his Fourteen Points.

The League to Enforce Peace was very active in America in 1917 and 1918 and gained large numbers of adherents. The idea swept England even more completely. A report to the United States State Department from England in early 1918 says: "Interest in the League of Nations has become a veritable flood. It is being discussed everywhere. The *Times* [organ of the government] appears to give guarded approval and the House of Lords accepted a motion approving the principle of a League of Nations and 'commending to the Government a study of conditions required for its realization.' The Labor Conference [in January] was for the proposal in vigorous language."

In the early spring of 1918 the British Government appointed a committee of distinguished international lawyers to draw up a document embodying a definite plan. In May, 1918, the report of that committee—known as the "Phillimore Report," from its chairman, Baron Phillimore—was sent to the War Cabinet and to the President of the United States and other leaders. It became one of the principal bases for the final League Constitution. It was not, strictly speaking, original either; but it put into correct legal terms the most practical suggestions from the various proposals already presented.

In June, 1918, Wilson began his study for a specific working plan. Colonel House assisted him with this, consulting Elihu Root, William H. Taft, and others. The two main documents used were the Phillimore Report and the Constitution of the American League to Enforce Peace. The French Minister Léon Bourgeois also sent over a draft on which he had been working with a group in his country for some years. There was a Swiss plan, a Belgian plan, an Italian plan, and numbers of others. It is therefore nonsense to repeat—as many writers and commentators do to this day—that "the Senate heard for the first time in the spring of 1919 that a league of nations was being promoted at the Peace Conference" or that "President Wilson rushed the League through in a few short weeks."

The League of Nations was one of the Fourteen Points accepted by the Senate and the American people and the Allies and the enemy and the whole world as the basis of peace and all postwar arrangements. For an entire year before the Peace Conference it was continuously put before the people in a series of public addresses by the President. The Constitution of the League represented the best thought and research of a large number of distinguished men—American, English, European, and Asiatic—over a long period of time, and the active preparation of certain men like Bourgeois and Cecil ever since the Hague Conferences of 1899 and 1907. Wilson had been working on his own plan for six months. So it is no good trying to saddle him with a hasty, ill-hatched project.

When Mr. Wilson went to Paris he took with him his first draft of a "Covenant" (his own term), which he and Colonel House had worked out. On arrival, he studied the plans brought by other delegates. General Smuts's plan had some points that impressed the President very much, and he incorporated them in his own draft as presented to the Commission: particularly the smaller (Executive) Council of the League in addition to the large Assembly, and the system of mandates which gave practical implementation to Point Five in Wilson's program. It appeared easier to amalgamate the American and British views than the French and Italian. After preliminary discussions both the President and the British prepared new drafts, and these were eventually consolidated by the American and British legal advisers into a composite draft which was finally accepted as the basis for discussion when the League of Nations Commission met on February 3rd.

How many of us have ever stopped to think of all that goes into the making of a great international document—what it means to get fifty or even thirty or even ten nations to bind themselves to certain action and to set the signatures and seals of their nations to that agreement? Consider those nineteen men gathered round the table in Paris to draw up the most important international document ever conceived: a covenant for a league of nations. Look at those men: two from each of the Great Powers—America, Great Britain, France, Italy, Japan; one each from Belgium, Brazil, China, Portugal, Serbia, and later four more from Greece, Poland, Rumania, Czechoslovakia. Each of them represents a completely different culture, tradition, and political system, different ideas on education, family relations, morals, and values. Each is there to represent a special nation with its special needs and fears and desires—vehemently conveyed to him every hour. Each has his own little personal quirks and prejudices and eccentricities. It's a wonder you get any international agreement at all, let alone a unanimous one by twenty-seven nations for a world constitution embodying twenty-six Articles on a series of involved and highly complicated questions.

The President redrafted his own plan four times, the British redrafted theirs twice, and there had been several redrafts of the consolidated plan before the Commission ever sat down to discuss the official "draft Covenant." Then the Commission members spent long hours of combined study and debate on this draft, Article by Article. They met in a large room in the Hôtel Crillon, the American headquarters building. The delegates gathered round a huge table in the center of the room, with President Wilson in the chairman's seat. At his left sat Colonel House, next him Cecil and Smuts; on the other side Orlando and the other Italian and the Small Powers delegates, with Bourgeois and Larnaude down at the far end. To one side was a smaller table where the drafting committee, the legal advisers and experts sat, and a third table for the secretaries. The President held in his hand the working-draft Covenant and read aloud one by one the Articles as they were submitted for discussion.

The first seven Articles of the Covenant deal with organization and administration: membership, voting, and procedure, machinery of the Assembly, Council, and Secretariat. Articles I and II passed with little objection. The first lively argument came on Article III and the question of representation of the Small Powers on the League Council, or Executive Body. Every country was to have representation on the larger body of the Assembly, but Cecil and others had proposed that the Council should be made up only of the Great Powers. Representatives of the Small Powers vigorously protested this point and were supported by Messrs. Bourgeois and Orlando of the larger governments. President Wilson had favored the small Council principally as a time-saving device; but he agreed to expand it to include Small-Power representation, and four Small Powers were added, making originally an Executive Council of nine, though the Council has at times reached a maximum of fifteen members. The Assembly votes on what Small Powers are to sit on the Council. These are elected for a period of three years, and certain Powers, such as Spain and Poland, came to be regarded as semipermanent members.

Articles VIII and IX deal with reduction of armaments and a permanent military commission. "The Council . . . shall formulate plans for such reduction, for the consideration and action of the several governments;" the Governments, after such plans have been adopted, shall not arm themselves beyong these limits without concurrence of the Council. The Military Commission will advise on the execution of these provisions.

Then comes the famous *Article X*, on which there was such violent discussion in the United States, though surprisingly little in the Commission: "The members of the League undertake to respect and preserve against external aggression the territorial integrity and existing political independence of all members of the League. In case of any such aggression or in case of any threat or danger of such aggression the Council shall advise upon the means by which this obligation shall be fulfilled."

Article XI is perhaps the most impressive Article in the Covenant and the most thrilling statement in the history of international life: "Any war or threat of war . . . is hereby declared a matter of concern to the whole League and the League shall take any action that may be deemed wise and effectual to safeguard the peace of nations. . . . It is declared also to be the friendly right of each member of the League to bring to the attention of the Assembly or of the Council any circumstance whatever affecting international relations which threatens to disturb international peace or the good understanding between nations on which peace depends."

The Covenant then goes on in *Articles XII-XV* to discuss the various types of arbitration by which disputes shall be settled instead of by war; these include the establishment by the Council of a World Court, which of course was subsequently done in 1920 at The Hague.

Articles XVI and XVII contain the famous "sanctions" or penalties to be imposed upon the aggressor—implementing Article X—the rules to be observed in breaking off economic and financial relations and a general boycott of the aggressor State. Here the French brought forward their proposal for an international military force, which the British and Americans at that time (also later at the Disarmament Conference) flatly refused to consider. The debate on this matter was the most intense of the first set of meetings and at one point threatened real trouble.

"The most serious hitch," wrote Wickham Steed in the Paris *Daily Mail* at the time, "came on February 11th when Wilson absolutely declined to accept the French demand for the creation of an international force that should operate under the executive control of the League of Nations. Monsieur Bourgeois urged the French view with much eloquence and pertinacity. Wilson claimed that the Constitution of the United States did not permit any such limitation upon its sovereignty and Lord Robert Cecil took a similar view in regard to the British Empire. . . . The French were willing to accept such limitation for the sake of security. They stood their ground and declined to surrender the claim which in their view alone could prevent the League of Nations Covenant from being 'a philosophical treatise devoid of authority.' The sitting broke up toward midnight with the position very strained."

The French—realists ever, rather than the rabid militarists

they were accused of being—asserted that an international instrument not backed by military force to cow the aggressor would have little weight with such countries as Germany. France urged this again at the Disarmament Conference of 1932 and offered to put all her bombers at the disposal of an international air force—surely the acid test. Spain, Sweden, and eight of the Small Powers pressed for this. England and America refused. One American delegate in 1932 declared that "this is not a realistic proposal." Hitler was even then building his gigantic armaments, but appeasement and peace at any price dominated Anglo-Saxon thinking.

If America had joined the League and such a force had existed —written into the Covenant when France first pleaded for it— history might have been completely different. The world might have swept forward in a vast and glorious advance instead of suffering the destruction known these past twenty-five years. As it was, the motion was lost.

The remaining Articles went through more rapidly. *Numbers XVIII-XX* deal with treaties and international obligations. *Article XXI*, on the Monroe Doctrine was added later. General Smuts, Chairman of the Mandates Subcommittee, presented *Article XXII*—the Article on Mandates. His words regarding the Article might well have been read to the United States Senate, later, apropos of the entire Covenant:

> For the last month we have worked out the provisions of the Article . . . day and night; we have weighed every sentence, every word, indeed I may say every letter, because we were of the opinion that if we succeeded it would be the cornerstone of a new and better world structure. . . . If you give your sanction to our work you will demonstrate that world public opinion is in favor of the ultimate self-government of all peoples without distinction as to race, religion, or color or previous conditions of servitude. . . . If you pull out a single plank, the whole edifice will come crashing down.

Peace-Maker

The Conference had anticipated a great fight on this Article. When the time came there was some discussion, but the Commission accepted the Article on both the first and the second readings, without any substantial changes.

A dramatic and splendid Article is *Number XXIII*, defining the social activities of the League. Lord Cecil introduced the Labor Clause, which the British Ministry of Labor originally proposed: "The Members of the League will endeavor to secure and maintain fair and humane conditions of labor for men, women, and children . . . both in their own countries and in all countries . . ." "To undertake to secure just treatment of the native inhabitants of territories under their control" was an important clause subsequently added. Clauses providing for international supervision of the drugs traffic, traffic in women and children, control of disease, and several other matters also came under this Article.

Article XXIV places under the League all international bureaus which are already established by international treaties or which may be constituted in the future. In *Article XXV* the members agree to encourage and promote voluntary national Red Cross organizations for "improvement of health . . . and mitigation of suffering throughout the world."

Article XXVI, on amendments, completes the document. An interesting discussion appears in the minutes on this: some favored a two-thirds, some a three-quarters vote on amendments to the Covenant. The Article finally reads that amendments shall take effect when ratified by the members of the Council and a majority of the members of the Assembly.

It is a remarkably simple document, considering the variety, complexity, and importance of the subjects treated. An article on religious liberty was proposed but later dropped. At the tenth meeting Baron Makino introduced a note on race equality, which he proposed as an amendment to Article XXI. The Baron brought this up again at the final meeting, pleading for its insertion as part of the Preamble to the Covenant. It was a plea of dignity and reasonableness supported by the French, Italian, and a number of other delegates—indeed by a final vote of 11

The Story of Woodrow Wilson

out of 17. The Americans and the British voted in the negative. Wilson approved in principle but feared harm to the Covenant as a whole through the introduction of such a controversial subject. Many letters from American friends of the League warned him against it. He expected that racial questions would be taken up naturally within the League after it was established. The subject was also a very delicate one for the British Government. Wilson finally ruled that the motion was lost, since it was not unanimous. The decision brought considerable criticism and charges of Anglo-American hypocrisy.

This is the way imperfect but invaluable international agreements are born. "Sorry, your Excellency, I couldn't get our people to agree to that . . . I am afraid my Government will insist . . . The Italian delegation would be obliged to add . . . The British Government will certainly refuse to . . . but if the Commission would agree to a slight modification of the second paragraph . . . yes, I think if that change were made, it would be all right."

Patiently, clause by clause, tedious hour after hour they built it up—the famous Covenant which was to become the target of sneering lesser men, ready so swiftly to tear down what others had tried conscientiously and sincerely to create for the good of humankind. Every man round that table (with the exception of Colonel House) had had long and arduous training in government, in the framing of both national and international policy, and in practical administration. They brought to their task the fruit of those years of precious experience and diplomatic insight, quickly seizing each question, adapting themselves to each new situation; yielding where they could, insisting firmly where they must: masters as well as servants in that most difficult of fields—international relations.

Being human, they had their moments of impatience, even exasperation with one another. These occasionally bordered on a first-class row, as when Lord Cecil—whose biting tongue belied his angelic countenance—told Mr. Larnaude there were absolutely no words in which he might appropriately do justice to the latter's legalistic and linguistic powers; or when Mr. Larnaude shook his fist across the table at a member and shouted: "I go—but I warn you I shall resume at the Plenary. I do not retire, Mr. President—I shall take it up again at the Plenary!"

Then they would calm down and apologize, each declaring the other was a grand fellow whom he had always admired with all his heart—and the meeting would go on again. As time passed, they developed some well-worn puns and some family jokes— Mr. Hughes's ear trumpet, Mr. Larnaude's late train to the country. They ended with real respect and in some cases strong affection for one another.

This was also true of the Big Four. "How do you like Wilson?" Clemenceau asked Lloyd George one day abruptly. "I like him. I like him better than when we started," said Lloyd George. "So do I," said Clemenceau

V

DURING their first months in Paris President and Mrs. Wilson lived in the magnificent house of Prince Murat in the Rue Monceau. Special police guarded it day and night. There was a sentrybox outside, and inside a small army of liveried lackeys to attend them—very different from the simple ways of the White House. Some of the beautiful rooms had been transformed into offices where busy typewriters clicked day and night. Mrs. Wilson's apartments were in "heavenly blue" and bright with flowers. The President's study was a comfortable book-lined room with big windows opening onto the garden and thick-padded crimson curtains to shut out the noise and distractions of the city.

Here every day came Clemenceau and Lloyd George and Orlando, accompanied by their secretaries and experts and various assistants doing special research on the many intricate technical questions. Mrs. Wilson sometimes came home to find the four men down on the floor with maps spread out before them, trying to work out new boundaries or tangled problems of

The Story of Woodrow Wilson

economic frontiers. "You look like a lot of little boys playing a game," she would laugh at them.

"Alas"—her husband shook his head, smiling, "the most serious game ever undertaken. On it may hang the peace of future generations!"

To this room—up the thick-carpeted stairs of the Palace Murat—wound a strange assortment of persons, races, types, and characters: peasants with the strong odor of the earth on their leather leggings; convalescent soldiers smelling of iodine; priests, farmers, scholars, astronomers, an old chauffeur from Brooklyn; women-suffragists, reporters just in from Archangel or Smyrna; French savants from the Sorbonne, Greeks, Poles, Lithuanians, Senegalese. . . . That quiet room and the slender man sitting quiet and attentive in the middle of it, had become the center of the universe. One of the most touching aspects of the Peace Conference was the absolute confidence people had in the President. Every man, woman, and child within a thousand miles of Paris felt that if they could just get to Wilson their troubles would be solved. And they did very often succeed in reaching him.

"He breakfasts at eight-thirty," Mrs. Wilson wrote to one of his daughters, "dictates and reads letters and important matters that have been referred to him until ten-thirty when he goes to the Council of Ten which lasts till one-thirty. Comes home for lunch. Goes back at three—and if he has a minute between lunch and three there are twenty people begging to see him, and the same later in the afternoon when he gets back before dinner. And then he goes back at eight-thirty to stay till midnight and after." Had it not been for "dear faithful Dr. Grayson who goes with him and watches over him every moment," she added, "I don't believe that he or anyone else could stand it."

His mail in itself was a major problem. First the bulky pile of domestic business sent to and from Washington—bills pending in Congress, appointments . . . he had to pick a new Attorney-General; correspondence with Senators and Representatives—a score of special issues on which even from this distance he was keeping a keen personal watch. Then the business of the American Commission in Paris—all the messages, letters, documents in connection with the daily meetings and the Peace Conference. Another set of messages and reports came from officials and special investigators in the field—Ellis Dresel reporting on Germany, Dr. Willoughby on China, Mr. Perks on Armenia. Finally the vast bulk of personal letters from apparently all the human beings in the universe—at any rate, several hundred thousand from every country. All these, neatly filed in separate folders under each succeeding day, form a precious résumé of the President's life and duties, the multitudinous affairs and interests pressing on his mind and heart at that hectic period.

Under a single date, January 18th, we find several letters from French towns naming streets after him; the same from parents naming children for him; requests to dedicate statues, to confer degrees, to receive deputations wishing to present albums, pictures, memorials; a letter from a group of French Senators and Deputies urging him to visit the devastated regions and see for himself "the destruction coldly committed by the enemy"; a letter from the Committee of Mutilated and Wounded Soldiers of Milan (very fine and infinitely touching); letters from the National Union of Railwaymen in England, conveying a heart-warming resolution, and from "the Worshipful Company of Plumbers, 38 Fish Street Hill, London."

From the President went letters of thanks to a signora for a penholder; to a French veteran for a ship model, artfully constructed; to a lady for a Bible "to use at the Peace Conference" (and sadly needed); to a gentleman in the Jura for a portrait pipe with the President's features carved upon it. Letters came to him from the Patriarch of Russia, from the porcelain manufactory at Sevres, from a French soldier who had lost both legs and begged President Wilson to send him orthopedic equipment. From the National Association of Serbs, Croats, and Slovenes—Yugoslavs in Paris—came a letter protesting against Italy's taking possession of the evacuated territories of Austria; a letter (sent on to the State Department in Washington) regarding treatment of destitute Russian prisoners of war; another regarding German ships taken over by the Spanish Government. A memorandum from Balfour urged Russia to cease fighting before the Peace Conference began, stating that Estonia and Lithuania were threatened with extermination; during the next few weeks, a French memo on German reparations; a memo from the Commission on Belgian Affairs urging revision of the Treaty of 1909 on her territories; a note from Colonel House suggesting what the President shall say in his opening address to the Peace Conference; and a message from F. Ziegfeld opposing a 20 per cent instead of a 10 per cent tax on theater tickets—"which will be a deathblow to the theater!"

To the United States went a message from the President to Senator Simmons: "I am very much disturbed by the deadlock that has occurred in connection with revenue bill on the subject of the postal zone amendment . . . earnest hope and advice that the Senate bill be accepted by the House conferees . . . public interest calls for agreement on this all-important bill. . . ." A message to Tumulty for modification of cereals in the manufacture of beverages—and for Mr. Ziegfeld and the theatrical profession. Cables to several Senators urging support of the woman-suffrage bill. A cable to Secretary Baker concerning possible use of our troops to garrison portions of the Turkish Empire. A cable to Secretary Redfield answering a message from the Secretary regarding certain postwar recommendations about unemployment and boosting business, backed by Mr. Baruch. A cable to Secretary of the Treasury Glass to meet deficiencies for allotments of families of soldiers, the deficit being over twenty-two millions. Most interesting of all perhaps was a cable to the Columbia Clearing House Association, Columbia, S. C.: "Cotton may now be exported to all neutral countries in amounts adequate to their needs"—from Tommy Wilson, who used to line his trousers with cotton pads at the mill on his way back from playing hooky with the other boys, and who had spent anguished months and years in the early part of the war trying to get justice for his Southern friends, then under the boycott imposed by the British, who later became our allies.

Hundreds of requests came for the President and Mrs. Wilson to visit French charities and philanthropic works in Paris and to

receive all manner of worthy delegations. One of the most significant of these, as it turned out, was the request that the President
attend a "manifestation" representing five hundred thousand
workingwomen of France at the Trocadero. Delegations of some
ten thousand were to await the President in the Hall—groups of
social workers, laboring women, feminists, and university women.
In the square outside many thousands of workingwomen wanted
to honor the President. A bas-relief would be presented to him
by the workingwomen of France "for the humane role he has
played in the war and the new hope for the future of which he
is the incarnation." Two or three delegates would make addresses
on the theme: "Our hope is in you for the constitution of a
Society of Nations. Your proposals are supported by all the
women who have endured the sufferings of the war in the hope
that the causes of war may now disappear and that a new world
based on justice may be created."

The President, deeply touched, accepted this invitation. But
a few days before the meeting Mr. Bullitt, of our Embassy, wrote
him that the French Government would permit the affair only
if it was turned into an innocuous "thank you" for the return of
Alsace-Lorraine, with a bouquet presented by some children
and with society ladies occupying the main seats—the workingwomen relegated to one obscure section. The workingwomen
therefore decided to call the whole thing off, and simply went
as a small group to his house and presented the statue privately.
The President was profoundly depressed over this and several
other incidents which showed that he was being deliberately and
systematically kept from the people.

On another occasion, when he was returning from a trip to the
devastated areas, his car had passed through Soissons and found
the town virtually deserted. On leaving, his chauffeur took the
regular road out but was soon warned to go no further as an
ammunition dump had accidentally been set on fire and the road
was unsafe. So the party went back again to Soissons. Here, to
the President's surprise, he found the streets—a few minutes
before empty—now alive with French troops. They crowded
around the car in the friendliest way, one soldier shouting that

his comrades believed in the peace the President was fighting for but not the peace their own Government was trying to gain. They cried to him to make them a little speech.

Where, he asked, had these soldiers been when he was in the town before? In their billets, they said, their officers having ordered them there when they heard that the President of the United States was coming. As soon as his car had disappeared— for good, as they thought—the soldiers were set at liberty. "But fate stepped in and brought you back to us!" they said. Of course under the circumstances there was nothing the President could say except to thank the men for their welcome. But the episode disturbed him greatly. It was of a piece with the incident of the workingwomen's meeting and with the constant attacks of the French press—clever, witty, indirect, but devastating; done so well and so incessantly that it was evident the journalists had powerful friends in the Conference who were feeding them inside information. Wilson actually received a confidential memorandum from one of his aides showing that the French press had specific instructions from the Government (possibly from Poincaré, who hated him) to play up American opposition to his ideas and program. At one point the President threatened to move the Conference to Geneva if this sort of thing was not stopped.

Meanwhile, he was driving ahead with the Covenant, meeting daily with the Council of Ten, and keeping generally abreast of his heavy program. When he first went to Paris he had hoped to get the major terms of the peace completed before his return home on March 4th for the adjournment of Congress. But the wasted month after his arrival scotched that plan. Now he was driving every hour to make up for it.

His main object was to get the League Covenant finished and approved by the Conference in first-draft form. He could then lay the tentative draft before the Foreign Relations Committee while he was in Washington, get their suggestion for any desired changes, and bring these back with him to Paris on his return. He explained to his inner circle that he wanted to put everything squarely before the Foreign Relations Committee and that it would be natural for the Senators to want to make their own suggestions. The President was confident that he would be able to meet those suggestions and to obtain the desired changes. This, he said, would assure the satisfaction and co-operation of the Committee and would go a long way towards eventual ratification.

VI

AT LAST came the momentous day when Wilson was to present the finished Constitution to the Peace Conference. The meeting was held in the Room of the Clock at the French Foreign Office.

Under the imposing timepiece from which that chamber takes its name the heads of the Commissions sat at a long table. The other delegates occupied seats in the center of the room. At the far end, facing the clock and the conference table, heavy red brocaded curtains concealed a small alcove. In this alcove, though most of the Conference did not know it, the wife of the President looked on, as every eye in the room centered on her husband.

Quiet and assured, he stood there, giving a sense of steady power: the power of a man who has come to the hour for which he was born, and who is ready for it. In his hand he held a copy of the draft Covenant.

"Mr. Chairman, I have the honor and as I esteem it the very great privilege of reporting in the name of the Commission constituted by this conference on the formulation of a plan for the League of Nations. I am happy to say that it is a unanimous report . . . from the representatives of fourteen nations."

He then read the Articles of the Covenant, looking out upon a league of nations there before him as he spoke: Portuguese and Australians, Brazilians and Chinese, Czechs and New Zealanders; olive-skinned men from Syria, amber-skinned Mongolians, ruddy-cheeked Britishers, wind-tanned Arabs, fresh-faced Canadians and Americans: all watching him intently, expectantly.

The Story of Woodrow Wilson

And beyond them that "great cloud of witnesses" of which he was always conscious: those thousands and millions who had looked to him during these anxious months and years, who were counting on him not to fail them.

"We represent, as we sit round this table, more than twelve hundred million people." The Commission had worked to give them, he said, "not merely a League to secure the peace of the world" but "a League which can be used for co-operation in any international matter."

He spoke of the general Assembly and organization of the League—all the different kinds of help and co-operation it offered. He spoke of the clause for helping the laboring people of the world—"people who go to bed tired and wake up without the stimulation of lively hope . . . these people will be drawn into the field of international consultation and help . . . wards of the combined governments of the world." (And they have been: the League and its affiliated International Labor Office passed sixty-seven international agreements during the twenty-five years following 1919.)

He spoke of the mandates clause—the obligation upon us to look after the interests of the helpless peoples before we use them for our own interest.

We are done with annexations of helpless peoples meant by some Powers to be used merely for exploitation. . . . The conscience of the world has long been prepared [for such a declaration]. We are simply expressing [what] has been long felt. Many terrible things have come out of this war, gentlemen, but some very beautiful things have come out of it. Wrong has been defeated but the rest of the world has been more conscious than ever it was before of the majesty of Right. People that were suspicious of each other can now live as friends and comrades in a single family, and desire to do so. The miasma of distrust, of intrigue, is cleared away. Men are looking eye to eye and saying: "We are brothers and have a common purpose. We did not realize it before but now we do realize it and this is our Covenant of fraternity and of friendship."

Other speeches followed—by Cecil, Orlando, Bourgeois, Wellington Koo—warmly supporting the League principle and the Constitution just completed, and some calling attention to points of special concern to their country. But it was Wilson's day. Delegates rushed to grasp his hand, with congratulations, emotion, excitement. For those who had worked side by side round the commission table during those arduous weeks, it was a happy moment. For the man who had led them, and led this fight from the beginning, it must have been the headiest moment of his personal and political existence.

On the way home in the car he said to his wife: "This is the first real step forward, for I now realize more than ever before that, once established, the League can arbitrate and correct mistakes inevitable in the Treaty we are trying to make at this time. The resentments and injustices caused by the war are still too poignant and the wounds too fresh. They must have time to heal, and when they have done so one by one the mistakes can be brought to the League for readjustment and the League will act as a permanent clearinghouse where every nation can come, the small as well as the great." Then he added with a contented sigh, "It will be good to go home for a few days feeling I have kept faith with the people—and particularly with those boys, God bless them!"

A few hours later he was on the *George Washington*, bound for America.

Before he left he had sent a cable requesting Tumulty to invite all the Senators and Representatives of the Foreign Relations Committees of both Houses to meet him for a dinner conference at the White House immediately upon his arrival.

The Peace Conference had opened on January 18th. On February 15th, less than a month later, Woodrow Wilson was on his way home with his cherished Covenant. Consider for a moment what that means: Here was an American, of the notoriously naïve and inexperienced breed, encountering old-school diplomats and trained negotiators—on their ground, not his. Yet in one short month and against all opposition, open and secret, he had put through a practical plan for world organization that the nations of the world had accepted willingly.

Certain revisions had been made, certain changes incorporated—some of which he welcomed. But he had carried it through, in one month, thanks of course to long months of preparation and to the solid work and help of other great men, especially Smuts and Cecil. *But he had carried it through.* This was hardly a man who "had the wool pulled over his eyes by foreign diplomats."

"Wilson had achieved a notable, almost an astounding triumph," says Dr. Seymour of Yale, who was present as a member of the American Inquiry. "In the face of apathy and increasing opposition he had translated his idea of an international order into concrete terms. At the moment when the materialistic reaction inevitable after four years of war threatened to capture the conference, he had successfully emphasized the higher purposes of mankind and pointed the way to a safer and better future."

The day after the session of February 14th Wickham Steed wrote:

> It was impossible to listen to the document which President Wilson read, to his comments upon it, and to the declarations of the Allied representatives, without feeling that the affairs of the world were being lifted into new dimensions. The old dimensions of national individualisms, forcible annexations for selfish purposes, and unqualified State sovereignty, were raised if only for an instant to a higher plane on which the organized moral conscience of peoples, the publicity of international engagements, and of government by consent of the governed and for the good of the governed became prospective realities.
>
> How long will the instant last? . . . No man can yet say. All that can be said is that yesterday a sense that something new, something irrevocable had been done, pervaded the

conference hall. All the speeches were made in the tone of men who were not afraid of their own handiwork but were obviously conscious of attempting to frame a new charter for civilized and uncivilized humanity.

The hour of splendor, of exaltation; then the inevitable reaction. With Wilson gone, the Allied leaders reverted to their own persistent interests and demands. Wilson had got what he wanted. They hadn't, and they saw no means of turning his League and his program to their uses and getting either the kind of security they needed or the territorial and economic prizes which under the old secret treaties they had hoped to receive. They were supposed during the President's absence to prepare military, naval, and air terms that might go into a preliminary peace treaty. Why not ease into that treaty the various things that meant so much to them: boundaries, reparations, colonies —in fact, why not write the whole peace into this preliminary treaty, letting the League—which was created to deal with many of these matters—take its chance at some postwar conference in the future?

It seemed as though every selfish nationalist instinct came to the surface the minute Wilson departed—like a caldron with the lid pressed down too hard. As soon as the chief removed his firm hand, the lid blew off with a bang. Lloyd George also went home, and instead of leaving in Paris liberals like Cecil and Smuts, he sent over the pugnacious and at that time anti-League Winston Churchill to sit side by side with the gentle and somewhat skeptical Balfour. In the Supreme War Council Sir Robert Borden of Canada kept the claims of the Dominion leaders, with their desire for the instant partition of the German colonies, ever to the fore.

French replacements also undermined Wilson's work. Four days after the President's departure Clemenceau was shot by an anarchist and had to stay in bed for several weeks. This left the reactionary Pichon at the head of the French delegation, with the conservative Balfour in charge of the English. Orlando, who represented the Italian liberal forces, had gone home, and

Sonnino, a strong Italian nationalist, remained to represent his country, Secretary of State Lansing, never sympathetic with the League or Wilson's peace program, now headed the American delegation. An extraordinary setup—as though the devil himself had framed it with the deliberate intention of tearing down everything Wilson had built up during those arduous first weeks.

On February 22nd Mr. Balfour introduced a resolution providing that the Council proceed without delay—not to the discussion of naval and military terms but to the consideration of "other preliminary peace terms with Germany," including frontiers, financial and economic arrangements, responsibility for breaches of the laws of war, and colonies. Monsieur Pichon supported Mr. Balfour and said he expressed Mr. Clemenceau's view. Mr. Lansing "agreed with Mr. Clemenceau" and said he "would prefer to embody all the terms of a preliminary peace in one document"—thus turning his back on the League and the President's entire scheme of things. The Japanese put out a feeler about colonies and Shantung (the first move in the settlement which later made so much trouble for Wilson) and received gratifying reassurances from Mr. Balfour. Lord Milner alone stood solidly and emphatically behind the President's ideas and urged that the Conference now take up, as it was supposed to do, the final naval and military terms with Germany.

Colonel House made a characteristic contribution by remarking that he was sure everybody really agreed with everybody else. After Lord Milner's plea, "Mr. House," says the Secret Minutes record, "persisted in his opinion that the Conference should go back to Mr. Balfour's original proposal as regards Germany." When Lord Milner stoutly urged adherence to the President's program Colonel House said that he was sure that "in reality there was no difference of opinion between the members of the Conference."

In reality there were deep and vital differences of basic principle. "Colonel House," says Mr. R. S. Baker, who observed him throughout the Conference, "never really seemed to see the great stark lines of the conflict or to realize what, by these sinuous and subtle moves, the 'old order' was trying to accomplish. He . . . thought he was truly serving the President's interests; sent the President long cablegrams as to what was going on in Paris. But the real effect of his action here as later at the Conference was to confuse everything, and . . . to serve exactly the contrary purpose from the one the President had in view."

"House expressed House's view—which was not the President's at all; but he gave it as the President's. This caused a maze of misunderstanding and confusion," one of the French delegates told the present writer. It must be said in the Colonel's defense that, as usual, the President had gone away leaving him with no formal written instructions—just the usual large "you know what I want—our minds always work the same way on these matters." This trusting carte blanche might do at lesser moments, even in attempts at wartime mediation; it was mortally dangerous in the present crucial hour.

VII

MEANTIME the President had arrived back in America. Sailing with him on this voyage were the Assistant Secretary of the Navy, Franklin Delano Roosevelt, and Mrs. Roosevelt, whom the Wilsons called "very delightful companions." What an experience if, as those two men paced the deck talking together of a world association of nations, they could have looked ahead twenty-five years! Mercifully, they could not; and the twenty-eighth and thirty-second Presidents of the United States walked up and down for exhilarating hours talking earnestly of the good things they hoped the world would soon see.

On February 24th they landed at Boston, Henry Cabot Lodge's home town. Calvin Coolidge, then Governor of Massachusetts, met the President and escorted him from the dock through cheering throngs to Mechanics Hall, which was packed to the rafters. Mr. Coolidge, at that time a supporter of the League, said in his speech of introduction: "We welcome him as the representative of a great people, as a great statesman, as one to whom we have entrusted our destinies, and one we will support in the future working out of those destinies as Massachusetts has supported him in the past." Mayor Peters in his speech of welcome said that "the League Covenant was an instrument that would go down in history with the Magna Charta and the Declaration of Independence—the more so as it did not supersede these instruments but merely completed them as milestones on the road to human progress."

The President in reply said with one of those impulsive intimate flashes that sometimes broke his habitual reserve: "I wonder if you are half as glad to see me as I am to see you? It warms my heart to see a great body of my fellow citizens again—because in some respects during recent months I have been very lonely indeed without your comradeship and counsel. . . ." He went on to describe the days in Paris and the feeling of all the people of the world regarding America. "I do not mean any disrespect to any other great people when I say that America is the hope of the world. And if she does not justify that hope . . . men will be thrown back upon bitterness of disappointment, bitterness of despair. All nations will be set up as hostile camps again; men at the Peace Conference will go home with their heads upon their breasts, knowing they have failed." But we would justify it, he said. "We set this nation up to make men free . . . and now we will make men free."

When he had finished the President got a real ovation. He left at once for Washington. Newspaper comment indicated that Boston's enthusiastic reception showed the preponderant sentiment in favor of the League. "It was a tremendous demonstration of loyalty, affection, and good feeling," said the Boston *Herald*, ". . . the proverbial coldness and reserve of New Englanders had no place yesterday. . . . Everywhere he went he met with hearty acclaim." "When Wilson brought to a close his speech in Mechanics Hall in Boston," said the *Christian Science Monitor*, "it is safe to say that in spite of anything that may be said in Washington, he had secured the acceptance of the League of Nations by the American people."

Peace-Maker

Wilson was pleased because he felt that once again his favorite theory was vindicated: whenever he could put his case direct to the people, the people responded, giving him the support he sought. If only Congress would prove as responsive!

On February 26th he met the members of the Foreign Relations Committees for the desired dinner conference. The White House was ablaze with light in the first official party in two years. Thirty-six persons gathered round the gala table in the state dining room. The die-hard isolationist Borah had refused to come. Senator Fall also stayed away. Senator Lodge, as ranking guest, escorted Mrs. Wilson. Dinner was gay and delightful. Mrs. Wilson—always beautiful to look at and witty to talk to—was at her best. As for the President, he had evidently decided to forget all old scores tonight and deal with men as he had dealt with issues, in a big way.

After dinner the guests adjourned to the East Room and got down to business. "Well, gentlemen, I bring you the Covenant," said the President, "approved by twenty-seven nations at the Peace Conference. It is not a perfect document—few are—but it is a good first draft. I have come now for your criticisms and suggestions."

Three hours of detailed discussion followed, with many questions, frank criticism. The President kept careful notes and gave keen attention and utmost courtesy to each questioner. "He showed not the slightest vexation even when Senator Brandegee was pressing him rather closely on certain of the difficulties in his mind," writes one of the Republican Representatives, Mr. John Rogers. "I never saw Mr. Wilson appear so human or so attractive as on that night."

"Ask anything you want to know, gentlemen, and ask it as freely as you wish. I will answer you very frankly." Wilson said he wanted to meet every point of view if possible and hoped that no one would hold back. Many members took advantage of the request and asked for enlightenment or expressed objections. A number voiced their fears, especially on territorial guarantees and the possible embarrassment in connection with

The Story of Woodrow Wilson

Article X. Only two Senators sat pointedly silent—Senator Lodge and Senator Knox. "Have you no suggestions, Senator?" the President asked Senator Lodge. "We have no comment to make," was the reply.

"Well, gentlemen, I am going to do my best with this document," said the President, when the time finally came for breaking up. "I shall go back to Paris and put these changes you have recommended to my colleagues at the Peace Conference. I have some pretty stubborn men to deal with, but I shall do my best. Senator Lodge"—again he turned to the Chairman of the Foreign Relations Committee—"do you think that with these changes and if the Foreign Relations Committee approves it, the Senate will ratify the Covenant?"

Mr. Lodge replied: "If the Foreign Relations Committee approves it I think there is no doubt of ratification." Other Senators had said they would support it if certain changes were made. "Very well, then," said the President, "I consider that armed with your approval I can go back and work feeling that you and your associates are behind me." Lodge bowed his head.

"If the Foreign Relations Committee approves it . . ." Mr. Wilson was too honest and open a person to read into this statement all the subtle insinuation it contained. Lodge and his colleagues already intended to block ratification in the Committee and on the floor. They had simply gone to the dinner to get ammunition to enable them to do this more effectively. On February 28th, two days after the dinner, Senator Lodge spoke against the League in the Senate, in a comparatively mild address, containing certain "constructive proposals" as well as criticisms. A much more violent attack from Senator Knox followed on March 1st. But it was the wily Brandegee who planned the first really deadly move: the famous Senatorial "round robin."

Brandegee proposed that a public statement be issued at once, before the President's return to Paris, announcing that more than the necessary one-third of the Senate opposed the League in the form of the present Covenant and that concessions and changes would have to be made before the Senate could approve the scheme at all. Lodge was "very much struck by the proposition" and says that Brandegee "had no difficulty in convincing me of its . . . vital importance." But how to put this through before the adjournment of Congress? To carry weight it must be made part of the Senate proceedings, and there were only a few days left.

They managed it, as that group of men so often did things, by a trick. Lodge on the last day of the session introduced a resolution so obviously out of order that the conspirators were sure some Democratic Senator would oppose it, and one did. The resolution declared in part "that it is the sense of the Senate that . . . the Constitution of the League of Nations in the form now proposed to the Peace Conference should not be accepted by the United States; and . . . that the negotiations on the part of the United States should immediately be directed to the utmost expedition of the urgent business of negotiating peace terms with Germany satisfactory to the United States and the nations with whom the United States is associated in the war against the German Government and that the proposal for a league of nations to ensure the permanent peace of the world should then be taken up for careful consideration." "I ask," said Senator Lodge, "unanimous consent for the present consideration of this resolution."

Senator Swanson of Virginia objected to the resolution, as they had anticipated. Senator Lodge then said that he accepted the objection but wished to add by way of explanation that "the undersigned Senators . . . Members, and Members-Elect of the Sixty-sixth Congress hereby declare that if they had had the opportunity they would have voted for the proposed resolution":

Henry Cabot Lodge	William M. Calder
Philander C. Knox	Henry W. Keyes
Lawrence Y. Sherman	Boies Penrose
Harry S. New	George P. McClean
George H. Moses	Carroll S. Page
J. W. Wadsworth, Jr.	Joseph Irwin France
Bert M. Fernald	Medill McCormick

The Story of Woodrow Wilson

Albert B. Cummins
F. E. Warren
James E. Watson
Thomas Sterling
J. S. Frelinghuysen
W. G. Harding
Frederick Hale
William E. Borah
Walter E. Edge
Reed Smoot
Asle J. Gronna
Frank B. Brandegee
Charles Curtis
Lawrence C. Phipps
Selden P. Spencer
Hiram W. Johnson
Charles E. Townsend
William P. Dillingham
I. L. Lenroot
Miles Poindexter
Howard Sutherland
Truman H. Newberry
L. Heisler Ball

The names of David Elkins of West Virginia and Albert B. Fall of New Mexico were added the following day, bringing the total number to thirty-nine, two more than the necessary one third needed to defeat a Treaty. All the signatories were Republicans. Not a single Democrat signed, nor did eleven Republican Senators—some of them, Lodge said, because they were away from Washington and had not been consulted.

It was a hard blow for the President, from the men who a few nights before had blandly eaten his salt and exchanged affabilities, who had had "no comment to make" when he generously invited it. But Wilson was optimistic, nevertheless. He believed this opposition was "politics" and did not represent the sentiment of the country. Mr. Taft had just come back from a long speaking tour in favor of the League and reported that the people in general seemed definitely for it. The press of the country confirmed him.

The President concluded his official business in connection with the closing of Congress and prepared to return to Paris. On the night of his departure he gave a rousing speech at the Metropolitan Opera House in New York. Mr. Taft presided. Both he and Mr. Wilson took up objections to the League one by one, refuting them with such success that the crowd from time to time broke into prolonged cheering. The reception given the President that night was even more enthusiastic than the one in Boston. Many people were thoroughly angered at the action of the Senators. That action had done him perhaps more good than harm with the mass of the people. Wilson told them not to be downhearted or to imagine that he was. The band struck up "Over There," and he promised not to come back "till it *is* over, over there" and till he could bring with him a League Covenant that the American people could wholeheartedly and conscientiously support. Fifteen thousand people sent him away with a great roar of approbation.

He was relaxed and happy on the return voyage. He knew he had a fight on his hands in the Senate, but he believed that the majority of the people were with him and that he would win, as he had won with the tariff and the currency bills and other big issues. He must win on this greatest issue of all. "It is beyond human power to satisfy everyone," he said to his wife, as they walked the deck together. "All these oppressed peoples look to me to fight for them. The people at home expect me to protect their traditional interests. God knows I wish I could give all of them all they hope for—but only God Himself could do that."

Colonel House met him at Brest. The President talked with him alone for several hours in his stateroom, long after everyone else had gone to bed. Finally the door opened and the Colonel took his leave. When Mrs. Wilson went to speak to the President she was shocked at his appearance. He seemed to have aged ten years, and his jaw was set "in that way he had when he was making a superhuman effort to control himself." "What is the matter?" asked his wife. "What has happened?"

"House has given away everything I had won before we left Paris. He has compromised on every side, and so I have to start all over again—and this time it will be harder, as he has given the impression that my delegates are not in sympathy with me. His own explanation of his compromises is that with a hostile press in the United States expressing disapproval of the League as part of the Treaty he thought it best to yield some other points lest the Conference withdraw its approval altogether. So now he has yielded till there is nothing left."

This was doubly bitter as the majority of the press in America at that time was definitely for the League. But the President threw back his head, the light of battle in his eye. "Well," he said, "thank God I can still fight. And I'll win them back or never look those boys I sent over here in the face again. They lost battles but won the war. So will I."

American newspapermen who landed with him were greeted by their French colleagues with a genial "Well, so your League is dead!" When the President reached Paris he found things even worse than the Colonel's report indicated. The Senate round robin plus the reactionary leaders at the Conference had done their undermining very well indeed. Wilson took off his coat and set to work to regain his position. He began with an immediate bold statement to the press: "The decision made at the Peace Conference in its plenary session of January 25, 1919, to the effect that the establishment of the League of Nations should be made an integral part of the Treaty is of final force and there is no basis whatsoever for the reports that a change in this decision is contemplated."

The statement caused a sensation. French and Italian papers had begun to oppose the League and a moderate workable peace. Partisan opposition had increased at home. Henry White, the Republican member of the American Commission, sent a desperate personal message to Lodge begging him to forward Republican suggestions for the desired revisions in the Covenant. Lodge refused.

The President, resuming his meetings with the Council of Ten, had his hands full. The fight was now on with Clemenceau over the Rhineland; with Foch, who wanted to lead a huge military force into Russia to subdue the Soviets; with the Poles, who were making exaggerated demands, with French backing; and always with Orlando on the Austrian coastline. The uproar in the Council of Ten grew unmanageable. All the experts, secretaries, and interpreters had now transformed the Council into a roomful of fifty or sixty people. The leaders therefore decided to transfer their business to a Council of Four. Wilson, Clemenceau, Orlando, and Lloyd George then fought it out together through long toilsome hours. The energy the President had stored up on his ocean voyages quickly disappeared. A severe attack of grippe laid him low. Even then he saw the Ministers every day in his bedroom, while he lay with a swimming head and a temperature. Things were at such a point that he dare not relax his personal hold. Finally Grayson put his foot down and shut everybody out for a day or two.

Taking advantage of the President's illness, Clemenceau pressed his claim for an uncollectable sum of reparations—at the same time, the Italians urged their claim to Fiume. The President of course opposed both these things. And he particularly opposed Clemenceau's pet project, the "Rhineland Republic," for which Colonel House had generously promised Tardieu the President's interest and co-operation.

When Wilson began to get better and to realize what had gone on during his illness he found the news so grave that he came to a grave decision. Looking up from a sheaf of staggering reports, the first morning he was allowed out of bed, he rose to his feet—pale but determined—and said firmly: "I can never sign a treaty made on these lines. If the rest of the delegates have determined on this, I will not be a party to it. If I have lost my fight—which I would not have done had I been on my feet—I will retire in good order." He called Admiral Grayson, on April 7th, and told him to order the *George Washington*, then in dry dock, to sail for Brest at once. The President of the United States was going home!

The news had an electrifying effect. The heads of Commissions rushed to see him, consternation in their faces. Statesmen big and little wrote letters begging him to remain, and holding out hopes for adjustment of conflicting views. Clemenceau, Lloyd George, and Orlando, for all their natural but aggressive desires to get everything they could for their countries, gave proof that they respected and trusted the President and were ready to meet him halfway—three quarters of the way, even. The small nations looked to him as their one hope.

The President did not want to leave if there was a fighting chance for terms he could sanction. He therefore rescinded the order for the *George Washington*, and as soon as the doctor permitted he resumed his task. Tumulty, in a great state over the proposed "coming home in a huff," was told by one of the Americans on the spot not to worry—that "more had been accomplished in two days since the threat of home-going than in all the weeks of the Conference. You know," the message concluded, "the French are the champion time-wasters of the universe!"

The plain truth was that everybody knew that without Wilson and the fight he was making for a just peace and a workable treaty, the chances were ten to one against the signing of any treaty or any peace. After one of their very worst tussles Clemenceau, who had left the house in a fury, returned to say with a sigh: "You are a good man, Mr. President—and you are a great man. But I wish you were less like Jesus Christ and more like Clemenceau!" Wilson returned to his work, the most urgent matter now being the desired American revisions of the Covenant.

VIII

ON THE return voyage to France the President had studied various suggestions and criticisms. By the time he reached Paris he knew the principal changes that must be made to satisfy American opinion. He worked over these with painstaking thoroughness. A week after his return he presented them in the form of Amendments to the League Commission of the Peace Conference.

The desired changes were summed up in a letter from Democratic Senator Hitchcock of Nebraska, who afterwards led the fight for the Treaty in the Senate; in the President's own notes of the recommendations and objections of the Senators and Representatives at the dinner conference; and in several cables from Mr. Taft reflecting the opinion of the groups that had supported the League to Enforce Peace and the entire movement for an international organization from the beginning.

Senator Hitchcock's letter stated the principal objections

raised against the Covenant by the Republican Senators and suggested six corresponding amendments. *The President accepted and put through every one of these amendments.* Mr. Taft and his group recommended five changes, three of which were similar to three of Senator Hitchcock's main points. *The President accepted and put through every one of the changes suggested by Mr. Taft and his colleagues.* He also incorporated three of the four "constructive proposals" made by Senator Lodge regarding changes in the Covenant, in his February 28th speech. All this by the "uncompromising and inflexible President Wilson" who, we are still told by noted columnists and commentators, "set his face like flint and obstinately refused a single change or alteration in his precious Treaty."

He not only accepted these changes: he fought for them as only men can realize who have themselves fought for special issues at an international conference, where every sentence has to be translated and retranslated a dozen times and every phrase and comma is hotly contested. He fought for them, and he carried them through, past the opposition of nineteen determined men; carried them through though he did not approve of them and though they weakened both the Treaty and his own power at the Conference—enormously. "I am yielding," he said, "to the judgment of men [the Republican Senators] who have little knowledge of the world situation but who alas control votes."

These amendments are worth studying, as the same points are still brought forward by the die-hards and isolationists in connection with America's now entering an international organization. The amendments suggested by Senator Hitchcock as meeting the chief objections of the Republican Senators were as follows:

"1. Specific Reservation on the Montroe Doctrine.
"2. Reservation excluding 'purely domestic questions' from arbitration or jurisdiction by the League Council.
"3. Provision for Withdrawal from the League.
"4. Acceptance of a Mandate shall be optional.

Also 2 suggestions for adding certain words in Articles 15 and 22—both adopted.

In addition Mr. Taft requested:

1. Unanimity Vote in both Assembly and Council.
2. Limit for Duration of the League.
3. Limit of Armaments.

"If you make these reservations," Mr. Taft cabled, March 18, 1919, "the ground will be completely cut from under the opponents of the League in the Senate. Monroe Doctrine alone would probably carry Treaty but others will make it certain."

The "constructive proposals" suggested by Mr. Lodge in his Senate speech of February 28th were:

"1. Put three lines into the draft of the League which would preserve the Monroe Doctrine.
"2. Exclude completely from League jurisdiction such questions as immigration.
"3. Provide for peaceful withdrawal.
"4. State whether the League was to have an international force of its own or to have the power to summon the armed forces of the different members."

The President explained the desired changes to Clemenceau and Lloyd George and the other delegates and the important bearing these would have in determining the American attitude to the final ratification of the Treaty. On the evening of March 24th he formally submitted the amendments to the League of Nations Commission. The Commission had now to review the entire Covenant and resubmit it to the Conference.

Once again the Commission gathered round its big table at the Crillon—Cecil, Colonel House, Bourgeois, and Larnaude, the Italians, the slightly ironic Japanese, and the others, all in their places. But the atmosphere had subtly but definitely altered. Everybody was aware of Wilson's awkward position in view of American criticism of the first draft and the round robin resolution of the thirty-nine Senators. The demand from America opened the way, as he had known it would, for demands from the other governments. "We shall now," predicted the President, "have a veritable flood of changes and amendments."

Lloyd George and Clemenceau had also, it seemed, been having their difficulties back home. Many groups in the French Chamber had denounced Clemenceau for his apparent failure to secure the Rhineland and other vital interests of France. Orlando was being booed in Rome. "The hard-driven war premiers are saying that the wishes of their people expressed in legislature or public meeting have to be considered quite as much as the will of the American people and their Congress," wrote a Paris reporter at the time. "If I help you, will you help me?" was the question more or less openly asked by the chief delegates when the President approached them on these mooted changes.

The French immediately sharpened their demands on the Rhine frontier, and Lloyd George was candidly trying to secure a commitment on naval equality in return for his acquiescence on the Monroe Doctrine reservation. Sonnino also insisted more emphatically on his Adriatic claims. In other words, the spirit of bargaining that he had tried so hard to banish from international negotiations was now forced upon Mr. Wilson himself, where before—at least in the League Commission and where the President was concerned—there had been a spirit of broad general co-operation. "The President will win," said one of the American delegation, "but he will have to make concessions, even give hostages. Whatever may have been their purpose, the recalcitrant Senators have handicapped him in his fight to make the world safe for democracy."

Three of the proposed American amendments aroused especially bitter opposition in Paris: the Monroe Doctrine reservation, the weakening of Article X, and the clause on withdrawal from the League. These drew scathing comment from the French delegates and the French press. "The President initiated a Covenant and now he smashes it!" said one delegate. "We were told that the Covenant was something sacramental—by it the peace of God would be secured. Now it appears it is just another temporary convenience."

The Story of Woodrow Wilson

At first the proposal was that withdrawal might come at the end of ten years. "If the people of France who are staking their future security on the League," said Mr. Larnaude passionately, "thought that the League was to last only ten years, they would regard it as bankrupt from the beginning." Mr. Wilson tried to soothe him: "Of course nobody intends that. This is just to satisfy certain overfearful people." "Then if nobody intends it, why put it in?" snapped the little Frenchman with some reason.

"Still," said the soft-spoken Orlando, "however precious the privilege of membership may seem today, it is a comfort to know you can divest yourself of this membership and its responsibilities in case you want to [as his country ultimately did]. I mean, in case the new society doesn't work out as we all hope it will." Wilson writhed. It is hard to say which embarrassed him more—the French with their violent opposition, or Orlando with his frank opportunism and delight that Italy could get out any time she wanted.

"Notice of withdrawal by a major power would throw the League into confusion," argued other delegates. "There might even be a combination of non-Member countries against the League!" Others pointed out that provision for withdrawal after ten years of service might be interpreted as anticipating a breakup and that an attempt was being made to hold them unwillingly meanwhile. Ultimately an agreement was reached to insert a provision allowing withdrawal after two years' notice. But even this brought tremendous opposition and another furious onslaught from the French press.

"The President has defeated his own Covenant," they said. "We were told that the old order was ended—pacts and agreements which men and nations kept only so long as it was to their advantage. The President said that his Covenant was to bring us a new era of peace and international co-operation. But now it appears it is only binding for twenty-four months. You can stay in or get out as your national interests dictate." "It is no more binding than a common trade agreement," said one powerful journal. "It is merely another 'scrap of paper.'" All this was hard to take, for the Scotch Covenanter who in his heart agreed with his critics. But he was President of the United States as well as world leader. He stood by what his people wished of him in this crisis, though it went against his personal conviction.

Feeling ran high too on the reservation the Americans requested on mandates. "Acceptance of a mandate is optional— no Power need accept a mandate unless it so chooses." Twenty-five years later the United States might not have objected to having a mandate for the Carolines or the Marshalls or the Marianas Islands, which the Japanese affably accepted. "But surely," protested the non-American delegates, "all the enlightened and democratic peoples should share in this work and this responsibility for those who are not yet fit to govern themselves. Certainly all the big nations should accept their fair share of the duties of trusteeship."

Colonel House tactfully suggested that the American form of government is not considered suitable for people of different mentality and traditions and that many Americans had not liked our stewardship in the Philippines because they felt it came dangerously close to "imperial appendages." He feared that "unless these prejudices of the Americans are humored, the Senate and even the American people will not subscribe to Article X on which our hope of world peace and national security depends."

There was another battle over the proposed paragraph for Article XV, to satisfy the Senators on domestic questions: "The Council is to make no recommendations in cases affecting a member's domestic jurisdiction." This included, of course, for the Americans the tariff and immigration, which non-Americans dryly point out have assumed rather large international aspects. The Japanese were deeply disappointed over this change. Baron Makino protested with considerable feeling to Colonel House. "My dear Baron, without these explanatory clauses," the Colonel again said deprecatingly, "the Congress of the United States will not I fear accept the New Order or enter the League. It is as simple as that. We can take it or leave it." The Japanese took it, but they did not forget.

The greatest fight of all was on the Monroe Doctrine reservation, at first inserted in Article X, later made Article XXI of the Covenant, where it still stands. The French felt that this reservation greatly weakened the guarantees of security promised them, and fervently opposed its inclusion. "Nothing in the Covenant shall be deemed to affect the validity of international engagements such as treaties of arbitration or regional understandings like the Monroe Doctrine for securing the maintenance of peace." Thus reads the reservation. The President told the Commission that "the Covenant is an international extension of the great principle" of the Monroe Doctrine, just as he had told the Senate in his speech of January 22, 1917. "The Covenant provides that the members of the League will mutually defend each other in respect of their political and their territorial integrity," he explained, "much as the United States said that it would protect the political independence and the territorial integrity of other American States."

The French felt that such protection was far from certain for them and seized this favorable moment to press again their beloved proposal for an international army on the Rhine frontier. The British opposed this and tried to turn discussion away from it. Bourgeois came back to his pet topic stubbornly. "The Americans," he said, "seem to think they are entitled to reservations and concessions exactly as they want them. Will they then be willing to allow some reservations and concessions desired with equal fervor for the people of other countries? If not, how can they insist upon their own?" From March 22nd to April 28th the battle raged. Night after night they returned to it, like seasoned gladiators to their arena. No wonder Wilson grew thin and became ill, worn out by this and other tussles in the Council of Four. Between the French on the one side and the American Senators on the other, he was taking a pretty stiff battering.

Not all the fights were on the American proposals. Other delegates introduced other amendments: a military commission under Article VIII, an expansion of Article XXIII to take in other social problems besides labor.

The French proposed a new Article to establish an economic section of the League, to ensure freedom of transit and equitable treatment of commerce for all members. The Belgians proposed a clause dealing with international agriculture. The location of the League provoked warm discussion. Hymans, the Belgian delegate, pleaded for Brussels, but Geneva was finally chosen.

The Portuguese delegate was scandalized at the idea of a Treaty or a Covenant being concluded with no mention of the Deity or the Church and kept trying to the last minute to have at least some mention of the Holy Trinity included. The Japanese again tried, with considerable dignity but no success, to introduce a clause guaranteeing racial equality. The position of women in the new world order was introduced by a very able group from the International Council of Women, who appeared before the Commission and got a clause incorporated whereby "all positions in the League are open to both men and women."

The British at the eleventh hour asked to have certain words changed under the Membership Article, so that each Dominion could vote. Wilson felt he must meet this request—the British having met a number of our own—though it made sore trouble for him in the future. "England has five votes to our one. The British will try to run us and tell us what to do. Fine thing our President's letting us in for!" Under the actual terms of the Covenant, of course, no nation could possibly tell another nation what to do, since there has to be a unanimous vote on all questions. America or any nation therefore could kill any vote of which she disapproved. This vital fact our opposition Senators always overlooked in their violent attacks on the voting matter.

When it came to a question of really serious first-rank importance in relation to the British—as when Lloyd George tried to bargain regarding our shipbuilding program in return for supporting the Monroe Doctrine—Wilson stood very firm indeed. "I have been unable to see any connection between the two questions," Colonel House wrote Cecil, under the President's instruction. "We would like your support [on the

Monroe Doctrine reservation] but of course you can oppose it if you see fit." When the time came, Cecil remained silent, thus implying consent. Most of the delegates were not so disturbed as the French on the Monroe Doctrine reservation. They argued that it had not kept the Americans out of war in 1917 and that it would not keep them out again if it was to their interest to go in.

Wilson believed, as Taft did, that the language of the Covenant did not justify American fears and that the effort to revise the Treaty in order specifically to mention the Monroe Doctrine would lead to great difficulties and weaken the American position at Paris, which it did. But having committed himself to fight for it, he did the best he could. Wilson built his whole peace program on the Monroe Doctrine in its wider meaning—not just the protection of the weaker South and Central American States but responsibility of the strong for the safety and welfare of the weak everywhere. On the evening of April 10th, after interminable hours of argument, he made an eloquent short speech on it:

> A century ago when the nations of Europe were crushed by absolutism the United States declared that the system should not prevail in the Western hemisphere . . . in this last war against absolutism the United States entered the war and fought for these same principles. Is she to be denied the small gift of a few words which after all only state the undoubted fact that her policy of the past hundred years has been devoted to principles of liberty and independence? Are we not assembled here to consecrate and extend the horizons of this document as a perpetual charter for all the world?

He thought that speech would end it. But the Frenchmen still persisted. Finally Wilson bluntly asked Monsieur Larnaude why France distrusted the United States, and "did France wish to stop the United States from signing the Covenant?" That question—ironically enough, as things turned out—settled the matter. On April 28th at the Plenary Session, after this long and bitter fight—*and with every one of the American amendments included in it*—the final Covenant of the League of Nations was formally and unanimously adopted and became an integral part of the Treaty.

It was a triumph, but not a triumph of which we need be proud. We held a pistol at the head of Europe: "Make these changes or America will stay out." Then we stayed out anyway. "Such and such Articles must be amended or America won't sign." Articles I, VIII, X, XV, XXII were amended in accordance with American requests and over the protests of the delegates of twenty-seven countries. Then, when the Treaty came before the American Senators in September they demanded fifteen more reservations and forty-six amendments. And America didn't sign—even after all the original demands were met and after all the other governments had ratified.

The American people never knew the true story of these amendments or of Wilson's fight at Paris to try to satisfy the American viewpoint and the American Senate. They didn't know because Wilson could never dramatize himself or his actions, and he balked when other people tried to dramatize him. Imagine what Theodore Roosevelt would have made of such a situation. Wilson proceeded on an entirely impersonal basis.

The President was trying to get a broad general agreement, a constitution for a working organization on which twenty-seven nations could agree, and within which they could then work out the various problems that confronted them. Because of the fears and demands from home, he had to weaken his document almost to the breaking point; to weaken confidence in it and in himself from the people of the world, who had followed him enthusiastically to that point. And he did not succeed in the end in the main purpose for which he yielded—to carry the Treaty and the Covenant through the Senate. The enemies of the Treaty and failure to get the necessary two-thirds vote blocked that.

Our Senators and our people can learn some precious lessons

from this experience. We can learn that the important thing in a peace-making is an agreement on broad lines that all can and will accept; an agreement that mirrors not the petty fears and apprehensions of each nation but its faiths and trusts—in the agreement itself and in the men who made it, their own national representatives, who will carry it out under the accepted rules of democratic procedure. By trying to cross every *t* and dot every *i* in advance you may have left only the *t*'s and the *i*'s—and bitterness.

IX

THE man who stood before the Conference on April 28th presenting the revised Covenant was not the flushed and smiling conqueror of the glorious session of February 14th. The man of April 28th was a soberer, wiser man, but steadier too, perhaps. His precious Covenant had undergone some changes that made him wince. "Wilson the uncompromising" had been forced to accept—and indeed himself had to insert—compromises he detested. His shining peace with far-flung banners had acquired some streaks of earth; even had raised, some declared, new problems that might breed trouble. But the Covenant still stood. That was the all-important point. The League would soon be a concrete functioning organization. And the League would in God's good time, if not in his, see those wrongs rectified, and all lesser matters set straight. In this he did triumph. The Covenant stood—and stood as part of the Treaty.

He explained the changes to the Conference briefly and without apology, closing with a motion to adopt the amended document and a resolution to appoint an organizing Committee of Nine to prepare for the establishment of the League and the agenda for the first meeting. The Conference passed the amended Covenant and the resolution by a unanimous vote. And the desire of his heart became fact.

Suppose it hadn't? Think for a moment when people are saying, "He should have done this—he should have done that"

—suppose there had been no Wilson. Or suppose he had washed his hands of the whole thing and gone home, as he must many times have been tempted to do, as once he almost did. What would have happened to the world? The final section in this book describes an amazing list of things that would not have happened.

"If Wilson had withdrawn," said one man who was present, "there would have been no treaty. Europe and the whole world would have been plunged in anarchy. The predatory powers would have pitched in and taken what they wanted—and the democracies America was supposed to help and had certainly promised to help would have been despoiled." People seldom think of the blank alternative.

As the Treaty neared completion Wilson had a sheaf of other problems and crises confronting him, besides the League. There was "the Italian crisis" and the matter of Fiume. The President felt that by rights this port belonged to the new Yugoslav State. France and England concurred, but let Wilson do most of the fighting and bear all the obloquy. In Italy his picture was torn down, the candles were trampled underfoot. The easily swayed Italian crowds that two months ago had wildly cheered, now hissed and hated him. Orlando begged and pleaded, in vain.

On the twenty-third of April Orlando and several of his colleagues summoned a special train with the intention of going home, prepared to abandon the Conference. Just before they boarded the train Orlando received a statement from Balfour formally declaring the position of England and France in accord with Mr. Wilson, but neither Balfour nor Orlando gave this to the newspapers. Wilson still had to bear the brunt of Italian fury. Clemenceau and Lloyd George tried to persuade him to yield. He refused. There was nothing for Orlando to do but to come back if he wished to sign the Treaty. He came and was comforted by the President "over by the window," where he was frankly weeping like a little boy. "Poor fellow—of course his Government gave him the devil!" Wilson said afterward.

There was "the Japanese crisis" and the matter of Shantung. In this the President yielded most reluctantly. Shantung, formerly in possession of Germany, had been taken over by Japan in 1917. The Japanese insisted on keeping it but agreed to return it to China within two years. The Japanese delegates had been ordered by their Government not to sign the Treaty unless this question was settled to their liking. Under the secret treaties of 1917 Lloyd George and Clemenceau were bound to give them Shantung.

Wilson yielded because thereby he could preserve the Conference and the Covenant of the League. If Japan refused to sign the Treaty she would in all likelihood ally herself with Germany and Russia and create a powerful anti-League bloc. In no case would China regain her sovereignty over the leased territory. Lodge and his Republican Senators made this matter of Shantung an eternal scandal, having never uttered a murmur when Germany snatched the province from China in the first place. But Wilson hoped through his decision—and it seemed the only hope—to get back China's territory for her.

"The only way," he told a friend at the time, "is to keep the world together, get the League of Nations with Japan in it, and then try to secure justice for the Chinese—not only as regards Japan but England, France, Russia too; all of them have concessions in China." Wonderful to relate, Japan kept her word and evacuated Shantung before the two years were up.

There was the matter of reparations, and the great question of Germany's economic future. Wilson thought the terms too severe, but he had not been able to prevail with Clemenceau. Was France herself to pay the reconstruction expenses, for rebuilding the factories and railroads the enemy had destroyed? Was Germany, who had pillaged and looted and burned and raped, to be allowed to get away with it economically also? "I don't care what you do so long as you let me strangle Germany!" one of the American delegates heard Clemenceau say to Wilson. Was she strangled?

A number of Americans at the Conference considered it a capital mistake to impose such heavy penalties on Germany—penalties which it was humanly impossible to pay and which "prepared the soil" of bitterness and resentment in which Hitler planted his deadly propaganda. The Conference was breaking up at the point where many of the American delegates thought it should begin all over again. Others thought—especially after the studied rudeness of the German deputation at the May meetings—that there was no hope for these people any way you fixed it, that they were not going to change their spots no matter what was done for them, that the harsher the terms the better, since that sort of treatment was apparently the only thing they understood. They would make trouble for the world again, as long as the world gave them an inch of latitude.

On May 7th the Treaty was formally presented to the Germans at the Trianon Palace, in Versailles. It comprised a book of 214 pages, 440 Articles. The Germans were given fifteen days in which to submit comments, to receive the Allies' answer in writing, and to say whether they would sign. On May 29th came their answer. You would have thought, from reading it, that Germany had won the war—certainly that she stood on the same basis of negotiations with the other Powers.

The Germans argued their case from the platform of the Fourteen Points and the alleged discrepancies in the actual peace terms. They protested the changes regarding Alsace-Lorraine and the Polish Corridor, dubbed the League of Nations a "hostile coalition," recalled Wilson's differentiation between the German Government and the German people, and declared that it would be the people who would have to suffer and to bear the crushing burden of these terms.

The reply of the Allies—an itemized, stern arraignment of all that Germany had done and made other people suffer—was sent them on June 16th. They were given five days in which to sign the Treaty. The fifth day arrived—but no decision. Marshal Foch started military preparations in the Rhine Valley. Paris was in a state of high excitement; there were rumors of remobilization, fighting perhaps already begun. On the sixth day the German Government fell. In view of this the Allies granted a time extension. On June 23rd word came that the new Government accepted the Treaty and would send two delegates to sign. Joy took the place of gloom, flags waved again, and Paris prepared for her greatest of all historic fetes.

Red carpets came out; the Palace of Versailles put on gala attire. Thousands of people lined the highroad from Paris. From the Versailles city gate all the way up to the palace imposing lines of French cavalry were drawn up, their lances shining in the sun. A few favored personages besides the delegates received invitations to witness the signing ceremony in the Hall of Mirrors, and the palace gardens were given over to the rapturous French populace. Fancy Marie Antoinette looking out of her windows upon "the people," now sauntering at ease along those royal paths and themselves included in an international treaty with kings and potentates!

On the stairs where in 1789 the royal bodyguard made its last stand were now stationed double rows of the superb Garde Républicaine in gleaming cuirasses and crested helmets, with their picturesque black and red horsehair streamers. Straight up the steps from the main doorway to the Hall of Mirrors they stood, swords in front of them ready for salute, behind them the flags of the Allies against the splendid tapestries of the great gilded hall. What a day for France! What a day for old Clemenceau!

Up those stairs strode Bismarck when he made the French sign the proclamation of Germany's triumph in 1871; there, two centuries before, Louis XIV greeted Condé on his victory over the Germans. "Victor" after "victor" had stalked up the magnificent staircase to the vast room of mirrors reflecting the triumphal spectacle—uniforms, decorations, elegant dresses, silks, jewels.

But wait—three special guests have just come in, escorted to one of the velvet-covered benches in a place of honor: "three ghastly masks of men with eyes unsocketed, with twisted jaws, their faces plowed with scars"—the perennial heroes, the unknown warriors who (whatever the current name of the "conqueror") win the fight and pay the bill. "Heroic friends, we salute you!" cries Clemenceau, describing that grim entry. "We present ourselves at your judgment seat. Speak, great scar-branded witnesses made judges of the battle, and tell us what would have come to pass had you refused!"

The Allied leaders came up the grand staircase through the central aisle, escorted by military attendants to their seats behind the table where the signing was to take place. A pause, then the hall grew absolutely still as the two Germans, unfortunate men no one had ever heard of before, were led in from an inconspicuous door and took their places, deathly pale and intensely nervous. Tension grew while the Allied Powers were signing the treaty. President Wilson signed first, then Clemenceau, then Lloyd George and Orlando. Finally came the turn of the white-faced Dr. Bell and Herr Müller.

The instant they had affixed their signatures, as from some electric signal the guns of Saint-Cyr boomed loud. Then fort after fort from the hills around Paris roared its triumphant salute. The fountains, which had not played since the beginning of the war, flung their dazzling spray to the sky. A wild shout went up, and the throngs in the gardens and all over Versailles and Paris broke into the tempestuous bars of the "Marseillaise." *Le jour de gloire* indeed!

The marble satyrs presiding over those shady groves must have quirked a sardonic eyebrow—anticipating out of their long and varied experience with so many régimes what might come in another twenty years, when another set of haughty "conquerors" would stride in. Perhaps some shining invisible figures looked on—more sadly; the wise men who had tried from time to time through the centuries, patiently but unsuccessfully, to show the world a better way.

On June 29th the President sailed for home. "His nerves were worn," said Charles Seymour, "and his physique was shaken, but his spirits were high. If he guessed anything of the struggle that lay before him in the United States he concealed this suspicion. The feeling of those who accompanied him on the boat was that the Senate must and would ratify the Treaty, that the country would enter enthusiastically upon the venture of the League of Nations."

The ship was packed with happy American soldiers on their way home. The man who had sent them forth two years before was happier than they, knowing that in a few more weeks all the remaining American men in France would be back in their homes—those, at least, who were not in hospitals. Hundreds of wounded on board reminded him, if he needed reminding, of the responsibility he had assumed and never indeed forgot day or night—the duty he and all the American people owed those boys. He spent many hours talking to them, and on the Fourth of July, while they were still at sea, he made them a stirring address.

On July 8th he landed in New York. A fleet of destroyers met the ship off Sandy Hook. In the harbor Vice-President Marshall and members of the Cabinet with Governor Alfred E. Smith of New York welcomed him. Thousands waited to shout a frenzied welcome as he drove through the city—along West Twenty-third Street and up Fifth Avenue.

"They saw in him," said the New York *Tribune* next day, "the symbol of victory and of the peace. Children shouted, and white-haired women leaned from boardinghouse windows, tears streaming down their faces, to throw him a 'God bless you'!"

Flags, handkerchiefs, cheering crowds, bands, huzzahs. . . . When the party reached the Waldorf Hotel, where a suite was reserved for them, the President's daughter Margaret (so she told me) could hardly wait for the door to close before she threw her arms round her father.

"Oh, darling, wasn't it *wonderful?* All those thousands of people crying, waving their hats in the air, yelling—all for *you!* There never was such a triumph, such a home-coming!"

He looked at her—with a look she said she never would forget.

"Wait till they turn," he said quietly.

Peace-Maker

X

ON JULY 10th, the day after his return, the President laid the Treaty before the Senate. Triumphal entries were one thing; now came the real encounter. Strange to be back in Washington—the simplicity of the White House and the Senate Room after the gray carpets and Old World luxury of the Quai d'Orsay; those rows of American faces before him, some eager and friendly, others hard and hostile, after months at the Peace Conference confronting all the varied types and features of the world.

Wilson faced them forthrightly. "Gentlemen of the Senate: the Treaty of Peace with Germany was signed at Versailles on the twenty-eighth of June. I avail myself of the earliest opportunity to lay the Treaty before you and to inform you with regard to the work of the Conference by which that Treaty was formulated."

It had not been easy to make, he said, and he went back over the demoralizing conditions, the maze of secret treaties which appeared, and the political reconstruction necessary in the larger half of Europe.

> The difficulties encountered were very many. Sometimes they seemed insuperable. It was impossible to accommodate the interests of so great a body of nations—interests which directly or indirectly affected almost every nation in the world—without many minor compromises.

> This Treaty as a result is not exactly what we would have written. It is probably not what any one of the national delegations would have written. But results were worked out which on the whole bear test. I think it will be found that the compromises which were accepted as inevitable nowhere cut to the heart of any principle.

He reviewed some of the main features of the settlement—protection of religious and racial minorities, limitation and regulation of military establishments, better channels of trade for the various nations, international pledges for the protection of labor. That there should be a league of nations to maintain these understandings and guarantee the peace had been one of the agreements accepted from the first as the basis of peace with the Central Powers. The statesmen of all the belligerent countries were agreed that such a league must be created. With the difficult work of arranging world affairs actually in hand, the League was found to be an indispensable instrument.

This was not the time to go into a detailed discussion of the League or the Covenant. He would merely state that the League was the permanent and practical part of the Treaty, agreed upon by all for the satisfactory fulfillment of its provisions.

> The League was the practical statesman's hope of success in many of the most difficult things he was attempting. It has assumed proportions much bigger than a mere instrument for carrying out of the provisions of a particular treaty. The peoples of the world . . . have demanded it. A cry had gone out from every home in every stricken land that such a sacrifice should never again be exacted. . . . The League of Nations was not merely an instrument to adjust and remedy old wrongs under a new treaty of peace; it was the only hope for mankind.

He did not refer to objections or reservations in his address, although in a talk with the press that morning he had explained the very serious difficulties that would attend any reservations. Every nation would have to agree to them, and while this slow process was going on—even assuming they all would agree—the United States would remain at war with Germany. He believed that even what seemed innocuous amendments would cause great trouble.

He paid a moving tribute to the troops: "the compulsion of what they stood for was upon us at the peace table." He spoke of the special role America had played at the Peace Conference, of the work of his American colleagues—"the fine group who have constantly sought to justify the confidence reposed in them"; of the history of America in the past, then of the expectations of the whole world from America for the future.

"Our isolation was ended twenty years ago when war with Spain put us unexpectedly in possession of islands of the Philippines and in the West Indies in association with other Powers. People have learned not to fear America, or the possibility of American aggression. Weak peoples everywhere look to us for guidance and protection. There can be no question of our ceasing to be a world power. The only question is whether we can refuse the moral leadership which is offered us, whether we shall accept or reject the confidence of the world?"

Earlier he had said: "My services and all the information I possess will be at your disposal and at the disposal of your Committee on Foreign Relations at any time, either informally or in session as you may prefer, and I hope that you will not hesitate to make use of them."

Many days passed before the Senators chose to act on this suggestion.

XI

THE phrase "psychological warfare" had not come into general use in 1919, but the thing itself was in deadly and intensive operation. The struggle for the control of the mind of the country at that time is a story to be pondered over and remembered by every thoughtful American. In 1918 and early 1919 the American people were overwhelmingly in favor of a league of nations. At the 1918 convention of the League to Enforce Peace, in Philadelphia, two thousand of our most distinguished citizens and leaders from all walks of life strongly supported the proposal. Ninety-six per cent of the Chambers of Commerce in the country had voted in favor of it. Thirty-four State legislatures had passed favoring resolutions. Thirty-three Governors of States had come out publicly for it. Teachers, preachers, scientists like Thomas Edison and Alexander Graham

The Story of Woodrow Wilson

Bell, businessmen like Judge Gary, head of United States Steel, and Darwin Kingsley, President of the New York Life Insurance Company; railroad presidents, bankers, labor leaders, farmers— the whole country was behind the League, even though Senator Lodge regarded this opinion as "very ill informed."

The little group of powerful opponents asked themselves how to beat it. On May 19th the special session of Congress convened, forced by that group through the March filibuster for the special purpose of fighting the League issue. Senator Lodge arrived back in Washington three weeks ahead of time to marshal the forces. He was now both majority Republican leader and Chairman of the strategic Foreign Relations Committee. The day after his return he had a conversation with Senator Borah "to talk over the course to be pursued." This conversation and the moves which resulted are described in Senator Lodge's book, *The Senate and the League of Nations.*

"I said to him," states Senator Lodge, "that I desired his opinion upon the situation as it appeared to me and that the following conditions as I saw them existed. The great mass of the people, the man in the street to use a common expression, the farmers, the shopkeepers, the men in small business, clerks and the like . . . did not understand the treaty at all . . . but their natural feeling was 'now the war is over and let us have peace as quickly as possible.'" Therefore they believed themselves in favor of the League.

In addition, "the vocal classes of the community, most of the clergymen . . . a large element in the teaching force of the universities, a large proportion of the newspaper editors . . . were friendly to the League and were advocating it. With these conditions existing, I said to Senator Borah, it seemed perfectly obvious to me that any attempt to defeat the Treaty of Versailles with the League by a straight vote in the Senate if taken immediately would be hopeless."

Note that "if taken immediately." He therefore proposed beating it by the slow-death process of amendments and reservations. Senator Borah "agreed entirely with my description of the situation. . . . He did not believe the Treaty could possibly

This picture was made to contradict rumors that Wilson was too ill to fulfill his presidential duties. Mrs. Wilson holds an official document which the President's paralyzed left arm is unable to steady. *Photo: Harris & Ewing*

The Big Four at Versailles:

oyd George, Vittorio E. Orlando, Georges Clemenceau, and
Woodrow Wilson. *Photo: Harris & Ewing*

One of many stops on Wilson's cross-country "League Tour."
Both of these photos were taken in Columbus, Ohio. *International News Photos*

be beaten by a direct vote." Note again this agreement between the two ranking Republican Senators that they could not beat the Treaty by direct vote because the people were overwhelmingly for it; therefore they would proceed to go against the will of the people and beat it by political manipulation and maneuvering. And Senator Lodge talks in his book of his colleagues, "the high-minded men who had no thought of self but of serving the best interests of their country"!

Senator Borah said he was "against the Treaty in any form whatever" and would vote against it in the final vote. But he was entirely ready meanwhile "to support any amendments or reservations which I [Senator Lodge] and those who agreed with me should offer."

In other words, Senator Borah was ready to kill the League by adding his vote to the reservations, which would appear to satisfy those who were for the Treaty, long enough to pass the reservations; then he would vote against the whole thing in the end. This from our "open, straightforward Americans" who railed against "the secret plots and maneuvers of scheming European statesmen."

"This conversation," Lodge tells us, "was followed by many others with other Senators . . . who would not under any circumstances vote for the Treaty but were willing to acquiesce in perfecting amendments or reservations, and also the support of the Republican majority in the Senate . . . anxious to adopt the Treaty if it could be done with safety to the United States." Lodge always presented these amendments and reservations as clauses he "sincerely believed would make the Treaty safe for this country."

"The first step," he told Senator Borah, "must be the organization of the Senate. We [the Republicans] had only two majority but we were entitled to the control of the Senate and the appointment of committees and it was very necessary that this matter should be successfully disposed of. With this of course Senator Borah entirely agreed."

According to the Senate's own Rule 24, members and heads of committees are elected by the Senate. According to actual procedure and long tradition, committee personnel is chosen by caucus and a prearranged slate is submitted which the Senate accepts as a mere formality. The Committee on Committees (of the party in power) is practically all-powerful in the matter of appointments.

"We were in session three minutes and a half," said the elder La Follette, describing one of these party caucuses. "A motion was made that somebody preside. Then a motion was made that whoever presided should appoint a Committee on Committees, and a motion was made that we adjourn. Then and there the fate of all the legislation of this session was decided."

In 1879 a young Princeton student spoke in stronger terms of these "methods of Congressional management," of which "too few Americans take the trouble to inform themselves"; therefore "not many have perceived that almost absolute power has fallen into the hands of men whose irresponsibility prevents the regulation of their conduct by the people from whom they derive their authority." If this condition went on, he continued, "our dangers may overwhelm us, our political maladies prove incurable."

He was twenty-three when he wrote that—his first published work. Forty years later he was to prove his own thesis in a personal encounter with some of the irresponsible men he had assailed, among them the editor who bought his original article!

The custom of appointment by seniority, "with the rights and privileges pertaining thereto," places a few older men in a position of immense—Wilson thought inordinate and unwise—influence. Geographical sections are also considered, in the making of appointments; also party harmony and the adjustment of various inner-party groups. In general, however, seniority and rank are the deciding factors.

Treaties and germane bills, resolutions and nominations go to the Foreign Relations Committee before being considered in the Senate. Most meetings are private. *The Chairman determines what shall be placed on the agenda* and may himself smother a bill by refusing to bring it before the Committee. Or the Committee may smother it by failing to report it back to the Senate.

Peace-Maker

The Committee may report a bill favorably or unfavorably as it stands, or it may report it with reservations, amendments, and interpretations. This last is the method most often used when the Senate wants to clip the wings of the Executive, as Dr. Eleanor E. Dennison shows it did with the Treaty of Versailles.

The Chairman has entire power in the appointment of members of the Committee: he may appoint or reject whom he pleases. Each of these sentences, it seems, should be written in letters of fire, such is their vital significance for the nation. Senator Lodge had four vacancies to fill when he became Chairman. Senator Frank Kellogg of Minnesota (afterwards Secretary of State in Hoover's Cabinet) would normally have been the first to be appointed, by virtue of seniority and previous service. But Senator Kellogg had made a speech in favor of a league of nations and had refused to sign the round robin. Senator Lodge had a talk with Senator Kellogg and told him he could arrange the appointment provided he could count on Mr. Kellogg to support his decisions and policies. Not the Republican party's decisions and policies, mind you, but his. When this agreement was not forthcoming Lodge expressed his regret and said that under the circumstances he was sure Mr. Kellogg would understand that he could not appoint him to the Foreign Relations Committee.

Senator Moses received the appointment, though he had been in the Senate only four months and his term would expire in two years. The other three Senators appointed were Warren G. Harding of Ohio, Harry S. New of Indiana, and Hiram Johnson of California—all of whom Senator Lodge could count on. This packing of the Committee with "Senators whose opposition to the Treaty has been pronounced" was publicly assailed by Mr. Taft and on the Senate floor by Senator Hitchcock, who said he "knew Republicans on the other side of this Chamber who feel just as I feel—indignant that agreement with the leaders on the Treaty should be made a test of whether a Senator goes on the Foreign Relations Committee or not."

All of which worried the Chairman and his inner circle not a particle. The full list of Foreign Relations Committee members was: Republicans—Lodge, Borah, Brandegee, Fall, Knox, Harding, Johnson, McCumber, Moses, and New; Democrats—Hitchcock, Pittman, Pomerene, Shields, Smith, Swanson, Williams. "It will be seen at once," writes the Chairman, "that this is a strong committee and such as conditions demanded." From Mr. Lodge's point of view it certainly was. He had now enough members to assure a majority without the vote of Republican Senator McCumber—a strong League supporter. The Committee numbered seventeen. With the four new appointees Lodge had nine votes of which he could always be sure. From that moment the fate of the Treaty was sealed. The drama played out before the world in the Senate chamber over the next twelve months was so much high comedy in which many of the actors spoke their lines by careful and often highly amused prearrangement.

Witness the account by Senator James Watson, Senator Lodge's colleague and chief henchman. On page 190 of his book *As I Knew Them* Senator Watson tells that Senator Lodge sent for him early in the fight.

He said . . . he wanted me as his special representative to have charge of the organization in the Senate of the League of Nations fight. He asked me to keep mum on this assignment and to report to nobody but him. . . .

"Senator," I said to him, "I don't see how we are ever going to defeat this proposition. . . . Eighty per cent of the people are for it. Fully that percentage of the preachers are right now advocating it . . . all the people who have been burdened and oppressed by this awful tragedy of war are for it. . . . I don't see how it is possible to defeat it."

He turned to me and said "Ah my dear James, I do not propose to try to beat it by direct frontal attack but by the indirect method of reservations."

He then went on to explain how we would demand a reservation on the subject of a mandate over Armenia for example. . . . "We can debate that for days and hold up the dangers it will involve." Senator Lodge then went on for two hours to explain other reservations and the details of the situation that would thus be evolved—until I became thoroughly satisfied that the Treaty could be beaten in that way. And that is the way it was fought through in the Senate—the debate covering about two months time. . . .

Senator Lodge high-mindedly records in his book that he "voted twice for the Treaty with reservations and gave to the reservations and to the Treaty with reservations genuine support. I believed that the reservations approved by the Committee . . . made the League safe for the United States."

The two sets of statements make very interesting comparative reading. Certainly both these men could not be telling the truth.

XII

THE Senate debate actually began in February, when Senator Lodge and Senator Knox spoke against the Covenant in first-draft form as Mr. Wilson brought it to America, and warned the European statesmen that the Senate, not the President, would have the final word. Lodge at that time urged the American people to look very carefully into this matter of the League, to investigate thoroughly and make sure just what they were getting into. He implied that the President himself did not know.

"It is no idle thing to abandon entirely the policy laid down by Washington in his Farewell Address and by the Monroe Doctrine," said Senator Lodge. This machinery of the League would, in his opinion, not promote the peace of the world but would on the contrary betray our political traditions and take away our traditional liberties. Every American politician knows the effect of this line of argument.

In that February speech the Senator made several "constructive proposals." The President then went back to Paris and put through nearly all of them. This might have made things awkward—but not for Lodge! The minute the revised Treaty was published he indignantly declared that the amended draft was worse than the first. The Monroe Doctrine, for instance, on which Senator Lodge had asked to have "three lines inserted in the Covenant to preserve it" now had those three lines. He declared that they "put us in a far worse position than the first draft—and that was bad enough!" Article X and the provision for withdrawal also met his emphatic disapproval; so did the Article on domestic legislation. "England and the League Council would now be telling us what to do," and that would not be tolerated by any self-respecting American. Nor should it be, but it is something which could not possibly happen under the provisions of the League Constitution, as Mr. Lodge well knew.

The language in which the Covenant was framed also offended him. It was "crude," "lacks precision," "demands interpretation." "As an English product it does not rank high. It might pass at Princeton but not at Harvard," he said. There were moments when Mr. Lodge was really delightful. Mr. John W. Davis, one of our most distinguished international lawyers, and at that time Ambassador to Great Britain, observed to Henry White that "after much polishing our own Constitution had given the courts work for 130 years in effort to fathom its meaning." He also gave it as his opinion that "the Senator's mind whether he realizes it or not was bent not upon amendments which would render the present scheme acceptable but upon objections which would render it or any substitute impossible."

Senators Knox and Hiram Johnson upheld Senator Lodge in his attacks, warning the Peace Conference while it was still in session to divorce the Covenant from the Treaty and that in their opinion this was not the moment to seek to create a league of nations. When twenty-eight prominent Republicans—lawyers, bankers, former Cabinet ministers, and others—protested that "political partisanship should have no place in the consideration on its merits" of the League Constitution, Senator Borah declared that if the Republican party did not make an issue of the League a new party would be created to do so. Throughout May and June the attacks and counterattacks continued, the fanfare of the President's home-coming and his own address to the Senate affording a mere momentary interlude. Mr. Lodge now had his Committee and his party leaders fully organized. The cohorts were lined up. The battle was drawn.

On July 14th the debate was formally opened by Senator Swanson of Virginia. He analyzed the various Articles of the Covenant, the objections raised to it, its advantages to the United States, including the advantages of the disputed Article X. The war had proved the dangers that might arise from lack of machinery for collective action in time of crisis. "Here," urged the Senator, "is machinery for such action and for a real peace program. If we do not accept it, we can expect another cataclysm which will overturn the whole social order and affect territories far wider than the conflict just ending."

Senator Kellogg and Senator Pittman followed with discussion of the contractual side of the Treaty; Senator Pittman contended that "there is not a reservation or amendment we can place in this Treaty that does not necessitate a renegotiation and reconsideration by every contracting power." Every one of the contracting powers must agree even on changes of wording. "Otherwise it is not a contract." Senator McCormick of Illinois then swung into a bitter diatribe on the Shantung question, and the debate was on in full force.

The debaters fell into three main groups on the League issue: For, Against, and Conditional or With Reservations. The Reservationists again were divided into two groups: Lodge Reservationists and Mild Reservationists. Then there were the Irreconcilables, against the League in any form whatsoever. All the Senators opposed were by no means of the Lodge and Knox variety. Some genuinely disapproved the idea of the United States' entering into any permanent international organization. Others favored going in "with protective safeguards." But their limited knowledge of international affairs prevented them from seeing that some of the very safeguards they favored would in reality thwart and render ineffectual the desired organization.

Ignorance, of various sorts, was the main trouble with America in 1919. The ignorance of the people was such that mistaken or deliberately falsifying arguments could be palmed off on them if repeated often and vigorously enough—a method perfected twenty years later by Herr Hitler. There was some conscientious analysis and inquiry on the part of opposing Senators, but there was plenty of double-dealing and duplicity too.

Some of the arguments were not very high-flown. Senator Hiram Johnson called the League a "gigantic War Trust." Senator Poindexter warned against "tariff tinkering" by the League, although President Wilson had inserted an amendment on that very point. Senator Borah called Wilson "Britain's tool—a dodger and a cheater." Senator Reed declared that "while the President talks much about sacrifice he rides at government expense on special trains, lives in palaces of princes, and accepts presents from foreign diplomats worth hundreds of thousands of dollars." In Senator Penrose's speech their worth had gone up to "more than a million" and included jewelry and extravagant gifts from the "crowned heads." (These finally proved to be a few bits of lace and other small articles of very modest value.)

At a moment when the whole world was crying for peace and the President had spent patient months of earnest effort sincerely trying to get it, these arguments did not impress the American people as reasons for repudiating the Treaty. More impressive were the points about sovereignty—preserving our national independence; shall our boys be ordered by a foreign council to fight Europe's wars on the seven seas (which, strangely, they seem to have been ordered to do twice in a quarter of a century *without* such an international agency); Britain's five votes to our one, and so on.

"The President in violation of his word and the American people, is trying to impose his arbitrary will on the nation," said Senator Hiram Johnson. "He is seeking to hand over American destiny to the secret councils of Europe." But the Constitution of the League provided that its councils should be public and open.

"The good things that the League may do in future are purely imaginary. The bad things that it is doing now are actual. The experience of history proves that any such centralized control invariably develops tyranny, bitterness, and bloodshed," said Senator Poindexter.

Peace-Maker

The "remarkable and brilliant debate" Senator Lodge and his friends speak of so admiringly indeed contained some gems that should be preserved for posterity. The Senator from Illinois declared that "nothing required us to scatter our strength over the earth and dissipate our energies and resources crusading in the affairs of every warring people except an impossible idealism drunk with phrase-making and cajoled by European diplomats into spending our national strength to underwrite the war risks of Europe, Asia, and Africa."

Senator Borah said: "We have come in contact with two evil forces of the old world—Prussianism and Internationalism. Both doctrines contemplate world domination and the utter destruction of the national spirit everywhere. . . . If you think you can do what the almighty God has not been able to do—what He in His inscrutable wisdom did when He planted race prejudice in the hearts of men and stamped color on the faces of men, then give us your prospectus!" It was noticeable that the Republicans in the debate called on the Almighty a good deal more than did the Democrats; perhaps they needed Him more.

Other picturesque contributions came from Senator Sherman, who said (in a filibuster) that the League was "a Pandora's box of evils"; that "it would empty upon the American peoples the aggregated calamities of the world and send the Angel of Death into every American home"; that it would "embargo our commerce, close our exchanges, destroy our credits, leave our merchandise rotting on our piers, shut the Isthmian canal, order Congress to declare war, levy taxes, appropriate money, raise and support armies and navies, dispatch our men to any part of the globe to fight because an alien Council so willed." The Senator again omitted—as the opposing Senators repeatedly omitted from their attacks—that no such situation as they described could have arisen because no League Council, Assembly, Commission, or other League organ could "make" us do anything since every vote on every question had to be unanimous and include our own.

Senator Spencer introduced into the Congressional Record a long list of probable expenses of the League (prepared by an accountant) purporting to show that the annual expense would be about $1,194,591,000. The actual budget of the League in normal times came to about six million dollars.

In addition to the blustering and berating, both sides did deliver some fine speeches, showing deep thought and considerable mental anguish and soul-searching. Some of the best pro-League speeches came from Republicans. Senator Colt, Republican, of Rhode Island said: "The League of Nations is in its essence simply an association of free nations. Its object is to prevent war through international co-operation. Broadly speaking, it covers three basic principles: obligatory conference when war is threatened; compulsory submission of every international dispute to some form of arbitration or investigation and report before resorting to war; and reduction of armaments." Senator Colt thought the arguments about a superstate restricting our independence and sovereignty were groundless, since all power that might be exercised by the League had to be by unanimous consent of all the co-operating nations. The great mass of the people, he said, "want something done to prevent future wars and believe that the League of Nations is the best solution to avoid the horrors of the past five years."

Senator John Sharp Williams of Mississippi made a telling speech attacking the reservationists and irreconcilables—the attitude that leads a man or a nation to say, "I do not want to enter into any entangling agreement with anybody to do anything, whether it is right or wrong; I want to be left free at the time to judge for myself." What sort of municipal society, what sort of Federal Union of these United States could you have, made up of individuals proceeding on that basis?

Senator Beckham of Kentucky urged the Senators to rise above partisanship and personalities and to consider the real merits of the document before them. Granted that there were objections to the Covenant and to the Treaty, he reminded them of similar objections—on the part of such persons as Thomas Jefferson and James Monroe—to our own Constitution. Jefferson in the beginning tended to fight it but on May 17, 1788, wrote: "There are indeed some faults, which revolted me a good deal in the first moment, but we must be contented to travel toward perfection step by step. We must be contented with the ground which this Constitution will gain for us and hope that a favorable moment will come for correcting what is amiss with it."

A number of Senators took up the argument about departing from the policies laid down by Washington; they pointed to the complete transformation of the world since Washington's day and commented that Washington himself, progressive and forward-looking as he was, would have been the first to emphasize this. Senator Knute Nelson of Minnesota spoke of the stake the United States has in this modern world: our resources and activities are so vast that we now require a world for our development and expansion, with a fifth of the world's trade ours, and Europe in particular absorbing half our foreign commerce. "I confess," said Senator Nelson, "I cannot take much stock in the 'entangling alliance' argument. Having become entangled by sending our soldiers to Europe to fight, had we not far better become entangled in arrangements to preserve peace than in arrangements merely for making war?" It would be one or the other.

Senator Ransdell of Louisiana reviewed the costs of war in life and money: 7,500,000 lives, 186,000,000,000 dollars. How could people fail to be moved by the overwhelming necessity of avoiding similar waste of youth and wealth in the future? Our people, he said, have not really waked up to the frightful costs of war. We can afford our slice of the money cost, and because death losses have not actually resulted in every home in the country we did not realize what war meant to the major section of the human race. "To large numbers of elderly Americans the war has been an exciting and profitable interlude ending pleasantly and gloriously." They sat in armchairs or behind comfortable office desks and spoke cheerfully of what "our side" had won today, as though it were a football game!

The next war, he went on to say, that nineteenth of July twenty-five years ago, would be destructive beyond imagination. Were Americans indeed so lacking in imagination that they could not look ahead and see what would come? American cities had not been under constant shellfire or in nightly terror of bomb and gas attacks from the air. "The composure of Americans had never for one moment been disturbed by the presence of a single invader or the sound of a hostile shot." Therefore we were unconcerned and complacent about the future.

Yes, we had some far-seeing, astute Senators in 1919. But much good it did us, with the Chairman and the controlling Foreign Relations Committee able to thwart all their efforts, to cancel out every constructive move. On August 12th Senator Lodge himself addressed the Senate in a long, very "America-First" speech, aimed largely at groups of veteran soldiers and sailors who happened by some peculiarly fortuitous coincidence on that particular day to be stationed in the public galleries, and who applauded vociferously.

He was answered incisively by Senator Williams: "The Senator from Massachusetts speaks of the right of all the Powers to call out American sailors and soldiers. I wish that the Senator . . . would tell me where that Treaty at any place gives any right to the League to 'call out American soldiers and sailors.' He cannot do it because it is not in the Treaty and the Senator from Massachusetts knows it is not in the Treaty as well as I do."

The last speech of the month and one of the shortest ever made in the Senate was given by Senator Sheppard of Texas— author of the Eighteenth Amendment. Replying to a newspaper statement that he intended to introduce an amendment to the Covenant calling for international prohibition, Senator Sheppard said: "Mr. President, this is an error. I have never at any time had any intention of offering an amendment to the Covenant of the League of Nations. I regard it as the sublimest document in history, since the Declaration of Independence and the American Constitution, and I regard the opposition to it as one of the most unfortunate and depressing episodes in American or world annals. I am for the Covenant without amendments or reservations."

Peace-Maker

XIII

Toward the middle of August the Foreign Relations Committee finally got around to accepting the President's offer of his services. Earlier in the month the Committee conducted an inquiry, calling certain persons who had been present at the Peace Conference to testify on various points; among them were Mr. Bernard Baruch, Mr. Norman Davis, Secretary Lansing, and Mr. David Hunter Miller. Somebody asked Senator Hitchock if he did not think it would help matters to have Colonel House come from Paris to give further information. "I do not believe," said the Senator, "that any testimony which could be produced could change one vote in the Committee either way. Every member has his mind made up just how he will vote on every question. Frankly I expect the Treaty to be manhandled in committee. It will be amended or reserved to death."

Failing to gain much useful information through these hearings, the Committee decided to question the President and to make it a public conference. Mr. Lodge asked Mr. Wilson to set a time, and the President responded immediately, fixing August 19th at ten A.M. He also invited the Committee to lunch with him afterwards. The conference was held in the East Room, with the Senators grouped around the President in order of precedence. Stenographers sent the proceedings on down to the newspapermen in the basement, and thus a verbatim report went out while the conference was actually going on: an unprecedented occurrence in those prebroadcasting days, and one which roused great excitement and interest throughout the nation.

"Well, gentlemen, I am most happy to see you!" No one could surpass the Virginia-born President in cordial hospitality on his own ground. "I am absolutely glad that the Committee should have responded in this way to my intimation that I would like to be of service to it." (He gracefully overlooked the fact that they had taken five weeks before responding.) "I

365

welcome the opportunity for a frank and full interchange of views."

He had taken the liberty, he said, of preparing a brief written statement which might expedite the discussion and which he proceeded to read. It began with a summary of the many phases of life that waited upon the ratification of the Treaty and his hope that this conference would hasten it and enable both the United States and the world to get back to normal living. "Nothing, I am led to believe, stands in the way of ratification of the Treaty except certain doubts with regard to the meaning and implication of certain Articles of the Covenant of the League of Nations—and I must frankly say that I am unable to understand why such doubts should be entertained."

Pencils flew. The Senators listened; some bored, some sympathetic, some sardonic—even contemptuous. "You will recall that when I had the pleasure of a conference with your Committee and with the Committee of the House of Representatives on Foreign Affairs at the White House in March last, the questions now most frequently asked about the League of Nations were all canvassed with a view to their immediate clarification. *The Covenant of the League was then in its first draft and subject to revision.*" He spoke the words slowly and with particular emphasis.

The Senators at that time "pointed out that no express recognition was given to the Monroe Doctrine, that it was not expressly provided that the League should have no authority to act or to express a judgment on matters of domestic policy; that the right to withdraw from the League was not expressly recognized and that the Constitutional right of the Congress to determine all questions of peace and war was not sufficiently safeguarded. On my return to Paris all these matters were taken up again by the Commission on the League of Nations and *every suggestion of the United States was accepted.*" Again the impressive emphasis, to which, Democratic Senators noted later, Mr. Lodge returned "a blank stare." "The Monroe Doctrine is expressly mentioned," continued the President. The domestic questions clause had been inserted and the withdrawal provision specifically defined.

He then went on to discussion of the much-disputed Article X. Its meaning, he said, is in no respect doubtful when read in the light of the whole Covenant. The Council of the League can only "advise upon" the means by which the obligations of that great Article are to be given effect. Unless the United States is a party to the policy or action in question, her own affirmative vote is necessary before any advice can be given—*for a unanimous vote of the Council is required.* If she is a party, the trouble is hers anyhow. And the unanimous vote of the Council is only advice in any case. Each government is free to reject it if it pleases. Nothing could have been made more clear to the Conference than the right of our Congress under our Constitution to exercise its independent judgment in all matters of peace and war. This cut the ground from under the feet of the Lodge contingent. They attempted no further argument that day on Article X.

The President went on to speak of reservations. Most of the interpretations of the Covenant which had been suggested seemed to him to embody what was "the plain meaning" of the Covenant. There could be no objection to such interpretations accompanying the act of ratification *provided they were stated as a separate resolution*—not as amendments or reservations to the document itself. "If the United States were to qualify the document in any way," he said, "I am confident from what I know of the many conferences and debates which accompanied the formulation of the Treaty that our example would be followed in many quarters—in some instances with very serious reservations—and that the meaning and operative force of the Treaty would be clouded from one end of its clauses to the other."

This, of course, was a point which the Lodge cohorts blandly ignored. They took the position that the other nations would be delighted to get the United States into their association on any terms we might wish to offer. Senator Knox went so far as to say once that "there were only five nations whose approval was really necessary anyway—the rest we didn't care about!"

The Story of Woodrow Wilson

But the conference was not proceeding along the lines that the opposition desired. When the time came for general discussion they tried to get in their belated innings. They asked the President hundreds of questions: questions on secret treaties, on mandates, when the Treaty came into force, how the Peace Conference operated, and what records were kept. Mr. Lodge was particularly persistent with questions as to the drafting of the Covenant, especially Article X. He believed that the President insisted on this Article so strongly, not because it was (as everybody knew) the backbone of the entire document, but because Wilson himself had originated it. Lodge was determined to track him down and to kill the Article. Indeed, as one studies the detailed proceedings of that inquiry, one is struck with its resemblance to the proceedings of a criminal court.

Senator Lodge records that the President took the three and a half hours' grilling in good part, though at the end of it "he looked very much fatigued." He betrayed no irritation or impatience at any moment. But in the privacy of a Democratic powwow with some of his colleagues he once said, apropos of the remarks of some of the Senators, that evidently the Lord had put heads on some men not to hold anything like a mind, but "just to keep them from raveling out at the top!" Senator Harding's questions in particular were almost unbelievably obtuse.

Senator Lodge thought the President "appeared in a very poor light" during the cross-examination. The New York *Times*, however, in its editorial of August 20th said: "In his address and in his frank answers to innumerable questions it seems to us and we are altogether confident it will seem to the country that Mr. Wilson met and disposed of every reasonable objection that has been advanced against particular provisions of the Treaty." However, the Senators on return to their own offices gave no signs of having changed their individual views. The line-up of Fors and Againsts was just the same as before the conference.

The President's foes were greatly disappointed at the results of the inquiry. They had expected to obtain valuable data to

368

bolster their accusations against him and their attack on the Covenant. They left the conference very meagerly provided. Wilson had met them cordially, submitted himself to their barrage for hours, and foiled them by his candid replies—obviously a man who did not need to defend himself or his cause but could simply let the facts speak for themselves.

Two new plans of attack were quickly instituted. The first was Senator Knox's project for a speaking campaign, in which Johnson, Poindexter, and others would cover the Middle and Far Western States—especially those where there appeared a chance of winning reservationist Senators to an outright rejection standpoint. Even though the League was so popular with the country, the wily Knox reminded them that they needed to convert only a third of the Senate to defeat the project. The speakers prepared to start as soon as the Treaty was reported by the Committee.

The second move, which the antis considered a real stroke of genius, was the holding of an American Peace Conference of their own. Representatives of seventeen peoples had established headquarters in Washington—peoples seeking to define their rights under the President's doctrine of self-determination, and dissatisfied with the results of the Paris Conference as far as they were concerned. Lithuania, Latvia, Estonia, and Albania were some of these, not to mention the Irish-Americans and groups nearer home. The Foreign Relations Committee announced that it would give a day in court to each of these dissatisfied groups. The hearings would give more time for developing hostility to the League. They also gave large groups of foreign-descended Americans the impression that the Senate Foreign Relations Committee was a fair and just body lending a sympathetic ear to the grievances of their people in the old country.

"The forces of hyphenism were boldly called into being," says Mr. George Creel, "and no effort was spared to revive and exaggerate the divisive prejudices of American life. The men who, like Lodge, intended to keep the rule of the country forever and ever in the hands of their special ruling caste, have time and again not hesitated to call upon and use those alien foreign groups to achieve their ends."

They appealed to the voters of German birth to oppose "Wilson's League" because he had waged war on Germany; they suppressed all that he had done for the German people straight through the war and at the Peace Conference. They appealed to the Irish on the ground that Wilson had refused to demand the freedom of Ireland before consenting to co-operate with Lloyd George; they ignored the fact that his policy led the way to Home Rule for Ireland and made possible Ireland's eventual membership in the League of Nations (she became a member in 1923). They roused the Italians against Wilson's League and Wilson's party because he had given Fiume to Yugoslavia. The debate in the Senate and this poison-propaganda program went along in parallel lines all summer. Largely in order to let the propaganda work, many thought, the Senate dawdled and procrastinated. Wilson demanded quick action for an exhausted and desperate world. The Senate's answer was hearings, hagglings, criticism, delay.

Meanwhile the President pursued his usual open and straight-forward course. He held conferences, wrote letters, interviewed Senators—especially Republicans who opposed the League in principle, or who had points they wanted cleared up. He talked with fourteen of the opposition Senators—for which he was sharply assailed by Senator Lodge and the very people who had also complained of his "persistent ignoring of the Senate."

He also had domestic problems to work out—railroad strikes, race riots, the punishment of food profiteers. He addressed Congress on the high cost of living, recommendations on railway wage differences, and other measures to improve domestic economy. Still the hours of argument and explanation of the Treaty continued.

The heat of a Washington summer, added to the strain of the past eight months, told on the President's health, but he refused to take a vacation. Reports from the Senate were anything but encouraging. The opposition was spreading its damaging propaganda in the smallest hamlets as well as in the cities and the capital.

Towards the end of August he came to a decision: he too would go to the hamlets and the small towns and the far-off places. He would go to the court of last appeal, which had never failed him. The President would go to the people.

XIV

THE first week in September the President left Washington on a nation-wide speaking tour. He would put the issues up to the country, explain to the people what failure to ratify the Treaty would mean. With public opinion powerfully behind him, he believed the Senate would be obliged to yield.

Dr. Grayson strongly opposed the trip. Mr. Wilson's health, after the prolonged strain of the Peace Conference plus his exertions and anxieties of subsequent months, caused serious concern. What would it be after more weeks of constant strain and travel—luncheons, dinners, speeches, parades, and perpetual talking and hand-shaking? "You can't do it, sir. It might be the death of you!" Grayson protested.

The President was looking out the White House windows, over the wide sweep of lawn to the gleaming shaft of Washington's monument. "Yes," he said, "that's all true. But my own health is not to be considered when the future peace and security of the world are at stake. If the Treaty is not ratified by the Senate the war will have been fought in vain and the world will be thrown into chaos. I promised our soldiers when I asked them to take up arms that it was a war to end wars, and if I do not do all in my power to put the Treaty into effect I will be a slacker and never able to look those boys in the eye. I must go."

The last week in August the President and Mrs. Wilson gave a lawn party at the White House for the wounded boys of the Walter Reed and Naval Hospitals. On September 3rd the President's special train left Washington. It carried more cars than usual, for one hundred reporters and photographers accompanied him, as well as Mrs. Wilson, Dr. Grayson, Mr. Tumulty, and the usual secret-service men, servants, and secretaries. His itinerary ranged from Ohio and Indiana to Missouri, Iowa, Minnesota, and the Western States. He traveled almost ten thousand miles and made over a hundred speeches (including the informal talks) in twenty-two days. Senators Borah, Hiram Johnson, and Poindexter trailed him, making counterspeeches in many places.

"Never have I seen the President look so weary as on the night we left Washington," says Mr. Tumulty. "When we were about to board our special train, the President turned to me and said, 'I am in a nice fix. I am scheduled between now and the twenty-eighth of September to make in the neighborhood of a hundred speeches. . . . But the pressure has been so great I have not had a single minute to prepare my speeches. I do not know how I shall get the time.' " He said he had been suffering from daily headaches but hoped the night's rest would make him fit for the work tomorrow.

No weariness was apparent in his opening speech at Columbus next day. "With its beautiful phrasing and effective delivery, it seemed to have been carefully prepared."

The Columbus *Evening Dispatch* of September 4, 1919, said that cheers and applause greeted the President throughout his visit in Columbus (Senator Harding's home territory). Other papers said that "the audience showed marked approval." His speeches and references to the League were interrupted frequently by applause.

At Indianapolis—home of another opponent, Senator New—twelve thousand people packed the building to hear him, shouting, "Wilson! We want Wilson!" and refusing to hear Senator New's friend the Governor, who was trying to make a speech of introduction.

At St. Louis—where one of his bitterest enemies, Senator Reed, was constantly trying to stir public sentiment against the President and the League—Mr. Wilson received his greatest ovation since his return from Europe. Twelve hundred businessmen of the Chamber of Commerce met him at luncheon and applauded enthusiastically his statement that "business was vitally interested in the swift ratification of the Treaty" and that "business in the United States was not separated from the rest of the world, commercially, individually, or financially."

That night twelve thousand people heard him, while other disappointed thousands tried to gain admission. Newspapermen traveling with the Presidential party reported that in Ohio and Indiana the crowds had been more or less apathetic about the League, their interest focused on the President rather than on the Treaty. But Missouri, thanks to Senator Reed's activities, was found to be "keenly interested and sharply divided," with a preponderance in the League's favor. And as the tour progressed, interest and enthusiasm increased.

"The President was tremendously pleased with his reception in Republican St. Louis and showed it," said the St. Louis *Globe Democrat*. "He was working at his typewriter as the train pulled out." He worked late and early, organizing his next address while traveling from one city to another, and between all the parties, interviews, and parades. Each day the program was repeated—sometimes several times over: a small local committee from the next town would meet him and accompany the party from the town before. This meant constant entertaining on the train, and there were no air-conditioned cars in those days. The dust and heat were sometimes almost unbearable.

The headaches became more severe, but he never allowed them to interfere with the business of the day or to intrude in any way on the rest of the party. "He would appear regularly at each meal," says Tumulty, ". . . always gracious, always good-natured, smiling; responding to every call from the outside for speeches—calls which came from early morning till late at night, from the plain people grouped around every station and water-tower. When he was 'half-fit,' as he expressed it, he was the best fellow in the group . . . full of anecdotes and repartee, always thinking of the comfort and pleasure of the men gathered about him."

The fact that his talks were so well received and that he was winning adherents for the League all along the line of course cheered the President tremendously. In his speeches he took up the various arguments that had been brought against the League —points about the Monroe Doctrine, domestic questions, Shantung, Article X—and answered them frankly and persuasively.

In the first place he would call his audience's attention to the League as a great human document and to the fact that it contained twenty-six great Articles which should be studied, not simply the four or five on which the dissenters had concentrated their attack. The central theme of the document was arbitration instead of armament—a powerfully armed nation inevitably came under the domination of the military caste, the only men who knew how to control the war machinery. Did the world want to live under a huge war machinery or a comprehensive peace machinery? If we did not organize under a peace machinery like the League "the world will have to contend with some nation dominated by evil passions of war just as soon as recovery comes."

The Monroe Doctrine was specifically mentioned and for the first time expressly adopted and authenticated by all the great nations of the world; this, he thought, was more important than matters of style and phrasing which seemed so desperately to worry some gentlemen. The proposal to be more specific about domestic questions (to be excluded from arbitration or interference by the League) he thought was unwise because almost invariably we would leave out the very question we might later most ardently wish to have included. Anyhow, the other nations were just as jealous of their sovereignty as was the United States. None of them had the slightest idea of surrendering their domestic concerns.

As for the Shantung settlement, he said that he himself had been far from pleased with it. But he told the story of the systematic despoiling of China by the various countries since 1898, also the story of the elements he had had to face at Paris. He then asked his audience to decide whether China's best interests were served through the League or through scrapping the settlement—having Japan refuse to sign and then form a "second league" with Germany and other disaffected nations.

Speaking of Article X, he said it was not only the inevitable, logical center of the whole Covenant but the fulfillment of promises made to our fighting men. "This Treaty," said the President in his great speech at Reno, "was not written, essentially speaking, at Paris. It was written at Château-Thierry and in Belleau Wood and in the Argonne. Our men did not fight over there with the purpose of coming back and letting the same thing happen again."

His constant theme from first to last was that the eight million men who had fought for us all in that war must not be betrayed. They had given their lives not for just a military peace with some economic prizes, but for a new world—the sort of world embodied in the League Covenant. He had promised our own boys when he sent them forth that that was the world they would be getting. If that promise should be broken, he warned the American people with all earnestness: "There will come sometime . . . another struggle in which, not a few hundred thousand fine men from America will have to die, but as many millions as are necessary to accomplish the final freedom of the world." Today these words come back to us with a good deal more significance than the irreconcilable Senators' constant warnings about entangling alliances.

The Irreconcilables of course would have people believe that the President's tour was a failure. "It became very obvious," wrote Senator Lodge, "that he was not meeting with the reception he expected or awakening the enthusiasm for the League which he anticipated. As a whole the meetings and events of the trip were disappointing."

The newspapers of the time tell a different story. As the President sped westward the crowds grew increasingly enthusiastic. A Des Moines, Iowa, paper declared: "The Middle West is for speedy ratification of the Treaty, including the Covenant of the League. . . . The people of Iowa, mostly farmers, strong Republicans, and representative Americans, apparently favor the League." In North Dakota, Governor Frazier said in introducing the President that he believed the majority sentiment in the State favored ratification of the League "with reservations"— but that if reservations would cause delay they were for immediate ratification without reservations, leaving changes for a later date.

In Minnesota "great crowds greeted the President everywhere with enthusiasm." Fifteen thousand heard him at St. Paul. "At the conclusion of the President's speech the Mayor asked for a vote for ratification with or without reservations. The 'ayes' came back in a great chorus. Only a few 'noes' were heard." "Minnesota was a Republican State in the last election," said one paper, "but it is not Republican in this fight to the extent that it is willing to permit politics to enter the question of the League or to follow any leadership which would advise a course to destroy the Peace Treaty."

In Oregon it was reported that "Portland throngs cheer his every appearance. . . . League sentiment strong. . . . The State of Oregon is apparently sound League of Nations territory."

Oddly enough, the warmest support seemed to come from strong Republican centers and from Republican leaders and newspapers. This was true in Missouri, Minnesota, Oregon, California, Iowa, Utah. Where there was opposition—which he encountered only once or twice on the tour—it came from places with a strong German or Irish population, which the Irreconcilables had played upon from the first. Nebraska was one such section; there the voting population was about 25 per cent of German origin. Northern California and parts of Missouri, with large Irish populations, were others.

But in other regions the expected opposition did not materialize. Senator Poindexter's home city of Spokane gave the President a rousing welcome. So did Tacoma, where twenty thousand school children greeted him with songs and flowers, surrounded by their cheering parents. At Seattle he reviewed the Fleet— a thrilling experience, which had the added advantage of giving him two nights in a hotel. Then on down the Coast to his great receptions in Oregon and California.

XV

MEANWHILE the Senators back in Washington had not sat idly by while the President held the spotlight. On September 10th the Foreign Relations Committee made its report to the Senate on the Treaty. The Committee recommended ratification with forty-nine amendments and four reservations.

While officially recommending "ratification" with these changes, the gentlemen responsible for the majority report made the spirit and purpose of rejection too plain to doubt. The report denounced the League as an alliance and a war-breeder. The amendments covered various points that had been especially stressed by League opponents—equality of voting, an amendment on the Shantung matter, an amendment to relieve the United States from representation on the various commissions established under the League, and an especially important reservation in regard to Article X.

In presenting these amendments the Senators declared that they would not, as frequently stated, cause delay or a resummoning of the Peace Conference, since the Conference was still in session in Paris. This of course was intended to mislead, for the limited bodies left at Paris to deliberate on special issues were not qualified to act on such amendments, as the Lodge contingent well knew. It was simply their way of strengthening prejudice and appealing to jingoism.

"Equally unfitting," the report continued, "is the attempt to frighten the unthinking by suggesting that if the Senate adopts amendments or reservations the United States may be excluded from the League. . . . That is the one thing that will certainly not happen. . . . The other nations will take us on our own terms, for without us their League is a wreck and all their gains for a victorious peace are imperiled."

What a statement to go out as representing the American point of view, and to build international good will and understanding. Few Prussian statements ever matched it for arrogance and downright stupidity. But Senator Lodge wrote the report and all Republican Senators on the Committee except Senator McCumber signed it and supported the amendments.

The Democratic members of the Committee submitted a minority report urging the ratification of the Treaty without change. They declared that the reservations were the work of Senators who had chosen this means of destroying the League and defeating the Treaty. The opponents of the League, perceiving that they could not win with a frontal attack, chose the indirect approach instead.

Senator McCumber, sole pro-League Republican on the Committee, filed another minority report denouncing the Committee and the Lodge group. McCumber described the majority attitude toward certain points as "selfish, immoral, and dishonorable." He denounced the Lodge group for ignoring the great purposes of the Covenant and said that it was shocking to the country that a matter so foreign to partisanship should be influenced "by hostility to the President of the United States" and in callous indifference to "the aspirations and hopes of a wounded and bleeding world."

While the President made his swing around the Northwest and down the Pacific Coast the debate in the Senate entered into a new and more intensive phase. The League opponents counted on this and on their Senators' speaking tours to counteract the President's triumphs. Their hopes were apparently not realized. On September 13, 1919, when Senator Borah was calling on the people "not merely to amend but to wreck the League Covenant," the New York *Times* reported that in Borah's own town of Coeur d'Alene, Idaho, "Wilson was heartily cheered. . . . Borah's home town applauded Wilson's attacks on those who were willing to destroy the Treaty. . . . It does not seem that the majority are willing to follow Borah's leadership to the point of preventing American participation in the League."

Senator Hiram Johnson was declaring that "public sentiment against the League is growing stronger every day and is fast assuming the proportions of a revolution. . . . Give the people sixty days and they will tear the League to pieces." But at the same time the papers in Johnson's home State of California said: "Great throngs of wildly cheering people greeted the President." "The ovation was unexpected in its exuberance and magnitude," said the San Francisco *Chronicle*. "Twelve thousand people heard him at the San Francisco Auditorium, while half as many outside gave him four successive salvos of greeting. 'Are We With Him?' shouted a man from the gallery. 'WE ARE!' was hurled back from thousands of voices."

In Oakland eight thousand dock workers stopped work to give him a hearty cheer. " 'That's the boy!' the crowd shouted delightedly to the President along a ten-mile parade in Los Angeles amid a din of applause," records the Los Angeles *Times*. The tour reached its climax at San Diego, where a crowd of fifty thousand heard the President as amplifiers carried his words to vast out-of-doors throngs. "If any doubt remained that Southern California stands closer to President Wilson than to Senator Johnson in his extreme opposition, it was dispelled today," wrote a Los Angeles correspondent of the New York *Herald* on September 21, 1919. "Reception here indicates that Southern California is supporting him and is in favor of the League."

Johnson and Borah could stir the crowds by appealing to deep-rooted prejudices and jingo patriotism; they had a hundred clever oratorical tricks, utterly unknown to Mr. Wilson, for moving primitive passions. But he had two things they lacked: straightforwardness and sincerity. He was not always wise in his allusions to his opponents. There were phrases occasionally that his friends wished he had omitted—as, for example, his "Let them put up or shut up," at Kansas City, and his statement that "when in the annals of mankind they [the opposition] are gibbeted they will regret that the gibbet is so high." Some of his references to politicians and to the Senators—whom, after all, he wanted to win to his side—were unfortunate. But for a man laboring under such a terrific strain, after having "fought, bled, and died" at Paris to put through the amendments the Senators asked for—only to come home to hear a shout for forty-nine more—it was a wonder he did as well.

The crowds grew ever larger and more enthusiastic, the wear

and tear on the President worse. To stand for hours every day in a swaying automobile while the deafening yells and whistles and calls of the populace beat on his eardrums and vast hordes of emotionally wrought-up human beings perpetually milled round him—certainly this was not the best thing for a man already suffering from prolonged nervous tension. He would come in from the incessant parades and bands and din and shouting, throw himself down in a chair, and groan: "They mean so well—but they are killing me!"

The gifts alone were a major problem—chrysanthemums twelve feet high, grapes that weighed a hundred pounds, prize deer, livestock, and tributes of all sorts jammed the Presidential car and apartments wherever he went till there was almost no place left for the party to sit down, much less relax and rest. The headaches increased, sometimes almost blinding him. "Coming in from a reception or dinner," said his wife, "I have seen him sit with his head bowed on the back of a chair in front of him while trying to dictate and keep abreast of his enormous mail. He lost weight and his physician grew increasingly anxious. The President tried to joke about it and laughingly said, when the newspapermen sympathized with him, 'Well, my constitution may not be very good but I ought to get along for a good while on my by-laws.' "

The severest ordeal came at Salt Lake City, where he had to speak in the Mormon tabernacle to fifteen thousand people for two hours, without a particle of air or ventilation. It was an important meeting. Senator Reed Smoot had declared that the leaders of the Mormon Church all opposed the League. The President's welcome was a strong disproof of this. On his arrival he was assured that a large majority of the Mormon Church were League supporters, that the head of the Church the Sunday before had made a declaration in favor of the League and urged members to work for it. "The official news organ of the Church is behind it and the *Tribune*—the Republican paper—is fighting for the League and says that the people of Utah are supporters of President Wilson."

Peace-Maker

On September 18th Charles Grasty reported from the Presidential train, now swinging into its return circle: "Belief in the League found to be nation-wide. Resubmission scouted. . . . Mass of people not keen for any changes . . . personal triumph for the President all the way from Columbus to San Francisco. They are not willing to take it out of his hands and give it to Johnson, Borah, or Reed." On September 19th the New York *Times* records: "Lodge summons Johnson and Poindexter to cut tours and return to Washington."

Then came the mortal blow—and the saving stroke for the Irreconcilables. After the speech at the Mormon Temple the President went back to the hotel completely exhausted, soaked through with perspiration and too weary to pretend any longer that he was not ill. He spoke at Cheyenne next afternoon, at Denver the following morning; then on to Pueblo, where he arrived for a big meeting at the fair grounds at three in the afternoon. He looked so badly that his wife pleaded with him to take a few days' rest, but he said, "No—no, I have caught the imagination of the people. They are eager to hear what the League stands for and I should fail in my duty if I disappointed them. Wait till we get back to Washington—then I promise you I will take a holiday." But even he knew that the time had come when he must slow up a little.

"This will have to be a short speech," he said as he took the stand that day at Pueblo. Then—nodding to the men in the press box who had followed him more than nine thousand miles and listened to all his speeches—"Aren't you fellows getting pretty sick of this?" Strangely enough, the speech that followed was one of the longest and most touching that he made during the entire tour. As he warmed to his subject the President's weariness seemed to drop from him. His eloquence that day had a quality which those who listened to him never forgot. The vast audience gathered at the Pueblo Auditorium rose and cheered for more than ten minutes when he appeared and "roared its approval time and time again," said the local paper, "as the speech proceeded."

The Story of Woodrow Wilson

There seems to me [he said] to stand between us and the rejection or qualification of this Treaty the serried ranks of those boys in khaki . . . who went forth to fight in order that other boys should not have to go on a similar errand in future. . . . What of our pledges to those men? We said that they went over there not just to prove the prowess of America but to see to it that there never was such a war again. . . .

Mothers who lost their sons in France have come to me and, taking my hand, have not only shed tears on it but they have said "God bless you, Mr. President!" Why, my fellow citizens, should they pray God to bless me? . . . I ordered their sons overseas. I consented to their sons being put in the most difficult parts of the battle-line, where death was certain. Why should they weep upon my hand and call down the blessings of God upon me? Because they believe that their boys died for something that vastly transcends any of the immediate and palpable objects of the war. They believe . . . that their sons saved the liberty of the world. They believe that wrapped up with the liberty of the world is the continuous protection of that liberty by the concerted powers of all civilized people. They believe that this sacrifice was made in order that other sons should not be called upon for a similar gift of life.

He recalled the Decoration Day ceremonies at Suresnes Cemetery, where our boys in France are buried. "I wish that some of the men who are now opposing the settlement for which those men died could visit such a spot as that . . . I wish that they could feel the moral obligation that rests upon us not to go back on those boys, but to see the thing through to the end and make good their redemption of the world."

It was his last speech. That night at about eleven-thirty, as their train sped through to the next stopping place, he knocked at his wife's door and asked her to come to him. He was feeling very ill. The pain in his head was so bad he could not lie down. Mrs. Wilson called Dr. Grayson. The night wore on in a long vigil for the three of them. Finally sleep came—but the end had come also. Dr. Grayson warned that to continue the trip might bring disastrous, even fatal, consequences. He simply must cancel the rest of the tour and take a vacation.

When the President was told this he flatly refused. "No—no, I must keep on. Don't you see if I cancel this trip our enemies will say I am a quitter and that the Western trip was a failure—and the Treaty will be lost. Just postpone the trip twenty-four hours and I will be all right." Finally his wife had to tell him: the fight was over. It was an agonizing hour for both of them, but at last it was done. "The seal he put on his lips in that hour," says Mrs. Wilson, "was never broken in all the long hard years ahead. Never once did he voice a syllable of self-pity, complaint, or regret."

At the next stop—Wichita, Kansas—the news of what had happened was flashed to the country. Mr. Tumulty told the reception committee and the press that the President was ill and Dr. Grayson had ordered him to Washington for a complete rest. Tracks were cleared, and, with a pilot engine running ahead to blaze the way, the President's train left on its mournful return journey. "It seemed," said one member of the party, "almost like a funeral cortege—with the lowered blinds and deathly silence, after all the usual noise and excitement." Certainly for one man it was the death of all his hopes and everything he had worked for.

On Sunday morning, September 28th, the train pulled into Washington. Motors were waiting, and soon the sick man was back within the shelter of the White House. He saw the members of his family. He talked and made plans with them—all playing up, trying to act as though the structure of his life were not lying in ruins. The awful pain in his head prevented him even from reading.

Next day he seemed a little better. He went for a drive and in the evening saw a motion picture in the East Room with some of the family. This went off so well that the President was delighted and insisted he would read Mrs. Wilson his usual chapter from the Bible before retiring. He stood under the center light in her room with the Book in one hand and the other resting on a table beside the big couch where she sat. His voice was as strong and vibrant as she had ever heard it. When he finished he put the Bible on the table and they talked a little. Then he went to his own room and to bed.

Mrs. Wilson looked in once or twice during the night, and he seemed to be sleeping normally. But at eight the next morning when she went to his room she found him seated on the side of the bed trying to reach a water bottle. His left hand hung loosely. "I have no feeling in that hand," he said. "Will you rub it?"

She left him for a moment to telephone the doctor. While she was at the telephone she heard a noise and, rushing back to her husband's room, found him on the bathroom floor, unconscious. He had suffered a stroke which paralyzed the left side of his body. One arm and one leg were useless, but the brain was clear and untouched.

Such is the tragic story of that morning of October 2, 1919. The climax of the tragedy was that every member of the tour who had watched the mounting enthusiasm of the President's audiences said that if he could have continued just two or three more weeks the League and all that he had fought for would have won through to victory.

XVI

For days the President lay at the point of death. Then the will to live and continue his fight gradually gained over the disease. He showed a little improvement. Grave questions confronted his physicians and those nearest to him. "Ought not the President to resign?" Mrs. Wilson asked. "Should not Mr. Marshall succeed to the office and allow Mr. Wilson to get the quiet and rest essential to his very life?"

The doctors said no: for Mr. Wilson to resign would have a bad effect upon the country as well as upon the patient. "He has staked his life and made his promise to the world to get the Treaty ratified and make the League of Nations complete. If he resigns the greatest incentive to recovery is gone. His mind is clear as crystal, and he can still do more than anyone else—even with a maimed body."

Pasteur, they told Mrs. Wilson, stricken in exactly the same way, did his best work afterwards. But for the best and quickest cure, the President must be shielded from every disturbance and harassing problem. The doctors had a plan to propose. "He has the utmost confidence in you," they said to Mrs. Wilson. "Have everything brought to you, weigh the importance of each question, and see if it is not possible with the heads of the Departments to solve many of these matters without the guidance of your husband. His nerves are crying for rest, and any excitement or disturbance is torture to him."

So began this difficult stewardship. Mrs. Wilson, in addition to her hours of anxious watching in the sickroom, studied every paper sent from the different Secretaries and Senators and tried to digest and present in tabloid form the matters that absolutely had to go to the President. The long evenings with the Drawer and four years of intensive work by his side formed a precious background of experience and discipline. She herself, however, never made a decision regarding public affairs. She decided only what was important and what was not, and at what moment to present to her husband the vital matters that he had to see.

A great many cruel and bitter things have been said about this stewardship—some of them by certain of Mr. Wilson's associates who opposed his second marriage from the beginning. A great deal has been said about "the second Mrs. Wilson"—not all of it kind, some of it harshly critical. But when you follow the course of her life with the President, as this writer has done for many months, studying their day-by-day existence, reading documents, letters, diaries, memoranda, you can only join with one of the Paris newspapermen of the Peace Conference who recently declared: "After an acquaintance of twenty-five years and an ever-increasing admiration, I just want to say—I take off my hat to her!"

This we know from the documentary record: she filled the

The Story of Woodrow Wilson

difficult duties of her position during the President's illness with utmost conscientiousness and a deep sense of responsibility. "Her high intelligence and her extraordinary memory," says Mr. Tumulty, "enabled her to report to him daily, in lucid detail, weighty matters of state brought to her by officials for transmission to him. At the proper time, when he was least in pain and least exhausted, she would present a clear oral résumé of each case and lay the documents before him. When it became possible for him to see people, she, in counsel with Admiral Grayson, would arrange for conferences—and carefully watch her husband to see that those who talked with him did not trespass too long on his limited energy. There never was an entire week during the whole of his illness when he was not in touch with all the most important matters of state." Surely his private secretary should know.

As the President improved he asked hundreds of questions and insisted upon knowing everything—especially about the Treaty. He would dictate notes to key people. He would tell Mrs. Wilson what Senators to send for and what suggestions he had to make to them. Imagine the torment to a man of Wilson's drive and fighting spirit: his tour a success—public sentiment responding eagerly to his vivid explanations on the League; friendly Senators anxious to press their advantage; and then—the President stricken, ruled out of the fight which he had come so close to winning.

Now was the time for the Irreconcilables to send up shouts of rejoicing. The campaign to rouse the country to "the crimes of Wilson" went on in spite of the President's illness; indeed, hate increased, seemingly, with his plight. All the pent-up fury of weeks of jealous onlooking during his triumphs was concentrated in the diatribe by Harvey in *Harper's Weekly* (October 4, 1919), only two days after he was stricken: "He has gained the immense gratification of holding the center of the stage for a time in the full glare of the limelight. . . . He has received a considerable share of the adulation which is ever so dear to his heart. . . . Undoubtedly he has had the time of his life 'slangwhanging' the United States Senate and insulting every

American citizen who ventured to disagree with him. . . . He has had his say. He has shot his bolt. He has done his worst. . . . Now let the Senate act."

The Senate was even then acting. The amendments proposed by the Foreign Relations Committee were voted upon in early October and were all defeated. The Committee then turned to the framing of reservations. "Some of the Senators," says Mr. Lodge, "feared that 'amendments' might keep the other Powers from accepting the changes." so he substituted the word "reservations." They comprised very much the same things—reservation on arbitration, reservation on withdrawal, reservation on Monroe Doctrine, reservation on Article X—only the name was different. The language was toned down a bit, but there was the same general stand on the same issues.

On November 6th Mr. Lodge reported the resolution of ratification together with these fourteen reservations—one for each of the detested Fourteen Points (including the four that were recommended in the report of September 10th). The little group of stonily determined men set grimly about the business of seeing to it that this time they should go through. As the matter came up before the Senate formally for a second time, petitions and messages poured in from all over the Country, from all classes and types of people, beseeching the Senators to consider the great issues at stake, the great basic purposes of the Treaty and the League, to cease quibbling and arguing and give the country and the world the peace they longed for. "Ratification without reservations" was the phrase urged again and again.

Europe, meanwhile, was plunged in disorder and violence. The Germans under General von der Goltz had captured the city of Riga, and it looked as though the Junkers might be restored to power. Italy gloated over her seizure of Fiume. The Rumanians, defying the decisions of the Peace Conference, took what they wanted and did what they liked in Hungary. French extremists were ready to oust Clemenceau and pursue a similar policy in Germany. Greece had her eye on Bulgaria, Poland again on Germany. One or two more such acts of defiance might completely demolish the Versailles Treaty.

These things did not disturb the Senators leading the attack at Washington. Senator McCormick found in them added reason for rejection. Senator Lodge marked the first anniversary of the Armistice with a speech of withering ridicule for the President's efforts at moderate settlements. The Senator advocated conquests by the Allies which would almost certainly lead to further wars.

Lodge and his friends now intensified the "wearing down" maneuvers at which they were expert. Anything to confuse and exhaust the people: amendments, reservations—Lodge reservations—mild reservations—Article This—Article That. And always the persistent cry: "The President obstinately refuses to consent to any changes. He demands the Treaty precisely as he brought it back with him from Paris." This is still said today, by people who should know better.

The facts are that the President four times publicly expressed his willingness for changes in the Treaty to satisfy the American viewpoint: first, when he laid the first-draft Covenant before the Senators at the dinner conference in February and went back to Paris and put through the amendments then requested; second, on August 19th, when he expressed to the Foreign Relations Committee his willingness for a "covering resolution" to accompany ratification—"interpretive reservations" including each of the main issues in regard to which the Senators desired special interpretation for America; third, when, before leaving Washington on his Western speaking tour (September, 1919), he wrote Senator Hitchcock a letter-memorandum, setting forth the reservations he himself would be willing to agree to; and fourth, on January 28, 1920, in another letter to Senator Hitchcock when he wrote: "I am happy to be able to add, therefore, that I have once more gone over the reservations proposed by yourself, the copy of which I return herewith, and am glad to say that I can accept them as they stand."

The "Hitchcock reservations," representing the interpretive or covering resolution which the President felt was the only wise type of statement that could be appended to the Treaty, were presented to the Senate on November 13th in the midst of the debate on the Lodge reservations and were voted down; many Senators did not entirely understand what they contained or how far they met what most of the reservationists actually desired. By this time the Lodge prescription was beginning to work. The politicians and the people alike were beginning to accept the oft-repeated statement about the President's stubborn obstinacy and "the dangers of the Covenant to the American people."

The President—with a mind which Newton Baker said was "ten times clearer sick than that of any other man well"—could not understand how so many intelligent men could fail to see what to him was so obvious. "But I did ask them for their amendments," he would say—"we did go back to the Powers and put those amendments through. I *am* willing for a general resolution covering the points they now raise. Can't they see that we have no right to go back asking for more changes unless we give every other Power the same right—to amend and reserve and alter the Covenant as *they* please? And then where will the peace and the entire Treaty be? It beats me that they can't see it!"

His jaw grew longer and his determination more grim as the days and Lodge's campaign wore on. There was one man Mr. Lodge and his tactics could not wear down: a man who lay flat on his back at the White House but whose brain remained alert as ever. Many trials came to test him. With the leader struck down, the League forces lost ground. The great gains of the tour faded. So did former adherents. Senators who had refused to vote for amendments voted for reservations without a blush. Lodge's program went through triumphantly. Between November 8th and November 13th the fourteen reservations were voted through one after the other. The Hitchcock interpretive reservations were defeated. The day was approaching for the final decision. Would the President yield?

"If you want your League to go through, Mr. President, you'll have to take it with the Lodge reservations!" one adviser after another said to him. On the very eve of the vote the Executive Council of the League to Enforce Peace announced its decision to accept the Lodge reservations on the plea of "better ratification with reservations than no ratification at all." This announcement arrived on November 18th and was jubilantly read in the Senate. Another blow for the hard-beset President: his stanchest helper, Mr. Taft, gone over to the enemy! He lay in his bed, helpless, while the fight raged at the other end of Pennsylvania Avenue and the opposition circulated all sorts of rumors about him, including even suspicion as to his sanity.

The Senate was to vote on November 19th. On the eighteenth Senator Hitchcock went to see Mrs. Wilson and told her that unless the Administration forces would accept the reservations, the Treaty would be beaten, the struggle having narrowed to a personal fight against the President by Senator Lodge and his supporters. Mrs. Wilson went in to her husband's bedside and told him what the Senator had said. "For my sake," she asked him, "won't you yield a little and get this terrible thing settled?"

He turned his head with a look of amazement. "Don't *you* turn against me—I couldn't stand that! Can't you see that I have no moral right to accept any change in a treaty I signed as head of this nation without giving every other signatory—even Germany—the right to do the same thing? It is not I that will not accept—it is the nation's honor that is at stake." Then he added, more quietly: "Better a thousand times go down fighting than to dip your colors in dishonorable compromise!" The whole of Woodrow Wilson is in that sentence.

She went back and told Senator Hitchcock. Later in the day the President dictated a letter to the Senator in which he said: "In my opinion the resolution in that form [i.e., embodying the Lodge reservations] does not provide for ratification but rather for nullification of the Treaty. . . . I trust that all true friends of the Treaty will refuse to support the Lodge resolution."

That same day the Senate voted. The Administration forces voting against ratification with the Lodge reservations won: 55 to 39. The vote was then taken on the ratification of the Treaty without reservations, as the President had brought it from France. The result was defeat—by eight votes, under the rule requiring a two-thirds majority. The vote stood 53 for the Treaty, 38 against. Yet, so strange is our American Constitution, a minority of reactionary opponents won over a substantial majority of fifteen Senators and the general desire of the American people.

It was feared that the news might have a serious effect upon the sick President. When his wife told him he was silent for a few minutes. Then he said: "All the more reason I must get well and try again to bring this country to a sense of its great opportunity and greater responsibility."

What can you do with a man like that? A quarter of a century has proved one thing: you cannot beat him.

XVII

M R. LODGE declared that it was the President, not the Senate or the Senate's leader, who nullified the Treaty. "He and he alone is responsible," said Mr. Lodge. "He was determined to have the treaty exactly as he had approved it in Paris."

Not merely as he had approved it, but as it had been formally voted in the official Peace Conference, *after* the amendments requested by members of the Senate Foreign Relations Committee and by him presented to the delegates at the Paris Conference had been incorporated. This is a point which present-day writers and commentators, apparently taking their cue from Mr. Lodge, ignore when they refer to "President Wilson's obstinacy about refusing any changes for his Treaty." One could not go on indefinitely making amendments and asking for changes.

The vital question is this: Did or did not these reservations nullify the Treaty and the Covenant of the League as agreed upon and voted by the nations at the Paris Peace Conference? Here are the reservations—here is the Covenant. Let the reader judge.

THE LEAGUE COVENANT

Any Member of the League may, after two years notice **Article 1**
of its intention to do so, withdraw from the League,
provided that all its international obligations and all its
obligations under this Covenant shall have been fulfilled at the time of its withdrawal.

The Members of the League undertake to preserve **Article 10**
and respect as against external aggression the territorial
integrity and existing political independence of all
Members of the League. In case of any such aggression the Council shall advise upon the means by which
this obligation shall be fulfilled.

... Peoples not yet able to stand by themselves ... should **Article 22**
be entrusted to the tutelage of advanced nations who
by reason of their resources, their experience or their
geographical position can best undertake this responsibility, and who are willing to accept it ... this tutelage
should be exercised by them as Mandatories on behalf
of the League.

If the dispute between the parties is claimed by one of **Article 15**
them, and is found by the Council, to arise out of a matter
which by international law is solely within the domestic
jurisdiction of that party, the Council shall so report,
and shall make no recommendation as to its settlement.

The Members of the League agree that if there should **Article 12**
arise between them any dispute likely to lead to a
rupture, they will submit the matter either to arbitration
or to judicial settlement or to inquiry by the Council.

THE LODGE RESERVATIONS

Reservation 1
Withdrawal

In case of notice of withdrawal from the League of Nations . . . the United States shall be the sole judge as to whether all its international obligations . . . under the said Covenant have been fulfilled, and notice of withdrawal . . . may be given by a concurrent resolution of the Congress of the United States.

Reservation 2
Territorial Integrity

The United States assumes no obligation to preserve the territorial integrity or political independence of any other country . . . or to interfere in any way in controversies between nations . . . unless . . . the Congress . . . shall, in the exercise of full liberty of action . . . by act or joint resolution so provide.

Reservation 3
Mandates

No mandate shall be accepted by the United States . . . except by action of the Congress of the United States.

Reservation 4
Domestic Questions

The United States reserves to itself exclusively the right to decide what questions are within its domestic jurisdiction and declares that all . . . questions relating . . . to . . . immigration, labor, coastwise traffic, commerce, the suppression of traffic in women and children and in opium and other dangerous drugs . . . are solely within the jurisdiction of the United States and are not . . . to be submitted either to arbitration or to the consideration of the Council or the Assembly of the League of Nations.

Reservation 5
Monroe Doctrine

The United States will not submit to arbitration or inquiry . . . any questions which . . . depend upon or relate to . . . the Monroe Doctrine; said doctrine . . . to be interpreted by the United States alone and . . . declared to be wholly outside the jurisdiction of said League of Nations.

All matters of procedure at meetings of the Assembly Article 5
or of the Council, including the appointment of Committees to investigate particular matters, shall be regu-
lated by the Assembly or by the Council and may be
decided by a majority of the Members of the League
represented at the meeting.

The expenses of the League shall be borne by the Article 6
Members of the League in the proportion decided by
the Assembly.

The Members of the League recognize that the mainte- Article 8
nance of peace requires the reduction of national armaments ... and the enforcement of action by international
obligations. The Council ... shall formulate plans for
such reduction ... the limits of armaments therein fixed
shall not be exceeded without the concurrence of the
Council.

THE LODGE RESERVATIONS

Reservation 6
Shantung

The United States withholds its assent to articles *156, 157*, and *158* [*the Shantung provisions*], and reserves full liberty of action with respect to any controversy which may arise under said articles.

Reservation 7
Appointments

The Congress of the United States will provide ... for the appointment of the representatives of the United States in the Assembly and Council of the League of Nations, and for the appointment of members of ... commissions, committees, tribunals, courts, councils or conferences and until such ... appointment ... and the powers and duties of such representatives have been defined by law ... no citizen of the United States shall be selected or appointed as a member of said commissions, committees, tribunals.

Reservation 8
Reparations

The Reparations Commission will regulate or interfere with exports [between the United States and Germany] only when the United States by act or joint resolution of Congress approves such regulation or interference.

Reservation 9
**League
Expenses**

The United States shall not be obligated to contribute to any expenses of the League of Nations ... unless and until an appropriation of funds available for such expenses shall have been made by the Congress of the United States.

Reservation 10
**Arms
Limitation**

No plan for the limitation of armaments proposed by the Council of the League of Nations ... shall be held as binding the United States until the same shall have been accepted by Congress, and the United States reserves the right to increase its armament without the consent of the Council whenever the United States is threatened with invasion or engaged in war.

THE LEAGUE COVENANT

Should any Member of the League resort to war...it **Article 16** shall...be deemed...to have committed an act of war against all other Members of the League, which hereby undertake immediately to subject it to the severance of all trade and financial relations, the prohibition of all intercourse between their nationals and the nationals of the Covenant-breaking State.

The Members of the League will endeavor to secure **Article 23** and maintain fair and humane conditions of labor for men, women and children, both in their own countries and in all countries...and for that purpose will establish and maintain the necessary international organization.

THE LODGE RESERVATIONS

Reservation 11
The Boycott

The United States reserves the right to permit ... the nationals of a covenant-breaking state ... to continue their commercial, financial and personal relations with the nationals of the United States.

Reservation 12
Debts of Nationals

Nothing in ... any article ... of the treaty of peace shall ... be ... taken to mean any confirmation ... or approval of any act otherwise illegal or in contravention of the rights of citizens of the United States.

Reservation 13
International Labor Organization

The United States withholds its assent to Part XIII [Articles dealing with the International Labor Organization] unless Congress shall hereafter make provision for representation in the organization ... and in such event the participation of the United States will be governed and conditioned by the provisions of such act or joint resolution.

Reservation 14
British Dominion Votes

Until ... the Covenant of the League of Nations shall be so amended as to provide that the United States shall be entitled to cast a number of votes equal to that which any member of the League and its self-governing dominions ... shall be entitled to cast, the United States assumes no obligation to be bound ... by any election, decision, report or finding of the council or assembly in which any member of the League and its self-governing dominions ... in the aggregate have cast more than one vote.

Do these reservations nullify the Covenant or do they not? If every Power or even every Great Power should make similar reservations—as many of them wanted to do, as they would obviously have the right to do if America demanded that right—what would your Treaty be worth, or your system of "collective security"? Of course Senator Lodge and his associates were not thinking of other countries. They were thinking only of America.

The only question in any reasonable person's mind after reading these reservations is: Why would America want to join a League at all, and what would she be joining? By these reservations Articles I, V, VI, VIII, X, XII, XIII, XIV, XV, XVI, XVII, and XXII are severally declared null and void so far as America is concerned. There is little left except the Articles on social problems and administration and procedure—and even some of these are affected.

The Lodge reservations were responsible for one of the great tragedies of history. At the same time they are surely one of the most comic documents of history. How the gentlemen of the inner circle could keep a straight face while solemnly debating them week after week passes comprehension. For in reality they say: "We will join your organization on condition that we are free to abstain from doing all the things your organization is set up for: that we shall use our own discretion about our dealings with people who may prove active enemies of your organization; and that we shall appoint all our own people on all bodies of your organization and control all their funds and their actions. On these conditions we shall be delighted to come in."

It never seemed to occur to the Senators that the other nations might refuse to have us on these terms—might even (oh, sardonic revenge) veto our entrance into the League. One single refusal of one country on one reservation was all that was needed. At the time it was not put to the test, for the President refused to sign the amended Treaty or to return it to the Powers as amended. But in 1926, when the question of our joining the World Court came up, with the Senate again appending the inevitable reservations, these gentlemen got a severe shock. Of the forty-eight nations to whom the Senators' terms were sent, only the five smallest accepted them unconditionally. Forty-three rejected them. Counterreservations were proposed by the September, 1926, conference of twenty-two League States, and the United States was invited to confer in the light of the two sets of recommendations. The gasp from Capitol Hill must have reverberated the world around. After that the Senatorial attitude underwent a decided change. When the Kellogg Pact came along even Senator Borah, after two years' salutary reflection, said he was "not willing to do anything" which could be represented abroad *as a change or reservation*. It had been used to our detriment abroad and had "produced a serious situation." Unfortunately, in Mr. Wilson's day this chastening experience had not yet occurred.

XVIII

THE country was stunned by the Senate vote. Jubilation reigned in some quarters, a sense of shame and national disgrace in others. Senator Borah declared it "the greatest victory since Appomattox." "A twin victory of independence and democracy," said the Cleveland *News*. In the eyes of the St. Louis *Star* the Senate had destroyed our prestige and given us the role of "chief international cynic."

Many refused to believe that the rejection could be final, and predicted a compromise. And indeed reasonable men on both sides lost no time in moving towards such agreement. Senator Colt of Rhode Island—a firm Republican advocate of the League—got hold of Senator McKellar, Democrat from Tennessee. "You know," he said, laying his arm round McKellar's shoulder, "you and I could get together and adjust the differences about reservations and we could confirm this Treaty, including the League." They went into Colt's office and talked it over.

"He called in Senator Kenyon, I called in Senator Kendrick," writes McKellar. Later they called in Senator Lenroot and Senator Simmons, afterwards Senator Kellogg and Senator Walsh of Montana, and this informal conference reached a tentative understanding. "We made such progress," says McKellar, "that it was concluded we should call in our respective leaders. So our Republican friends called in Senator Lodge and my Democratic colleagues and myself called in Senator Hitchcock."

"After much discussion among individual Senators," writes Lodge in a characteristically misleading statement, "I called together what was known as the Bi-Partisan Conference." Only because he was forced to do so, only after other Senators had done all the conciliatory work, and with full intent on Lodge's part that their efforts should be fruitless.

The Lodge Republicans had gone too far to turn back. They were determined that if a league of nations ever existed, it should bear their hallmark. The long years of Democratic supremacy had been galling years for the Republican Senators. If Wilson could be defeated and discredited on this great issue, all signs would point to a Republican return to power. Hence the edict of *no compromise*. The fourteen reservations were the final terms. "The door is closed," Senator Lodge said to Senator Swanson when the vote was taken. "Take it or leave it," said Senator Edge, "that or nothing."

When the demand for compromise grew so strong that his own party leaders forced him into conference, Lodge went through the motions, actually intending to yield nothing whatsoever. If the Democrats wanted to save their treaty they would have to accept his terms. Early in the regular session in December the Bi-Partisan Conference was set up. Lodge had no idea of permitting it to accomplish anything. He assured the bitterenders, according to his own statement, "that there was not the slightest danger of our conceding anything more than a change in wording." He had brought the irreconcilable Senator New to replace Senator Colt in the conference. He also dropped Senator Kenyon, who had been active in moves for compromise.

"This conference . . . sat constantly for two weeks," Lodge records, "and considered all the reservations. We came to tentative agreements on certain changes in the wording . . . but we could not agree on . . . the Monroe Doctrine, or the reservation pertaining to . . . equality of voting, and . . . conspicuously and emphatically . . . on the reservation relating to Article X." Lodge was adamant on this last, as in his opinion Wilson's insistence on it was due to his "pride of authorship" in the Article. To kill it was therefore the way to hurt Wilson.

"There was another object which I had very much at heart," he adds with extraordinary candor, "and that was that if we were successful in putting on reservations we should create a situation where if the Treaty were defeated the Democratic party and especially Mr. Wilson's friends should be responsible for its defeat and not the opponents of the Treaty . . ." What a colleague such a man would have made at a peace table!

"His hatred of Wilson is very deep," said Senator Hitchcock to a friend at the time. "At first," said the Senator, "I had the impression that he merely wished to weave into the Covenant some of his great thoughts [to capture some of the prestige for the Republican party]. . . . But when I ask him to get down to cases and state what changes he would suggest, his attitude stiffens and his face hardens. . . . My conviction deepens that whatever may have been his purpose two months ago today Lodge has decided to defeat the Treaty and the Covenant if he can. . . . His chief talking point is that as the President did not permit any real Republicans to participate in the drafting of the Treaty, they have a perfectly free hand in the matter of ratification."

"He didn't bother to take us along when he was drafting it"— there you have the crux of the matter. "Lodge is hurt in his vanity, which is enormous," wrote a correspondent of the time. That is the real reason for all his reservations and obstructions, his intricate arguments or lack of arguments; and, it may be, the real reason why the United States never joined the League of Nations and had to enter World War II.

The sincere men who originated the Bi-Partisan Conference hadn't a chance from the beginning. Party politics and party jealousies swiftly thwarted any possible adjustment. The Irreconcilables told their Republican colleagues that if all Republicans stood together on the Lodge reservations they might cause a split in the Democratic party. The country would press for ratification, forcing the Democratic leaders to yield. The President would probably then drop the Treaty and there would be "a rift in the Democratic Party" excellent for Republican fortunes in the approaching campaign.

For those who wanted ratification of the Treaty, the argument was different. The "mild reservationists"—those who wanted a change of wording—were told to look out: a change of words might mean switching the credit for those words to another political party. If the reservations bore Lodge's name, the country would note that they were Republican reservations, but should the wording be changed they might then be known as the Hitchcock reservations and credit would go to the Democrats. Such were the arguments that decided the peace of the world and the life—or death—of future generations.

In Europe, meanwhile, nations were flocking into the League —twenty-three original members, ten others rapidly following. Thirty-three countries did not hesitate to risk their national honor and independence in the association which so frightened the American Senators. Spain was the first to ratify. Great Britain ratified in July, by an almost unanimous vote; France on October 4th, by a vote of 372 to 53. Guatemala, Uruguay, Paraguay, Brazil, Colombia, and Peru followed. All the American States except Costa Rica, Santo Domingo, the United States, and Mexico ratified. So did all the States invited to join: Switzerland, Holland, Denmark, Norway, and Sweden.

By late November the Treaty had been ratified by a sufficient number of nations to make the League operative. To President Wilson fell the honor of issuing the call for the first meeting of the League Council. This cheered and pleased him very much. He drafted the call, appointing Paris as the place and January 16, 1920, as the date. One of the many disappointments of his life at that time was that he could not be present at the first historic meeting, which took place in the Room of the Clock where he first presented the Covenant and made his great appeal for it.

Ironically, at the very moment of its first meeting, the institution which was to ensure the peace and save the world was still being torn to pieces in the Senate room at Washington. The President, ill though he was, followed the fight with closest attention. Every day he insisted on being taken in his invalid chair along the White House portico to the window of Tumulty's office.

> There [says his secretary], day after day in the coldest weather I conferred with him and discussed every phase of the fight on the Hill. He would sit in his chair, wrapped in blankets and though [physically] hardly able to discuss these matters he showed in every way a tremendous interest. . . . Whenever there was the slightest rise in the tide for the League a smile would break over his face and weak and broken though he was he evidenced his great pleasure at the news. Time and time again during the critical days of the Treaty fight the President would appear outside my office seated in the old wheel chair, to make inquiry regarding the progress.

There was little that was encouraging to tell him. The Bi-Partisan Conference broke down completely. A public letter from Lord Grey defending the Lodge reservations—after he had spent considerable time with Lodge during a four months' visit to America—gave strength to the opposition and credence to the view that other countries would not object to the reservations. Some of our own commentators today make much of this letter. Grey wrote it, to the London *Times*, as a private citizen after he had ceased to be a government representative. Neither Lloyd George nor Clemenceau nor any government official who had drawn up the Treaty ever endorsed Grey's view. On the contrary—the writer has it from officials of Great Britain and of France in office at the time—"Europe viewed with utmost consternation these reports of still more American amendments and reservations that might be asked of us."

On February 9th the Senate voted to reconsider the Treaty and referred it again to the Committee. It was reported back again next day with the Lodge reservations. Debate was resumed and continued for a month, during which time the reservations were made rather more than less objectionable to the President. In his letter to Senator Hitchcock on January 28th he had said: "Any reservation or resolution stating that 'the United States assumes no obligation under such and such an Article unless or except' would, I am sure, chill our relationship with the nations with which we expect to be associated in the great enterprise of maintaining the world's peace."

On March 8th he repeated to the Senator that deliberation convinced him that "practically every so-called reservation is in effect a rather sweeping nullification of the treaty itself"; he heard of "reservationists" and "mild reservationists," but he could not understand the difference between a "nullifier and a mild nullifier." Our responsibility at this turning point in history is an overwhelming one, he said, and he begged everyone concerned "to consider the matter in the light of what it is possible to accomplish for humanity, rather than in the light of special national interests."

On March 19, 1920, the Treaty met its final defeat at the hands of the United States Senate, after a series of maneuvers which should be studied by every thoughtful American and every young person who is to become an American citizen: for its commentary on our laws, our representatives, and the power we give them over our destiny at crucial moments; the infringement of our rights under the two-thirds majority vote, and its bearing on the fate and future of our country. On March 19th a little group of obdurate men triumphed over the will of the majority of the Senate, the majority of the House of Representatives, the majority of our leaders—church, university, press, business, labor—and the will of the vast majority of the American people. Committee rule—anathema to the young Wilson of 1879—defeated Wilson the world leader.

The President took the news calmly, believing that in the long run history would vindicate him and prove his adversaries mistaken. When Tumulty told him, his only comment was: "They have shamed us in the eyes of the world." At this zero hour the faithful secretary showed wonderful tact and imagination. "Governor," he said, drawing a book from under his arm, "I want to read you something—a chapter from your *History of the American People*—if it will not tire you?" The old warrior propped against his pillows, his profile sharpened by the months of pain and disappointment, nodded his consent.

Tumulty opened the volume and read, in Wilson's own words, the account of the famous John Jay Treaty in defense of which Alexander Hamilton was stoned while he was upholding it on the steps of the New York City Hall. There was indeed a remarkable similarity between the two fights. He read the whole chapter, including this passage.

> Slowly the storm blew off. The country had obviously gained more than it had conceded, and tardily saw the debt it owed Mr. Jay and to the Administration, whose firmness and prudence had made his mission possible. But in the meantime things had been said which could not be forgotten. Washington had been assailed with unbridled license, as an enemy and a traitor to the country; had even been charged with embezzling public moneys during the Revolution, was madly threatened with impeachment, and even with assassination, and had cried amidst the bitterness of it all that "he would rather be in his grave than in the presidency."
>
> The country knew its mind about him once again when the end of his term came and it was about to lose him. He refused to stand for another election. His farewell address with its unmistakable tone of majesty and its solemn force of affection and admonition, seemed an epitome of the man's character and achievements, and every man's heart smote him to think that Washington was actually gone from the nation's counsels.

When Tumulty finished reading the President said, "Thank you—it is mighty generous of you to compare my disappointment over the Treaty with that of Washington. You have placed me in mighty good company!"

On May 15, 1920, the Congress of the United States decreed the end of the war between the United States and Germany and declared that America, though she had not ratified the Treaty of Versailles, was not called on to waive any of "the rights, privileges, indemnities, reparations, or advantages claimed by her or her nationals under the terms of the Armistice signed November 11, 1918, or any extension or modification thereof, which under the Treaty of Versailles have been stipulated for her benefit as one of the principal Allied and Associated Powers." In other words, while repudiating the Treaty her President had signed, she did not propose to give up any of the advantages of that Treaty to herself. The special Treaty with France—in consideration of which France had yielded point after point of her own rights and privileges at the Peace Conference—was also repudiated.

President Wilson refused to sign the resolution passed by Congress. He stated his position in the following letter dated from the White House, May 27, 1920:

To the House of Representatives:

I have not felt at liberty to sign this resolution because I cannot bring myself to become party to an action which would place an uneffaceable stain upon the gallantry and honor of the United States. The resolution seeks to establish peace with the German Empire without exacting from the German Government any action by way of setting right the infinite wrongs which it did to the peoples whom it attacked, and whom we professed it our purpose to assist when we entered the war.

A Treaty of peace was signed at Versailles on the twenty-eighth of June last which did seek to accomplish the objects which we had declared to be in our minds because all the great governments and peoples which united against Germany had adopted our declarations of purpose as their own and had in solemn form embodied them in communications to the German Government preliminary to the Armistice of November 11, 1918. But the Treaty as signed at Versailles has been rejected by the Senate of the United States though it has been ratified by Germany. By that rejection and by its methods we had, in effect, declared that we wish to draw apart and pursue objects and interests of our own, unhampered by any connections of interest or of purpose with other governments and peoples. . . . Such a peace with Germany—a peace in which none of the essential interests which we had at heart when we entered the war is safeguarded—is, or ought to be, inconceivable, is inconsistent with the dignity of the United States, with the rights and liberties of her citizens, and with the very fundamental conditions of civilization.

I hope that in these statements I have sufficiently set forth the reasons why I have felt it incumbent on me to withhold my signature.

Woodrow Wilson

Clemenceau, commenting on the situation, says in his book *Grandeur and Misery of Victory*:

I confess that President Wilson's criticism seems to me unanswerable. American Comrades, you arrived on the battlefield when the war was nearing its end. But in the discussion of the peace treaty yours was a deciding share. It was the head of your Government who claimed to settle, in full accord with you, the results of the war. It was he who claimed to solve, and with the authority he derived from you, did solve, problems of the much-hoped-for stabilization of Europe—problems before which our statesmen were at a standstill. . . .

And now after the work has been toilsomely accomplished, not merely do you smash it to pieces of your own motion but further, make on your own initiative a *separate peace* that is an American Mutilation—you usurp the rights won

The Story of Woodrow Wilson

by the soldiers of Europe on the battlefield during four interminable years to make defeated Germany recognize the *"rights, privileges, indemnities, reparations, or advantages"* gained with our blood after the destruction of our possessions.

That was a high emprise of downright materialism the like of which has never been seen. Never did a Peace based upon a breaking up of solidarity, upon a dissociation of interests as strongly deserve the title of *separate peace*—since you propose to secure the profits of it after puffing into thin air the advantages your own President had proffered to us in your name. And what am I to add when you present us with an account on which to these profits of *yours* are added *our* losses, for which you request us to indemnify you! If this American Peace is not a *separate peace* I wonder what description can possibly be applied to it?

He adds a warning: "You have rid yourselves of the ties of solidarity with Europe with which the war involved you . . . [but] do not despise Europe. Do not treat us too badly. . . . A weaker brother is often useful in time of need. . . . Do you not think that the general break-up of solidarity that you have so vociferously let loose may one day in Europe or in the Far East bring us all again in dangerous straits?"

What would old Clemenceau have thought on the day of Pearl Harbor! How he must have cursed himself back in 1920 for not having better heeded his own advice at the beginning of the Peace Conference when he said to his colleagues: "Why pay so much attention to Wilson? He is a fine man but his Senate can undo everything he negotiates here—and probably will." It could and it did, shaming not only Wilson the President but the entire country of which he was the head and every one of the humble folk to the uttermost parts of the earth who had trusted in his program and in America.

Several years before the struggle over the Versailles Treaty, an American Senator eloquently spoke as follows:

Peace-Maker

I am a strong party man [he said]. I believe in government by parties and party responsibility. To thwart the
purpose or discredit the official head of a political party is
legitimate political warfare. To discredit or break down the
President of the United States upon a question of foreign
policy is quite another thing, never to be undertaken except
for very grave reasons. In the one case we overthrow a party
leader and political chief within the area where the American people alone sit in judgment. In the other we break
down and discredit the representative of the whole country
in the great forum of the nations of the earth, and paralyze
his future power and usefulness in that field—where he and
he alone can declare and represent the policies and the
honor and the dignity of the United States.

The man who uttered these words, with so much grandeur
and good sense, was Henry Cabot Lodge, speaking in the United
States Senate in support of President Wilson in the Panama
Canal tolls debate in April, 1914.

XIX

I T IS an injustice and an inaccuracy to blame the United States
Senate for the defeat of the Treaty and the repudiation of
the League in 1920. As we have seen, a majority of the Senators
were honestly and sincerely in favor of ratification, and worked
for it with a disinterested spirit that was in some cases remarkable. After prolonged study of the debate and conferences of
that time, one's dominant impression is how many fine Senators
we had back in 1919, but how powerless they were in face of
the mechanism of committee government and the unscrupulous
small group who took advantage of it.

The real reason for the defeat of the Treaty was not the
Monroe Doctrine or Article X, this reservation or that amendment. The real reason was partisan politics and personal hatred
of the President: hatred so intense that it swallowed up all

national loyalty and human feeling. The three men really to blame were the three who hated most: Henry Cabot Lodge, Philander C. Knox, and George Harvey, followed by their group of lesser lights—Brandegee, Watson, Reed, McCormick, Harding, Fall, and New.

"They were small mean men," an eminent editor of the time observed to the present writer, "eaten up with jealousy and fears for their own and their party's future. They didn't care for the country, they didn't care for the peace of the world, they didn't care for the millions of American boys who in another twenty years would have to be marched out and shot down again —which Mr. Wilson warned them would happen, and which has happened. They didn't care for one damned thing except to 'get' Woodrow Wilson—to beat that man in the White House!"

Consider the men who made up that defeating group: "the vicious narrowness of Reed, the explosive ignorance of Poindexter, the ponderous Websterian language and lack of stamina of Borah, the vanity of Lodge . . . the selfishness, laziness, and narrow lawyerlike acuteness of Knox . . . the utter nothingness of Fall, in the face of this great world's crisis." These are not the words of a Democrat or a Wilsonite but of the affable Republican Mr. Taft.

Call the roll of the defeaters: Boies Penrose, most notorious of all the political bosses; Medill McCormick, with a record perilously reminiscent of Senator Newberry's, who was forced to resign from the Senate; Senator Brandegee, who committed suicide, his affairs hopelessly involved; Senator Fall, who was sentenced to the penitentiary; Senator Harding, within whose Cabinet later occurred the greatest scandal in Presidential history. Place beside this group the "weak Wilson men": Hitchcock, McKellar, Owen, Underwood, Beckham, Nugent, John Sharp Williams. Whose leadership would you trust? Whose values and decisions would you credit?

Senator Watson—whose colleagues in Valhalla must have had a few things to say to him—makes some revealing disclosures on Borah and Reed. "Reed," says Senator Watson, "is a master of ridicule and irony. . . . He rarely proposed anything but with tremendous vigor he opposed anything he disliked. . . . Both he and Borah are at home *only in antagonism* [italics added]. They excel as opponents rather than as proponents." When the elder La Follette died, Reed made a memorial speech about him in the Senate. "Well, Jim, I expect you are damned glad to hear me say anything good about anybody," said Reed to Watson.

"That is true, and I am sorry you had to waste it on a dead man!" retorted his friend. "Borah has been in the Senate over twenty-five years," continues Watson. "It is doubtful whether . . . any measure of major importance . . . carries his name . . . though his voice has been heard on nearly every proposition of importance in all those years. . . . Both he and Reed understood that the man who assails is more apt to get the headlines. . . ."

These are the men, we are told, who would have assured us a "real peace" and "a league that would have worked"—if only Mr. Wilson had consulted them more and taken them with him to Paris. They would have stuck a knife in his back at the Peace Conference in January instead of in the Senate in November; that would have been the only difference. We should have had no League and no Peace Treaty whatever.

All were men with some personal weakness of character. To no one of Wilson's bitter opponents could one point and say, "Yes, there's a fine, well-balanced, clear-headed individual whom we've got to admire. If *he* found Wilson wrong and the League plan dangerous, there must have been some truth to it." On the contrary, if any of these men *had* admired him one would have had cause for anxiety. As one of the small-town papers, the Fulton *Gazette* of Fulton, Missouri, wrote at the time: "If Lodge did approve of him we would have been worried."

Their personal frustrations accentuated their hatred for a really big man. "After having spent more than thirty years in Washington," writes David Lawrence, "I am convinced that some of the tangles we have in public life can be traced back to frustrations in the individual. . . . Pride is perhaps the most vicious of all. The pride motive is more dangerous than the profit motive. Men will do things in their quest for power that they will not do in their quest for profits ... and in the battle of Washington it is the battle between people for power—and between groups."

Pride and a devouring jealousy were certainly dominant motives in the battle against Wilson, especially as regards Harvey, Lodge, and Theodore Roosevelt. Lodge had an almost morbid jealousy of Wilson and some peculiar personal twists and complexes concerning him. John Singer Sargent, the artist, told Henry White a story which illustrates this. The night before Sargent went to stay at the White House to paint the President's portrait, Lodge invited him to dinner. "I am delighted that you are going to do President Wilson's portrait," said the Senator; "it presents a great opportunity for you to serve our party."

Everyone knew Sargent's ability to find in human beings the counterpart of animals and thus reveal some hidden beastly trait. Lodge said he knew there was something sinister hidden in Wilson and that he looked to Sargent to reveal it to the world. "I therefore," Sargent told Mr. White, "studied the man with intensity. I tried to probe his very soul. But I could find nothing hidden or unworthy." Lodge couldn't understand the source of Wilson's power. Not understanding it, or being unable to account for it, he attributed it to secret questionable motives and traits.

Wilson of course was a continual affront to Lodge. Before Wilson's advent Lodge was the scholar of Washington—the official classicist and purist—as well as the treaty-maker. Naturally, he did not fancy being set aside. Some of his comments in his book reveal this annoyance rather naïvely. Lodge observes that Mr. Wilson "was not a scholar in the true sense at all, although the newspapers were fond of applying that term to him as they are apt to apply it to anyone who has held a position of educational importance." He notes only one "classical allusion" in Mr. Wilson's speeches, and that an incorrect one (it had to do with a legend of Hercules). "He very rarely made a literary quotation," Lodge also remarks. "This would seem to indicate that Mr. Wilson ... was not a widely read man, for a lover of literature and letters instinctively and almost inevitably thinks of the words of the poet or great prose writer which express better than

he can in writing or speaking the idea he is trying to enforce."
So he does, unless he himself happens to have great powers of
expression. The Gettysburg Address and the Second Inaugural
of Lincoln contain no classical allusions. They became classics.
So did some of Mr. Wilson's great speeches and public documents. As we have seen in the appraisal of his writings, literary
critics considered that Mr. Wilson made too much use of quotation in his early days (twenty-five quotations in one essay) and
that his style became truly great only when—as statesman and
President—he dropped such extensive quotation and presented
his own views with stark simplicity and vigor.

"Mr. Wilson was a master of the rhetorical use of idealism,"
says Lodge; "he convinced many people who were content with
words that he was a man of vision. . . . But no one who ever
studied Mr. Wilson's acts . . . could fail to perceive that . . . Mr.
Wilson always had in view some material and definite purposes
which might result in benefit to the world but certainly in benefit to himself." Yet Tumulty, who saw him every day for ten
years, and Burleson and Vance McCormick and others complain
that "his chief fault was that he never thought of himself."

Senator Lodge's book furnishes a fascinating case history for
the psychiatrist. All the attributes persistently accredited to Mr.
Wilson were attributes characteristic of Mr. Lodge. "Mr. Wilson
was devoured by a desire for power. . . . Mr. Wilson in dealing
with every great question thought first of himself. . . . Mr. Wilson's passionate absorption . . . in his own interests and ambitions
. . . He wished to have a League of Nations of which it was generally expected, I suppose by himself as well as by others, that he
would be the head. Therefore he went to Paris. Therefore all the
negotiations for peace were hampered and delayed. . . ."

Of course there was no permanent President or head of the
League of Nations, nor was such an office ever contemplated,
which anyone claiming to be as thoroughly informed on the
League as Mr. Lodge must have known. The President of the
Assembly is elected for each session by the usual democratic
procedure of balloting. The Presidency of the Council passes—
also for a single year—to the member countries in rotation. The

The Story of Woodrow Wilson

Secretary-General of the permanent Civil Service, or Secretariat, holds an administrative routine position which Mr. Wilson would have detested and for which neither he nor any of the Big Four statesmen at Paris was ever mentioned. Mr. Lodge, however, read into Wilson's mind the thoughts and aims that would have been in his own had he been in Wilson's shoes and in charge of the negotiations at such a time.

Lodge constantly ascribed to Wilson the motives and emotions that ruled himself, including the obsessing hate that went beyond love of country, love of humanity—everything. "But, Senator," said Watson anxiously at one stage of the game, "suppose the Senate actually adopts the reservations and we really did then join the League?" "My dear James," answered Lodge, "you do not take into consideration the hatred that Woodrow Wilson has for me personally. Never . . . could he be induced to accept a treaty with the Lodge reservations appended to it." "That seems to me . . . rather a slender thread on which to hang so great a cause," Watson replied. Lodge shook his head. "As strong as any cable with its strands wired and twisted together!" He should know.

Wilson certainly hated Lodge's principles and everything Lodge stood for. But it was simply not in his make-up to feel or be motivated by the small personal hate and pettiness that animated Lodge and the Brandegee-Knox-Harvey cabal. The "sound and accurate estimate" Lodge was so sure he had formed of him was far from accurate at this point—at almost any point.

"The soundness of my estimate . . . the accuracy of my judgment and correctness of my analysis . . . and I was not mistaken in my analysis of him . . ." This constantly repeated self-bolstering throughout Lodge's book shows the inner doubt and lack of assurance, the annoyance that he could *not* be sure his estimate was correct; that actually the man left him baffled and still wondering.

The final paragraph of his book is particularly revealing:

> There are those still extant who speak of Mr. Wilson as "a very great man." An able man in certain ways, an

ambitious man in all ways he certainly was. But "very great men" are extremely rare—Mr. Wilson was not one of them. He was given the greatest opportunity ever given to any public man in modern times. . . . Having this opportunity he tried to use it and failed. The failure necessarily equaled the opportunity in magnitude and the failure was complete and was all his own. No one could have destroyed such a vast opportunity except the man to whom it was given and in this work of destruction unaided and alone Mr. Wilson was entirely successful. Difficult as such an achievement in the face of such an opportunity was, it does not warrant describing the man who wrought the destruction in any sense as "a great man."

You are too modest, Mr. Lodge. Remember your own statement to Mr. Watson: "I propose to beat it by the indirect method of reservations." And your conferences with Theodore Roosevelt on December 17, 1918, and with Senator Borah on April 29, 1919; and your own daughter's statement: "My father hated and feared the League. . . . The object of his reservations was so to emasculate the Wilson pact that if it did pass it would be valueless."

Ah, no—in this destruction, planned so far back, executed with such unflagging ardor and adroitness, *you* were the successful one. And to that success, as your biographer Mr. Schriftgiesser has recently stated, your monument is the second World War.

XX

I N JUNE, 1920, the Republicans chose "that great and good man Warren G. Harding" as their Presidential candidate to defeat Wilsonism and all it stood for. The President himself might be out of the running, but his influence was still powerful. "The Republican party is the only force that can defeat Wilson and his objectionable policies," Harvey told Lodge, who emphatically agreed. Lodge was chairman of the Republican Convention, which met in June in Chicago, and he dominated it as completely as he had the Senate fight.

Senator Murray Crane, Senator Kellogg, and others led a vigorous battle for a strong League plank in the platform. Lodge threw his whole weight against them and against any endorsement of the reservations he had sponsored for so long. He said he would leave the chair and fight from the floor any move to support ratification of the League, even with his own reservations. Yet he "had given the reservations, and the Treaty with reservations, genuine support"! Having dumped the Treaty back in Wilson's lap, he was not going to risk losing his precious victory. Borah and Johnson threatened to bolt the party if the platform gave any sort of approval to the League. Senator Root offered a compromise plank which was accepted and saved the party from a split like that of 1912.

The Republican platform contained carefully worded statements to satisfy both Leaguers and bitter-enders. There were some handsome phrases about "an international association based upon justice and . . . to secure instant action and general conference whenever peace shall be threatened." In other paragraphs strong condemnation of the League was found. Thus all factions were satisfied. When it came to the choice of a candidate the Republicans made the rather significant statement that "any one of a number of men would do." However, they were astute in choosing a man about whom there could be no disagreement or rift in the party. Age defeated some candidates. Mr. Lodge, he regretfully admitted, was nearing seventy. Mr. Knox had already passed that deadline. General Wood, Governor Lowden of Illinois, Senator Hiram Johnson were possible choices and runners-up. The man finally chosen was chiefly distinguished by party regularity on the League and other questions.

At the final session of decision in a private room of the convention hotel the usual inner circle were present: Harvey, Lodge, Brandegee, Watson, McCormick, James Wadsworth of New York. "Here's the Senate in epitome," observed Senator Watson, "with a non-Senator in place of the Vice-President in the chair." It was extraordinary how Harvey influenced that group. He had ruled from behind the scenes all through the 1918-20 drama, although he was not, precisely speaking, a politician. His hatred had more explosive power than Lodge's; he also possessed an exuberant vocabulary, unhampered by the elegancies of Beacon Hill.

Harvey had made his choice long since. More than a year before, he had predicted that Harding would be the Republican candidate for the Presidency. He had the privilege of notifying Mr. Harding of his prospective nomination, in a remarkable scene involving solemn assurances by Mr. Harding on his own moral character after a period of twenty minutes' reflection in an adjoining room. Mr. Harding later expressed his appreciation by appointing Mr. Harvey Ambassador to Great Britain. Harding and Coolidge were nominated on the Republican ticket; Governor James M. Cox of Ohio and Franklin Delano Roosevelt of New York on the Democratic.

Mr. Harding followed the platform and waged a two-way campaign calculated to win all types of voters. In one sentence he flatly condemned the League; in the next he suggested that something along that line, only more effective, might be produced by his Administration. In a speech at Des Moines Harding declared: "It is not interpretation but rejection that I am seeking"—only to declare in the next breath that directly after election he would "consult with the best minds . . . to the end that we shall have an association of nations for the promotion of international peace."

Declaring that "the original League" had "undoubtedly passed beyond the power of restoration," he proposed to put in its place "a world court of justice supplemented by a world association for conference" to take from "the failed League of Versailles . . . all that is good and excise all that is bad." This might seem a rather complex operation—particularly as forty-eight nations were by this time members of the Versailles League and actively engaged in making it an effective world organization. But never fear—Mr. Harding could manage it. And he would generously use all that had been contributed by Mr. Wilson, after thirty years of painstaking study and preparation, and by other Ministers of State after their years of protracted research and effort.

"If the League which has heretofore riveted our considerations and apprehensions has been so entwined and interwoven with the peace of Europe that its good must be preserved . . . then it can be amended or revised," said Mr. Harding magnanimously, "so that we may still have a remnant of world aspirations in 1919 builded into the world's highest conception of helpful co-operation in the ultimate realization."

Harding—this was the man whom thirty-one outstanding American citizens, under the leadership of shrewd Elihu Root, announced that they intended to vote for and urged the rest of the country to do the same: Nicholas Murray Butler, Robert S. Brookings, Paul Cravath, Herbert Hoover, Charles Evans Hughes, Henry L. Stimson, George Wickersham, Lawrence Lowell, Henry W. Taft, and others. And while Hiram Johnson in California was telling his audiences that he could assure them that Harding's election meant "the death of the League," the thirty-one quoted Harding's speech expressing willingness "to take and combine all that is good" from both the League and the Court, and called for his election which they believed would "most effectively advance the cause of international co-operation to promote peace."

Governor Cox in his campaign came out clear and strong for the League—stating his willingness to accept "interpretive" reservations and making it clear that the first duty of his Administration would be the ratification of the Treaty. In this his running mate, Mr. Franklin Roosevelt, stoutly upheld him. But the chances against him were too heavy. The country by this time was sick to death of the whole League fight—worn out with the long twelve months' battle in the Senate, the arguments and arraignments, hashed and rehashed; the confusing proposals of reservationists, mild reservationists, ratifiers, and Irreconcilables. People wanted a change and to forget the whole subject.

The canny Mr. Lodge had asked only for time—time and talk

—and the inevitable wearing down of human emotions and nervous systems. Every move of the Lodge campaign—from the initial raising of a mild skepticism in the public mind, on to the carefully built up prejudice, distrust, and the steadily increasing antagonism and hostility—was as carefully thought out, as precisely and knowingly manipulated, as the most delicate machinery of a master mechanic. Hatred against Wilson was fanned to fever heat again during the 1920 Presidential campaign. The Irish, the Italians, and the German-Americans didn't know much about Governor Cox, but they favored any party rather than Wilson's party. Postwar reaction and resentment of various other groups, disgruntled by government policy, were turned to good account. "Mr. Cox may be a very fine gentleman, but we want no more Democratic Presidents for a generation!" was the war cry.

A violent reaction against Wilson seemed to sweep the nation. Malice and slander attended the very mention of his name. Lifelong friendships broke up, relatives left each other's dinner tables, business associations were dissolved. The seething fury recalled the days when Lincoln was screamed at as "the gorilla" and "Illinois ape" and threatened with assassination not only by the South but by the people of his own State and of neighboring Ohio. It was like the stoning of Alexander Hamilton, Washington threatened with impeachment. All of which suggested that Wilson was in line for next place among American immortals: such is our quaint and peculiarly American preamble to enthroning our national heroes.

The Springfield *Republican* on October 30, 1920, forecast this shadow of future greatness in words that strike home today: "His enemies by their assaults compel the perpetual identification of the President's name with an ideal of international organization that is simply deathless. Even the killing of 'Wilson's League' in a tempest of passion will ensure his survival . . . for when war next comes on a large scale the thought that it might have been prevented by the assassinated 'Wilson's League' will capture the imagination of posterity."

Meantime the voters of 1920 were captured by the vastly clever phrase "Back to Normalcy," and in November Harding was elected by an unprecedented plurality of 16,152,220 votes to Cox's 9,147,553.

The President, with his unquenchable faith in the people, was confident to the last that Governor Cox would be elected. "I do not care what Republican propaganda may seek to do," he said, "I am sure that the hearts of the people are right on the great issue, and that we can confidently look forward to triumph." When they lost, he took his medicine manfully. "Of course I am disappointed by the results of the election," he admitted to his friends, "for I felt sure that a great program that sought to bring peace to the world would arouse American idealism and that the nation's support would be given it.

"It is a difficult thing, however," he went on, "to lead a nation so variously constituted as ours quickly to accept a program such as the League of Nations. The enemies of this enterprise cleverly roused every racial passion and prejudice, and made it appear that the League would crush and destroy instead of save and bring peace. . . . Now the people will have to learn by bitter experience just what they have lost."

The fourth of March dawned. The President rose early, put on his official cutaway, and quietly sat in his study awaiting the arrival of the President-Elect, with whom he was to ride to the Capitol. Hard to believe, looking out those familiar windows toward the Potomac, that after having been head of a great nation for eight years, in a few hours one would slip back into the role of private citizen. What events and memories must have filled his mind during those last few moments.

Presently he was notified that Mr. Harding had arrived in the Blue Room. Leaning on the blackthorn stick that he affectionately called his "third leg," Wilson made his way to the elevator and was soon cordially greeting his successor. The President was suffering considerable pain at this time, but he absolutely refused to give up the trip to the Capitol. He was a sportsman and would show Mr. Harding every courtesy and perform the last duties of his office properly, no matter what it cost him.

As the two got into the car together—the one ruddy and handsome, the picture of health and vigor; the other gray and battle-scarred—no one would have dreamed that Wilson would outlive Harding and that the next procession in which the two rode together would be Harding's funeral procession, which Wilson followed from the White House to the Capitol two years later. Wilson has a stubborn Scots habit of winning in the long run.

On that brilliant inauguration morning all the odds seemed with the other man. Crowds cheered the car as it advanced down Pennsylvania Avenue. The President, assuming that the cheers and the day were Harding's, gazed straight ahead. He must have remembered the many drives he had taken down that Avenue: before his own inaugurations; on the momentous day of the break with Germany; on the day of the declaration of war; his trips to the Senate in the interests of his great legislative measures; his pilgrimage on foot, Memorial Day, 1918, when he led the soldiers, in the full prime of his own health and vigor. And now this—the final journey.

When they reached the Capitol the President went to the President's Room, Mr. Harding taking a seat in the background. Senators and Representatives came to confer about bills in which they were interested and which the President had to sign before the old clock in the corner struck twelve and marked the end of the official relationship of Woodrow Wilson with the affairs of the United States.

Other Senators and Congressmen of both parties flocked into the room to say good-by. It was amazing how many friendships this man had who was "the enemy of the country" and "had led the nation from the right road into dark and devious ways toward destruction."

At the close of each session of Congress a joint committee of both Houses notifies the Executive that the Congress has completed the business before it and now stands ready to adjourn unless the President has any further message to communicate. The chairman of this committee is generally the Chairman of the Senate Foreign Relations Committee, an office at this time still held by Senator Henry Cabot Lodge.

At a few minutes before twelve there appeared in the doorway a short, gray-haired man of imperious manner. "Mr. President, we have come as a committee of the Senate to notify you that the Senate and House are about to adjourn and await your pleasure."

Mr. Wilson turned toward the man who had led the fight against the Treaty. For a moment his face hardened, then the ghost of a smile hovered over his face. "Senator Lodge, I have no further communication to make," he said calmly. "I thank you. Good morning."

His arch-enemy confronted him to the final moment. He had to drink his bitter dose to the last galling drop.

XXI

BUT Wilson did not grow bitter. He went into the new life cheerfully—happily, even—delighted with his attractive house in a beautiful part of Washington and with his freedom to think and read and be with his wife. He was an invalid with an invalid's schedule; but he gave some hours each day to his voluminous mail, to appointments with some of the people who still flocked to see him, and to talks with old friends. Every day he took a drive. Sometimes he watched movies in his own library; sometimes he went to Keith's vaudeville, which he greatly enjoyed.

His family wished him to have some active interest. There had been talk of a possible law partnership with his former Secretary of State, Bainbridge Colby. An office was indeed set up under the name of Wilson and Colby. Many cases were offered —some at huge fees; but they were not of a nature that a former President and Secretary of State could accept. Many had to do with the Government. The partnership was reluctantly dissolved.

Numerous offers for literary work also arrived. His family and physicians wished that he might accept some of them. But his health did not permit any long-sustained effort. His one literary contribution during his retirement was "The Road away from

Revolution," an essay which he sent to the *Atlantic Monthly* and which was published in August, 1923.

"That was so characteristic of Mr. Wilson," one of the *Atlantic* editors of the time told the present writer. "He could have sold that article to one of the mass circulation magazines for thousands of dollars, but sent it on his own initiative to the *Atlantic* which paid only in the hundreds. But that was the place Wilson felt he belonged."

Most of his activity went into his letters. People from all over the country wrote to him on all sorts of subjects, asking for all sorts of things: how to vote, what to name their children, what to do for the prevention of juvenile crime, how to get inventions patented, how to bring their cousin to America. He was asked to comment and present his views on all sorts of schemes—prevention of war, race suicide, the education of orphan boys. He was asked for money—and frequently sent it, as neat entries in his checkbook show: checks for five, twenty-five, and fifty dollars, made out to various individuals and philanthropies. He was asked for messages to be read at public meetings. Some urged him to express his political views—to attack the new Administration, to "strafe" President Harding. "You could put him in a hole by dumping the whole Versailles Treaty on his doorstep," one of Mr. Wilson's friends said indignantly.

"But I do not wish to put Mr. Harding in a hole," was the instant reply. "The situation of the nation and of the world is too serious to make it thinkable that I or any other good citizen should desire to hamper him. I should like to help Mr. Harding and I hope that every good citizen will try to help him." In striking contrast with other former Presidents, he uttered no criticism of his opponent's policies and offered no comment on current affairs. Asked to do so by Cornelius Vanderbilt, Jr., in connection with the Four-Power Treaty, he declined. "It would seem to me very ill-advised for me to attempt at this time to influence the action of the Senate," said Mr. Wilson. Imagine what Theodore Roosevelt would have done in a similar position.

Mr. Wilson's way was very different. This man whom Mr. Lodge declared "consumed by hatred" spoke no word of censure and attempted no interference with the party in power. He believed that the Democratic party should have strong leadership and wanted to help give it, though not in an autocratic fashion or single-handed. On November 15, 1922, he wrote Frank Cobb: "The Democrats must offer the country in 1924 a constructive program which will clear the air of all the mists and doubts and ineptitudes of the last two years and also a candidate who can be counted on with reasonable confidence to carry such a program out." Cobb told him "the only man who can present such a program that will attract nation-wide attention is yourself."

The ex-President gathered round him some of his most trusted colleagues of former years—Bernard Baruch, David Houston, Newton Baker, Justice Brandeis, Bainbridge Colby, Norman Davis. This eminent company thereupon began to prepare a document to set forth the principles and policies of the Democratic party. Each man was to furnish a statement on that phase of national affairs with which he was most familiar—one on railroads, one on taxation, another on the needs of the farmer, and so forth. These statements were then to be discussed and approved and rewritten as part of the general document and used to promote the Democratic interests at all times, but especially in the approaching campaigns. The chief question was the most effective time and place to launch it. "Ammunition so potent should not be dissipated," said Justice Brandeis.

A surprising amount of suggestion, correlation, and revision was done by Mr. Wilson himself—astonishing, in view of the rigid discipline of his invalid state and the gradual failing of his bodily strength. "Please remember in noting the typographical blunders that I had the use of only one hand in using the typewriter," he commented in a rather touching note to Mr. Baruch on March 31, 1922. However, as he got into the game again he felt better than he had for a long time.

"My pulses are quickened by the prospect of battle!" he wrote characteristically. What looked like the greatest improvement in his health came just at that time. "I have gone over and assembled the material of the document which you put into such convenient shape for my examination," he wrote Mr. Colby on

April 6, 1922, "and believe you will find the enclosed to contain our materials in a natural order and in sufficiently clear form. It reads to me like a very impressive declaration of clear and definite purpose." But he died before it was completed or published.

Various events checkered those final months of his life: the burial of the Unknown Soldier at Arlington, when Mr. Wilson took part in the procession; the thousands of pilgrimages to the door of his own home, in tribute to the living hero; the establishment of the Woodrow Wilson Foundation on his birthday, December 28, 1922; the funeral of President Harding; a visit from Lord Cecil, who came to receive the first Woodrow Wilson Foundation award. There were visits from Clemenceau and Lloyd George also; a genuine affection seemed to have survived the stormy Peace Conference days. The old Tiger, scorning the elevator, bounded up the stairs to the library and embraced Mr. Wilson heartily in characteristic French fashion. He was gentle and full of tact with the invalid, whom last he had encountered in fierce combat over the Rhineland and those American amendments—which turned out not to have mattered so much, after all. Many people said to have hated Mr. Wilson took the trouble to look him up, to come and see him—and to stay as long as they possibly could. Almost always they came downstairs laughing over one of his good stories, told usually at his own expense.

He talked with Norman Davis and other friends long and earnestly about the League. He corresponded with the League of Nations Union in England and with the leaders who were setting up the cherished institution in Geneva. He was deeply moved when Americans returning from abroad told him of the progress the League was making. Over and over he expressed his faith that the people would ultimately choose rightly in the matter of the League of Nations. They had been deceived and in error, but eventually they would see the thing clear.

Some of his friends spoke with great bitterness and indignation. "No—don't feel that way," he said to more than one of them, and to his own daughter. "Probably in the long run it is best that things should have happened as they did. If the American people had gone into the League now they would have done it out of loyalty to me. If ever they do go in in the future it will be because they have 'seen' it and chosen it for themselves and seen that it is the best way for them and for the whole world." It was a great man who could say that—not after twenty or thirty years, but in the full sting of immediate defeat.

"I tell you," he repeated again and again, "the principles we have fought for can never be beaten. They will prevail as surely as God reigns." Surrounded by familiar things he loved—the pictures of his wife and children, the old desk he had brought from Princeton, and a bookcase with his favorite books, his Bible and a small volume of daily texts in which he liked to read—he sat looking out onto the garden at the back of his house and beyond to the proud city of Washington; reading, thinking, reflecting—thus he passed those last months before the final date of his life: February 3, 1924.

He refused to make any published comment either on his life or the cause he had fought for. Lansing, Lodge, Page, House, all wrote books telling how it all happened, what should have been done, what was wrong. But not Wilson. He wrote no memoirs. "He uttered no complaint, suffered no pity, displayed no vainglory," said his friend and valedictorian Dr. Alderman. "It was as though a great gentleman 'weary of the weight of this unintelligible world' sought his peace at last in a quiet home luminous with love and perfect care, and shut out at last from the noises and the storm. . . . The very depth and dignity of his silence won through to the imagination of men and when he spoke the world stood at attention.

"As death enfolded him in its shadows, men paused in their busy lives and came to comprehend that a man of great faith had lived in their era, akin in heart and blood to John Milton and John Hampden, Mazzini and Luther, that a prophet had guided their country and stirred the heart of mankind in an hour of destiny, and that an incorruptible liberal aflame with will to advance the slow ascent of man had joined those whom men call immortal and stood among that high fellowship

> Constant as the Northern Star
> Of whose true fixed and lasting quality
> There is no fellow in the firmament."

CHAPTER VI

LEGACY: HIS

LEAGUE

THAT "FAILED"

I

ON NOVEMBER 15, 1920, at eleven o'clock in the morning, the church bells of the city of Geneva rang out in honor of the first meeting of the Assembly of the League of Nations. The man who had fought to establish it was not present. Woodrow Wilson never saw the organization he fathered. That seems the greatest tragedy of all.

What a thrill it would have given him to see his dream come true; to drive through the flag-decked streets to the Assembly Hall on Opening Day, stand among his colleagues of many nations, smiling and handshaking; to watch the Foreign Ministers of fifty countries mount the tribunal, cast their ballots, and

428

Legacy: His League That "Failed"

address the world in this first actual Parliament of Man. To address it himself: what a climax for the life of the Princeton student who toiled so hard over his political science and his oratory!

Then to sit in at a session of one of the League Commissions —planning fairer treatment for minorities, schools for backward peoples, better conditions for diamond miners in South Africa or coal miners in South Wales. "Humanity First!" Woodrow Wilson's great cry. Here it took concrete practical form.

"The League is now deceased," announced Senator Harding pontifically in 1920. "The League of Nations is harmless," wrote Senator Lodge condescendingly in 1924. "Its occasional conferences or conversations may be beneficial, probably won't do any harm."

This represents pretty much the average American view. We hear it so often. "The League? A debating society, wasn't it, largely? Results mostly negative . . . The League never accomplished anything—a little social work perhaps . . . Oh, certainly the League failed. Just a talkfest."

Let us look at the actual record of "Wilson's League" during its twenty-five years, and then form our judgment.

As soon as enough nations had signed the Treaty to make the League operative, Sir Eric Drummond—named in the Annex of the Covenant as the first Secretary-General—began to organize his forces. He drew around him an extraordinary band of able men and women from the various countries. Sir Arthur Salter—head of Inter-Allied Shipping during the war—became Chief of the Economic Section of the League and held that post for twelve years. A little later Mr. de Madariaga, one of the outstanding personalities of Spain, became Chief of the Disarmament Section; Mr. William Rappard, of Switzerland, Chief of the Mandates. Dame Rachel Crowdy, head of the British WAACs in the last war, was chief of the Social Section, dealing particularly with the problems of women and children. An American, Raymond Fosdick, served as Under Secretary General from 1919 to 1920.

The Story of Woodrow Wilson

The last war left Europe in indescribable confusion. Millions of homeless refugees wandered about without passports or money. Millions of ragged soldiers waited to be repatriated. Millions of women, dazed by privation and abuse, had become prostitutes. Typhus and smallpox, raging in Eastern Europe, were being brought back to the Western countries by returning refugees. Dangerous epidemics threatened to engulf the whole world.

The newly organized League forces threw themselves into the rescue work with a miraculous sort of courage and boldness. During its first year the League repatriated half a million prisoners of war and rescued thousands of distraught women from whom all hope had fled. It also arranged for the relief and resettlement of several million refugees, giving them passport certificates, legal status, transportation, and financial help. The Refugee Bureau of the League, under the direction of the beloved Dr. Fridtjof Nansen, became famous for this great humanitarian work. Countless despairing people were set on their feet again; families and individuals got a fresh start in life. The League Health Organization, with emergency posts quickly set up in the different countries, organized stations for disinfecting travelers on their way from one country to another, effectively stamped out the typhus and smallpox epidemics, sent groups of doctors to help the countries in the worst plight, and launched a world-wide campaign for the conquest of fatal diseases.

Physical misery resulted largely from economic chaos. Austria, Greece, and Rumania faced ruin. The League laid the bases for the financial reconstruction of Europe at a conference held in Brussels in 1920, and then for economic reconstruction at the Barcelona Conference in 1921, which resulted in reopening Europe's system of communications. Under its newly established machinery of the Financial Committee the League reconstructed the finances of nine countries.

The League Economic Section assisted substantially in the re-establishment of international trade relations, which the war had completely disorganized. A great World Economic Center was set up at Geneva to gather statistics from all countries for the scientific treatment of economic and financial problems.

In 1921 the Social Section organized a Conference on Traffic in Women and Children. The Second Assembly turned the recommendations of that conference into an international agreement whereby forty-eight nations bound themselves to prosecute persons attempting to procure women and girls for immoral purposes, to punish people attempting to use employment agencies illicitly in this respect, and to adopt laws for regulating emigration and immigration so as to check the traffic. Before the advent of the League there had been some discussion but little action to combat the international white-slave traffic, and the secrecy and fear instilled into the victims made it a particularly difficult problem. Various philanthropic organizations had passed resolutions and attempted some desultory rescue work, but the League put through the first real international action, and continued and expanded its work through twenty-five years.

With the same efficiency it attacked the international drug traffic. At the Hague Conference in 1912 an international agreement for controlling the traffic was signed, but the war had interfered with its ratification and enforcement. When the Peace Treaty was drawn up at Paris the League was entrusted with the task of supervising the execution of any international agreement, past or future, that might be made to control the drug traffic. During the first four years that the League drugs-control system was in operation the quantity of morphine produced in licensed factories declined 50 per cent. The production of heroin and cocaine also decreased sharply. The estimated number of drug addicts in the United States dropped from one hundred thousand to fifty thousand; other countries also showed substantial reductions.

Over five hundred international treaties, covering a tremendous variety of human interests, operate through the League.

In the meantime, set up by the Peace Treaties as "part of the organization of the League of Nations," the International Labor Office was established with its own building adjacent to the League Secretariat, following upon the first Labor Conference in 1919. The World Court, provided under Article XIV of the Covenant—with its fifteen judges and its own secretarial staff and organization—was established with headquarters at the Hague Peace Palace. The great International Civil Service of the Secretariat—which organized the work of all the different sections, Assemblies, and Council meetings, and acted as permanent liaison for the whole structure—was carefully chosen and assembled.

Within one year after its defeat in the United States Senate "Wilson's League" was functioning as a smooth-running concern, thanks not to his own compatriots but to a "decadent, effete, and militaristic Europe," as the Senators called it—particularly to Great Britain and the British genius for political organization and diplomatic efficiency. Within the twenty-five years of its existence the League has settled thirty-six disputes between countries and has helped to settle many more. It worked out a system for the government of Upper Silesia, with its High Commissioner in Danzig. It administered the Saar territory, a point of friction between France and Germany, for fifteen years; and the Leticia territory for one year during a dispute between Colombia and Peru that the League finally settled. It conducted the Saar plebiscite with model skill; order was maintained by an international force to which four countries contributed. It organized the first great series of meetings and consultations in connection with proposals for the Federation of Europe.

Altogether, the League has conducted over fifty international conferences resulting in several hundred international agreements and treaties still in force. It has set up a World Center for Children, where blind, illegitimate, and other handicapped children are helped and where the problems of children are studied on a world scale, with centers in every country of the globe comparing notes, telling of successful methods, and sharing experiences. It has brought about the revision of school textbooks and a new and different teaching of history so that young people of the different nations grow up with understanding and sympathy instead of hatred and hostility for one another.

Legacy: His League That "Failed"

The League Health Organization has helped more than a dozen countries to organize a modern health service; has fostered —together with the Economic Section—the universal movement for better nutrition and the creation of national nutrition committees in thirty countries; has brought about a world standardization of remedies, so that the same high-standard drugs may be obtained in every country. The League succeeded for the first time in history in bringing cholera, bubonic plague, and other deadly epidemics under control. Its Malaria Commission is the recognized world authority in that field.

The League has assisted thousands of refugees expatriated by Hitler. It has transferred and settled in Syria some ten thousand persecuted Assyrian Christians, providing them with food, dwellings, agricultural equipment, medical care, and education. It has made scientific studies, on an international scale, of a vast range of human questions, such as housing, migration, and population problems, fiscal and monetary matters, restrictions on international trade, propaganda and the influencing of the public mind, and has passed on its findings to governments and to the general public. Its publications have gone to school-teachers, missionaries, doctors, and scientists in the farthest outposts of civilization and brought back their precious information and reports so that the rest of the world might learn of them.

The World Court has handed down sixty decisions settling disputes between nations, and its decisions have never been challenged. The disputes had to do with such delicate questions as foreign loans, frontiers, and conflicting territorial claims. The International Labor Organization has put through sixty-seven agreements providing better conditions for working people all over the world: reasonable working hours, security against accidents in dangerous trades, minimum rest periods and vacations, care of women before and after childbirth, abolition of forced labor and exploitation of downtrodden people unable to speak for themselves. . . .

This is the record of the League that "failed." Is there a record in human history to match it?

The Story of Woodrow Wilson

II

Yes, but it didn't fulfill the most important thing it was created for: it didn't end war. This humanitarian and health and social work is all very well," people say, "but you have to admit that the peace machinery of the League of Nations was a failure. What did the League do for Poland, for Czechoslovakia, for Austria, and all the little nations that fell one by one to Hitler? What did it do for China and Ethiopia? The League certainly failed politically, whatever it may have done socially and educationally."

There are a number of answers to this. The League has settled thirty-six of the sixty-three political disputes submitted to it in the course of its history. One of these—the dispute between Yugoslavia and Hungary in 1934—the League settled when war was imminent; another—the dispute between Greece and Bulgaria in 1925—it adjusted when hostilities had actually begun. The League assisted in arbitrating eighteen other disputes. Only nine of the sixty-three remained unsettled. These included the famous conflicts of Manchuria and Ethiopia.

Manchuria and Ethiopia were left undefended not because the League machinery was used and failed, but because it was *not* used. The Great Powers, not the League, failed in both instances. The Covenant of the League still stood; nothing had happened to the Covenant or to Article X or Article XVI, which if properly enforced would have stopped both these wars in their very first stages. Nothing had happened to the structure of the League. What happened was that the governments of England and France and the other Powers following their lead did not in time of crisis employ the instrument they themselves had set up. Instead they reverted to the old methods of diplomacy.

One must say in their defense that without the presence of the largest Great Power—the United States of America—it had become increasingly difficult to make these Articles, or the boycotts and embargoes provided for by them, effective; and the burden thrown upon each big Power was such as any government might reasonably refuse to assume. William Martin, editor of Geneva's leading newspaper, speaking of how seriously the absence of the United States weakened the League, said in 1931:

> If the United States were in the League, the system of penalties provided for in the Covenant would be effective; and if it were not considered strong enough Great Britain (sure of the position of the American Fleet) would not object to strengthening the system. The obstacle which has been wrecking all efforts has been Great Britain's repugnance to accept any new obligations whatsoever without being certain beforehand that in case of international conflict the British Fleet would not be on the other side from that of the United States.

At every League meeting America was always the incalculable and demoralizing factor. In the early days of the Manchurian affair hope ran high. Encouraging reports from America led to the belief that the United States would back the League in firm action to punish and halt the aggressor. "Don't you worry —there isn't going to be a war!" men in the inner circles would declare after a Council meeting. Then, all at once, things changed. On October 9 a cable came from the United States Secretary of State, Mr. Stimson, saying: "The United States can take no official action on Manchuria until Congress meets in December." From that moment weakening began. The tone of the representatives of the Great Powers, which had been severe to Japan in Council meetings, became milder, the tone of the Japanese representative daily more arrogant. Englishmen and Americans returning from Japan a few weeks later reported that the Japanese had been thoroughly frightened when at first the Powers appeared prepared to apply sanctions and to use the League machinery against them. They believed they would have to withdraw from Manchuria. Later, when the backing-down process began, the astonished but delighted Japanese thumbed their noses at the world and swept ahead triumphantly.

The matter was closed with the face-saving device of the

The Story of Woodrow Wilson

Lytton Commission of Investigation, which old-school diplomats recognized as a "first-class burial." Lord Lytton and his colleagues took their mission seriously, performed it with great care and conscientiousness, and turned in their report after months of hard work in Manchuria itself. The League Assembly, like the Commission, unanimously voted Japan guilty. But while the Commission's findings were adopted, its recommendations for active settlement were adjourned indefinitely. Responsibility for this rested with the Foreign Ministers and governments of the Great Powers. "The matter had to be dropped," said Lord Lytton, "when the Foreign Minister of Great Britain, Sir John Simon, declared in the House of Commons that however the matter was handled he did not intend that his country should get into trouble about it." One wonders what comment Sir John's compatriots at the fall of Hong-Kong would have had to make. France, of course, followed Britain's lead. The smaller nations had no choice but to do the same. Thus the Great Powers turned their backs on the Covenant, left China to fight her own battle, and the Manchurian incident was officially closed.

It was the same story in Ethiopia, which Italy had long regarded covetously. After a series of gradual encroachments the Italians used a trumpery border incident as an excuse for entering Ethiopia, declaring they were prepared to spend $850,000,000 in a two-year campaign "to obtain satisfaction from Ethiopia," and forthwith launched their aggressive war. In this case the League both voted and applied sanctions; Article XVI of the Covenant, which provided for economic and financial boycott of an aggressor, was put into actual operation. A League Committee of eighteen toiled faithfully for weeks, working out the regulations. The Member-States prepared in very good spirit to apply them: a blanket boycott of all Italian imports, and prohibition of exports to Italy of all war materials and other essentials. Then, despite all this good work, Sir Samuel Hoare and Mr. Laval produced their barefaced plan for handing over large sections of Ethiopia to Italy on a platter. A furious British public demanded Hoare's resignation. He quit, but reactionary

Legacy: His League That "Failed"

leaders still dominated. Italy triumphed. Sanctions were withdrawn.

On May 9, 1936, Italy formally annexed Ethiopia. The Emperor Haile Selassie fled. On June 30th he made his historic speech to the Assembly, interrupted by the whistling and cat-calls of Italian journalists from the press gallery. The Emperor —a noble figure in his pale gold robes—continued calmly in prophetic words: "The problem submitted to the Assembly today is a much wider one than the mere question of the settlement of Italian aggression. It is collective security itself . . . it is international morality that is at stake. . . . We have come here before this great body, confident that justice will be done and the honor of the nations vindicated. We have stated our case. We await our answer." It never came—till July, 1940, when Haile Selassie was taken into the cloakroom of a Cairo hotel, reinvested with his uniform, and gratefully acknowledged as a fighting ally of the British in North Africa.

All this happened not because the League machinery failed or because the majority of English and French people approved the Hoare-Laval procedure; it happened because of the leaders who were in power at the time and because the Ministers of two Great Powers did *not* use the League machinery to protect a fellow-member against aggression or apply the penalties as they had sworn to do.

The great responsibility for Manchuria and Ethiopia rests plainly and undeniably with the political leaders of Great Britain at those periods—with Sir John Simon, Stanley Baldwin (then Prime Minister), Sir Samuel Hoare, and other leaders of the Conservative party. Many good men attached to the League passionately disapproved the course followed and did their utmost to promote a different one. But they were powerless before the Ministries of the two big Powers. The trouble was with men—not with the League machinery—as it will be always, under whatever international or national machinery may be set up. The only way to get a different kind of action is to elect a different kind of men.

Americans, unhappily, cannot avoid their own heavy measure

437

of responsibility, not only in the cases of China and Ethiopia but on many other occasions. Time after time in League meetings I have heard the same question flung athwart some helpful proposal: "But what will be the position of the United States on this?" And the answer: "We don't know. We never know—where the United States is concerned."

America remained the eternal question mark, her declared policy (identical with that of the Lodge reservations) being always: "We shall make up our minds when the time comes. We shall not commit ourselves in advance. We shall enter into no agreement committing us to any future course of action." Suppose that each member of a board or business concern said this, or each citizen of a township at a town meeting. Or each State of the Federal Union: "We don't guarantee to stand by the other States in time of trouble—any of us. We'll see, when the time comes." What sort of town, State, or nation would the individual citizen have to live in? What sort of world has he to live in now as a result of this evasion of responsibility to the world commonwealth?

We refused to go in, yet we couldn't stay out. At every big meeting we were always there as "observers," visitors, sitters-in; complicating the machinery, having special rules and places made for us, special procedures, enjoying all the privileges while assuming none of the responsibilities of collective organization. At the time of the Manchurian crisis Mr. Prentiss Gilbert, United States Consul at Geneva, was sent as an "observer" to listen and report to the United States Government. At the later session in Paris Mr. Charles Dawes, then American Ambassador to Great Britain, was sent "to confer with members," though not to sit at the council table. This, we are told by an historian of the meetings, caused considerable confusion—creating really two conference headquarters, one in the official Room of the Clock at the Quai d'Orsay, the other in General Dawes's suite at the Ritz Hotel. Another American commentator caustically referred to "the sorry spectacle of the Ambassador of the United States peeping out of his hotel room while sixty nations sat in council over a major crisis in the life of the world." Then we stand off and speak disdainfully of the "failure" of the League of Nations!

Under the terms of her own choosing America should never have been allowed inside a meeting of the League of Nations—or have desired to attend one. Actually she has attended hundreds. Mr. George Harvey in the early days of his Ambassadorship to Great Britain (1921) declared in a public address: "The United States will have nothing to do with the League—with any committee or commission, department or board, or in any way, shape, or form whatsoever." In actual fact more than two hundred and fifty Americans have held salaried posts in the League and many hundreds more have participated in its activities as members of commissions and conferences, and as technical experts. In 1945 the Chairmen of two functioning League Committees (Fiscal and Economic) and the Vice-President of the Narcotics Supervisory Board were Americans.

Under the conditions of modern life an increasing amount of world business has to be transacted in common. America had to be present whether she would or no. In our own interest we had to go to these meetings though we went by the back door. American businessmen have used League material—especially the economic material and world surveys—as extensively as any people in the world. More Americans have attended the international schools and study courses in Geneva than the citizens of any other nation. We talk so much about "realism" and "taking a realistic view," but it took just twenty-five years and a second world war to wake us to an understanding of our real place and inescapable responsibility in the international scheme of things.

The real weaknesses of the League were, first, the absence of America; second, power politics and national selfishness. These same factors are present as we contemplate a new international venture today. Every country wants to belong to an international organization, "provided it does not mean giving up any part of our national sovereignty, or any threat to our national interests." In brief, nations want all the advantages of the co-operative system while renouncing none of the privileges of the independent State. It can't be done. And it is dangerous to continue the myth that it can be done. A nation does have to part with some of its sovereignty when it enters a world association, just as the individual States in America had to give up some of their state sovereignty when they entered the Federal Union. The question is, do the benefits outweight the sacrifice? The people who formed these United States evidently thought so.

However, fulfilling our international obligations does not, as many fear, work against our national interests. On the contrary. Where are the "British interests in North China" that Sir John Simon used to urge upon us so eloquently? If the nations had kept their pledged word to China they would have protected their own interests and possessions most securely. If we all had protected the Chinese people from Japanese bombings in 1932 the Japanese would not have bombed and bayonetted our own people in China and the South Pacific ten years later. Gradually it is dawning upon some of the citizens of the world that the moral law Woodrow Wilson fought for actually is, as he contended, the governing law of the universe, and that unity and interdependence are grim basic facts—basic to our survival as nations and as individuals. But it takes a long time for us to learn.

Another influence working constantly against the League was Mr. Wilson's old enemy, Vested Interests. Today in every country powerful interests organize to get special protection and privileges for themselves at the general expense. Governments are more and more affected by these opposing pressures. "After several years of trying to understand what was in the minds of the negotiators at Geneva," says Sir Arthur Salter, "I came to the conclusion that they were constantly calculating various political pressures and reactions. In other words a main reason why the representatives of one country could not agree with a representative of another was that governments are not masters in their own houses." At every crucial moment and at every big meeting on any vital question various interests turned up at

Geneva just as they did in Washington. The French and British delegates to the Disarmament Conference included some actual directors or large shareholders in munitions factories—Vickers, Armstrong and Schneider-Creusot. The American Mr. Shearer— friend of our own Mr. Schwab and the Bethlehem Steel magnates —attended, with large sums at his disposal for entertaining the delegates, until he was politely asked to leave. Similar influences were in evidence when other great questions came up for decision: forced labor, tariffs, drugs.

Human nature is to blame, not the League of Nations; not "England" or "France"—large and sometimes very misleading terms. These special groups of people and sets of interests exist in every country and will be no less evident in the future. In fact, groupings are rapidly becoming horizontal rather than perpendicular; ribbons of these same general types encircle the globe. We see this in the increasing power and activity of international cartels and the conspicuous grouping of the moneyed and fascist-minded class throughout the world.

III

In 1940, when Hitler was blasting his triumphant way across Western Europe, international co-operation seemed threatened with eclipse. Poland, Norway, Denmark, Holland, Belgium, and France had fallen in swift succession. An attack on Switzerland might come at any moment. Nobody knew what might happen to the League buildings or to personnel remaining in Geneva. Ironically enough, at that fateful hour when the League seemed about to die, it was invited to go to America to live.

Dr. Frank Aydelotte, President of the Institute for Advanced Study at Princeton, with several other devoted internationalists, promoted the plan to bring the non-political sections of the League to carry on their work in this country for the war's duration. A joint invitation from Dr. Aydelotte, the Trustees of Princeton University, and the Rockefeller Institute—which gave a grant for the purpose—resulted in grateful acceptance by

League officials. So by a certain poetic justice Wilson's League, rejected by America, came to take up its residence in America, and one section of it in the very town where Wilson fought some of his bitterest battles.

For five years, 1940-1945, the work of the Economic and Financial Sections was conducted from Princeton; part of the Drugs-Control work from a branch office at Washington; the Health Section work divided between Washington and Geneva. The International Labor Office had its wartime headquarters in Montreal. From these new bases the League carried on its activities, preparing world surveys and bulletins on vital questions, continuing its child welfare work—especially for children whose lives had been blighted by the war; its work for women, its far-reaching help to refugees.

In addition to its regular tasks it made valuable contributions to postwar efforts. During these years the League has furnished to the United Nations thousands of pages of material for use in wartime and postwar plans and operations. From its economic headquarters at Princeton it furnished substantial bases for the documentation and plans for the Food Conference at Hot Springs and the UNRRA Conference at Atlantic City. It has given to the State Department and to ex-Governor Lehman, to the Departments of Commerce and Labor, to Treasury officials and economic advisers of the Government masses of notes, figures, and comparative data as part of their essential documentation.

While Americans were placidly dismissing the League as extinct, "the fact is, we have never been so rushed in the history of this department," said Alexander Loveday, Chief of the League Economic Section. "Our staff has been busy day and night."

In most cases no public acknowledgment has been given for the use of this League material. Commentators and public speakers rather comically extol the vast improvement of various new agencies over "the old League," oblivious of the fact that these new agencies have frequently drawn three quarters of their material from League sources and from documents drafted by men with long League experience. League officials participated in the work of the Interim Commission on Food and Agriculture, attended the sessions of the UNRRA Council, the International Monetary Conference at Bretton Woods, and the San Francisco Conference—where they made substantial contributions to the new United Nations Charter.

In addition to privately furnished material the League has published between 1942 and 1945 a number of important studies on wartime rationing and consumption, money and banking relief, international currency, international raw materials, population problems in Europe and the Soviet Union, agricultural production, the economic transition from war to peace, and economic stability in the postwar world. Each of these studies serves a special purpose in connection with the plans of the United Nations to give effect to the Atlantic Charter and other declarations of joint policy.

Forty-five nations remained Members of the League in wartime. Crippled though they were, many of them contributed regularly to its modest wartime budget. The League building at Geneva remained open, with a nucleus of eighty officials working there. The last wartime Assembly was held in December, 1939, but a number of conferences of League experts and special Committees were held during the war years—mostly in cities of the western hemisphere.

As this book goes to press final meetings of the League of Nations Assembly will be in progress, to dissolve the old institution and to transfer many valuable assets to the United Nations. Embarking on a new experience with international machinery, we may wisely pause and look back at the international machinery that has operated for twenty-five years, on the whole, amazingly well.

The principle of League organization was the linking together of national governments for certain international purposes. Contrary to popular belief, the League was never intended to be a world government. As the Preamble to the Covenant said, it was created "to promote international co-operation" and to regulate on a just and orderly basis various phases of international life in which all governments had an interest. Before

The Story of Woodrow Wilson

Wilson's day international co-operation meant simply an occasional imposing conference ending in some pious resolutions. At the Hague conferences, for example—as Mr. Wilson rather impatiently pointed out to Mr. Bourgeois in 1919—there was much earnest talk, little concrete result. We have seen in how many phases international co-operation up to that time was desultory and unorganized.

With the advent of the League, representatives of governments met at regular periods under a regular procedure. This regularity is an important factor in achieving concerted government action. The frequent personal contact of the representative Ministers of the different countries in systematic consecutive work gradually promotes mutual understanding and personal friendship and lays a strong foundation for common undertakings. The permanent machinery of the League Secretariat existed before the Ministers met; it remained when they had departed. This insured the preparation of their work in advance on an international basis and also the execution of their decisions.

This same system of personal contact, preparation, and execution applied to a whole network of League Committees which dealt with economic, financial, and social matters on an international basis. Specialists from different countries met time after time round the same table. Thus the living tissue of a world organism grew gradually and naturally, not in some theoretical blueprint, or the vague imaginings of some amateur's brain, but round the table in actual day by day routine work.

The Economic Organization provides an excellent example of League machinery. Before the League came into being, small bureaus for compiling international trade statistics or executing specific agreements had existed; but the League established the first peacetime machinery for concerted action between governments covering the whole field of economics and finance. The Economic Committee concentrated on studies of international trade problems—commercial arbitration, credit control, export and import regulations. It arranged a number of international conferences which led to more than fifty international agreements. The Report of the Geneva Economic Conference of 1927 has been called by many foremost economists "An Economic Charter for the World."

The Financial Committee furnishes another good example of the League method. This Committee was made up of well-known bankers, high treasury officials, and financial experts, chosen for their individual capacity. The Committee successfully organized the financial reconstruction of nine separate countries and gave technical advice and assistance to several more.

The reader will remember the classic type of international financial transaction in the proposed Six-Power Loan to China which President Wilson refused to sanction, and which would have handed China's financial administration over to foreign officials. When a country applied for financial aid under the League, a League delegation conferred on the spot with the local bankers and other national leaders; it made its presence as unobtrusive and considerate as possible, and arranged every detail in the best interests of the country itself.

The League Health Organization gave its help in the same way. China, Greece, and many other countries profited by League assistance in reorganizing their public health services. Over three hundred doctors worked on the League Malaria Commission, pooling knowledge and experiment. They studied methods of mosquito-control, worked out a less costly substitute for quinine, organized courses in malariology followed by practical instruction in different areas. The work of the Sleeping Sickness, Cancer, and Leprosy Commissions has proved equally remarkable. And the League's Far-East Intelligence service always kept the entire world informed of dangerous epidemics which might be approaching from various countries, ships carrying cases of infectious disease, and quarantine measures immediately necessary. Thus shipowners have been saved millions of dollars; humankind, millions of precious lives.

"More lives have been saved by the League than were lost in World War I and so far in World War II," says Surgeon-Commander Best, chief of Canada's wartime medical staff. Most of them were saved through the Health Organization.

The Story of Woodrow Wilson

Space does not permit an account of all the various League mechanisms—the machinery for the improvement of communications and transit facilities, the Committee of Intellectual Co-operation on which Dr. James Shotwell has done such valuable work, and the highly efficient Drugs-Control machinery. Enough has been given to indicate the general scheme and the excellent results obtained. Underlying it all, and responsible for the success of all the different departments, was the permanent Secretariat, keeping its watchful eye on a hundred countries and territories, and thousands of special undertakings; reporting to the Council, chiding an offending government at first gently, then not so gently; carrying on a huge and complicated correspondence in a score of tongues.

"The secret of our success," says one executive of the Drugs Section, "was the permanent Secretariat. If its control were to be relaxed for one day, all the progress made during twenty years of arduous work would be lost."

Anyone who has seen the great mechanism of the League Secretariat in daily operation, with its army of devoted workers —their wide experience, their meticulous care, their constant faithfulness to the top-notch League standards—knows that there is literally no body of people in the world like them. Six hundred workers belong to this great International Civil Service—both men and women—most of them speaking from four to seven languages, thoroughly familiar with international procedure and with the customs and cultures of many different peoples. We saw the service they rendered after the first World War. What a service such a staff could render in the difficult reconstruction days ahead! It is to be hoped that many of them will be carried over into the United Nations.

IV

NO LESS significant than the new machinery was the new type of statesman who operated it. During the 1930's, the popular idea of an international statesman combined a vague idealist and an unscrupulous Machiavelli hatching dark plots and intricate schemes against the people. The alleged "failures" at Geneva were ascribed to this individual, who came to stand as the political demon of his time and was blamed for most of the agonies of the world.

It will simplify all our thinking on international affairs, both past and future, if we get it firmly into our heads that there have been, as a matter of fact, two completely different types of international statesmen functioning at Geneva and elsewhere during these years, each type working actively and well. There were the Machiavellis, certainly—the classic old-style diplomats who attended meetings and voted for resolutions while each suavely pursued his own private path and methods of private understanding and negotiation on the side. But—and this is all-important—there was also the new-style leader: open, straightforward, selfless, with the welfare of the people of the world constantly and sincerely at heart; men who worked for us early and late, who gave their time, their energies, everything they had; who fought for us against our reactionary enemies. These men are a gold mine in this confused present-day world. They embody three literally priceless qualities: administrative experience, technical knowledge, personal disinterestedness.

Consider, for example, a man like Sir Arthur Salter. For twelve years Salter headed the Economic Section of the League, where the world's economic panorama daily spread out before him. He knew prices, statistics, fluctuations of markets in your country better than did your own businessmen. The nine financial reconstruction schemes of the League were largely his personal achievement. He twice helped reconstruct the finances of China and India and thus knows the problems of Asia and the Far East, where he has a host of friends. Member of Parliament for Oxford, head of Britain's Rail and Road Transport Commission for some years—such a man hardly seems a dreaming idealist or subtle Machiavelli. Here is a supremely practical statesman and an eminently experienced one. Salter had been from the beginning one of the pillars of the League, and one of its most active and devoted partisans.

The Story of Woodrow Wilson

Or consider Edward Phelan, Acting Director of the International Labor Office. After passing the stiff Civil Service examinations in England, Phelan spent his early life in many parts of the globe, studying the lives of his fellow-beings. In 1913 Lloyd George put him onto a special job of inquiry into the housing conditions of working people. He was loaned to the Department of Labour in 1916, sent to Russia with Bruce Lockart in 1917, and at the end of the war served on the staff of the British Delegation to the Peace Conference.

While a young beginner in the service, Phelan conceived the idea of an international labor organization—a three-division body to be composed of workers, employers, and governments meeting at regular intervals to study their common problems and maintaining a permanent secretariat. He put his idea to the British Department of Labour, which got it incorporated in the peace proposals of the British delegation at Versailles. Mr. Phelan and others were appointed to draw up a constitution, and thus this great body came into being. Ever since, he has watched over it, guided and served it with utmost devotion, though never accepting first place for himself.

Again, take the Norwegian Carl Hambro, head of the League Supervisory Committee, which handles all questions of the budget and finances of the League organization. Dr. Hambro has been President of the Norwegian Parliament for eighteen years and was also head of the Conservative party and Chairman of the Foreign Relations Committee of Norway. He represented his country in the League of Nations from 1920 to 1945 and was President of the last Assembly in 1939. It was Hambro who got the King and the Parliament away into safety in England at the time of the Nazi invasion, after two months of incessant danger. He also helped save the four-million-ton Norwegian merchant marine and the hundred-million gold reserves. Is this a practical man?

Take Eduard Beneš, heroic President of Czechoslovakia, President of the Council in 1935, many times president of committees and special meetings. Take Anthony Eden, Foreign Minister of Great Britain, hated by the fascists above all others for his loyalty to the League, and his valiant efforts to adhere to League rulings and agreements in connection with sanctions and Ethiopia. Take Madariaga of Spain. Ambassador to this country and three years Ambassador to France under the first Spanish Republic—one of the most devoted workers the League has ever seen. From the Manchurian conferences in 1931 straight through the Disarmament Conference, the Ethiopian negotiations, and every crucial League meeting, Madariaga fought with all his strength for the use of League methods and strict adherence to the Covenant. When one of the old-style officials said to him angrily, "You will break the League with this constant harping on the Covenant!" Madariaga replied, "You have already broken it!"

We must remember who stood "for" and who "against" on these international issues just as definitely as on our national issues here at home. It will become increasingly important to know who stands for liberalism, who is reactionary, in the international as in the national field during these next years. Every little while call the roll:

Maxim Litvinoff: no stancher advocate than he of collective security and cleaving to the Covenant and the principles of the League. Whatever might be the position of his country or the momentary attitude of the outside world, Litvinoff himself never wavered. The writer heard every speech Mr. Litvinoff delivered in the big meetings over the period of his service as Russia's Geneva representative. Every one of them impressed his hearers by its courage, conviction, and sincerity.

Amé-Leroy—Briand's faithful colleague and co-worker of Léon Bourgeois for many years—is another. French Ambassador to Norway, last Ambassador to Portugal, French Minister to Bavaria during Hitler's rise to power—time and again he warned his countrymen of Hitler's war preparations. One of the few great French liberals still alive and free and who has stood by his guns to the last ditch. Amé-Leroy represented his country at Geneva for thirteen years.

Two stout-hearted Irishmen also served the League well—Eamon de Valera and Sean Lester—the latter as Acting Secretary-General from 1940 to 1945. And Münch of Denmark and Te Water, High Commissioner of South Africa, who alone and in spite of the color problem in his own country raised his voice on behalf of Ethiopia at the final Assembly when all hope had gone. And Alexander Loveday, first-rank economist, has been responsible for the statistical work of many years and for much of the valuable material furnished recently to the United Nations. Our own John Winant, present Ambassador to Great Britain and former Governor of New Hampshire, was the greatly liked Director of the International Labor Office for several years. And there was Arthur Sweetser, invaluable American who served on the Information Section for twenty years; and Branting of Sweden, Rappard of Switzerland, the Rumanian Titulesco, the Chinese Wellington Koo, the Dutch Colijn; never forgetting the great roster of the past—Briand, Cecil, Nansen, Apponyi.

These are the men who built the League, who made possible its great achievements, who defended it and upheld it against all attacks and desertions and attempted weakenings. These are the new statesmen who have taken their stand for the people of the world and international order.

V

THE real worth of the organization at Geneva will be better appraised—and appreciated—fifty years from now in the light of historical perspective. Already these specific contributions appear: the development of a new and expert political machinery; a new type of political leader; a new method and technique in the handling of international affairs. No one can say any longer that world organization or world machinery is an impractical dream. Any one of the League departments disproves it. An international civil service has been established, a system of international standarized research and education set up on which a sound international life can be based. The League men and women who set it up will go down in history as pioneers who took the first vitally important step.

Legacy: His League That "Failed"

Nine tenths of our present international thinking and planning is based, unconsciously, on League precedent. We use its phrases, its terms, its methods and habits continually. Before the advent of Article X in the League Covenant such a thing as trying to halt an aggressor in war was never heard of. Any war—a war of conquest or a war of defense—could break out at any moment, with no thought of opposition or concern by the rest of the world. In the thousands of years of world history no concerted effort had been made to stop wars, let alone written into concrete political terms and embodied in an international organization. And it would not have come into being in 1919 except for the determination of the "obstinate" Woodrow Wilson. The Eight Points of the Atlantic Charter, Dumbarton Oaks, the Declarations of Moscow, Yalta, and San Francisco rest upon the Fourteen Points and the League Covenant. If you do not believe it, re-read them.

The new United Nations Charter is extraordinarily like the League Covenant. There are 111 Articles instead of 26; it makes explicit many things that the Covenant stated implicitly. But there is the same general structure: the Assembly, the Council, the Economic and Social Organization, the World Court. Mandates become "Trusteeships," but remain much the same in concept and administration. The Court makes a slight change of name but none in nature. The Economic and Social Council at first seems something new, but we find it also harks back directly to a League conception.

In 1939 just before the outbreak of war, the League had arranged to set up a "Central Committee," as it was called, to deal with economic and social questions, and with almost exactly the same powers as the present Council. It was to be composed of twenty-four governments and a certain number of experts. The new Economic and Social Council is composed of eighteen governments. That is virtually its only difference from the proposed League Committee. Again, the Military Staff Committee of the Charter is the direct descendant of the Military Commission of the League.

The main differences between the two documents are the

majority vote, armed force behind decisions, and the concentration of power in the hands of the Security Council. The new organization has more power, but that power cannot be used so universally. Only the Great Powers can use it—and a Great Power can veto any disciplinary action against itself. League men see danger in this proviso. Under the League, in the event of aggression or dispute, all powers had the right to vote except the powers party to the dispute. Under the Charter only the Big Powers vote and any Big Power can void any punitive measures against itself by simply using its veto.

Furthermore, the Covenant did and the Charter does not guarantee territorial integrity. Mr. Lodge at long last has triumphed in the matter of Article X. The French, too, have won their historic battle for armed force behind the international organization. But of what use will this be to an invaded country if the five Big Powers do not choose to penalize the invader? Smaller Powers cannot even bring up the matter of an aggression or dispute. The Council, not the Assembly, determines such matters.

The Charter throws complete responsibility on the Great Powers—where in the last analysis it must belong—and where it also belonged under the League, had the Great Powers chosen to act. It remains to be seen whether they will now accept this responsibility in time of crisis, instead of evading as they did in the past. As General Smuts said, reviewing the instrument, "The question now is, *will they use it?*"

If the Great Powers would not use the economic weapons of the League to punish an aggressor, will they be more apt to use the new military force to do so, should they find it inexpedient or against their interests at the moment? This is the great issue which remains to be proved. It rests with the everyday citizens of each country to see to it that this time their statesmen shall be obliged by force of public opinion to live up to their agreements.

Meanwhile, standing with our feet proudly planted on the League-begotten Charter, we declare the League is finished and a failure. "What will become of the buildings?" Eight million dollars' worth of white magnificence, a royal library and priceless archives. . . . Whatever may happen to its buildings, whatever happens to the original organization, nothing that is ever done can kill the League. It is built into the lives of millions of better-off, better-fed, better-educated, and happier men and women of a hundred lands and in the lives of their children and children's children. The League's immortality, like Woodrow Wilson's, is assured.

"Don't you get awfully discouraged?" someone asked a well-known League man in Geneva during the trying summer of 1937. "You slave here day after day—wear yourself out at all these meetings and conferences. What is there to show for it—all this 'internationalism'? After these months and years and efforts—what happens?"

"The most important thing in the world happens," replied the statesman: *the formation of a new habit.* For thousands of years humankind has settled its disputes by prompt resort to physical blows. The sword or the gun was the prevailing habit. During a brief twenty years has come a new order: gathering round a table to talk things over—trying to see the other person's point of view, wanting to see the other side, and to modify one's course accordingly. If this had happened only once—at a single meeting of the nations—it would have been a landmark in human history. But it has happened again and again. It happens every time the Council meets—or any smallest League committee. It has now—in spite of all immediate appearances, wars and dark forebodings—*become a habit.*"

The real internationalism, the real accomplishment of those twenty-five years, is found in this new spirit and method of approaching and handling human problems and human beings—this new attitude in human affairs. This attitude is not confined to Geneva. From Geneva it has spread all over the world and flows from all the world back to the central focusing spot.

The great thing in the history of the League negotiations on Ethiopia was not the sorry betrayal of Ethiopia at the council table but the fact that for the first time in history there *was* a table where the oppressed and attacked could come and state their case before the world. When the President of the Council gave that historic invitation—"I now therefore call Ethiopia to the council table"—and the Ethiopian delegate came forward and took his place, all the oppressed and downtrodden of the earth seemed to stand there in that one small figure, during the attentive hush with which the Ministers of sixty nations listened to his words. Not even the ultimate betrayal, tragic as it was, could destroy the dignity and greatness of that moment. For what has happened once will happen again—next time with a worthier conclusion.

Again, in the Manchurian failure the most important item was not the evasion and timidity of the old-style diplomats, their mistaken efforts at "protecting the interests" of their respective countries. It was the historic roll-call when nation after nation answered "yes—yes—yes" to the resolution condemning the invasion of an unoffending country, and calling for immediate cessation of hostilities. Not a dissenting voice was heard. The solid bloc of world opinion rendered a moral verdict of the first order.

We complain of our times, shake our heads over the age we live in, moan over our problems—and they are heavy enough, in all conscience. But some of the most glorious pages of history are being written in this same age—and at Geneva. When you see men and women of Sweden, Spain, Holland, Brazil, and twenty other countries discussing with fiery sympathy in a League Commission the conditions of Singhalese coaling coolies, of children in Egypt or Persian rug-weavers in Iran, insisting on action with regard to these and a score of other pressing human problems; when you watch men of fifty countries greeting each other at the opening of an Assembly, coming in like brothers, arms around each other's shoulders, faces alight, brown, black, white, yellow; when you see them walking around the Assembly building arm in arm during intermission, laughing and chatting, or grave and concerned, studying the fate of some people in danger—that's the League. That's what has happened amid all the strife and disappointments and turmoil of these twenty-five years. That's internationalism—as American democracy is Jim and Henry chatting on their way home from the town meeting—not the sorry deals and dickerings of convention hotels and political back offices. That is what Woodrow Wilson died to create, and that will go down in history as the birth of a new era.

VI

"I am content to leave my reputation to the verdict of history," said Wilson. Well he might. History never discredits a principle or betrays a man's integrity. History acted more quickly in Wilson's case than in many. Every tenet he fought for is being welded into our lives today. The peace of 1945 rests upon the principles Wilson laid down in 1919. Indeed, the history of America's foreign policy during these twenty-five years might be called "Growing Up To Woodrow Wilson."

What Wilson said of Hamilton could well be said of himself: "Nobody could defeat Alexander Hamilton . . . because he alone had the constructive program, and they had either to submit to chaos or to follow Hamilton." Has that not proved true for us in our belated following of Wilson's program today?

As we run through Wilson's life, chapter by chapter, we note certain dominant recurring themes: the theme of *Service*, ruling his every hour and every measure; the theme of *Democracy* as an active living reality—democracy in education, in government, in religion, in world affairs; but with its balancing theme of *Responsibility*, the responsibility that goes with the privileges of education and freedom: the *noblesse oblige* of the democratic world.

Wilson was out to serve the people genuinely, sincerely. He kept repeating the phrase, "in the public interest." And he meant it. All that he was and had was at the people's disposal at any moment. This, and his determination to make moral principle the basis of practical politics, were the two great sources of his strength. For generations people had said, "High principles

The Story of Woodrow Wilson

in politics? It can't be done!" Wilson did it, and thrilled the world with the spectacle.

"But if only he had been more flexible—if he had unbent a little more—if he could have managed Lodge and those other Senators a little more cleverly. . . ."

If only human beings were perfect—which no one is, but which somehow Americans always expect their leaders to be. Under our democratic system we incessantly find fault with our great men but seldom stop to consider their positive performances.

Can any American read the story of Woodrow Wilson's achievements and not stand abashed before such a record of concrete accomplishment and disinterested service? Reform of the American educational system—almost every university in the country uses Wilson's "quad" system today; reform of the laws of the State of New Jersey—the primary elections law, employers' liability law, laws curbing corporation abuses, laws giving a public commission instead of the bosses control over public utilities; and then as President—tariff reform, Federal Reserve Act, Workmen's Compensation Act, Farm Loan Act, woman suffrage, anti-trust legislation, the Federal Trade Commission, Child Labor Bill, eight-hour day; the good-neighbor policy with Latin America—today a commonplace, but revolutionary when Wilson first proposed it and put it into practice. Finally, the first concerted world act to establish an international peace organization: the League of Nations.

Was it possible that a single being in a single lifetime could have accomplished so much? Always working for the people's causes, always with power and money banked high against him; beset by radicals on the one hand, reactionaries on the other. Yet always in the end putting the thing through. "Princeton in the nation's service" . . . "the government in the service of America" . . . "America in the service of the world" . . . "all the nations of the world serving humanity. . . ."

"I am going," said the boy Woodrow, "to be a great statesman."
He was.

ACKNOWLEDGMENTS

THANKS ARE DUE especially to Mrs. Woodrow Wilson for access to Mr. Wilson's papers in the Library of Congress; to Dr. St. George L. Sioussat, Chief of the Manuscript Division of the Library, and assistant members of his staff; and particularly to Katherine E. Brand, Custodian of the Wilson Collection, whose assistance with both preparatory research and final criticism has been invaluable. Also to the Woodrow Wilson Foundation in New York for most generous use of books and records, and especially to Harriet Van Wyck, Librarian of the Foundation, and Mrs. Quincy Wright, its former President, for initial help and suggestions.

The writer is indebted to League of Nations officials—in particular to Mr. Alexander Loveday and Mr. Martin Hill—for much valuable information and checking of facts and figures; to Ethel M. Young for devoted and tireless assistance in months of special research; and to Frank Barth, former research expert of the Woodrow Wilson Foundation, for much kind help and advice on special points.

Every writer who has had access to the Ray Stannard Baker papers in the Library of Congress owes an unpayable debt to Mr. Baker; an even greater debt for his biography of the great President, with the wealth of source material which he so generously puts at the disposal of others. If the present volume succeeds in stimulating its readers to embark upon a fuller study of Wilson in Mr. Baker's splendid books, this writer will be profoundly content.

Much of the material in the early sections of this book was drawn from Mr. Baker's volumes, with his kind consent. Dr. Denna F. Fleming was equally generous in permitting use of material from his exhaustive work on the League and the Senate fight. Mr. George Creel handsomely permitted the incorporation of a substantial portion of one of his chapters in *The War, the World, and Wilson,* to which the reader is

457

Acknowledgments

recommended for a stirring account of America's record in the first World War.

Special acknowledgment is also due the Honorable Josephus Daniels, Secretary of the Navy in Wilson's Cabinet, and Ambassador to Mexico for Franklin D. Roosevelt, for valuable data in his two books, *The Wilson Era* and *The Life of Woodrow Wilson*; to Mrs. Wilson and Mrs. Eleanor Wilson McAdoo for kind permission to draw from incidents and descriptions in their books, *My Memoir* and *The Woodrow Wilsons*; to Mrs. Edith Gittings Reid, Mr. Wilson's friend of early days, for the portrait from her book, *Wilson, the Caricature, the Myth, and the Man*; and to Stephen Bonsal, David Loth, and many others for helpful background material contained in their excellent volumes.

The author feels a special gratitude for David Hunter Miller's invaluable Minutes of the Paris Peace Conference in his volumes on *The Drafting of the Covenant*, and for *The Public Papers of Woodrow Wilson* edited by Ray Stannard Baker and William E. Dodd; also for Dr. Eleanor E. Dennison's small but very valuable book, *The Senate Foreign Relations Committee*—which every American should read in its entirety.

Memoranda and letters furnished by Joseph E. Davies, A. Howard Maneely, William C. Redfield, and Bainbridge Colby have been particularly helpful with specific sections of this writing.

Thanks are tendered to the following publishers through whose courtesy quotations and reprints appear in this volume:

Bobbs-Merrill Company:

 As I Knew Them by James E. Watson, 1936

 My Memoir by Edith Bolling Wilson, 1939

Doubleday, Doran and Co.:

 Woodrow Wilson and World Settlement by Ray Stannard Baker, 1922

 Life and Letters of Woodrow Wilson by Ray Stannard Baker: Vol. I, 1927; II, 1927; III, 1931; IV, 1931; V, 1935; VI, 1937; VII, 1939; VIII, 1939

Acknowledgments

Unfinished Business by Stephen Bonsal, 1944

An Adventure in Constructive Finance by Carter Glass, 1927

Woodrow Wilson As I Knew Him by Joseph P. Tumulty, 1921

E. P. Dutton and Co.:

Cobb of the World by John L. Heaton, 1924

Harper and Bros.:

The War, the World, and Wilson by George Creel, 1920

Harcourt Brace and Co.:

Grandeur and Misery of Victory by Georges Clemenceau, 1920

Houghton Mifflin Company:

Crowded Years by William Gibbs McAdoo, 1931

The Intimate Papers of Colonel House. Edited by Charles Seymour,
    Vols. I & II 1926; III & IV, 1928

J. B. Lippincott & Company:

The Bridge to France by Edward M. Hurley, 1927

Woodrow Wilson: The Fifteenth Point by David Loth, 1941

Macmillan and Company:

The Woodrow Wilsons by Eleanor Wilson McAdoo and Margaret
    Gaffey, 1937

Oxford University Press:

Wilson, the Caricature, the Myth, and the Man by Edith Gittings
    Reid, 1934

G. P. Putnam's Sons:

The United States and the League of Nations by Denna F. Fleming,
    1932

Charles Scribner's Sons:

The Senate and the League of Nations by Henry Cabot Lodge, 1925

My Brother: Theodore Roosevelt by Corinne Douglas Robinson, 1921

Stanford University Press:

The Senate Foreign Relations Committee by Eleanor E. Dennison,
    1942

APPENDIX

THE FOURTEEN POINTS

1. Open covenants of peace openly arrived at, after which there shall be no private international understandings of any kind, but diplomacy shall proceed always frankly and in the public view.

2. Absolute freedom of navigation upon the seas outside territorial waters alike in peace and in war, except as the seas may be closed in whole or in part by international action or the enforcement of international covenants [similar to Atlantic Charter Pt. 7].

3. The removal, so far as possible, of all economic barriers and the establishment of an equality of trade conditions among all nations consenting to the peace and associating themselves for its maintenance. [Corresponds with Point 5 of Atlantic Charter.]

4. Adequate guarantees given and taken that national armaments will be reduced to the lowest point consistent with domestic safety.

5. A free, open-minded and absolutely impartial adjustment of all colonial claims based upon a strict observance of the principle that in determining all such questions of sovereignty the interests of the populations concerned must have equal weight with the equitable claims of the government whose title is to be determined. [A.C.-3.]

6. The evacuation of all Russian territory, and such a settlement of all questions affecting Russia as will secure the best and freest co-operation of the other nations of the world in obtaining for her an unhampered and unembarrassed opportunity for the independent determination of her own political development and national policy, and assure her of a sincere welcome into the society of free nations under institutions of her own choosing; and, more than a welcome, assistance also of every kind that she may need and may herself desire. The treatment accorded Russia by her sister nations in the months to come

will be the acid test of their good-will, of their comprehension of her needs as distinguished from their own interests, and of their intelligent and unselfish sympathy.

7. Belgium, the whole world will agree, must be evacuated and restored, without any attempt to limit the sovereignty which she enjoys in common with all other free nations. No other single act will serve as this will serve to restore confidence among the nations in the laws which they have themselves set and determined for the government of their relations with one another. Without this healing act the whole structure and validity of international law is forever impaired.

8. All French territory should be freed and the invaded portions restored, and the wrong done to France by Prussia in 1871 in the matter of Alsace-Lorraine which has unsettled the peace of the world for nearly fifty years, should be righted, in order that peace may once more be secure in the interest of all.

9. A readjustment of the frontiers of Italy should be effected along clearly recognizable lines of nationality.

10. The peoples of Austria-Hungary, whose place among the nations we wish to see safeguarded and assured, should be accorded the freest opportunity of autonomous development.

11. Rumania, Serbia, and Montenegro should be evacuted; occupied territories restored; Serbia accorded free and secure access to the sea; and the relations of the several Balkan States to one another determined by friendly counsel along historically established lines of allegiance and nationality; and international guarantees of the political and economic independence and territorial integrity of the several Balkan States should be entered upon.

12. The Turkish portions of the present Ottoman Empire should be assured a secure sovereignty, but the other nationalities which are now under Turkish rule should be assured an undoubted security of life and an absolutely unmolested opportunity of autonomous development, and the Dardanelles should be permanently opened as a free

passage to the ships and commerce of all nations under international guarantees.

13. An independent Polish State should be erected which should include territories inhabited by indisputably Polish populations, which should be assured a free and secure access to the sea, and whose political and economic independence and territorial integrity should be guaranteed by international covenant.

14. A general association of nations must be formed under specific covenants for the purpose of affording mutual guarantees of political independence and territorial integrity to great and small States alike.

THE EIGHT POINTS

OF THE

ATLANTIC CHARTER

The President of the United States of America and the Prime Minister, Mr. Churchill, representing his Majesty's Government in the United Kingdom, being met together, deem it right to make known certain common principles in the national policies of their respective countries on which they base their hopes for a better future for the world.

1. Their countries seek no aggrandizement, territorial or other.

2. They desire to see no territorial changes that do not accord with the freely expressed wishes of the peoples concerned.

3. They respect the right of all peoples to choose the form of government under which they will live; and they wish to see sovereign rights and self-government restored to those who have been forcibly deprived of them.

4. They will endeavor, with due respect for their existing obligations, to further the enjoyment by all States, great or small, victor or van-

Appendix

quished, of access, on equal terms, to the trade and to the raw materials of the world which are needed for their economic prosperity.

5. They desire to bring about the fullest collaboration between all nations in the economic field with the object of securing, for all, improved labor standards, economic advancement, and social security.

6. After the final destruction of the Nazi tyranny, they hope to see established a peace which will afford to all nations the means of dwelling in safety within their own boundaries, and which will afford assurance that all the men in all the lands may live out their lives in freedom from fear and want.

7. Such a peace should enable all men to traverse the high seas and oceans without hindrance.

8. They believe that all of the nations of the world, for realistic as well as spiritual reasons, must come to the abandonment of the use of force. Since no future peace can be maintained if land, sea, or air armaments continue to be employed by nations which threaten, or may threaten, aggression outside of their frontiers, they believe, pending the establishment of a wider and permanent system of general security, that the disarmament of such nations is essential. They will likewise aid and encourage all other practicable measures which will lighten for peace-loving peoples the crushing burden of armaments.

August 14, 1941

Franklin D. Roosevelt
Winston S. Churchill

INDEX

465

Index

British Dominions, Claims of,
298-99
Brooke (Friend of Wilson at Columbia, S. C.), 13
Bruce, Cabell, 26
Bryan William J.,
leads the West, 93 f.
and Wilson's nomination, 99 f.
supports Wilson, 104 ff.
and appointments, 119
Secretary of State, 121
and foreign policy, 124 ff.
and Federal Reserve Act, 145
and "Lusitania" case, 183
resigns as Secretary of State, 184
heads Pacifists, 188
Bryce, Lord, 36, 41, 175, 283
Bryn Mawr College, Wilson joins Faculty, 41-43
Burleson, Albert (Postmaster-General), 93, 119 f., 122
Byrd, Richard, 26

"Calendar of Great Americans," 58
Capelle, von (German admiral), 220
Carranza, Venustiano (President of Mexico), 130 ff., 154
Cecil, Lord,
confers with House, 283
member of British delegation, 290
member of Draft Commission, 305, 310
and international police force, 307
receives first Woodrow Wilson Foundation award, 425
Chadwick, Rear-Admiral, 41
Chamberlain, Senator, 242 f., 265
Charlottesville, Va., 25
China,
Six Power Loan, 126

China—*(Continued)*
Wilson protects independence, 126
Shantung question, 343-44, 374
Chinda, Viscount (Japanese delegate), 290
Churchill, Winston, 172, 321
Civil War, 10
Clark, Champ (Speaker of the House), 102 f., 140, 142, 265
Clayton Anti-trust Bill, 152
Clemenceau, Georges,
personality of, 290
on Wilson's arrival in Paris, 292
Chairman of Peace Conference, 297
on Wilson, 311, 332
wounded by anarchist, 321
and Rhineland, 330, 335
on United States' separate peace, 407
visits Wilson, 425
Cobb, Frank, 226
Colby, Bainbridge, 207 f., 422, 424
College of New Jersey, *see* Princeton University
Colt, Senator, 362, 399
Columbia, So. Carolina, 11
Columbia University, Wilson lectures at, 56
Columbus Evening Dispatch, 372
Conference on traffic in women and children, 431
"Congressional Government," 40
"Constitutional Government in the United States," 56
Coolidge, Calvin, 323, 417
"Council of Four," 293, 330, 338
"Council of Ten," 285, 298, 330
Covenant, *see* League of Nations
Cox, James M., 417 ff.
Crane, Charles, 102
Creel, George, 369
Crillon, Hotel, 285

466

Index

467

Index

Index

Index

Index

Index

Index

Index

Index

475

Index

Index

Index

About the Author

Ruth Cranston has lived in eighteen countries and fifteen different States of the Union. Her family took her to the Far East at the age of eight. She attended school in Switzerland; went to college with Woodrow Wilson's daughters. Her father became a friend of the President and when she went overseas during World War I she carried with her a letter of commendation from Mr. Wilson himself. During the years between the wars she worked with many League of Nations officials at Geneva and wrote extensively—novels and fiction for women's magazines; articles and correspondence for the *Christian Science Monitor, Harper's,* and *Century*. She has lectured on international affairs and organized forums and discussion groups. In preparing this book she has had access to the vast collection of Woodrow Wilson's private papers in Washington and to the President's personal notes on the Paris Peace Conference.